TASTE AND THE HOUSEHOLD

TASTE

AND

THE HOUSEHOLD

The Domestic Aesthetic and Moral Reasoning

JANET MCCRACKEN

State University of New York Press

Published by
State University of New York Press, Albany

For information, address the State University of New York Press,
90 State Street, Suite 700, Albany, NY 12207

Production by Marilyn P. Semerad
Marketing by Fran Keneston

Library of Congress Cataloging-in-Publication Data

McCracken, Janet.
    Taste and the household : the domestic aesthetic and moral reasoning /
Janet McCracken.
       p. cm.
    Includes bibliographical references and index.
    ISBN 0-7914-5105-4 (alk. paper) — ISBN 0-7914-5106-2 (pbk. : alk. paper)
    1. Judgment (Aesthetics) 2. Judgment (Ethics) 3. Popular culture—
Influence. 4. Women in popular culture. I. Title.
BH301.J8 M29 2001
170'.42—dc21   00-066071

10 9 8 7 6 5 4 3 2 1

To Mom and Dad, and Tante Annie

CONTENTS

PREFACE

In a much longer and very different form, this book served as my doctoral dissertation in philosophy at the University of Texas at Austin. It has been a long time since I first formulated the claims I make here. Mindful of the passage of time and of the change of audience, I have changed the book a great deal, updated many of the examples, reorganized my thought, and shored up a lot of the prose in order to make more enjoyable reading than a dissertation committee can expect.

Still, there are some things I'd like to say to readers before they get started. First, this work touches on questions in ethics, aesthetics, and cultural criticism; it is not a work in political science or political theory or normative ethics. As I am going to argue here, the popular tendency to conflate political, aesthetic, and ethical reasoning is related to what I call "fashion tactics," a kind of mass production of opinions on issues of the day. I think fashion tactics debase aesthetic appreciation, ethical life, and political relations, by emptying them all of the concrete subjective qualities that ought to accompany them, and replacing these qualities with vague, bald, power alliances; bitterness; confusion. Today's habits of discourse can empty many words of any but their politically fashionable meanings. But as I argue in several places, the sort of "moral epistemology" I put forward here is consistent with both relativist and absolutist moral theories: People reason about the good domestically-aesthetically, and in complicated and nuanced ways, I claim, whatever their particular conceptions of goodness—aesthetic, moral, and political. My claims here are consistent, therefore, with many specific political and ethical positions, and I think are best understood in light of their being so.

Second, I recognize that readers may find themselves asking if my claims can be applied to x person or character by attributing her behavior to y domestic aesthetic choice. For instance, one might wonder if some behavior one finds morally abhorrent can be traced to a domestic practice one finds aesthetically abhorrent. Or, vice versa, one might wonder if my claims can be tested by finding some domestic aesthetic triumph at the heart of a moral disaster. *No they cannot!* If you start to think this is what I'm arguing, think again. Come back to this page and reread this paragraph. Or refer to pages 11–16, 33–37, 64–67, 100–02, 197–201, the conclusion, and so forth, where I try hard to dispel this interpretation.

Third, this is a critical thesis. I have not indicated any positive project for improving moral decision making. This may disappoint some readers. Philosophical discourse, however, presupposes the value of participating in pure criticism and analysis. Here, I hope that by speculating on people's reasons for even misguided choices, I can demonstrate that people always have their reasons for behaving as they do, reasons that others can appreciate (aesthetically, ethically, intellectually), even if they do not agree with them.

Acknowledgments

I am very grateful for the assistance, helpful advice, and constructive criticism of Jane Bunker, acquisitions editor, her assistant, Katy Leonard, as well as Marilyn Semerad, production editor; all at the State University of New York Press, and Therese Myers, copyeditor, and cover designer Ken Schrider, with whom I have corresponded and worked while preparing this manuscript for publication. Thanks too, to readers Donald Abel and Albert Hayward for their very helpful remarks.

Long ago, this was originally a dissertation—a much longer and rather cumbersome one to read. I was very fortunate to have patient committee members who went far beyond the call of duty by reading and rereading, commenting upon, and improving this work. I consider myself lucky, and my philosophical work enormously better, for my knowing them: A thousand thank-yous to my committee chair, Douglas Kellner, and to Greg Urban in the department of anthropology, and to my friends Kathleen Higgins, Louis Mackey, and Robert C. Solomon in the department of philosophy, all at the University of Texas at Austin.

I never would have actually finished this, even as a dissertation, if I hadn't been employed at Lake Forest College. Special thanks to Lou Lombardi for all his support over the years I've been here. Thanks too, to Dean Galovich and President Spadafora at Lake Forest, who helped provide the time for me to work over the last seven years, especially the Hotchkiss Fellowship in fall 1997.

This book has been long in the evolution, and many friends' and family members' thoughts have contributed to it. Many thanks to my sisters and brother, Anne Wares, Hugo Flesch, Jill Flesch, Kate Flesch Portillo, and Abby Flesch Connors, and their families. Many thanks also to Teri Ager, Ed Allaire, Roger Gathmann, Jill Glenn, Jill Gordon, Monte Hull, Pierre LaMarche, Abba Lessing, Mike Kash, Dan LeMahieu,

Al Martinich, Chuck Miller, Nader Nazmi, Ahmad Sadri, Darlene Schmurr-Stewart, Homayoon Sepasi, Jim Siebach, Brian K. Smith, Derek Stanovsky, Tom Szentgyorgyi, Wesley Tate, Carolyn Tuttle, Emrys Westacott, and Joseph Weh. Special thanks to Ellen Handler Spitz, whose reading and comments on an early version of the manuscript were exceptionally helpful, and to Otto Bohlmann for putting me in touch with her. I also need to thank the students and recent alumni in my three Gender and Character classes at Lake Forest College, who helped me formulate some of my thoughts for the final revision, and those who assisted me on this and other projects during the time I have been writing: Heather Brown, Yancy Dominick, Sarah Drehobl, Doug Ehrman, MariClare Kzryzewski, Geoff McNeil, Alicia Witten, and Adriana Wojcik.

There are three people I need especially to thank: Susan Heckler and Jennifer O'Brien, my best friends, without whom I would not be able to do much at all, and for bringing me to the big game and to my senses, my husband, my coach, my giant love, Chad.

INTRODUCTION

If nature had been comfortable, mankind would never have invented architecture, and I prefer houses to the open air. . . . Egotism itself, which is so necessary to a proper sense of human dignity, is entirely the result of indoor life.

—Oscar Wilde, "The Decay of Lying"

When the woman saw that the fruit of the tree was good to eat, and that it was pleasing to the eye and tempting to contemplate, she took some and ate it. She also gave her husband some and he ate it. Then the eyes of both of them were opened and they saw that they were naked. . . .

God answered, "Who told you that you were naked? Have you eaten from the tree which I forbade you?" . . .

Unto Adam also and to his wife did the Lord God make coats of skins and clothed them.

And the Lord God said, "Behold, the man has become as one of us, to know good and evil."

—Gen. 3:6–22

Perhaps it is curious that we find in Genesis a statement to the effect that the moral consciousness that many people take to be the human being's definitive—if cursed—characteristic has so much to do with why we wear clothes. Nonetheless, if we read the rest of the Adam and Eve story and others, we will find the biblical authors indicating repeatedly that morality has something to do with why we grow, herd, and cook our food; why we weave, sew, and wear clothing; and why we build, furnish, and decorate homes in which we may live together.

Indeed, it is quite obvious that human life is all tied up with cooking and dining; tailoring and dressing; upholstering and lounging.

Just the amount of time we spend deliberating about what to wear or eat or where to sit, shows, if not that such considerations are as important as, say, whether it is permissible to lie, at least that they occupy our thinking considerably more than we tend to recognize and more than those we normally call specifically *moral* deliberations. My purpose here is to show that how one satisfies one's basic survival needs (i.e., how one eats, dresses, and shelters oneself) is fundamental to one's moral character, from which even more purely moral choices spring. That most people today, including moral philosophers, do not believe morality or politics to be "about" these things, then, is a matter of deep concern, a concern that motivates the present investigation.

In part I of this book, I locate the relation between human nature and moral reasoning in what I call *domestic aesthetic skill*. I argue that this skill, which brings together moral and aesthetic judgment about little things close to home, develops moral reasoning much as the continued practice of drills and scales develops concert piano playing. I will discuss two ancient and fundamental theories of human nature—Plato's and Aristotle's—and show how they support my claims by providing two exemplary ways of understanding how and why our domestic aesthetic choices contribute to our moral ones. Their examples can, I believe, be useful in reviving what I take to be the fading art of considered decision making.

In part II of the book, I investigate how some important modern philosophers have had the perhaps unintended effect of encouraging ordinary moral practitioners to abandon their domestic aesthetic orientation and to base their decisions instead on an abstract notion of the individual that cannot be aesthetically realized. Despite some severe criticisms of his *After Virtue,* I argue that Alasdair MacIntyre is right in stating that our particular weaknesses in ethical reasoning stem in large part from our abandonment, as a culture, of the notion of virtue as skill. Criticisms of Enlightenment moral theory such as MacIntyre's, however, could not by themselves adequately or sympathetically explain the spirit of the contemporary age even if they were all perfectly on target. Because, at least as I will argue, moral choices are realized aesthetically as well as socially, and are, consequently, manifested not only in human relations, but also in our relations with material objects such as clothes and food and furniture, the study of modern moral theory should be combined with the study of modern economics if we want to understand the way people today decide how to behave. In other words, one needs to look at economic assumptions as well as ethical ones and at their effects on domestic and industrial design if one wants to really start to understand how heady theories became translated into everyday actions.

In parts III and IV of the book, I look at the effects on moral decision making of the tendencies I cite in part II; that is, these chapters consider the phenomenological effects of modern fashions and economic practice in dressing and cooking and arranging our homes. The way we characterize our choices of household objects, I argue, has habituated us in weak reasoning in a way that theory never could by surrounding us with nonsensical and unedifying objects for our concrete contemplation. In part III I investigate some of the mechanisms through which I believe contemporary moral reasoning has been debilitated. In particular, I believe the domestic aesthetic judgment that underlies moral reasoning has been profoundly dulled by the rhetorical methods of advertising, packaging, and display, and these fundamentally superficial rhetorics have insinuated themselves into the deep rhetoric of commodity design. I call this surface rhetoric *fashion tactics,* borrowing a term from Kennedy Fraser,[1] because I read them as sympathetic but short-sighted and desperate techniques for living. I do not, for instance, espouse the paranoid but popular belief that advertisers or television executives participate in some sort of malicious conspiracy in mass deception. Rather, I will argue, advertisers and television producers, and other purveyors of popular culture, themselves suffering from poor domestic aesthetic skill, simply churn out reproductions of the vague and ill-thought objects of choice that they, like their audience, find all around them. Designer Richard Buchanan claims that modern design is a kind of rhetoric or liberal art, which pervades human experience, as its teleological dimension.[2] I agree with Buchanan and some other contemporary philosophers of design in this fundamental insight about the profound role of design in human experience; but by itself, it cannot distinguish between the use of design in the service of selling and the use of design in the service of people's lives. Using fashion tactics, I claim, advertisers not only mislead their audience about the value and necessity of the products they endorse or sell. Through these benign misrepresentations, they also mislead us about what constitutes a good human life. Thus, the applied theory of the domestic aesthetic that I develop in part III essentially offers a historical-materialist explanation of why making everyday choices is really not so easy to do these days, and consequently why it often feels so very stressful and difficult.

In part IV I follow this deterioration of domestic aesthetic skill by reflection upon four of its aesthetic products. These four domestic aesthetic models, or four tropes, or *representative characters* (to borrow a term from MacIntyre), I claim, offer to us for our aesthetic, as well as moral, reflection visions of possible ways to live. Although I follow MacIntyre in that I believe moral theory is socially embodied through character, I diverge from MacIntyre with regard to how character is developed. Consequently, I find MacIntyre's representative characters to be rather empty sociological placeholders; since I believe that moral reasoning develops through and alongside aesthetic judgment, the four women characters in my part IV are more like popular culture tropes, and in my characterization of them, I borrow not only from MacIntyre, but also from others, including Stanley Cavell, whose treatment of women characters in American movies, for instance, looks at their aesthetic contribution to the social drama.[3] I have chosen four representative *women* characters, first because I believe that it is through female figures that both women and men provide themselves very important current models of domestic aesthetic reasoning, and second because I believe that these very powerful female representative characters have often been overlooked by both philosophers and in popular culture to our detriment as a society.

One concern that turns immediately upon these claims is that women have wound up doing so much of our domestic aesthetic work. After all, in the biblical passage at the beginning of the introduction, it is Eve that serves up the fateful fruit, and undeniably for what I will call domestic aesthetic reasons; she finds it pleasant and thought provoking. To do justice to this concern, I take a careful look at the role of women with regard to the changing status of domestic aesthetic skill over history. My treatment of women's role in all this evades the "essentialist"/ "inessentialist" distinction by taking a more Aristotelian view that stresses the interdependence of nature and culture, individual and society. The question of the "escapability" or "inescapability" of what have come to be thought of as traditional feminine or masculine roles, which is often the upshot of the essentialism question, is certainly moot and possibly pernicious. Worrying about whether one can or ought to avoid playing a certain gender role or throw oneself into such a role detracts from one's reflection on the more fundamental issues about how one should behave, and about the extent of one's real capacity for free action and the concrete limits that one's society, geography, family, and so on impose upon it. I argue, instead, that a person's comportment of her gender, like her other moral decisions, is developed through domestic aesthetic practice. If I am right that domestic aesthetic skill founds moral reasoning, then it is simply incumbent upon all of us, men and women, to practice it and improve our skill. After all, again, despite Eve's initiative, Adam's final responsibility to clothe himself is equal to hers.

Perhaps—as one reading of the opening Genesis passage may indicate—women have some kind of affinity for domestic aesthetic choice. Perhaps not. Nonetheless, even if women have such a facility, it would not make the progressive increase of their responsibility for these activities either excusable or of happy consequence. If gender differences exist in the way human beings make judgments and act according to them, then all that follows from these differences is that men and women, by and large, bring different strengths and weaknesses to the project of living a good human life, that some of the requirements of that project may tend to be more difficult and others easier, all other things being equal, among members of one sex than of the other. My point is merely that whatever their historical roles or strengths, it is obvious that both men and women are allowing their domestic aesthetic skill to atrophy. To return our moral reasoning to the strength of which human beings are capable, we will all simply have to muster our forces and help reinstate the practice of this skill.

PART I

The Domestic Aesthetic Foundation of Moral Reasoning

I recall also watching Mr. George Bernard Shaw, the renowned playwright, at dinner one evening, examining closely the dessert spoon before him, hold it up to the light and comparing its surface to that of a nearby platter, quite oblivious to the company around him.

—Kazuo Ishiguro, *The Remains of the Day*

CHAPTER 1

WHAT IS THE "DOMESTIC AESTHETIC"?

The generic name which I will use to describe as a set the activities with which I am here concerned is *domestic aesthetics*. Domestic aesthetic activities are those whose object—in the sense of their end or goal—is a beautiful life (where *beautiful* is used both in its modern, roughly Kantian, sense of the object of aesthetic judgment and its classical, roughly Platonic, sense of the object of love). One's life is made livable in the first instance by securing one's survival (e.g., by feeding, clothing, and sheltering oneself to the extent made necessary by one's environment). In the second instance, however, life is made livable by securing one's survival pleasantly (e.g., by preparing food, sewing clothes, and building and furnishing houses).

Thus, those things toward which a life is first and foremost directed are those things whose shared center is at home, and they are therefore domestic in the broadest sense. Thus, one's primary choices, the first order of business of one's life, are not what one does for or with one's boss or one's government, but what one does for or with the members of one's household. Domestic aesthetic activities are those in which we engage in order to make and sustain households, that is, in order to make a pleasant shared life with those with whom we choose to share it.

Domestic aesthetic activities understood according to the classical sense of beauty are what we might want to call *gestures of love.* They are to be understood as gestures of love, however, only on a model of love wherein love is neither an end in itself nor something that takes only other human beings as its end. Rather, domestic aesthetic activities are gestures of love, where love itself is correctly understood to be a motivator or an instrument through which a human being (and perhaps a domestic animal as well) directs her life toward an end. Indeed, as I will soon discuss, this is what I take to be Plato's conception of love, at least in his *Symposium*, *Republic*, and *Gorgias*—"the desire for reproduction in beauty" (*Symposium,* 206e). This love, as I discuss, is at the same time something similar to the way a theatrical director (one worth her salt) directs a production, taking the production itself as an end, rather than her personal glory, a particular audience member, or a particular star.

I will flesh out these claims later; for now, however, consider as an example a rather standard scenario: a person faced with a decision about whether to lie to protect a friend who has committed a crime. Perhaps this situation can be adequately understood and resolved in terms of weighing conflicting duties, or maximizing pleasures, or manifesting virtues—some of the standard ethical analyses applied to such cases. Still, I think something is lost in our analysis if we do not acknowledge that the person in this situation, whatever she chooses, will be making a dramatic gesture, a gesture either of loving sacrifice of her own ordinary moral standards for the sake of her friend or of stern but noble devotion to the Law or to the Truth, even at her friend's expense. Seen as a dramatic gesture, this person's decision becomes a choice of what she loves the most—or perhaps of what she wants (or desires, or in other words, loves) to love the most. Her love, therefore, is both instrumental in her decision and expressed and refined by her decision, in the same way, I will argue, that both the mechanism and the result of one's domestic aesthetic choices is a certain degree of domestic aesthetic skill.

Despite the fact that they express love (or perhaps even because they do), domestic aesthetic activities include, of course, those through which we assert our independence within our personal relationships, such as for example when a husband buys a car stereo instead of the Revereware his wife would prefer, or when she cuts her hair in the new fashion despite his protests. With these sorts of activities, after all, one maintains oneself as a lover or beloved in the continuing relationship one deems necessary to the goodness of the life it fills. These gestures are sacrifices to love just as much as refraining from them would be. One often feels, for instance, that "one can't go on with" a particular person—one whom one deems necessary to a good life—unless she "allows one to be oneself." One insists on "being oneself" in the relationship, then, precisely to go on with her.

The domestic aesthetic is the ability to engage in the sorts of activities that will so allow her, an ability whose presence is felt only through engagement in the activities themselves. The ability is of the nature of a skill—and as such is always only a more or less developed ability—and the activities themselves are decorative. As a first effort, then, I will call the domestic aesthetic *a skill at choosing and decorating the things with which we live, such that we can continue long at living well.*

Phenomenological Intimacy and Distance

Although the word *skill* is often taken to mean good, but unreflective, doing or making—as though the pianist's skill were in her fingers alone—we would not want to call the pianist skillful unless she could recognize good and bad piano playing as well as play the piano. In fact, her ability to improve her piano playing comes from and with the ability to hear her own and others' mistakes and to hear when they have been corrected. As the pianist becomes better and better at piano playing, then, so also does she become a better and better judge of piano playing. The situation is the same if we consider something very plebeian, such as getting dressed in the morning, or shaving, or making coffee—in other words, domestic aesthetic activities. A person might easily live out her life doing one, two, or all of these things quite badly. But should she ever improve at these basic skills, to that extent she must also be a better judge of her own and of others' achievements. One learns to tie a tie from and as one learns to recognize shabbily and impeccably tied ties; one learns to shave better by and as one notices well and poorly cleaned chins and upper lips; one makes better coffee by and as one taste tests or polls one's guests.

An idiot savant, for instance, despite whatever impressive feats she may perform, is not able to make judgments about her performance or the performance of others. We would not want to say, then, that she exhibits a *skill* , but rather a tremendous *talent*. This is partly because without reflective judgment, she would not be able to improve or develop the talent; onlooking teachers would be amazed but helpless toward her. In addition, as I will argue presently, we consider the idiot savant unfortunate, or sad, or lost to human community, precisely to the extent that she is unable to reflect upon her talent critically, and thereby, to learn. In being a skill, the domestic aesthetic is reminiscent of the Aristotelian notion of virtue, or rather, what underlies virtue, practical wisdom. For Aristotle, morality is not the result of an innate absolute faculty, but of being able to overcome one's weaknesses by learning to do better.

A moral theory is inadequate if it cannot account for moral learning or moral teaching; that is, if it can neither account for nor therefore help initiate moral improvement in the face of mistakes. That practical wisdom is the result of moral practice is part of what gives Aristotle's notion its explanatory power.[1] That domestic aesthetic activities are skillful is therefore central to their ability to found moral reasoning because the domestic aesthetic view characterizes reason as something that one can do well or badly, rather than just as something that one can do or not do. To have a skill is to have both facility and reflective judgment, and therefore, to be capable of improving or degenerating in one's performance of an activity. In this doubly aspected sense, the domestic aesthetic is a skill.

Moral education, or education at any skill, requires that a connection be made in the mind of the agent between sensory experience and conceptions of ends, between what the agent takes to be the goal of an action and her interpretation of that action and its consequences. If the agent cannot judge both whether an action achieved what it was supposed to achieve and whether what it was supposed to achieve was really worthwhile, the agent cannot improve morally; she cannot either refine and revise her goals or correct her mistaken actions. This mental connection between concepts and the experience of objects can itself be strong or weak, and part of the process of learning a skill is forging a stronger, clearer such connection.

I call a strong ability to reflect in this way, to refer a concept of the good to the experiences of events or objects that purport to achieve it and vice versa, the *phenomenological intimacy* between one's concepts of goodness and one's judgments of particular objects and activities that do or may fill one's life. A weakness at such reflection then may be understood as stemming from a phenomenological distance between these things. If the reflective relationship between conceptions of goodness and the objects of experience to which they are applied and on the basis of which they are revised grows phenomenologically more distant, one's moral education is that much more in peril. The first job of a weak moral reasoner, then, is to establish a stronger phenomenological intimacy between her conceptions of goodness and the things and actions she experiences in the life whose goodness is at issue.

Strong phenomenological intimacy can only be achieved through exercise or practice in the skills it supports, just as a strong muscle is achieved by doing with it over and over what one does with strong muscles. Because of the need for exercise, one's ability to practice at the domestic aesthetic faces certain limitations. A particular person, for instance, may not be entirely free to exercise and improve her physical strength in the way she would like. She may have a disease that inhibits muscular movement, or she may be obliged to spend so much time at a desk that she has no time to exercise, or she may have in her home or neighborhood no place that accommodates the exercise she needs. Similarly, the ability to build up one's phenomenological intimacy can be limited by various factors. For instance, one's ability to judge the full connotations and effects of one's words is limited in languages in which one is less than fluent; one is limited in one's ability to practice "honoring one's father and mother" if one is an orphan; one's ability to be a good host is limited if one is homeless, and so forth.

To the extent, then, that one's current situation and state of character may affect her phenomenological intimacy, moral reasoning can be said to be subjective on the domestic aesthetic theory; to the extent that the quality of the objects from which one has to choose, the advice one gets from others, and so on affects her phenomenological intimacy, moral reasoning may be called historically and culturally relative; still, there may well be some ideal good that universally guides all these disparate practices. Since a domestic aesthetic notion of moral reasoning requires that an agent both glean from the objects of her experience their relative value and that she test her subjective concepts of goodness upon them, it assumes an interdependence and a dialogue between an individual's consciousness and the cultural artifacts with which she comes into contact. This dialogue makes a domestic aesthetic theory of moral reasoning adaptable to either moral relativism or absolutism (I discuss this in subsequent chapters), as well as making the essentialist/inessentialist question regarding femininity—or any quality of character for that matter—moot (as I mentioned earlier) because a person's idea of goodness takes a position in her phenomenological dialogue that is both given and changeable. One brings a certain vision of goodness in which one has implicit faith, or about which one has doubts, to one's contemplation on one's life, and at any particular moment one finds this idea of goodness verified or countered by one's experience. Thus, phenomenological distance and intimacy may equally well be conceived as a dialectic that heads toward an absolute good or as a perpetually open conversation.[2] In other words, the domestic aesthetic theory of moral reasoning would hold whether we take a particular person's conception of the good to be better or worse than another person's absolutely, or just *for her*.

Aristotle's analogies in the *Nicomachean Ethics* (1103b7), between learning to be virtuous and learning to play the lyre, and in the *Politics* (1325b35–1326a4), between statescraft and weaving and shipbuilding, put in relief the interdependence between one's concepts of goodness and the physical conditions in which she finds herself. The lyre player, for instance, cannot be expected to make a significant improvement practicing with a warped or waterlogged instrument; similarly, she cannot be expected to improve, even on a fine instrument, if she has no clear idea how good lyre music sounds. The case of domestic aesthetic skill is similar. One cannot be expected to know fully how to cook rice if one has never been exposed to any brand other than Success rice which comes out of the box in a plastic packet and is boiled through the plastic for the time indicated on the box, or if one has no concept of how well-cooked rice ought to taste.

Domestic aesthetic skill, therefore, will depend not only on the quality of the objects that fill a life and upon one's knowledge or ignorance about them, but also on the physical properties of the geographical area and the concrete cultural artifacts with which one lives surrounded. In the previous example, for instance, we could say that one reason a person might not know how good rice is supposed to taste is that she was raised in a strictly corn-growing, corn-eating region.[3] This implies that moral reasoning, too, again if I am right that it depends upon domestic aesthetic skill, is really tied to the place and time in which one lives, not through an attachment to the amorphous abstraction we call *culture*, but through one's sense experience of extended objects (i.e., aesthetically). Thus, if I can show that moral reasoning is dependent upon domestic aesthetic skill, then it follows that moral reasoning can be affected by the quality of the objects with which one's life is led, including the very landscape on which one's neighborhood is built, regardless of the relativity or universality of the good itself.

Because domestic aesthetic skill is independent of the absolute or relative nature of the good whose definition it is in the practice of refining, domestic aesthetic skill is clearly neither a necessary nor a sufficient condition for *making* moral decisions; if I am right in my present claims, it is rather a necessary—*and importantly not* sufficient—condition for *good* moral *reasoning*. It is certainly the case, in other words, that people make both domestic aesthetic judgments and moral decisions all the time and that onlookers might well judge a particular person's moral decision making to be miles ahead of her domestic aesthetic skill and vice versa. I am not claiming, then, that some direct relation exists between domestic aesthetic skill and particular moral decisions, such that philosophers could reliably discern the domestic aesthetic cause of every moral triumph or mistake. Rather I argue moral reasoning is influenced by its ongoing internal dialogue with domestic aesthetic skill in many ways, some probably quite subtle and nuanced. In a domestic aesthetic theory, the post hoc analysis of a moral decision, like the moral decision itself, is a matter of interpretation, a reflection—in this case on the part of the interpreter herself—upon an object of experience in light of current standards of judgment.

We can easily imagine, for example, a conscientious, effective mother who is oblivious to the poor quality of her own cooking. Such a person is not a counterexample to the domestic aesthetic theory. All other things being equal, all we could say about such a person is that she appears to us to be a good mother with an unrefined taste in food.

She may, for instance, have a raw talent for mothering, such as the above-mentioned idiot savant; or she may indeed have reflected very carefully on, say, the relative values of cultivating her taste and her various obligations to her children, or on her time and budget, or on her tolerance for practicing her cooking and tasting, and decided that the inattention she gives to the taste of food is acceptable, maybe even optimal, for her particular situation. Moreover, she may be discernibly satisfied with her behavior on these fronts or she may be slightly or seriously disappointed with it, and in either case, she may or may not attribute her feelings to this particular set of decisions.

Since her behavior, understood on its face without some further insight into her character, situation, and rationale, yields no evidence about the phenomenological intimacy or distance she brings to her decisions, we are simply not in a position to assess the present theory on its basis. To assess this apparent counterexample, one would need to know the extent to which this person's behavior was accidental or deliberate, and how satisfied she and the other members of her household are with the consequences of this and her other related behavior (e.g., perhaps they eat out every day or distribute the responsibility for cooking, and perhaps this is for reasons unrelated to the quality of her food; in other words, perhaps this person's unrefined taste is simply never an issue in the life of her household). The standards by which one would judge a particular person's decision with regard to her domestic aesthetic skill are not how good the decision is according to one's own conception of goodness, but how well it achieves the particular good at which the person making it aims, and how well that particular good accords with the conception she had, at the time she made the decision, of a good life; in other words, one would need to know how *well reasoned* the decision was. One would have to look at the agent's material situation, the duresses upon her choice, and her apparent happiness. Even with all that information available, one is still making a judgment about the person's decision, a judgment that one may want to revise in light of later reflection or information.

It may well be the case that if everyone had the most reflective and sharpest notion possible of the moral good, everyone's notion of the moral good would be the same; it may be that everyone's notion would be different. However, because we can observe that not everyone has the same conception of the moral good and because many people would admit that theirs is *not* the most reflective and sharpest concept of good possible, everyone must simply put her efforts into better thinking about the good. This book is an exercise in that effort, and my claim is that one's thinking about the moral good develops and degenerates through her aesthetic judgments of the material objects with which she shares her life.

PHENOMENOLOGICAL DISTANCE AND THE CONCEPT OF ALIENATION

My notion of phenomenological distance is reminiscent of, but not identical to, Marx's concept of economic "estrangement" (or "alienation"), and Hegel's notion of the "reflected self-consciousness" from which Marx's notion is in part derived, as well as to the more popularized existential and psychological notions of alienation. Because Hegel's and Marx's nineteenth-century terminology tends to influence contemporary talk about objects we make and buy, it is worth clarifying both the similarities and the differences between my view and theirs.

For Hegel, thinking undergoes progressively disruptive and unifying moments of consciousness as it endeavors to bring its conception of self into an equilibrium with its recognition of objects in the world as separate from it. Hegel implies that the only way to acknowledge objects other than oneself is to wrench one's perception of them from an initially chubby and contented self-consciousness, which imagines itself fully in possession of the world. Learning on this model consists in pushing and pulling consciousness from and to its objects, which it knows essentially as "not-itself."

For Marx the alienation of oneself from oneself occurs initially and paradigmatically only in the process of labor. The laborer, by investing her consciousness (time out of her life) into the making of a product, thereby comes to see herself through, or reflected in, this foreign object. For Marx, this alienation is essential to the nature of labor, but it is exacerbated by capitalism in that the object produced in a capitalist system is not only distinct from the worker, but cannot be reclaimed by her in ownership and consumption—"in it [capitalism]," Marx claims, "he [the worker] belongs, not to himself, but to another."[4] Thus, for Marx, the reunifying moments that Hegel ascribes to alienated self-consciousness—through which learning occurs—are inhibited in labor (which, because labor is necessary in order to live, means that it is inhibited in general), and particularly in labor under capitalist conditions.

Both Marx and Hegel suffer from a tendency, common also in recent psychologists and philosophers, to identify the notion of *self* with that of *goodness*. What is alienated from objects, for them, is always to be understood as the self and never as ideal or universally good qualities. Both assume, therefore, that the objectification in consciousness of things other than oneself—however appealing it may be to a lonely consciousness—is always more disturbing than it is consoling. This presupposition relies upon the equal or greater priority that they ascribe to the *I* over the *good*. This is of course made quite explicit in Hegel, since the goal or end of consciousness is for him full recognition of itself.

It may well be the case, though it is not necessarily so, that one's idea of oneself is phenomenologically or temporally prior to that of objects other than oneself. But it is very likely *not* the case that one's concept of oneself is *logically* prior to one's concept of goodness. Any agent believing herself less than perfect distinguishes within her consciousness the notion of her self from the notion of the good. Although surely an important object of consciousness is the self, it cannot be the only one. The self, or the agent, plays host to a variety of objects and concepts on which it reflects; it sometimes can and obviously does, therefore, take the part of a guest in its own home. The moments when it does so are moments of self-criticism. Only an agent with either a very tawdry notion of goodness or an extremely inflated sense of self-worth would judge goodness by the standard of her conception of her self.

Like Hegel and Marx, I will certainly claim that moral reason proceeds to an extent through a dialectic, in that it proceeds by resolving conflicts in consciousness. I do not, however, agree with them that the terms that reason dialectically opposes to each other are always reducible to *self* and *other*. On the contrary, I believe that dialectical reasoning is made possible because the self is a mediator between her concepts of goodness and the objects of her experience, only some of which are of her self. Hegel's and Marx's conflation of the notions of *goodness* and *self* create a theoretical atmosphere in which people are likely to find any activity to which they devote themselves to be exploitative, oppressive, drudgery. Indeed, this is how many people have come to think of the work they do around the house. As I develop my notion of domestic aesthetic skill here, however, it will become clear that while all work requires that its agent give up something of herself, not all work becomes oppressive or exploitative on this account precisely because it is the notion of goodness—and not her own interest—that is being refined through a person's work, and this process of refining allows her to better herself and her life.

The distinction, then, between exploitative and nonexploitative activity is not to be founded in a distinction between self and other (as *work-for-oneself* and *work-for-another*) but in a spectrum of qualitative distinctions judged reflectively in comparison to the agent's notion of goodness (e.g., good work, okay work, mediocre work, terrible work). A person assesses her own life, in part, through her judgment of her work (as, e.g., an important figure in her field, a respectworthy employee, an impostor, a lazy bum, a screw-up). An agent who finds she has devoted herself and her time to something she recognizes as good actually enlarges her notion of herself, because she has done something of which she can be proud. Through her association of herself with a good product, she is that much more fulfilled as a person and not, as Marx or Hegel might claim, that much more fractured (despite, as both admit would be good in this case, her recognition of herself in the object and the healing that this recognition may occasion).

An agent who devotes herself and her time to something that turns out terribly or turns out to have been futile, may feel very much exploited indeed. Hence, the oppression that constant and useless meetings pose to business people or that housework—understood solely as doing something demanded by television advertisements or by an inconsiderate or unappreciative household—poses to the contemporary domestic laborer. Useless, bad, or meaningless work does belittle or fracture us, not because it is work but because it is useless, bad, or meaningless. Marx sometimes takes a line similar to this, on which I spend some time later, but he never gives up his association of goodness with humanity, and this conceptual association makes gleaning an adequate criticism of capitalism from his theory difficult. It also makes it difficult to talk about alienation, exploitation, and oppression in any but black-and-white terms as mechanisms of the economic system. Surely, however, we can and do make distinctions of degree in how oppressive or exploitative or alienating an activity is for us, and these degrees are often marked by the relative worth of the object. Cooking delicious meals for a demonstrative, appreciative household is certainly less oppressive than cooking for an ungrateful mob; the ungrateful mob, however, may yet provide more fulfillment for a cook than an outrightly cruel employer, and so on. Studs Terkel's famous and insightful book of interviews, *Working*, to which I refer later, is a compendium of evidence that people's self-image depends on just these latter sorts of judgment, that is, on richly shaded judgments about the quality of their work.[5]

My notion of phenomenological intimacy and distance presupposes a consciousness able—at its best—to manipulate and order many, many, different concepts and objects of experience. Where choices are concerned, either moral or aesthetic, an agent orders the relevant objects of consciousness in relation to her conception of the good. Each object—to flesh out the spatial metaphor—must be held up next to her concept of goodness to see how similar the two are. When someone's conception of goodness is hard to find (i.e., where it is vague, particularly difficult to articulate, unusually complex or novel, rarely visited, or particularly off track) she will be woefully inept at making the comparison, although she may well still make a decision. This is phenomenological distance. Phenomenological intimacy is a facility at making this comparison. It is an indication of a sharp, clear field of vision between concepts of the good and objects of experience.[6] Moral learning takes place only when the concept and the object are clearly enough conceived to compare to one another; only then can the object be judged appropriately, or the concept revised, to accommodate the data. Perhaps we can never, even under the best conditions, fully articulate a concept of the good. Nonetheless, we can offer and recognize what we judge to be better and worse attempts, and we can take the best ones available as standards for new judgments.

This description might make it appear that our conceptions of the good are hypothetical imperatives, in the Kantian sense, but they are not.[7] Whereas functionally conceptions of the good may be revised, they cannot figure as hypotheses within an agent's consciousness throughout a lifetime and still hold for the agent as standards of judgment; hence, she will not pose her moral maxims as hypotheticals. It is true that according to a domestic aesthetic theory of moral reasoning, an agent's conception of goodness does not have the categorical status that Kant ascribed to moral imperatives, but this does not mean, as Kant claimed it would, that moral reasoning is purely instrumental. An agent's notion of goodness must be rationally compelling if she is really going to be able to strive to achieve it, but the maxim on which she bases her action need not be "universalizable," as Kant claimed— that is, it need not be a maxim that she could rationally will that everyone obey—in order for her notion of the good to achieve this authority. Rather, her maxims will speak to her with the authoritative voice of the premises of a convincing argument. This kind of authority is not unconditioned, as Kant claims in the *Groundwork* that it must be, but instead is conditioned by its phenomenological qualities through their reference to quality, or value, itself (i.e., an agent establishes the authority of the premises of her maxims through her judgment, not through her rational will). Because she will experience her maxims as having authority, following them will be perfectly rational, as Kant claimed following the categorical imperative is perfectly rational, but she cannot establish this rationality for herself except by her judgment.

Although one may read Kant's moral theory in such a way that it seems relatively sympathetic to the present one, the domestic aesthetic notion of moral reasoning is more readily comparable to Kant's idea of how we make judgments of *beauty*. Indeed, as Ted Cohen argues,

Kant's own notion of "the good will"—what Kant calls the only un-conditional moral value—may not really be intelligible except as it is symbolized in beautiful objects, which one judges to be "purposeful" yet without a "purpose" (i.e., free).[8] On a domestic aesthetic theory, the moral good, whose compelling authority is recognized through one's judgment, would, we might say, figure in an agent's conscious-ness as personified, or rather, dramatized; its status would be similar to that of our heroes or moral superiors: people of whose moral au-thority over us we are quite certain and to whom we believe ourselves to have a strict duty, but about whom occasional aberrant events do sometimes force us to rethink our allegiance. On this point, Cohen interprets an early and obscure passage from Kant's *Critique of Judg-ment* in which Kant discusses the certainty of judgments of beauty, stating that a judge will "often make mistakes, and thus lay down a mistaken judgment of taste."[9] Cohen wonders what Kant could mean by a "mistake" in this passage, since, according to Kant, there is no concept of beauty that might be wrongly or rightly applied in any case, and he resolves the matter by reference to Kant's moral theory, claiming that "beauty affords us a certainty we cannot have about goodness."[10] In other words for Cohen, it is precisely the greater au-thority over us that is exercised by beauty relative to duty that makes Kant's notion of a mistaken aesthetic judgment both puzzling and nontrivial and that informs our understanding of Kant's claim that "beauty is the symbol of morality."

A domestic aesthetic theory of moral reasoning is like Kant's moral theory, then, only when one takes very seriously Kant's indica-tion, in his aesthetics, that we reflect upon and deepen our notions of goodness through aesthetic judgment. But if we symbolize morality in beauty, as Kant implies, and yet we can make mistaken judgments about beauty even though we generally are very certain about it, as according to Cohen he also claims, then our symbolization to our-selves of the moral good, while generally very certain, can prompt perfectly rational action, yet be mistaken. Kant does not want to assert this, but I do. In fact, I believe that this last claim makes the difference between a moral theory that is satisfactory because it can account for moral learning, and one that is not, because, like Kant's moral theory, it cannot account for moral learning. Maybe the maxims of dutiful action would be universalizable if an agent had incontrovertible evi-dence that her concrete representation of the good will were perfectly accurate; but since we live without this evidence, we have no choice but to flesh out the emptiness of Kant's "good will" as best we can, which is a task for the aesthetic judgment. This is another way of saying that the absolute or relative truth of one's notion of goodness is not the point, even though there may be an absolute good, but rather its strength or weakness against challenges and its effectiveness in guiding a life toward its achievement.[11]

In this way conflicts in consciousness such as those Hegel and Marx described are resolved by learning about the good, which in turn is achieved by critical reflection on examples, both real and imagined (i.e., on the objects of consciousness). By reflection, agents learn about and choose both ends and means, both moral goodness and courses and styles of action. To reflect, however, we must have an object present to us, either imaginary or real. An agent, therefore, must be understood as *considering scenarios of action*, both those she has experienced in the past and those she is considering for the future, as objects for criticism, much as—or so I will argue—she would consider a date or a kitchen design or characters in a great novel: she judges it, in a sense, by imagining living with it.

That both moral agency and the aesthetic judgment of fine art involve envisioning scenarios of life speaks to the wide distinction between a domestic aesthetic view of moral reasoning and the unreflective advocacy of "having nice things" for which it may be mistaken by some. Human beings look for all kinds of things in a life, whether that life is lived by the agent or depicted in art, and having clean baseboards or Laura Ashley wallpaper is sometimes, but only occasionally, among them. In fact, as I argue later, the belief, largely instilled by advertisers, that these things will improve a life, often actually functions as an obstacle to reflection about the good. Fundamentally, human beings seek to fill their lives with things that move or inspire them. We judge to be good works of art those that are sad or funny, interesting or puzzling, admirable or cathartic, and so on, and the same with the decor in our houses or the clothes we pick for the day. Many people, for instance, could be said to decorate their lives or homes for tragic or comic effect. This book has room neither for an expanded aesthetic theory, nor for the defense of some particular aesthetic theory. I leave it that whatever aesthetic theory one may advocate, one may think of the aesthetic dimension of the domestic aesthetic as aesthetic in that same way.

This does not mean that there is no such thing as moral duty or that duty is reducible to some whimlike and mysterious standard such as cultural norms or preference or the eye of the beholder. As I have stated, although the claim that moral choice rests on phenomenological intimacy will found an explanation of the cultural and historical relativity of morality, I am not on that account committed to moral relativism. Indeed, I would grant that Kant may well be right in describing the call of duty as a "categorical imperative" (in other words, as absolute) and right again in conceptualizing the imperative as a universalizable and rational standard. What I believe Kant misanalyzes in his moral theory is what *universalizability* and *human ends mean* when an agent takes them as standards of action. What Kant calls the "maxim"—the rule, once articulated—of a dutiful action cannot be universalizable over all "rational beings," as Kant states it must be, because in choosing, an agent does not take rationality to be a given, but rather judges the very criteria for rationality. A woman, for instance, contemplating adultery, does not simply ask herself whether to fool around on her husband is rational, she also asks what the reasons for and within marriage are in the first place. Kant would claim that breaking the promise of fidelity made in the marriage vow logically presupposes the binding nature of the promise, and that therefore adultery is irrational and wrong. But he might have claimed, consistent with the rest of his moral theory, that a person may quite rationally decide in reflection that some particular promise (perhaps because of its particular circumstances, perhaps because of some social failing) is actually meaningless, that there is no real promise to break. This is why Kant's notion of the "reflective judgment," offered in this aesthetics, captures much better than his moral notion of universalizability the way agents actually carry their notion of the good, and it is his notion of reflective judgment, which I believe is similar to Aristotle's "practical wisdom," and to which I would loosely ally my notion of "phenomenological intimacy."[12]

The maxim of a worthy action, I claim, is better described as being universalizable over all *well-lived lives*. We see hints of this, of course, in Kant's second formulation of the categorical imperative— "Act in such a way that you treat humanity, whether in your own person or in the person of another, always at the same time as an end and never simply as a means"[13]—that is, Kant seems to find something in each of us that warrants treatment as an end, and yet something remains in each of us that is legitimately treated as a means. We find a similar hint in Kant's notion of "imperfect duty" (e.g., one has the duty to develop one's talents).[14] In this imperfect duty, we see that Kant well recognizes that even the "good will" cannot take the life of the individual to which it belongs as a finished or perfect affair. Thus, we need not abandon Kantian ethics in order to accommodate moral learning.

DECORATIVE ART AND THE DOMESTIC AESTHETIC

The domestic aesthetic is the skillful making and judging of food, clothing, shelter, and other basic human necessities. It is an addition, then, with a coincident judgment, that one makes to a necessity. Thus, the domestic aesthetic is a kind of decorative art that everyone applies to her life. In decoration necessary objects are made artful, and art is conditioned by usefulness. Decoration is distinguished from other sorts of art by its dependent relation to something that is decorated. In other words, decoration is an intentional art, it must be a decoration *of* something, not in the sense that it must have some representative content, but because it must be added to an otherwise complete (i.e., functional) object. In everyday conversation we usually speak of decoration as being of everyday sorts of objects: hats, lapels, upholstery, living rooms, and so forth. We do not ordinarily think of fine art-works—say, paintings or symphonies—as decorated, nor do we think of mere tools—say, hammers and nails or even computers—as decorated. These things are, however, decorated; indeed that they are decorated is an important part of what makes them recognizably the products of human beings.

In some cases, it is difficult to determine what it is precisely that is decorated, as in the case of a painting. Is it the canvas? The theme? The artist? In some cases, contrarily, we decorate things to look un-decorated and purely functional, as with hammers and nails and some-times computers and stereos. On further reflection, however, we can see that while particular fine artists or fine art critics may understand different things to be the object of a decoration (in the case of a paint-ing, some the canvas, some the theme, etc.) clearly, nonetheless, some-thing must bear the paint, or the notes of the symphony, or whatever, other than the paint or the notes themselves. The paint and the notes are applied to something. We can see, upon reflection, as the designers at Apple recently have done with their iMac and G4 models, that computers needn't be tidily bounded by their beige or gray plastic frames; nor do they need their trademarks lettered in a single font; nails needn't have different kinds of heads for use on the inside or outside of wooden furniture; hammers needn't have varnished handles or painted necks. They must be designed to fit their use, but they also must be decorated to look appealing, feel sleek, and so forth.

In the cases of both fine art and tools, then, something is deco-rated (even if it is hard to say precisely what). I am not prepared to say what the object of decoration is, even in general cases, precisely because decoration can take different objects; as for instance does love, with which—if I was right when I stated that the domestic aesthetic is prerequisite to moral reasoning and a gesture of love—decoration will be seen to have a great deal in common. Whatever a decorator takes as her object, however, in the act of doing so, she makes that object a tool, that is, she makes it an object functional toward whatever end or ends she will lead it toward through decoration. The good decorator understands a more beautiful object as a more functional object thereby; she sees the better functioning object as a more beautiful one thereby.

Obviously the decoration may be an instrument to another instrument—such as for instance when a computer is decorated to look functional—say, a monochromatic box—and looks functional to sell to its intended market, and sells to its intended market to help people do their work, and so on. It may, on the other hand, be an instrument to an ultimate end or to what the decorator takes to be an ultimate end, such as for instance when a deceased person is dressed in what was her nicest clothing so that her soul will make a better impression in the next world. The object of decoration, then, may be made a tool in the strictest, most rudimentary sense, such as when some early human first picked up a rock and used it as a hammer. We may, however, by decorating something, make it a tool in the more unusual, but quite appropriate, sense of making it instrumental to a happy life, that is, by making it a moral instrument.

As decoration the domestic aesthetic may or may not include the fine arts. Whether it does so depends, as with the bad cook in the earlier example, on the ends sought by the particular artist. I am not claiming, for instance, that Michelangelo's *David* was created for the sake of keeping Michelangelo's personal life together, nor even that the *David* is not a greater and more important work than breakfast. A fine art, say for the sake of consistency someone's concert piano playing, may be domestically aesthetic if, or to the extent that, it is serving the same function within her life as is, say, the aforementioned wife's fashionable new haircut. Piano playing is domestically aesthetic if, or to the extent that, it plays the role in the pianist's life of a decorated personal necessity. Otherwise, I am not talking about the fine arts. *David* is one of the things that made Michelangelo Michelangelo, but dining, dressing, and using furniture are some of the things that made Michelangelo a human being.

The domestic aesthetic does not, then, strictly speaking, include the fine arts. It is, rather, a series of exhibitions of artistic skill as a part of the general practice of seeking something good or useful. As a skill or craft, it has a history and a changing set of standards developed by its practitioners, which in its case is everybody. But this is not to say that the domestic aesthetic takes no part of art. On the contrary, the domestic aesthete is an artist, but she is a workaday, amateur kind of artist; she is neither an artist by vocation, nor does she devote any part of her life to art; rather, she uses art by way of and for the sake of carrying on her life. In other words, I grant that there are many contexts in which we can distinguish usefully between art and crafts, but these distinctions should not, as I believe they have in many modern aesthetic and moral theories, blind us to the fact that we practice both art and craft, however we distinguish them, in decoration and particularly in domestic aesthetic decoration. While an art/craft distinction is helpful for many philosophical purposes, it is almost always obscured in any actual art or craftsmanship. In decoration, the confluence between the two is most obvious. As long as we remain creatures with physical limits, we will be creatures with needs that we cannot fully satisfy, that is, with needs not just for food, clothes, and shelter, but with needs for beauty, goodness, and truth. As such, we will always artistically enhance the products of our industry, producing useful things that are also beautiful, and we will always require mundane skills in our fine-artistic endeavors, tuning the piano or guitar, mixing paint, and so on.

By applying decoration to an object and making it a tool, an agent works upon that object and thereby makes it her own. To decorate in the sense in which I use it, then, is an activity of which love and work are both aspects (here I intentionally echo Freud's notion of human happiness).[15] In Plato's *Symposium*, for instance—probably the first place to start for philosophical discussions of love—Socrates establishes, as I did here for decoration, that love is necessarily of something. It follows, according to Socrates, that a lover must lack whatever quality she loves in the object (200b), and that what the lover lacks is the continuing possession of the object's beauty or goodness (200d–201b). As with my claim about domestic aesthetic decoration, the object is taken by the lover to be a personal necessity—one feels desire as a need—and the love of the object is instrumental to a continually happy life with it. Consequently, Diotima—the woman from whom Socrates claimed he learned about love—establishes that love is of "reproduction in beauty" (206e). *Reproduction* here is meant to evoke Plato's theory of art, which he indicates is essentially imitation. Love then, at least for Plato, partakes of art; as I claimed about decoration, love takes an object and makes it an instrument for the eternal possession of its beauty, or, in other words, an instrument of its own beauty's reproduction. Love, at least on this Platonic version, appears to be an artistic makeover of a needed object such that it can eternally provide happiness for its lover. The lover, however, is not necessarily a fine artist. Rather, she envisions herself as a decorator who merely brings out the beauty already latent or potential within the beloved.

Note that the relevant distinction in this notion of love is not between love and work or between love and drudgery, that is, it is not between love and not love, nor is it the distinction between self and other, lover and beloved. Rather, the relevant distinctions in Plato's theory of love are those we make among the various better and worse objects of love, among the better and worse instances of loving work (e.g., work done well, adequately, poorly). The instances are frequent because we humans are, according to Plato, lovers by our very nature. Hence for Plato in the *Symposium*, love is at least partly decorative; love moves us to decorate our lives, to reproduce those things we must reproduce for our survival, but in beauty. Just as there are different types of love, however, depending upon their objects, so are there different types of decoration to which love moves us, depending on its objects.

Decoration cannot be avoided as long as we are the kind of creatures we are; neither can love. But because decoration makes its object an instrument, it is as much concerned with function as with pleasure, as much concerned with utility or morality as with aesthetics. Thus, the decorative aspect of love obscures the distinction we tend to make between desire and respect, as it does the distinction between industry and art. The lover needs, admires, and emulates the beloved, but always mixed to some degree with the determination to use the beloved to make a beautiful life with her. In that sense, the beloved is both an end of the lover's action and a means to the lover's ends; the love loses its quality as love if either of these aspects is missing. An instance of domestic aesthetic practice, then, is a gesture of love, one through which the agent seeks to improve her life and upon which she bases her reflection on the value of the good life she envisions. Without this domestic aesthetic or decorative aspect, none of the things we say about the love of inanimate objects make sense. If I say that I love coffee or that I love a particular coffee served at a particular café, need I be speaking only metaphorically? It would be very hard to convince me of this. Rather, I think, I would really mean here that I love coffee, but in a small derivative sense, derivative from my love of things I take to be more important, such as the study of philosophy, my husband, my dog, or even Mozart's *Requiem*. But I would really love coffee, and my love would be expressed through the gestures of ordering, buying, drinking, and savoring a cup of it, and perhaps even through a tip for the waiter. And these gestures are reproductions in beauty in that I order a cup of coffee for the sake of repeating the daily and necessary experience of drinking beverages, pleasantly. This is not categorically, but only different by degree, from, say, applying to graduate schools in philosophy, asking someone to marry me, adopting a dog, or buying a CD.

The beauty that the decorator seeks to bring out in the object is inevitably poorly defined for her as long as she doesn't have a good idea what the object is useful for. A reference to human needs must always focus and limit the moral reasoner, or the domestic aesthete. Without mastery of domestic decoration then, love is unguided by a clear concept of the good, and it becomes undisciplined, difficult, and ultimately unsatisfying. For instance, appreciating a computer or using it well is difficult when one doesn't have a clear idea what good its various features are for the things one wants to do with it; hence the idea that the design of computers should be "user friendly." As Albert Borgmann puts it, "designers are the guardians of common practical wisdom,"[16] and a computer whose particular use is obscured frustrates our efforts to use computers well in general, or to imagine more or better or more pleasant uses for computers. Similarly, the woman in my previous example who is contemplating lying to save a friend will have a more difficult time making her decision or reflecting upon the decision once made if she doesn't know whether she is a skillful enough liar to pull it off or if she is not really sure how good a friend her friend actually is. We suffer today from a profound unclarity about the usefulness of our actions, our household commodities, and even our friends in making our lives better than they might be without them. Certainly many aspects of homemaking—including skillful, long-term negotiation of the human relationships that go on in our households—have come to seem for many people to be an unsatisfying burden rather than something that we do as a gesture of love; it feels for many people like an unguided and often confusing habit that we just can't seem to shake.

Decoration, then, is also work, hence its occasional relation to drudgery. I think this is not only intuitively obvious, but also is borne out by philosophers of work. That love is work is also intuitively obvious; attraction may not require particular effort, but the moment we try to engage the object to which we are attracted, that is, the moment we begin to turn our attraction into love, through gestures, we are working. This is how we often talk about love, at least when we talk about love as an activity. A guy says to his buddy about a woman they have met at a party, "I'm working on her"; a frustrated wife says to her girlfriend about her marriage, "I'm the only one working on this relationship," and so on. As with expressions about the love of inanimate objects, it seems to me on the face of it quite unjustified to assume that such statements are metaphorical rather than derivative.

In addition to the previous more narrow claim I made that decoration is related to Marx's "estranged labor," we can see a notion of decoration at work in Aristotle's and Locke's labor theories. Locke envisions work as an agent making an object into her property. Neither property nor value, at least in the economic sense of that term, can be created, according to Locke, without human effort upon an object. For Locke the paradigmatic possession is land, whose natural fruits we bring out by working on it. For Aristotle, property is instrumental to activity, as is the ownership of a tool to a craft, or of land to citizenship. For Aristotle the good craftsperson is responsible for choosing good tools (i.e., tools that have the potential for making a good product). Thus, Aristotle's notion of work and ownership is distinct from Locke's and Marx's in that Aristotle requires the laborer to recognize a relationship to her product prior to working on it, and Aristotle thinks of the craftsperson as a responsible agent who chooses some tools and not others.

These differences point to important historical differences between classical and modern theories of labor and value that will be of interest later. For now, however, one can see that both Aristotle and Locke claim that the latent or potential value of an object is brought out or created by the laborer; neither the object nor its value is created ex nihilo. By contrast, God's creation ex nihilo is effortless—God cannot work because God's power to make things valuable is not limited by the possibilities of given, already existent, objects. Only God's creatures' power is so limited, and so only God's creatures need to work. This offers another piece of evidence that the notion of the domestic aesthetic can help us understand how moral reasoning can be affected by material conditions, while our notion of the good remains relatively more free of those constraints.

Work indicates a resistance to one's work on the part of the world. Where there is no counterforce to one's efforts, creation cannot be considered labor. We might want to think of love as an objectless or effortless creativity, but the comparison to decoration shows that erotic love, or desire, is work, and so it takes an object. Thus, again, we can see that artistic endeavors not bounded and guided whatsoever by necessity are not decorative and certainly not domestic decoration. Some sort of entirely free artistry may perhaps be what Kant intended by his appellation *genius*, to which he opposed skill in the arts.[17] Let us hope the moral reasoner need not be a genius. She does, however, and as Freud claimed, need to be a worker and a lover and, consequently, I claim, a decorator of her life.

THE LIFE OF A HOUSEHOLD

We see in both love and work the desire to see the chosen object bettered, made more beautiful and more useful again and again by virtue of its interaction with the agent. In the case of domestic decoration, the chosen objects are ones that are shared intimately, such as the taste of coffee or the look of a tie. In domestic decorating, one chooses an object with which she believes it will be ennobling to live; something whose beauty she believes herself able and willing to bring out, most likely—or at least with hope—to the credit of both herself and the object.

These things, these domestic objects with which one must of necessity fill her life, cannot be said to belong solely to the agent because, indeed, a person's life cannot be solely her own property. We may in the biographical retelling attach a life story to a particular person as its hero.[18] But it is a widespread and quite severe misapprehension of the facts to say that the hero of a piece *owns* it and may do with it as she pleases. We can imagine already the effect of such a belief on moral theory.[19] I am claiming, then, that a life is a shared object. It necessarily requires the participation of several people and things. Obviously, many of our current ways of thinking about what a life consists in are according to this analysis misguided. Thus, for instance, although I would never claim that a stream of consciousness or a subjectivity or even a soul can be shared, I also would not claim that a stream of consciousness or a subjectivity or even a soul is *a life*.[20]

All shared objects may be shared more or less intimately (in the physical and social senses of "intimate," and not the phenomenological one this time). Citizens of a state may share a representative in the U.S. Senate, yet be complete strangers to one another. Residents of a town may share a grocery store, yet never interact in any other way. Neighbors may share the services of the same mail carrier, and although they will probably interact otherwise, they may never actually meet or speak to one another. Roommates may share a house or apartment and maintain considerable social distance—as may members of an unhappy family—yet certain things unavoidably must be shared quite intimately, (e.g., physical space, the refrigerator, the television, the living room furniture). A closer household, whether filled with family members or roommates or some other combination of relations, will share more things more intimately still than the aforementioned socially distant roommates. They may share a bed, a bathroom, each other's clothing and, perhaps most important, considerable amounts of each other's time.

It is in the household that I believe one finds the unit to which we may ascribe human happiness or human unhappiness.[21] The household in which members share most fully their time and space throughout their shared life is the center of that life, the locus of its decision making. Its members are the major players in the piece, and they carry the primary responsibility for its moral success or failure. Only the person who lives alone approaches being an individual in the modern political sense, though even she does not fully achieve it. The rest of us do not even theoretically make our decisions under conditions of full autonomy, but rather under the influence of social spheres variously ordered in relation to us; and most important under that of our household. Even the classic rebellion of the adolescent is made by reference to, and is entirely swept up in, that against which she rebels.

Of course, some members of a household may (and usually do) branch off from this base and begin new households of their own (e.g., they grow up and move out, or they divorce and move out). That some members can pick up and leave does not, however, indicate that people are more properly understood as individuals than as members of households. When we start a new plant from a cutting, we do not thereby come to understand plants as loosely tied groups of cuttings. Those members who move on, quite contrary to indicating that households are not constitutive of lives, broaden the influence of their original household and mix it with other influences, precisely like an innovator in art. That all households are spin-offs of earlier households founds the continuity of human life, and whether we consider that continuity a curse or a blessing depends on the flexibility and adaptability of the institution of the household.

Thus, lives are shared most intimately emotionally, morally, and politically when they are shared most intimately physically, that is, when they share closely a particular physical space and physical objects over time. More important, members of a household share an end: pleasant economic survival.[22] The physical space and the physical objects in and around her household, including the bodies of other household members, together occasion more reflection more commonly for a particular consciousness than does anything else. It is through reflection on household objects that one develops one's phenomenological intimacy. It is with these objects that one first and foremost practices judgment. Sharing the use and appreciation of household objects is the library paste, the early glue, that holds people together in ethical relations. Designer Clive Dilnot makes a similar point when he implies that industrial designers do or ought to model their actions on gift givers: ". . . is not the work of the designer, at its best, nearer to the impulse that motivates the gift giver who gives out of love than to the huckster? . . . And is this not because objects work not only possessively for the individual subject who owns them, but also dialogically, that is, between subjects, working at once to aid subjects materially in how they live but working also as a means of establishing concrete relations with the other?"[23]

Although some people may be more naturally talented at reflection upon objects, better judges by nature than others, and although surely the way other household members interact with objects will, in addition to the objects themselves, affect a particular person's phenomenological intimacy, still the objects of her experience impose physical limits on one's ability to practice domestic aesthetic judgment. The limitations on judgment imposed by household objects offer a greater resistance to reflection upon them than do objects less common, less physically intimate. Thus, a person who comes into a household newly, whether as a new baby or as a new adult member, with a very poor, weak phenomenological intimacy may be aided or further impeded in sharpening her judgment by the objects that fill the household into which she comes including its human members. A person coming into a household with a very strong phenomenological intimacy runs a similar risk, but she is in a better position to calculate that risk and to bet accordingly. Dilnot speaks to this point when, even as he claims that the well-designed object is truly a gift, he derogates the "gift-article":

> We would never buy those we love a "gift-article" [a thing that is almost not a thing (as with the "gift book," for example, which is a book that is nearly not a book)]: only real and substantive things will do for those with whom we have a real and substantive relationship. . . . The state to which the gift-article is reduced mimics the generalized loss of a real relation to the subject which we find over and over again in the usual run of contemporary (sign-) products.[24]

The choice and judgment of these objects is that I call the *domestic aesthetic*, and its importance for moral reasoning, as the ward of the phenomenological intimacy on which the efficacy of moral reasoning depends, should be now dawning. When one chooses objects with which to fill her home (on the occasions that one can choose these) she chooses her primary moral influences. A great deal, consequently, rides upon these choices because they help form the environment in which our next choices will be made. Through our domestic aesthetic practice in a sense we make the results of our choices manifest in the world as new objects for reflection, new influences upon us. Thus, in domestic aesthetic practice, we engage our values with objects in the world, such that while our values influence our choices, the results of our choices become new occasions for us to revise or consolidate our notions of the good. That we can so engage with the world and revise our values is what enables us to learn from the things around us.

Because the domestic aesthetic gets at this reflective relation with things intimate to us in the world, it can base a theory of moral reasoning that can account for moral learning.

If one's conception of the good is fuzzy or otherwise badly thought, one may make the mistake of taking these objects to be themselves the criteria by which one ought to choose them; in other words, one may be guided in one's choice by the thing, rather than by its goodness. A passionate romance, for instance, often leads the participant to believe that her beloved—the person, rather than the quality of the life they dream about sharing—is the good. But the passionate lover in this sense demonstrates a weak judgment, a weakness that all too often results in an unreasonable expectation of her beloved and hence an unnecessary disappointment.

When a man of good domestic aesthetic skill falls in love with a woman, he no doubt admires her given attributes and takes them to be good influences with which to make a life; because of this and in addition to it, however, he also wants to some extent to change his life through her. He wants to spend his time with her and make her happy thereby, in which condition she will be a still better, more beautiful, more pleasant, and more sustaining participant in their shared life. Or, similarly, when a woman skilled in such choices falls in love with a house, she admires the floor plan and construction; but only insofar as she already can imagine what she's going to do with it. She loves the house as a potential home, which her love will actualize.[25] So are those people to whom we are attracted—when we are thinking well morally—potential members of our household, with whom we commit ourselves to work toward the good.

INTIMACY, DRAMA, AND RESPECT

To envision love and work as partly—importantly if not essentially—decorative and to think of aesthetic domesticity as the way we conduct our shared lives calls attention to a rather disconcerting fact: Whenever we work on something or love something, whenever we endeavor to live with something, we impose our style upon it. This fact brings out quite clearly a certain likely objection to the claims I have been developing. Mine seems a disrespectful and unromantic notion of love and community. It appears, as well, to deny that there is aesthetic tolerance within the home, as if *il n'ya pas que chaque un a son gout*. Furthermore, this view seems inconsistent with the Kantian notion of morality with which I have claimed it shares quite a bit, and with modern liberal political theories, because to impose one's style on another human being (in the case where another person is one of one's chosen love objects) is to make her a means to the achievement of one's own conception of the good life (i.e., it is to violate neutrality).

In a domestic aesthetic moral theory, the end of human action would not, it is true, be best conceptualized as a human being. Rather, the decorator makes both herself and the decorated object into means for the achievement of a good or beautiful or happy life lived together. Whether the human parties are respected in this arrangement hinges on whether that life can in principle be recognized as good by both of them; in other words, respect is a matter of sharing one another's conceptions of ends—as in presenting them for communal use or discussion, *not* as in agreement upon them—not of tolerating them. I want to claim that mutual respect in this sense is both achievable and desirable, even perhaps necessary, among members of households, and therefore that much of Kantian moral theory and modern liberal political theory are consistent with a domestic aesthetic moral theory. What I dispute in these theories is only their implied claim that such respect ought to attach to all and only individual human beings as ends in themselves.

To respect one another, or to put it in the terms of contemporary liberal theory, to respect one another's conceptions of ends, is not necessarily to *accept* one another's conceptions of ends. Rather, respecting another person or her concept of the good is, on my account, only to hold her to no greater or worse standard of goodness than that to which one holds oneself. This in turn amounts to a willingness to hear and to offer *reasons* for one another's choices.[26] Only this willingness can allow choices to be made together in any meaningful way, whether the choices are made together as colleagues, citizens, neighbors, or spouses. Consequently, the respect that any two persons owe to each other is always assessed alongside a judgment about the intimacy or distance appropriate to their social and physical positions with regard to each other. We should not be surprised, then, that respect in a domestic aesthetic version of morality will be owed to everyone and to certain nonhuman animals and inanimate objects as well, but demanded most often of and by members of one's household.[27]

To envision respect as acceptance or tolerance and, similarly, to envision respect as something due to humanity and only humanity, does a disservice to many of our most common experiences of the opposite of respect, violation. Why does the teenager feel violated, for instance, when her mother goes through her room looking for drugs or even just to get her laundry so that it can be washed? We tend to understand this, when we take it seriously at all, as a disrespect for the teenager's conception of ends or as the violation of some sort of tacit contract between mother and daughter. Where the teenager had expressed her conception of ends or where she and her mother have made some sort of explicit arrangement, these analyses seem to make sense. But they do not apply as well as we often pretend wherever, as is most often the case, no articulation of household members' intentions has occurred, and yet the teenager still feels violated. In their abstraction, these analyses overlook the concrete material qualities of the teenager's room, the qualities that make that room an extension or an instance of a conception the good life that, as a member of the same household as herself, the teenager had assumed her mother could understand, a conception that includes things such as having private spaces that look when one returns to them the way they looked when one left them, and that bear more of the marks of the style of one household member than of the others, things we do not generally envision for shared spaces.

One's conception of ends cannot be as well articulated as the Kantian notion of respect or as a contractarian theory would require, even hypothetically. Were our thinking about goodness so autonomous or so finished as they required, these analyses might be applicable, but because our moral reasoning is an ongoing reflection upon objects in our environment, we must understand respect and violation as fundamentally dramatic gestures, as I mentioned previously. The teenager's expectations of her mother's behavior in this example were not contractually based, even hypothetically, but she does have expectations, expectations that she thought her mother knew about. Thus, mother and daughter stand to each other more like actors in an improvisation. Certain elements of their roles have been set through their earlier interactions, including their use of space, and based on these precedent characterizations, mother and daughter have made judgments about how the improvisation will or should proceed if it is to reproduce in beauty. When the mother rifles through her daughter's room, her daughter perceives it as wrong in the sense that it is a gesture that fails to take the improvisation where she thought it ought to go. The mother's action seems, to the daughter, to be either out of character or in an all-too-familiar villainous character.

It is worth noting that we can easily imagine the mother in this scenario being quite surprised that her daughter has taken such offense at her action; she may well believe that her daughter shares her appreciation for clean clothes or that her daughter will be touched that her mother is worried about her possible drug use. Indeed, we can easily imagine a crowded or very intimate household in which no one is at all surprised or offended by one another's comings and goings in the various rooms of the house. We can easily imagine one or several members of the household changing from one position to the other over the course of time without any new arrangements being made, yet without causing any surprise for anyone involved. This cannot be explained by references to changes in tacit contracts, or at least not by such alone, but only by reference to perceptible changes in the character of household members, and consequently in the character of the household.

Although domestic aesthetic choice, and so moral choice, can be helpfully modeled on many kinds of artistic choices, then, I rely here on a long-standing and not unwarranted tradition of taking drama as a metaphor for human life. The metaphor already goes far toward expressing a real affinity between life and drama, which we express when we use the words *character* and *role* equally literally in the contexts of morality and of theater or literature. I have availed myself of this metaphor several times already, and I would like to expand on it here by way of demonstrating how life choices largely taken to be moral can be understood to be founded on aesthetic choices. Movie and theater critics often talk about actors' choices. What is an actor's choice? The content of her role is already given in the script and blocking. The actor is only in the most minimal sense choosing the content of the artwork (and in no sense, except in improvisational theater, choosing words); a raised eyebrow, perhaps, as she walks across the set according to the director's instructions. Actors primarily choose *how to deliver* the content of the script to others; they make choices of quality or style—or, we might say, form—not content.

Good actors make their choices not with regard to their own glorification, but with regard to the quality of the drama as a whole. Good actors, even when cast in leading roles, do not dominate the piece. The end of their action is shared with the director, the rest of the cast, and the crew or with their partners in improvisation. The end is the piece, not the actor herself. No matter how strictly or loosely her role may be drawn with regard to content, however, the choice of quality remains with the actor, and to the extent that she can make that choice well or badly, she is responsible for it. Hence, critics are within their rights crediting or blaming an actor for her performance even when her role has been tightly scripted or intrusively directed.

We can understand a domestic aesthetic choice on the model of an actor's choice. It is in a sense a generic choice, not itself either a purely aesthetic choice or a purely moral one, but rather the choice in which both moral and aesthetic choices participate, a formal choice. When the moral agent chooses how to behave, she uses qualitative criteria, not categorical or calculative ones. The moral agent confronted with the need to make a decision—when she is not acting thoughtlessly, which happens often enough—imagines her life with the upcoming scene written and played in various ways. This is what I meant earlier when I referred to the agent imagining living with the object. In this way, she chooses as best, not that which maximizes pleasure (because pleasure is not taken as a given by the artist, but is evaluated in the critical reflection that the artist applies to her own work and that of others), not that which her society condones (because again the criteria for a good society are not given, but are evaluated in reflection upon the objects of experience), but rather that which best exemplifies the way the best human being she can imagine being would live. Based on that judgment, she then seeks to do what it prescribes to the best of her ability.

One cannot imagine such a person—that best really possible person, on whose choices one models one's own—without reference to a conception of goodness, a working hypothesis about human nature, and a judgment about one's own capabilities. This quite complicated collection of notions on which choice depends is the result to date of the agent's lifetime reflections on the objects of experience. If that reflection has been ill informed or ill performed, the phenomenological materials with which the agent has to work at the time a decision needs to be made will be of poor quality, and the resulting decision, all other things being equal, is endangered. Similarly, we suspect the work of an actor or a director or a scriptwriter who hasn't watched a lot of movies or plays or who has watched exclusively schlock. Of course it is possible that such a person will produce a masterpiece; but in such a case, as in the case of the earlier-mentioned idiot savant, we would be disinclined, all other things being equal, to attribute the success of the project to skill, but would rather give credit to some kind of genius, a pure and great talent, an inspiration. And although we may endeavor successfully to learn dramatic skills from observing this inspired masterpiece, we could not hope on that basis to produce another good work of art in the same inspired way as the genius; we would hope to do by skill what this, our mentor in this case, did as if by magic.

That we can think of moral choices in terms of inspiration or talent is demonstrated in Plato's *Meno* (95b–100b), which focuses on the problem of teaching virtue. There Socrates and Meno tentatively conclude that because there are apparently men of great virtue and yet there are apparently no teachers of virtue, virtue must be acquired through divine inspiration. But the dialogue also leads the reader to believe that learning does occur and that learning virtue, therefore, may indeed be possible. If both claims are to be accepted, then learning virtue must occur, at least sometimes, without teachers. The divinely inspired virtuous man, then, though himself unable to offer a rule-based account of his behavior (i.e., unable to offer a reliable and universally usable recipe for or map of virtue and therefore unable to teach it), may nonetheless be a useful example from which the avid and determined student of virtue may study and learn, a true moral hero.

Aristotle states in his first discussion of virtue (*Nicomachean Ethics*, 1104a5) that "matters concerned with conduct and questions of what is good for us have no fixity," meaning something similar to the final claims of the *Meno*. In the discussion of practical wisdom (1140b1–5), Aristotle distinguishes it from scientific knowledge in this same way; its conclusions cannot be demonstrated as can those of science. Because practical wisdom is of this unscientific character, Aristotle must include in his definition of *virtue* that virtue is a capacity to act "as the man of practical wisdom *would*" *act* (1107a3). In other words, virtue cannot be taught, but it can be learned by the student able to judge examples qualitatively and act accordingly. Not surprisingly, we find Aristotle describing the man of practical wisdom as one who "is good at managing households" (1140b10). Thus, a conception of moral choice that grounds it in something such as dramatic choices demonstrates similarities between the domestic aesthetic theory of moral reasoning and ancient moral theories, and as with ancient moral theories, it can accommodate moral learning precisely because of its reliance on judgment.

Contrary to the usual reading of, say, Aristotle's notion of the virtuous character, the domestic aesthetic notion of moral reasoning allows for both a moral egalitarianism and a respect for individuals. We acclaim, after all, both tragedies and comedies, and similarly, we can see our way to acclaim both tragic and comic lives. We do, for instance, praise lives that end by death in battle for a noble cause (all other things being equal), and we do admire (again, all other things being equal) the happy-go-lucky life of the young aristocrat filled with zany antics and their minimally inconvenient consequences. We could imagine calling both an abjectly poor and an exquisitely embarrassing life "good," provided that the choices involved in producing it were ones whose criteria, or reasons, we could entertain and appreciate. Although it may be difficult to imagine either a melodrama or a farce sustained over a very long life, because poignant moments lose their poignancy if they continue too long unresolved, and although we may, ultimately, prefer a life with both tragic and comic elements, we can certainly understand how our judgments of lives correspond to our judgments of drama.[28]

One may object that by envisioning life as series of dramatic exercises I put too little value on sincerity and paint people, Sartre-like, as so radically free that they are not even bound by a conception of truth. In fact, probably the most fundamental and powerful objection that the ethicist brings to the aesthete is that the aesthete is a sophist, a cynic, a liar. The aesthete does, I admit, run the risk of insincerity. Philosophers such as Sartre and even MacIntyre (who, despite his moral-philosophical specialty does envision life as a drama and the Aesthete as the most honest about that fact) do come off as cynics.[29] I want to tread on very thin ice here, however, and claim not only that human life can be understood on the model of drama and yet have room for sincerity, but that a well-lived life must be sincere, or, to put *sincerity* in other words, it must take truth as its standard.

Thinkers such as Sartre and MacIntyre fail to tie aesthetics (which they do envision as integral to human life) to their notion of morality, at least to the obligation not to deceive, because they conceive actors as the only relevant participants in a dramatic production. For Sartre, explicitly, people are always and only actors in their own lives, and indeed if nobody were involved in a production besides the actors, the play would be radically free as Sartre envisions it, unbound by the script, the stage, and so forth. The real drama of a human life does not, however, proceed so freely or unreflectively: it is constantly referring to, and reflecting upon, objects both imagined and material. There all the agents involved are at once actors, authors, casting directors, directors, set designers, lighting technicians, and stage crew. They are limited in their choices by physical factors such as their budget, the size of their space, and the technology available to them. Furthermore, even as actors, and also in all the other roles we play, agents bring to the play a set of natural talents, looks, training, capabilities, and experience, as well as an idea of the way they would like the production to turn out. This is far more than just what Sartre calls their *facticity*.[30]

Certainly, some of these capabilities, talents, and so forth, are subject to change, and some of their changes can be attributed to voluntary acts of the actors. But even these relatively free choices, choices for which one can and ought to be held responsible, develop or deteriorate throughout the run of the play, as does the actor's ability to change them. One can, for instance, make decisions that place duress on one's other decisions, such as entering a romantic relationship or moving into a smaller house. In domestic aesthetic choice, as I have stated, prior choices can change the strength of one's phenomenological intimacy, too, and therefore affect one's future choices.

Each of the jobs that contribute to a production makes a different contribution to the honesty of the play; in particular, the director, the casting director, and the prop, costume, and set people are responsible for putting the actors and their surroundings in a play that complements their style, historical time period, culture, and talents. As director, casting director, and prop crew of the production that is her shared life (i.e., as a domestic aesthetic practitioner) everyone contributes integrally to its honesty and, indeed, is obliged to do so. The greater the degree to which we surround ourselves with people and things ill-suited to our capacities, attractions, ideals, and style, the greater the degree of contrivance in playing our role, the greater the deception about ourselves we impose on others, and the worse the piece. Unless we relied on some concept of aesthetic honesty in the way we understood people's characters, we would never be able to describe a person as "affected," or "phony," or "histrionic," and we would not be able to intend such terms as moral evaluations. But we do use such terms, and we use them effectively to make moral judgments of ourselves and others.

Sartre's cynicism—and his philosophical failure—comes from imagining everybody almost equally capable of playing all roles. Perhaps indeed we can play more roles than a very strictly cast society such as Aristotle's would imagine us able. Perhaps as well it is good for us to stretch our range as artists. But ignorance of one's limits stretches one to exhaustion. A kind of amorality comes from not believing that any roles are better for one than others. Not only does this make for insincerity—a moral failing in the deontological sense—it also makes for a bad production—a failing both moral and aesthetic whose end is unhappiness. When we choose a mate or a child to adopt or even a pet, then, we don our role as casting director of our household, a role that everybody in the household including the new member is also donning, which is one of the things that makes sharing a household so challenging.

We are responsible for that choice, which can indeed be made well or badly, where its goodness or badness is evaluated on the same scale as the agent evaluates herself. The standards of evaluation are best understood by the agent who places herself rightly on that scale in comparison to the potential object of choice, that is, by the agent who is least self-deceived. This is captured in part in Aristotle's conception of the virtue, "truthfulness." For Aristotle, lying is wrong, as it is according to Kant. But for Aristotle, *lying* is an expression of a dishonest character. To lie about anything, as Aristotle sees it, is in a way to misrepresent oneself, to feign an interest in one thing where one's real interest is otherwise. "The man who observes the mean [truthfulness] is one who calls a thing by its own name, . . . both in life and in word, owning to what he has, and neither more nor less. . . . But each man speaks and acts and lives in accordance with his character, if he is *not* acting for some ulterior object" (*Nicomachean Ethics*, 1127a24–30). For Aristotle, in other words, *truthfulness* is conceived precisely in dramatic terms, as "appropriateness to character," a requirement he imposes also on the playwright's vehicles (*Poetics*, 1454a20). To lie, then, is always to play one's part in an interaction insincerely, to present a different face to one member of the audience than to another, where one is oneself always a kind of audience to one's own actions and words.

A domestic aesthetic notion of moral reasoning is egalitarian, then, as well, but not in the awkward modern connotation of that word. To be morally equal surely cannot be to be morally identical. There is simply no way to make sense of a moral identity between people or even of some underlying part of people that can be said to be morally identical. Neither character, nor happiness, nor conceptions of goodness can be meaningfully identified from one person to the next. We are equal not by virtue of having the same quantity of rights or entitlements, then, but by virtue of having the same intention and obligation to make the life we share with others good. Just as all of the contributors to a good dramatic production are equally interested in and obliged to bring their differing talents and efforts to the aid of the production as a whole, regardless of their particular craft, we are all equally interested in and obliged to bring our differing domestic aesthetic skills and activities to the aid of our shared lives, regardless of our particular backgrounds. In other words, we are equally interested in and obliged to be happy, good people, able to live with others in households and neighborhoods.

Therefore, people may be created equal, in a sense, and yet still be better and worse for the roles for which they are considered. Thus we can safely say, for instance, that to buy a horse as a pet for a Manhattan apartment, or for a 97-pound, six-foot tall, adult man to go on a diet, are at least prima facie terrible and irresponsible choices, likely to make the lives to which they contribute worse than they might be otherwise.[31] These are easy calls, on which many people might be able to agree. There are very few such clear examples of poor choices, which may be one reason why neutrality is such an attractive position. However, we must be able to judge bad choices as such if we are going to try to meet our moral obligations well. We can and should, if we care about them, advise our friends against such choices. That these judgments are subtle and hard to make most of the time is evidence that doing so is a skill that requires practice and a refined imagination. In our interest in and obligation to make these judgments, in our obligation to give our best advice when it is called for, lies our equality; we all have the same obligation to make the best moral judgments we can.

Additionally, if one wants to live well in a community with others, one is obliged to respect others in the sense that one is obliged to appreciate that everyone is trying her best to live a good life and has reasons for living as she does, reasons that one can, at least in theory, discuss with her, influence, and be influenced by. Thus, respect is a necessary component of a domestic aesthetic theory as well, not respect for humanity as some abstract concept, but respect for the good life, the intention toward which we recognize in others, perhaps especially or most often in human beings. In this sense, too, then, I would claim, respect is better characterized by Kant in his aesthetic theory in his "Third Moment" of the "Analytic of the Beautiful," that what we judge to be beautiful exhibits "the form of purposefulness without a purpose."[32] In other words, we find in many things—among them, other human beings—the general ability to contribute to a good, shared life. We may not share with all these things and people a particular vision of what that life consists in, but we see in them the ability to engage with us in a kind of ongoing discussion about it (Dilnot describes this as a dialogue with objects) and we try to have that discussion through domestic aesthetic activities or in the terms I laid out earlier, through gestures of love toward them.

To avoid bad choices, a tremendous amount of honesty about one's own and others' situation and real capabilities is required. In fact, honesty itself is a choice; one that is limited as much as any other choice by the physical objects that have until that moment filled the agent's life. Here we return to my understanding of Hegel's notion of the reflected self-consciousness: If those objects, including other people, with which one has for whatever reasons found oneself to date surrounded, have so limited her ability to reflect upon goodness and upon their and her relation to it, she will be handicapped in her ability to evaluate herself honestly. She may even be so severely handicapped as to be unable to meet her obligation to "tell the truth" in her conduct; in other words, she may be unable both to improve herself and to inform others adequately about her appropriateness for the roles in which they might consider putting her. Consider, for example, the familiar trope of the executive who has surrounded herself with yesmen. This is a person whose choices to date have so arranged her surroundings that she will receive very little help from her coworkers in recognizing and correcting poor choices. Her increasing power, then, accompanies a weakening judgment and therefore increasingly misrepresents its own legitimacy, becoming increasingly dangerous to her.

In the extreme case, a person whose phenomenological intimacy has been developed almost entirely by reference to the results of poor choices, may, if unchecked, become an integral cog in a household, a community, or even a state, whose moral reasoning spirals downward uncontrollably. She may, quite without malicious intent, mislead others about the good in an increasingly damaging way. Such a person, indeed such a household, neighborhood, or culture, almost requires the intervention of a divinely inspired leader; or to use the less spectacular terms of Plato's *Meno*, they will need desperately some very good teachers. Because of this, however, people in such desperate circumstances are particularly vulnerable to political manipulations. In subsequent chapters I argue that, if unchecked, ours will be that household, that neighborhood, that culture. The twentieth century's trends in political candidates, the increased capacities for misrepresentation provided by modern media, the increased incidence of militia groups with charismatic but disturbing leaders, and the seeming desperation of our attachment to talk shows all seem to point to this conclusion.

WOMEN'S ROLES AND THE DOMESTIC AESTHETIC

I can no longer avoid facing the fact that the activities I have been describing as fundamental to moral reasoning are today, and have been for some time, overwhelmingly often performed by women. Furthermore, they are commonly thought to be the very activities through which women are oppressed. A word or two must be said here, then, about the relationship, if any, between what I call *domestic aesthetic skill*, the modern concept of *domesticity*, and the connotation of femininity that the domestic realm carries in our discourse. For *domesticity*, as the word is commonly used today, includes a plethora of activities that are not directly linked to the generic endeavor of choice I have defined.

Although my arguments are independent of any particular moral theory, they nonetheless presuppose that some conception of moral goodness can be imagined by almost everybody, under even the most slightly auspicious conditions for phenomenological intimacy, and that whatever conception of goodness a person holds, it obliges her to make choices according to it as a criterion. All moral theories, at least any that suppose all human beings to be capable of the good they delineate, must assume this much.

Consequently, whatever domestic aesthetic skill members of one sex or the other may be discovered to have and whatever their cause, these characteristics would not make either women or men any more or less obligated to conceptualize the good well and to make good judgments according to it than members of the other sex. For instance, we would still be likely to say that height is serviceable to a person (e.g., for putting her bags in the overhead compartment on an airplane) even if we established that men were as a general rule taller than women. Similarly, however, even if we were to recognize that tallness had its benefits, tall men and women would still have to take their height into consideration as a potential liability when, for example, they buy a car or a new suit. Thus, we could lay out a detailed theory of human characteristics and their moral liabilities and assets, as well as a theory of women's and men's differences from each other with particular attention to these characteristics, and still say nothing about the existence of different social roles or moral obligations based on gender. Yet, whatever facilities or weaknesses a woman may discover herself to have because of her gender, while they need not affect her notion of the good, they will certainly be included in her reflections as a factor in deciding how she will best be able to achieve that good. They are part of her capabilities "as an actor" in her life, and as a "director" she will need to consider them in choosing her roles.

If one, á la Hegel or Marx as I have described them, conflates one's notion of goodness with one's notion of one's own consciousness, then one is likely to apply moral connotations to one's gender per se, just as one might to one's height or one's talents in such a conflation in so far as gender is a part of almost any particular person's self-consciousness. If, however, one distinguishes one's consciousness of oneself from one's notion of the good or of the good life, or as I have described, conceives the end of one's actions as a life, which is modeled on goodness and beauty and is shared by members of a household, quite possibly both male and female, then one's gender per se may take on fewer, or at least more subtle and finely distinct, moral connotations. In such a case, the masculinity and femininity of any particular person are characterized, like any other physical or psychological characteristic, as but two factors to be assessed, pieces of material to be used, with a view to making a good life. Thus, femininity may or may not be an asset for a particular life lived at a particular time and place, and the same with masculinity; these characteristics may be assets or liabilities in both men or women, or only in one or the other. A person, for instance taking into account her social circle, her ideals, the constraints of her culture, and so forth, may judge it best to cultivate those characteristics in herself that she judges to be masculine, or she may decide it is better to cultivate what she takes to be her femininity or her androgyny, or she may decide it is best to forego believing in gender characteristics altogether and base her decisions on other criteria entirely.

Furthermore, it is important to an understanding of domestic aesthetic choice that whatever choices women and men may make in their endeavors to live well, once made these choices foreclose the freedom to do otherwise, at least temporarily. In other words, in addition to the oppression that may be suffered under conditions of direct coercion of our choices (with which I am unconcerned here), all choices sincerely made are in a certain sense constrictive; they all cut off certain opportunities that might otherwise have remained open. If one decides to run for president, one commits oneself to a fairly oppressive and difficult enterprise that may often feel like drudgery. One may have to defer or even cancel plans one had to do other important things, such as improve one's piano playing or have a child. Even under tremendous social pressure to fit into certain gender roles, in other words, we may consider men's and women's choices to be significantly freely made, yet, once made, constrictive. I think this is a consequence of the notion of *autonomy*, in Kantian moral theory, as "legislating the moral law to oneself"; we are free to legislate as we see fit, but because we are obliged by the laws we give ourselves, we freely limit our freedom.[33] Because all choices limit one's freedom, it is not really as important that our choices are made freely, in the sense of being unconstrained, as that our choices are made well. Weakness in one's ability to choose well, because of a phenomenological distance developed under the duress of a failed society and economy is, I will argue, a very serious limit to one's autonomy.

Aristotle recognized ignorance as a crucial duress on the will, and it is in this sense that phenomenological distance limits our choices (*Nicomachean Ethics*, 1109b30–1111b5). Where one makes a poorly thought-out choice, one fails to assess fully the dramatic impact of the character one dons through making it. I put this in the theatrical metaphor because I want to draw out the fact that whereas all choices limit one's freedom, the emotional affect of that constraint plays differently for different people. When a person makes a choice that actually makes the life she leads a better, more impressive one by her own good assessment, she is not necessarily any more or less limited in the ability to do otherwise, not necessarily any more or less regretful from time to time about opportunities passed by, not necessarily any more or less pleased from moment to moment than a person who has made a poor choice. Such a person, however, is *proud* of her choice and able always to refer to its reasons and to reaffirm them. To put it in Nietzschean fashion, she has the sense that she would make the same choice again and again.[34]

Someone who on reflection decides she has made a poor choice, on the other hand, is not proud of it, has lost track of its reasons, cannot reaffirm them, and consequently has little sense of how such a choice is to fit into her life from the present onward. Such a person may come to feel like a mere actor in someone else's play, even in a case where no external coercion has occurred. A person who makes a bad choice will not feel as responsible for it as a person who makes a more reflective choice. This is true even if the poorer choice is successful according to the agent's judgment at the time. For instance, a person who succeeds in attaining a promotion in a company with whose management policies she is constantly frustrated, may be pleased with her decision at the time, but she may still feel as if it were essentially just a savvy negotiation of a bad system from which she still feels alienated. Having gotten the promotion, she may look ahead vacantly, having no idea where to go from here, and her frustration with the company may be less likely to go away than it might have been. Particularly, a person who makes a bad choice and does not know how to avoid repeating it will feel very much a pawn in her own life. For instance, this woman may climb upward in this company year after year, yet never ease her fundamental distress; in fact, she may just exacerbate it. She may not be proud, for instance, of the way the management policy requires her to treat her increasing number of subordinates.

This seeming tangent has been by way of showing that the oppressiveness and coercion that many people today believe attaches to domestic pursuits does not attach to domestic aesthetic skill per se, nor even to the particular activities we have come to think must be done at home, at least not any more than in the generic sense that oppressiveness attaches to all moral choices for both men and women. Rather, domesticity has come to *feel* oppressive to many people because, through perhaps a whole series of socially habituated domestic aesthetic choices and as I will argue an overwhelmingly bad selection of economic and political possibilities from which to choose, particular domestic aesthetic choices that many people are making today are *bad ones for them*. Thus, women and men alike are finding that leading well-lived lives today is more difficult than they imagine should be the case, particularly in the sense that they find trying to do so a confusing enterprise. They are finding that reaffirming their decisions and using their past successes and mistakes to inform their present dilemmas is more difficult than they expected. They do not, in a sense, feel themselves to be in control of their own happiness, and they are complaining about this is a variety of ways.

In considering the historical and philosophical relationships between women and domesticity, we must rethink specifically what we want to mean by *domesticity* and to what we want to contrast it. In his fascinating book *Home*, Witold Rybczynski locates the origins of domesticity in seventeenth-century Holland.[35] Privacy, comfort, and family—as distinct notions separate from the shared space and responsibility, the social and religious significance of which were distinguishing characteristics of the ancient and medieval household—do not appear either in word or act, according to Rybczynski, until the bourgeois era. Yvon Thébert, considering the theoretical assumptions required to understand "Private Life and Domestic Architecture in Roman Africa," in Paul Veyne's *A History of Private Life*, thinks on the contrary that the roots of domesticity go back much further in history. "Private life," he claims, "is a product of social relations and a defining feature of every social formation."[36]

Regardless of the historical moment to which we attribute its derivation, however, the modern notion of *domesticity* does not primarily derive from abstract historical changes in policy, technological achievements, or political philosophy, but more often from physical changes in the surroundings in which people live. The activities we think of as domestic and the value we place on them are subject to the material conditions of domestic labor. They are not, of course, free from the effects of a particular society's system of ownership or of exchange value for work around the home, but they are far more heavily determined by the aesthetic, sensible qualities of this work than by its social status. The look, the size, the smell, the feel of houses and homes; the kind and number of people we find in them; their physical location in the neighborhood and city and country in which they are nestled; the amount of time we spend in them; and only consequently, the amount and type of labor that their maintenance requires: these factors, far more than the payment of household labor or the ownership of the plot, influence our conceptions of *domesticity* and of its social value and gender associations.

In myriad societies too many and various to discuss in detail, we find a great divergence in household structure from the homes to which we today have become accustomed. Wherever notions of *tribe* or *nation* supersede notions of family, for instance, we see very different physical groupings from those that figure around the nuclear family; responsibilities for work are shared in a variety of ways, although they still center on the provision of food and shelter, the decoration of surroundings, and religious dicta; the material qualities differ widely and in many ways from the decorations common in the modern West.

Of particular interest, perhaps, if we look at the development of modern European and U.S. households, are the ancient Greek, Roman, and medieval European constructions. The physical conditions of an ancient Greek household, for instance, exemplify a profound difference between their sensibilities and ours, and not just between our respective political systems. Their household was a fairly large plot of land on which were housed various family members, their slaves, and their guests with a shared responsibility for the cultivation of the land. The male head-of-household was the household supervisor as well as

the owner of the house and land, ultimately responsible for the production of food and the preparation of entertainments at important
public events. "A Roman household," writes Veyne, "consisted of a
number of domestic slaves or former slaves, a paterfamilias, his legitimate wife, and two or three sons and daughters, along with a few
dozen free men known as 'clients,' . . . A household was not a 'natural'
family."[37] Medieval European households, like their ancient predecessors, had large populations (25–30 people coming and going for different lengths of stay), although they shared sparsely decorated, cramped,
and cold quarters (usually one or two small, poorly heated rooms).
Household responsibilities, even in the cities, were shared by household members; even in later European cities that included private
homes, the bottom floor was often a public space. These, too, centered
on the provision of food and shelter (mostly heat) for their members.
The frequent entertainment of houseguests, friends, and neighbors was
common.

Thus, the private-public distinction, before the time we might
loosely call *modernity*, although it was important, did not *mean* the
same thing as it does today, even in the West. The gender differences
that, then as now attached to this distinction, therefore, did not signify
the same things even for our Western ancestors as they do for us. In
earlier eras, the household was often distinguished from the public
realm only vaguely and according to the different ends of each. The
household existed for the sake of *maintaining* the lives of its members
or of citizens in general (i.e., providing food, clothing, and shelter),
whereas the city or state existed for the sake of *cultivating* the lives of
citizens (i.e., providing law, ideals, order, education, and spaces for
social, political, and intellectual interaction among independent people).
Veyne states, "Roman nobles had a keen sense of the authority and
majesty of their Empire, but nothing like our notion of public service.
They made no clear distinction between public functions and private
rank, or between public finances and personal wealth."[38]

Today we have placed far in the background of our thoughts
those ends above and beyond physical survival, the responsibility for
which historically belonged to the state. Focusing nonetheless on public
utility and public notoriety, we have tended to give to the state those
functions formerly performed in the household of feeding, clothing,
and protecting our bodies. Under the auspices of increased individual
freedom, and perhaps through our interpretation of privacy as deriv-
ing from private property, we have yielded some of our personal responsibility for our lives and confused our concepts of private and
public ends or goods. Consequently, we are now under duress to make
the distinction between the public and private realms crudely, vaguely,

and in a way quite unlike that of our historical predecessors: according to the economic and scientistic criteria of contractual property ownership, legal guardianship, or romantic love and to overlook the obligations to take care of ourselves that fall to us in the realm that these borders represent.

Not until a group of people with the wherewithal and the desire to make private single-family spaces, such as are now our symbol of the private realm, came on the scene (i.e., the bourgeois) was there ever such a thing, and domesticity as we think of it today is still all tied up with the physical existence of private family spaces. Because of the strict protection of servants afforded in Dutch law, for instance, the bourgeois class organization in that country created a situation in which the woman of the house—a person in a position of authority, rather than a servant, and who now lived with her husband away during most of the day—cared for her own household.[39] The private ownership of modern capitalism was applied to the household, enabling craftsmen to build offices or to work in factories away or separate from their houses; consequently, it enabled household duties to be organized through a purely physical division of labor where provision for the members of the household became a distinct set of activities from the management of their activities and needs and where the two jobs could therefore be assigned to two individuals.

Ann Oakley, in her enlightening *Woman's Work*, analyzes the British development of domesticity as we know it into three stages, beginning in 1750, showing in the British context the historical origins of distinctions with which we are now so familiar as to imagine them primordial.[40] In the first stage, the fact that women who had spun and woven for their households moved out of the house to work in textile factories was taken as a promising sign for the financial security of the family and an opportunity for unmarried women to gain independence. This early industrialization also often physically separated wives and children from husbands to a much greater extent than previously. Consequently, the work each found to do differed in its style, type, and goals. Later, in the period between 1841 and 1914, according to Oakley, social and moral pressures in addition to some legal restrictions exacerbated women's condition in the home. Beyond the practical necessity of staying with the children, women faced for the first time a sense of moral obligation to "keep house" and a sense of inadequacy to bear the difficulties and filth of factory work. Class and social status were for the first time tied to domesticity and contributed to women's role in maintaining class conflict—single and working-class women still worked away from home. This period of history deeply influenced the current social distinctions between men and women and the consequent distinctions between their "proper" labor, ultimately creating the rift that still plagues us between upper-middle-class women who worked at home and lower-class women who left home to go to work. Between 1914 and 1950, according to Oakley, the moral and social association of women with the home was consolidated, despite a steady 25 to 45 percent of the paid labor force being comprised of women.[41] More people who could not afford servants could afford the houses and families that required them; women picked up the slack, doing more domestic labor than ever in addition to working outside the home. Although women gained considerable legal protection during this period, their social and moral positions became increasingly vulnerable, anxious, and ambiguous; women were torn between a desire for equality with men on the one hand and for the admiration of their peers for their stellar housekeeping and child rearing skills on the other.

Were it not for these very particular and contingent historical events in the physical conditions of work, economy, architecture, town planning, and so forth, many of the decisions we make about food, clothing, and shelter would not have come to seem like the feminine concerns they appear to be today. Obviously the good satisfaction of these basic human needs is everyone's concern and requires everyone's talents. In fact, to turn the tide on the way we read history for a moment, put this way it is obvious that people (in the modern era, primarily men) whose actions are unguided by the shared sustenance and goodness of the life of a household are derelict in duty and out of touch with their own history.

The moral, political, and aesthetic consequences of the historical regularity with which women have been associated with the home is far less clearly traceable than that regularity itself. What a woman considers "not feminine," may or may not also be considered by her to be "not good," depending on what she thinks femininity is and whether she thinks it is good: it also depends on how feminine, in her terms, she believes herself capable of being. Thus, although femininity has tended to be associated with being at home, that by itself does not constitute grounds for the belief that women's work is "marginal" or "valueless." No such evaluation can be rendered without reference to a particular historical time period, culture, and community and without moral reflection on the various qualities associated in that time and culture with the home and with femininity. Labor, character, and role can be and have been socially distributed in a vast variety of ways. Whether or how one society uses gender as a criterion for this distribution is an empirical matter, one whose evaluation requires careful reflection on its cultural costs and benefits. Furthermore, however precisely one pinpoints a culture or era, including our own, it is likely to have conflicting strains of moral and aesthetic opinion, including the opinions people hold regarding gender, manifested within it. Thus, the phenomena that present themselves for assessment are convoluted and indistinct.

We might point, then, to an early and widespread happenstance that women live physically close to children and therefore to the activities immediately concerned with feeding, clothing, and sheltering them. We might cite this happenstance as a contingent foundation for the various roles that women have come to play in the cultural evolutions of the Western tradition since the sixteenth century, which may be or may not be workable today. But we cannot point to any necessity, either for this happenstance (in fact, we do find male homebodies in many cultures including our own) or for the moral significance we have recently attached to it. The social acceptance and acclaim we tend to offer for men's and women's successes outside of or in the home (the latter of which is diminishing greatly today), can be considered no more than some among many duresses on choice that have fallen to individuals as a result of historical and cultural circumstance. In other words, no matter how narrow the social offerings and no matter how clearly a person may understand her own masculinity and femininity, the choices that an individual makes with regard to gender role will still be made somewhat freely and with an eye to goodness as long as her ability to reason about the good is still intact. And so the question of men's and women's proper roles will reduce to the question of what is a good path for any particular life to take and how one's understanding of that good can be influenced by one's surroundings.

Thus, although we may be able to make generalizations about the respect given to women or to household duties in particular societies and although reflection on these generalizations can greatly inform one's personal decisions, we should be very cautious about adopting positions thought to be either traditional or progressive. As I will argue, these essentially political positions toward moral questions and toward the study of history are ultimately just vague and disappointing substitutes for the well–thought conceptions of the good human life that ought to guide one's actions. In fact, I am inclined to believe and will argue later that the physical conditions of labor that have evolved since the seventeenth century have exacerbated both the distinctions and the enmity between men and women; they have exaggerated the symbolism with which we represent femininity and masculinity and skewed our moral evaluations of the activities of men and women.

However arbitrarily, the position in which the majority of women have found themselves in Western culture has ultimately given women, by now and as a group, more practice than men at making domestic aesthetic judgments, and this includes a greater involvement in the ongoing cultural institutions of this practice. Physical intimacy affects phenomenological intimacy, and because of their greater physical intimacy with household objects over this time period, many women—though of course not all—are in a different position today from which to make domestic aesthetic judgments than are men. Whoever makes decisions about the qualities of things in the home will remain responsible for their intimate scrutiny. Rotten or poisonous berries and nuts must be felt or smelled to be weeded out, both in the gathering and in the preparation; children's skin and hair quality, the tone of their voices, and the look and smell of their excrement must be scrutinized.[42] These are intimate, qualitatively based assessments requiring delicate aesthetic judgment. The job of making these judgments has tended to be designated to women. To the extent that women may have through the centuries had more practice at such things, we might expect that their judgments of objects of experience will be more refined than that of men.

While we may say that in a world of paid labor the unpaid labor we do around the house is exploitative, the fact that unpaid work done around the house *still gets done* at all, even in a world where it is widely recognized as exploitative, speaks to the simple necessity that we as a culture still attribute to at least certain types of domestic labor. Recognition of the unquestionable necessity of certain domestic labor may shed some light on its oppressiveness and freedom: No matter what else we may spend our pay on, we must eat, and *someone*, therefore, has to get the food on the table. This is the real bottom line. That we are oppressed by the fact that we must eat and clothe and shelter ourselves from the elements, that our possibilities are limited by our having to live in bodies, and that attending to the necessities imposed upon us by that fact is a struggle are simple facts that we all, men and women, must have faced since time immemorial. Furthermore, without this struggle, what *human dignity, character, virtue,* and other ethical terminology can really mean is not clear.

This—that the beauty and difficulty of having bodies is a vital part of what makes us moral creatures—is, I believe, the significance of Adam's and Eve's fig leaves in the Genesis passage with which I introduced my claims. It is a strange circumstance of our era that anyone can be deluded about these plain facts, that anyone can imagine that we are, or will ever, or would ever want to be, wildly free to pursue our professions or preferences without having to stop and eat, wipe our noses, clean up after ourselves, or wrap a towel around our wet bodies. In a world where the function of most of our activities, particularly our paid activities, is very obscure, the household marks an increasingly narrow realm of activities whose purposes can still be obvious to their practitioners. All things being equal—say, for instance, that *no* work was paid—to which activities would people then apply themselves? Although looking after the house is certainly a frustrating and unfair burden to bear alone, it is a more sensible, more clearly necessary burden than most of one's other obligations. And so we must turn there for a notion of simple skill and craftsmanship in a careless world.

In summary, then, we can say that the particular activities associated with domesticity today—housecleaning, making clothes, cooking, wearing appropriate outfits, caring for one's family in a private house—have come about as contingencies of history, sometimes falling to women and sometimes not. That these jobs have fallen most often today to women may have roots in some very common, perhaps universal, qualities of women's experience even if some or all of these qualities are also to be found in men's experience.

I think it undeniable, however, that both men's and women's moral skills, whatever their gender character and no matter their historical derivation, are needed in the achievement of impressive social characters and long-lasting happy households. Surely being physically near to household objects is not necessary in order to take the goodness of a household as a moral end, in fact it seems likely that being away from home and concentrating on less homely goods is a necessary part of leading a good life, both individually and for the sake of one's household. It is only because of the increasingly narrow focus placed in recent centuries on work done outside the house that we must now place a premium on domestic aesthetic practice.

✻

Thus we may come to some definition of the domestic aesthetic and some understanding of its relation to and distinction from other theories of moral, aesthetic, and psychological development. The domestic aesthetic is the skillful, and therefore critical, decoration of objects that an agent deems necessary to live a continuingly good human life, where human good is understood as shared in varying degrees by members of her social institutions, and most closely shared among members of her household. As such, it is work whereby one bestows gestures of love on objects with which she chooses to surround herself because she judges them able to satisfy her needs as she understands them and to satisfy these needs beautifully or pleasantly.

The domestic aesthetic takes as its objects potentially useful items and seeks to make them perfectly functional toward the good, that is, it seeks not only to make them functional, but also pleasantly or beautifully so. In this sense, the domestic aesthetic aims, as Aristotle claims cities should aim, "not at life only, but at the good life" (*Politics*, 1252b30). Because it is decoration, in domestic aesthetic choice beauty and utility are not clearly distinguished, but instead are both taken as indications of goodness in the general sense. The skillful domestic aesthete takes as objects those things (including people and actions) with which she can envision living happily. The good domestic aesthete, therefore, must be critically reflective, not only on the beauty and/or goodness of the decorated object, but also her own state of character. Therefore, we may say in a sense that in domestic aesthetic practice, agents take not only goodness and beauty, but also the truth as their guide in making choices.

As a last effort, then, with an understanding of all the constituent parts of the formula, let us define the *domestic aesthetic* as that more or less skillful practice through which agents develop, sharpen or slacken, and apply their notions of goodness, again and again, through the choice, judgment, and craftsmanship of things close to home.

CHAPTER 2

THAT MORAL REASONING IS DEVELOPED THROUGH THE EXERCISE OF DOMESTIC AESTHETIC SKILL

> Learning and the arts may be indispensable to living well, but they are not indispensable to living. In that sense, they can be considered a kind of luxury. Food, on the other hand, is essential to life. Nobody would turn to somebody else and ask him why he eats.
>
> —Keiji Nishitani, *Religion and Nothingness*

The domestic aesthetic is the catalytic skill of the skill that is moral reasoning. In showing this to be the case I remain neutral toward competing moral theories themselves; in other words, I believe that the domestic aesthetic develops or degenerates moral thinking whatever we think morality is. One could call the domestic aesthetic theory, then, not so much a moral theory as a developmental moral epistemology, a moral phenomenology. No matter what view one holds regarding the nature of goodness—its absolute truth or its relativity, its essence as pleasure or duty or happiness or truth, its independence or dependence on the mind, and so forth—the way one comes to think in such a way about the good, I will show, is modeled upon the way one makes domestic aesthetic judgments.

Having offered this reminder, however, I must begin my ruminations with a claim in the jurisdiction of moral theory, that is, that goodness simply *appears* in a reflection in consciousness between concepts and representations of objects (including actions, both of the agent and of others). This is to say that *things appear* to be good or bad, better or worse, to us; our very experience of things is of their being qualitatively better and worse things. Whether this appearance of goodness is all that goodness is, whether the true concept of goodness can change over time or in different cultures, and so on, needn't concern us here.

This appearance of goodness cannot be solely the responsibility of the object perceived (i.e., it cannot be directly caused by the object alone, or in other words, the appearance of good in objects cannot be wholly objective) because the same object appears differently good to different people or even to the same person at different times. When I bought this dress, I loved it. Now I think the feathers are too much. When I gave the stern assignment to my students, I thought it would build character. Now I am afraid it will scare them away from philosophy. Some factor other than the thing perceived must affect how good the thing appears to me to be. Perhaps these other factors, it may be claimed, are just the different surroundings or situations in which the object is found at different times or by different people. This is very likely partly the case; sensible qualities of things certainly change under different physical conditions and if the goodness of a particular object is sensible, then it may very well differ under different conditions. But because the situations, too, may appear differently, even to two people in the same one, the situation cannot account fully for the difference in their apprehension of goodness either. Twins share a piece of birthday cake made by their mom; one finds it delicious, the other, yucky. Two women, at the same time, from the same saleslady, get a free sample spritz of perfume. One finds it captivating, the other, saccharine. Thus, although changes in the physical situation will certainly affect the appearance of goodness, some other factor must play into the better and worse appearance of the object as well; it must be some capacities or ideas that are brought to the object and the situation by the agent who perceives and evaluates it. Thus far, then, quite in contrast to the Aristotelianism of my earlier discussion, a domestic aesthetic moral epistemology seems rather Kantian.

The agent, of course, cannot be held entirely responsible for the appearance of goodness, either, simply because the goodness *is apparently* the object's, that is, in the appearance of goodness, goodness *has the quality* of *belonging to* (if not exactly "being in") the object. Of course the whole configuration of experience may be attributable to the agent. Thus, further, and contrarily to Kant, the fact that the agent has anything at all to configure may be to the credit of the consciousness alone. Nonetheless, the fact that something has been configured that appears as other than the agent carries with it the transmission, if only in appearance, of some of the responsibility for the appearance of goodness to the configured experience; that is, even if representations of goodness originate in the agent, she could still not thereby control the appearance of goodness in the object by a pure force of her will. The objects of experience take on, or the agent gives them, an active contribution to the establishment in consciousness of their apparent goodness. The agent does not experience herself making up their goodness. Therefore, that goodness appears in things in the world, although it doesn't prove that goodness is as it seems, does prove that the agent does not appear in her own experience to make up goodness out of whole cloth, but rather to join with the objects of experience in formulating the experience of good qualities. Thus, both agent and object make contributions to the appearance of goodness. This again echoes what Dilnot called the "dialogic" relation we have with objects: even if one believes that all the "characters" in the "dialogue" are ideas of the agents', they would not all be equally under her control.[1]

Because sometimes—perhaps most of the time—one party to this effort is an inanimate object, its contribution cannot be a directly or intentionally conscious one; it will not contribute perceptions or judgments of goodness to the team effort that is the appearance of goodness in the object. Its perceptible qualities—which perhaps in part have been intentionally given it by an agent—but not its choices, figure into the resulting appearances of goodness. An inanimate object can only participate in the reflection in which goodness appears, as an occasion for it, a reflective surface. In an encounter where both objects are also agents, however, both contribute in each role; as both object and consciousness, both surface and depth. This can, of course, make for very complicated and rich reflections (e.g., when the description of the reflection of one becomes the occasion for the reflection of the other). On these occasions, the possibility opens up for help or misguidance in our reflections because of each agent's ability to affect how she appears to others.

This is, I hope, how we would want to envision a meeting or a conversation between two people. So long as our appearance and behavior presents empirical data to others, we cannot help but be judged as objects. So long as we are able to choose what data we present to others and so long as we are conscious recipients of whatever data they may present to us, we are free to make judgments about them and obliged to make them well. In contrast to Sartre's famous claim in *No Exit*, however, "other people" making judgments of us only becomes a "hell" when we lose faith in our ability as human beings to help one another correct wrong judgments. Similarly, a world in which all of us were fully agents toward one another and never objects—the sort of world many people might, offhand, believe to be desirable—would be a *practically* impossible world, in the sense of being an ethically impossible world. Although moral choice would be unnecessary in such a Kantian "kingdom of ends"—and hence it may seem inviting—so would human happiness be unnecessary there. In a meeting between two complete subjects, there is nothing for them to experience of each other;

there is no physical encounter between them, and as far as we can know, therefore, no physical distance between them to be overcome in their meeting. Whatever level of freedom might be achieved in such an encounter, it would be a freedom without moral content.

Thus, even the goodness of character of other people appears to consciousness in reflection, in this case a dual reflection, something like two mirrors facing each other. In such an encounter, just like that of the two mirrors, a tremendous reflective depth is created that does not take up any space. And, just like the two mirrors, and more so (because the two consciousnesses are not merely subject to physical laws but can play with the images they offer to each other) the obscurity and illusion possible within a single moment of reflection is compounded. Thus, the goodness that appears in such reflection may be even more difficult for judgment to ferret out than the goodness reflected in inanimate objects. This is to say that both the phenomenal qualities of the object and the agent's skill at judgment contribute to the agent's notions of goodness, both the goodness of that particular object and goodness in general.

REFLECTION AND MORAL LEARNING

This interaction between consciousnesses is the basis, in addition, of the possibility that nonhuman objects, too, can help or misguide us in our judgments. As Hegel and Marx both claim, man-made objects reflect human consciousness to their observers, the alienated consciousnesses of their makers.[2] Kant claims that in a sense the artificial and the natural are always analogs for us, at least when we approach them as judges: nature appears to the judgment, he claims, like art, and vice versa.[3] All three agree, then, that even inanimate things speak to us, *like*—if not, as for Kant, exactly *because of*—human beings. Similarly, as I discussed, for Kant in his "Third Moment" of the "Analytic of the Beautiful," one of the ways we can understand what objects say to judgment is that they are "purposeful in form" without revealing a specific purpose.[4] Thus, we may become confounded or deluded, in a sense, about the form of purposefulness even of inanimate objects. They can, like other people, and not just through other people, lie to us about themselves.

Just as visual reflections in mirrors or other shiny objects can be sharp or dull, so can reflection in consciousness be sharp or dull. In both cases, this quality of the reflection is also a team effort on the part of agent and object. Sometimes the mirror is dirty; sometimes it is polished especially well. Sometimes one gives it a passing glance or stares dully into it thinking of something else; sometimes one scrutinizes every pore and eyelash.[5] Similarly, the appearances of goodness that come about in reflection can be crystalline, wooden, or various qualities in between. And similarly, both agent and object contribute to this quality of apparent goodness. An old untuned piano with a beautiful tone, for instance, may sit unplayed in the back of the antique store, while this year's tinny-sounding model sells well from the front of the music store. That polyester is sturdy and very easy to clean does not enhance one's appreciation for Burger-King uniforms. The goodness that appears in reflections between objects and agents, then, is sometimes obscured by the dullness of the surfaces (even those surfaces behind which there is reflective depth, that is, agents) and sometimes especially clearly revealed by them. Well displayed, cleaned, or otherwise well-decorated objects, all other things being equal, demonstrate their goodness to agents better than hidden, obscured, or poorly decorated ones. Hence, Christ's exhortation "not to put your light under a bushel" may be interpreted at least in part as a reminder of one's obligation to present oneself clearly to others so that they may understand goodness better through reflection on one's own example.

This is so whether there is a lot of goodness in the apparent object, or very little. A well polished mirror will reflect both beauty and homeliness better than a dull one. Both an excellent and a mediocre recipe for seafood mousse will be better recognized as such when they are prepared properly by a skillful chef and served accessibly. Both a beautiful silk pair of pantyhose and a cheesy nylon pair will be better judged as such when they are taken out of their package, touched, and worn. Clearly recognized mediocrity is more useful, all other things being equal, than mediocrity that goes unrecognized. There is a better chance, as well, that an obviously or provocatively poor effort will lead to improvement in the agent's next attempt than a poor effort masquerading as a coup. We can say that a sharp reflection of an object's goodness is more likely productive, all other things being equal, of a better overall situation, whatever the object, than a dull one.[6]

A sharp reflection, then, can strengthen the phenomenological intimacy necessary for good judgment by better enabling consciousness to pick out the goodness of the object (i.e., what is good about it) from the object as a whole. This is similar to what Klaus Krippendorf calls the "self-evidence" of objects: "the efficient and instantaneous indication of what something is . . . an example of the 'correct' presentation" of its possible uses.[7] When sharply contrasted to the rest of the object, its good qualities are more easily held up in consciousness in comparison to the agent's prior conceptions of goodness than when the contrast is unclear. A slightly dull reflection may not affect a good judge very much, but it weakens a weak phenomenological intimacy by obscuring the contrasts between the object's goodness and its other qualities. The good qualities of an object made dusty by the build up of qualities irrelevant to or otherwise than its goodness can only with great difficulty be brought into consciousness to compare with prior notions of goodness. A pair of shoes bought from a mail-order catalogue, for instance, cannot be tried on; the texture of the leather cannot be felt; their comfort, beauty, and sturdiness, whether good or poor, cannot be well reflected in the catalogue format. A refrigerator with myriad special features (e.g., in-door ice maker, special glass door-in-door for immediate needs, hundreds of plastic drawers, glass shelves, plastic shelves, chrome shelves) may, unless the use of the features is clear, befuddle an investigation of its ability to store food and keep it cold. The various high-tech additions to a stereo, the enormous speakers and the plethora of gauges and knobs, may fill the mind of the listener with specifications and distract her, not only from the music itself, but also from the propriety of its quality and loudness to the room, or the neighborhood, in which she listens to it.[8]

The usefulness of an object for an agent's reflection upon it will also depend on both the clarity of the object's representation to consciousness and the current abilities of the agent. As is the case, for instance, in some Platonic dialogues, some of which I will discuss later, some people are able to make use of a conversation in which terms are not clearly defined, whereas some people need to stop and define terms before proceeding. Obviously, the need for clarity depends upon the strength of the judgment going into the experience of the object. The practice of judgment of a poor judge, in other words, may be bettered to some degree by a self-evidently good object and is likely worsened by a poor one whose poverty is obscured or masked; the judgment of a clearly poor object may still be good practice even for a very discerning judge, whereas the judgment of an only very obscurely good object may befuddle anyone who is not so discerning. A person who knows that the earth revolves around the sun will not be misled when told that the sun came up in the morning, but a person who is not sure about how morning comes about may take this figure of speech as a scientific truth. Similarly, the subtle reflections upon goodness that may be provoked for an experienced reader by an intricate novel may never arise for a reader unused to reflecting upon fiction. The experienced reader may have her wits sharpened by a fictional working of a moral failure; the novice may be confused or even misled by an attractive characters' misjudgment.

PRACTICING JUDGMENT

The appearances of goodness, then, as qualities of a reflection in which both objects and consciousness participate, both reveal goodness and at the very same time serve as material upon which reflection is practiced. The reflective agent, making judgments about the goodness of various objects, is a practitioner of judgment or possibly, therefore, of choice. Every choice is, then, a session of practice in which the agent may both take pride (or shame) and credit (or blame) for her performance, and learn how to make better choices in the future or, perhaps, grow more entrenched in habits of poor judgment. Thus, the objects themselves can be said to direct the agent's practice to some degree; they offer to consciousness occasions for reflection, possible foci for her attention. Like any teacher, the objects that surround consciousness may or may not be successful with the agent; she may or may not take the opportunities offered, may or may not make the most of those she does take up. Still, reflection on goodness can be neither practiced nor therefore honed without the object on which it partly depends; and so, the objects make a contribution to the direction of consciousness. As guides of consciousness, in this sense, all objects are our teachers.

There are good teachers and bad teachers, however, and the object that misguides the judgment by directing its attention away from the object's goodness can be said to be a bad teacher. The masterful practitioner of reflection, then, is a practitioner who is able to choose, among other things, good materials for her practice. In the same sense, teachers trust that a good student will come to class prepared with the right materials: a pen that works, perhaps, instead of a hidden comic book. Similarly, one sign of a good student is her ability to evaluate her teacher. A good judge will likely not settle for bad materials if she can help it. Therefore, working with useless or bad materials, no matter how abundant they may be, will signify a poor craftsman, economic austerity, or both. A state-of-the-art, well-stocked school library is no indication of a successful school board if the children in the district can't read or if all the books, though new, are uninteresting or badly written.

Furthermore, working with bad materials deteriorates the quality of the work and eventually the skill of the craftsperson. This is one reason why good craftspeople will not use them. Just as a person who is nearsighted or hard-of-hearing develops roundabout ways to compensate for her handicap, the practitioner of reflection about goodness without access to good materials develops roundabout habits of judgment perhaps becoming dependent on the decisions of external authorities to an unwholesome degree. If the heat doesn't work in one's apartment and the superintendent never fixes it, one lives through the winter with the oven open and comes to think of the kitchen as the only habitable room. If a woman with big shoulders can no longer purchase blouses without shoulder pads, she perhaps accustoms herself to surgically amending each new blouse. If a young man first living away from home tries his luck first at microwave dinners and never learns to cook, five years later he may have grown to love them and won't eat anything else.

Thus both agent and object not only contribute to the quality of the reflection at each particular occasion, but also contribute to the development of the judgment over time. If either the agent becomes a more skillful judge of apparent goodness or if the object comes to give a clearer image of goodness, the resulting reflections of that agent will be, all other things remaining equal, sharper than past reflections. To return to the mirror analogy, a mirror can be polished, and in a polished mirror, one's own image is not only clearer; one also comes to understand and use mirrors more effectively. A person who has come to make good use of a well-polished mirror, through the help of better objects, more clear reflections, her own determined apprenticeship, or all three in the future will recognize a dirty mirror and if appropriate, desirable, or necessary, know how to clean it. She will become a better judge of quality in herself and in objects other than herself.

This better judgment, which develops through good practice, is dependent on *phenomenological intimacy*, as I defined it earlier. The person better practiced in recognizing goodness is the person more facile at picking out goodness from the appearances of objects and comparing them in consciousness to her existing notions of the good. Furthermore, of course, one who is better able to work with objects to bring out their usefulness, desirability, propriety better also will be in a better position regarding the further formation of her own notions of goodness. This is the description of skill as both a facility and critical ability that I offered in chapter 1.

The better cook not only knows what spices give what tastes to food, she also knows how the various foods are supposed to taste. The good seamstress is not only the servant of the designer, but also the designer's advisor. The good potter not only picks wisely certain clays and glazes for certain pots, she also knows which kinds of pots are the best for which purposes and which uses of pots are most common and good for the people for whom she makes pots. I believe this is what Aristotle means when he claims in the *Politics* that the user should set the price of an object (*Politics*, 1282a20–24) or what Plato means when he so often has Socrates compare philosophy to a craft: skill is allied with judgment, and skillful practitioners, even if they are not highly educated in the fine arts or the sciences, must know not only about how to make good objects, but also about the good of the objects of their craft. Similarly, the person who has never owned a pair of shoes that fit or that lasted longer than six months, is likely to be a poor cobbler; the drinker weaned exclusively on *Ripple* or *Old Milwaukee* will have poor luck when she fulfills her lifelong dream of opening a vineyard or a brewery. An agent without skill at feeding, clothing, or decorating simply will not be an informed consumer. If she chooses really good objects with which to surround herself, ones with which she is really happy, it will not be by skill that she does so, but by dumb luck or divine inspiration.

Not only do objects teach us about their own goodness or the goodness of things of their type, they also occasion reflection about the nature of goodness itself. For over the course of her life, an agent obviously does not experience merely the occasional lousy or excellent thing, nor even merely a series of lousy or excellent examples of one type of thing. She experiences uncountably many things of uncountably many types (even if, as is most likely, what counts as a particular type of thing and how many of each are even worthy of attention is itself subject to each particular agent's judgment). Over the course of a life, the various apparent goodnesses of various objects and types of objects through comparison and reflection contribute to the agent's notion of goodness. In terms of the usual philosophical candidates for the moral good, we could say that various pleasant things contribute to her notion of pleasure, which the agent then finds to compare either well or badly with her notions of, say, beauty, goodwill, fulfillment, divinity, and so on, themselves developed in cooperation with the various objects with which they appeared throughout her life to date. Thus, the agent comes to commit herself to beliefs about the nature of the good, her allegiance with which, subject to the cautious interpretation of the continuing influx of data, she further consolidates or breaks faith.

Because moments of reflection upon goodness or upon the goodness of objects are sessions of practice, one's conceptions of ends have the strength of a level of mastery or the tautness of muscle. They express themselves as levels of knowledge of goodness, developed and maintained through practice or continued good use, or, contrarily they are weakened and atrophied by continued lack of practice or bad use. Accomplishment in the practice of judgment then, can be measured by the conception of ends, of good, to which it has brought a particular agent. If an agent's conceptions of ends are both appropriate to the kind of object being considered and clearly defined in her consciousness (i.e., if they are functional and can be maintained in the face of challenges) then we may assume that at least prima facie her reflective judgment is in fine fettle. Her "mirrors" have been polished enough or her attention has been paid sharply enough to make the agent's recurrent reflections on the whole progressively improve. If the agent's conceptions of ends are both inappropriate and fuzzy, that is, if they serve her poorly and cannot be sustained against challenges, then we may correctly assume that her reflective judgment is in poor shape. During the formation of her habits of judgment, her "mirrors" have been dusty, her attention has been spared, or both, and her reflection progressively deteriorates her judgment. The strength or weakness of one's conception of goodness is linked to one's phenomenological intimacy, like the reflections upon objects that they support. Just as an object whose goodness is more apparent is easier to "hold up" in comparison to one's conception of goodness than an object whose goodness is obscure for some reason, a clear, strong concept of the good is easier to "hold the goodness of objects up to" than is a weak or obscure concept of the good.

Consider, for instance, an act utilitarian who has a very clear, strong idea of what pleasure consists in; one that everybody she has ever talked to about it agrees with, for instance, or one whose promise has never in her experience failed to please. Such a utilitarian will have a considerably easier time making calculations of utility and justifying decisions for herself and to others, than will a utilitarian who is never able to articulate a notion of pleasure for which she can give reasons or to which she is strongly committed. An intelligent, well-versed utilitarian with a weak notion of pleasure will nonetheless make decisions, maybe even very assured ones, but the results of her decisions will serve her less well than they might. Assessing whether future decisions are consistent or inconsistent with them will be difficult, so that she gathers insufficient data about their adequacy and falls into a vicious circle. Or, take a Kantian who waffles about the narrowness or breadth of the maxims of action she articulates to herself. This weak and muddy notion of duty will have exactly the same effect in this life as a weak notion of pleasure does in the life of the utilitarian. As Alasdair MacIntyre noted, the Kantian with a strong notion of duty almost instinctively knows what maxims are appropriate and how to act in accordance with them.[9] This shows that what is most operative in her good decision is the clarity and strength of her notion of duty, not her Kantianism.

Because conceptions of ends are both the standard for and the result of practice with objects and because good objects are necessary to the good practice of judgment, we can say that if an agent has an appropriate and clear conception of goodness, it is because, *on the whole*, the objects of her prior experience (and, so, of her prior choices) have *represented goodness clearly and well* to her and because, *on the whole*, she has practiced carefully and well with them in her continuing judgments to develop further the skill of judgment, therewith to inform or consolidate further her conceptions of ends. If an agent has inappropriate and fuzzy conceptions of ends, we can say that it is because, *on the whole*, the objects of her experience and prior choice have *represented goodness vaguely and poorly* and because, *on the whole*, and perhaps because of their overall unclarity, she has been neither able to recognize their poorness nor therefore able to seek otherwise, nor therefore able to strengthen her conceptions of ends through them.

As in any practice taking a couple of days off or making do during a lean period with poorer materials than one would like makes little difference in the skill level of the craftsperson. A long period of unemployment, however, or an extended dearth of good materials will take a toll on even the most masterful practitioner. The amount of downtime that can be safely accommodated will vary with the skill level of the craftsperson in question. Arnold Schwarzenegger, for instance, although we may assume he never ignores his exercise routine for long, could laze longer without effect and require less work to recoup his strength than could George Wendt. Thus, the importance of practicing with good materials increases as the skill level of the practitioner decreases. Someone with very poor reflective judgment needs to start slowly, work hard, and take all the help she can get from the things with which she surrounds herself in order to improve significantly.

Thus, people who are well able to make judgments can be said, *on the whole*, to have been surrounded by things that occasion reflection upon goodness well—by being good, but more important, by being *clear* in their presentation of their own goodness—or by very good human teachers or both. Those who make poor choices, who reason badly about moral decisions, can be said *on the whole*, to have been surrounded by things that poorly occasion reflection about goodness—by being of poor quality, or again more important, by being *vague* in their presentation of their own goodness—or by poor human teachers or both.

This is true no matter whether we consider the objects as the chickens or the eggs. If we consider in the first moment the objects present to the agent, then we see their representations of goodness or paltriness partially informing her conceptions of ends, either for better or worse depending on the agent's acumen, and contributing thereby to the further development or deterioration of her judgment. If we consider in the first moment the judging subject, then we will see the state of her judgment partially determining the quality and clarity of objects with which she surrounds herself. In every choice, because it is an endeavor of the reflective judgment, both moments are at work, and thus in every choice both the agent's skill and the object's quality contribute a share to the value of the choice and its possibilities for education or foreclosure. The development of judgment occurs, then, in unsurprisingly Platonic and Hegelian terms through a dialectic between consciousness and representations of objects.

This is why, although questions of nature and nurture, heredity or upbringing, essentialism or inessentialism, and so forth, are not unimportant to our knowledge of how conceptions of ends are derived, they can never undermine the importance of practice. One's conceptions of goodness, the appearances of goodness in objects, and the phenomenological intimacy of the relation between them remain always at the risk of deterioration and with the hope of improvement. Upbringing, Kohlbergian stages, pure rationality, social convention—any of the various candidates that have been suggested as determining factors of moral reasoning—may indeed be, even as theories, objects of experience and occasions for reflection, very important to the development of that reasoning ability. None, however, can completely close the gap between a person's current moral reasoning—her state of character if you will—and the moral reasoning that she will apply to future behavior.

Because objects guide an agent's judgment of them and of goodness itself, they may be said to be her teachers about the good. If they are to be good teachers, they must improve the agent's skill at judgment, which will consist in improving the phenomenological intimacy between her conception of the good or of the good of the object, and her perception of the object. Because the ability of the object to improve judgment will depend on the clarity and accuracy of the object's representation of goodness to the agent, the object that serves as a good teacher about the good should clearly and accurately represent its own goodness to the agent over the course of her continued practice with it. While any object that represents its goodness clearly and accurately will be a better teacher about goodness than one that does so vaguely and inaccurately, a good object that represents its goodness well will, all other things being equal, be a better teacher about the good than a mediocre object that represents its mediocrity clearly and accurately because it will help the agent to develop a better notion of the good to serve as a standard of evaluation in other situations. Thus, for example, a bad cook who represents herself to her guests and family as such, and regularly suggests they go out for pizza, may well be as likely, all other things being equal, to raise gourmets as a person who is a very good cook but is usually too busy to prepare a meal. Only the latter, however, would be able, once she devoted the time, to teach her children to cook. A terrible cook who insists on preparing every meal and requires her guests to eat heartily and compliment the chef, however, is a sophist, doing nothing more than exercising her power as a hostess, parent, or actor to force people into confused habits of reflection about the good.

Consequent upon these reflections, then, and given the definitions of the domestic aesthetic from chapter 1—the choice and decoration of the objects that surround one with a view to their role in bettering a life—we can see that the domestic aesthetic is what fills this gap between a person's present character and the future development of her judgment. The domestic aesthetic is the practice of which each judgment, whether moral, aesthetic, or simple domestic aesthetic, is a session. The domestic aesthetic may be called, then, as another effort at its definition, the generic skill at judgment or choice from which both aesthetic and moral decision making get their exercise.

Through decoration, the domestic aesthete brings out in appearance, as clearly as is possible for her, the goodness of the objects with which she will most closely surround herself, and through critical reflection on those objects (some of which one may presume she chooses and some of which may appear accidentally to her choice) the domestic aesthete is educated in her conceptions of the good, which will be brought to bear in future judgments. These household objects, the things (and people and chores and activities) that fill her home life, are those things with which her domestic aesthetic practice is most often and most casually repeated. Hence, although we may want to say that those choices more properly and traditionally called *moral* and those likewise called *aesthetic* are indeed higher or more important kinds of choices and that they will occur regardless of the state of the agent's domestic aesthetic judgment, we still must face the fact that they rise and fall on the foundation of domestic aesthetic choices.

PRACTICE AND PLAY

Because I have described the domestic aesthetic as both work and gestures of love, as well as a dramatic exercise, picturing the domestic aesthetic as a kind of *play*, a word that carries connotations of all three of these practices, might be helpful at this juncture. In his "Creative Writers and Daydreaming," Freud derives the practice of, or the propensity for, imaginative writing from the activity of children's play in an effort to better understand both human psychological development and aesthetic judgment. There, he notes that children's play, far from being carefree or trivial, is earnest, effortful, and directed, and yet it is free in the sense of being openly expressive and not—or not very—repressed. Play, he claims, is a child's work, and yet for the child, play unburdens work of its drudgery. Play, Freud claims, is an activity through which we practice the skills we will need in later periods and wider arenas of life: adulthood. "A child's play is determined by wishes: in point of fact by a single wish—one that helps in his upbringing—the wish to be big and grown up. He is always playing at being "grown up," and in his games he imitates what he knows about the lives of his elders. He has no reason to conceal this wish. With the adult, the case is different."[10]

For Freud, also, the child casts himself as a kind of character in his play, just as he claims the creative writer writes himself into the characters of his story.[11] Thus, Freud thinks of childhood play as a kind of children's work or research, a learning process in which the child learns, among other things, how to grow up and behave acceptably. Although his interest in this particular essay is aesthetic, play, as well as adult fantasizing, clearly must also according to his theory function in moral development.

I understand the domestic aesthetic to be like Freud's notion of children's play; a generic practice of choice making in the senses both of dramatic and moral choices to which I have alluded. In the domestic aesthetic, we try out different social and moral roles and see how they fit our notions of ourselves and of goodness. That the sphere of domestic aesthetic practice is personal or private, accounts for its having the kind of openness that Freud attributes to child's play. Like child's play, however, domestic aesthetic judgments have repercussions and applications in the more traditionally moral (i.e., interpersonal or public) realm. For example, a woman considers, "Am I the kind of woman who can wear a strapless dress in public?" largely by imagining herself in such a dress at a public event or by trying on the dress at home or in a private fitting room and envisioning the figure she sees in the mirror going through the motions of a public occasion. In this way, however, she evaluates not only the way that dress fits her body, but also the way the *character* that she projects in that dress *fits her life*. A man who moves to a new neighborhood and dons the character of a weekend tinkerer about the house goes through a similar moral reflection; perhaps on the basis of his reflections he will incorporate this activity as a more or less indelible part of his character; perhaps he will instead laugh about it later with his pals who know him better. A divorced father asks himself, "Am I the kind of person who can shirk child-support payments?" in a sense fantasizing his demeanor as he faces his angry ex-wife. In an important sense, the only or best way to test one's moral character and so one's convictions in these sorts of instances is to play out the scenario of action to see how a certain decision fits in one's life, either in fantasy or some other safe venue for earnest play, that is, in private. In the domestic aesthetic, one tests the malleability of her character by discovering its limits, evaluating its achievements, and clarifying its goals in the safety and freedom of her home, or private ruminations.

This is a mixed judgment in the Kantian sense done not only for its own sake, but also for the sake of its consequences. As the activity in which work and play are undifferentiated, *play* in this sense captures the unalienated character of the domestic aesthetic. It comprises those activities that we do, in the same instant, both out of love for the object itself that we decorate and out of love for some higher end to which we hope to lead it. Domestic aesthetic activities, then, are those activities that, when they are done well, are done both for their own sake and for the sake of some other end. They may be understood, therefore, as those activities whose good is most apparently a part of one's own good or of *the* good. In this sense, as I mentioned, the object's use and its beauty meld in a decorative goodness that only the sort of creature we are can appreciate.

Lastly to understand the domestic aesthetic as play in this sense will pose it as a foil and a standard for various contemporary notions of both work and goodness, which I later criticize. The Derridean or deconstructionist notion of play, for instance, in which an uncontrolled and largely uncontrollable language teases and confuses our notions of goodness and truth, poses play as a contrast to the oppressiveness of language and of all structures generally understood as linguistic.[12] To submit ourselves playfully to the use of language and to play with it, is on this Derridean model a substitute for the genuine moral freedom that we imagine ourselves to have, but apparently do not. In the playful aspect of the domestic aesthetic, one is understood to play, indeed throughout one's lifetime and not just as a child, in order to practice and ideally to master how one influences and interacts with the world. The Derridean notion of play contrasts it to a notion of work that is irremediably alienated, the Freudian notion contrasts it to repression of our wishes. Domestic aesthetic skill founds the moral education through which we seek to remedy of its oppressiveness the work that is necessary to life by testing and appreciating its necessity and goodness. Our practice with domestic aesthetic objects, then, especially when they help improve judgment, may be helpfully understood as a very earnest kind of lifelong play.

Because judgment is a skill and so is bettered by practice, we may say not only that objects that teach better judgment are those that occasion better practice, but also that an object that occasions more, earlier, and more constant practice at judgment will be a better teacher about the good than one that is rarely attended to. Because the objects that occasion the most, the earliest, and the most frequent practice are the objects we find about the house, we may say that good and accurately assessable domestic objects are the foremost teachers we have about the good. Thus, I conclude domestic aesthetic practice is the elemental activity, the drills and scales through which judgment, both moral and aesthetic, is developed and refined. Domestic aesthetic activity is neither a cause nor a building block of the higher sorts of judgment it influences: just as, according to Freud, an adult will surely fantasize and indeed an artist may well create even (were it possible) in the absence of childhood play, everyone will make judgments whether or not they are well practiced in the domestic aesthetic. But it is through our evaluative and reflective interaction with household objects, probably as natural and unavoidable as child's play, that our capacity for judgment or moral reason is refined or atrophied.

CHAPTER 3

PLATONIC AND ARISTOTELIAN ETHICS AND THE DOMESTIC AESTHETIC

The Greeks took the question of leisure seriously. . . . Who today
would say that a nation could collapse because it didn't know
how to use its leisure?
—Sebastian DeGrazia, *Of Time, Work, and Leisure*

One of the ways that people apply and refine their notions of
goodness is by reading moral philosophy. Yet the little things we do
around the house, which I claim are so vitally important to the formulation of our notions of goodness, do not take up much space in the
pages of books and articles in contemporary ethics. In fact, they are
not much attended to in other philosophical specialties or academic
departments, except as an occasional, sometimes fashionable, slant
given to cultural studies, the problem of technology, or home economics classes.

The only places one tends to find these household matters discussed these days in any earnestness, with any real attention, are not
in academia; they are in fashion, cooking, or decorating magazines,
daytime television advertisements, some novels, and talk shows—the
major audience for which is women. Yet, if my understanding of moral
reasoning is even partly right, this state of affairs is very seriously
misguided. Not only should these household matters be as important
to men as to women, they should be as important to moral philosophers as to fashion models, hostesses, and handymen.[1]

I believe that the fact that contemporary moral philosophers do
not properly understand the role of the domestic aesthetic is due mostly
to the material historical circumstances in which we find ourselves
today, particularly to the easily accessible abundance of poor-quality,
vague, or otherwise useless food, clothes, and household items. This
is not, in the first instance, the fault of the Western canon of literature.
The modern mass production and sale of domestic aesthetic goods

have led to the neglect of both the importance and the practice of domestic aesthetic skill by modern moral and political philosophers. There are coherent and well-respected Western moral theories that respect and reflect upon the role of domestic aesthetic skill. In many ways, for instance, as I have already indicated, Kantian thought is perfectly consistent with a domestic aesthetic theory. I believe Plato's and Aristotle's moral and political theories, however, really give the domestic aesthetic its due. This is not to say that Plato and Aristotle held domestic aesthetic theories or even that the strains of domestic aesthetic theory in their works are among the most prominent or important. To even investigate, much less defend, claims of that order is far beyond the scope of this work. Here, rather, I pursue these two ancient and fundamental theories of human nature primarily as examples, because they carve out ways we might understand how and why our domestic aesthetic choices contribute to our moral ones. This is just one, however, among many strains in Platonic and Aristotelian thinking and perhaps an understated one.

PLATO

Plato's Socrates constantly harps on the topics of crafts and personal routines, particularly those relating to physical health and strength (medicine and gymnastic), and many of the dialogues take a position that acknowledges the importance of these crafts to moral reasoning.[2] I focus here on *Republic*, Book II, and *Gorgias* as particularly vivid accounts of the role of personal routines in virtue, particularly these dialogues' explicit discussions of cooking, clothing, and other decorative arts.

By Socrates's own admission, the most pressing concern of his life and study, and arguably the underlying concern of even the most metaphysically oriented dialogues, is an ethical one: the improvement of the soul. Why then the frequent return to the topics of cooking, weaving, cobblering, cosmetology, and so forth, that is, the occupations concerned with the health and beauty of the body, which according to many passages in the dialogues Plato seems to consider unworthy of philosophical concern? What place do such skills and routines occupy in the examined life? What role do they play in a specifically human life? Throughout the dialogues, it is not Socrates but the frustrated interlocutors, who fail to see the connection between cooking and cobbling, and so forth and the good life.

Crafts of the body and crafts aimed at pleasure, also called *routines*, are represented by Plato as "tools of tools" (the body is presumably itself a tool for living) and the discussions of them function in the Platonic dialogues in three ways.

First, the "routines" are explored as analogies and contrasts (in the *Gorgias* as imitations or shams) of the "true crafts"—the virtues—that are concerned with the health and beauty of the soul. In this sense, the discussions of these personal skills are used as teaching aids or rhetorical tools in the study of ethics.

Second, the routines are represented as sensible crafts, as opposed to the purely intelligible crafts of virtue, the crafts of the body serve as representative examples of practical knowledge. Plato implies that the virtues are crafts and indicates that craftspeople are the most knowledgeable, least self-deluded human individuals, short of philosophers (this is made very clear, for instance, in the *Apology*, 22d–e). Plato valorizes the crafts because (1) crafts are teachable skills, that is, they have rules;[3] (2) in crafts, unlike arts, an imitation is not easily mistaken for the thing imitated, that is, people are not easily confused or misled by crafts;[4] and (3) a product of craft is clearly both instrumental to and ordered in relation to its goal, the object that is created, bettered, or sustained by the craft.[5] The personal routines are examples of craftlike arts (i.e., teachable, rule-governed imitations or habits) from which we may learn about personal habits in general. By studying them the interlocutor and the reader unfamiliar with virtue can learn how to distinguish between good and mediocre practice and practitioners and in general about how people learn. In other words, the personal routines are practice at practice and so are the catalytic elements of moral learning.

Third, and most important for my purposes here, the discussions of these personal occupations show them to play a real and vital role, not just a didactic one, in the constitution of the soul because as long as one is human, Plato implies, falling into personal habits cannot be avoided. The flatteries or routines are the things this particular human animal must do and that, therefore, she is obliged to do knowledgeably and well. This third function of the discussion of the routines probably finds its most explicit expressions in the *Republic* and *Gorgias*, hence my focus on those dialogues here.

In *Republic*, Book II, Socrates builds a city in order to find Justice. Farming, weaving, building, and cobblering, he claims, are the first crafts and the building blocks of civilization because they are concerned with satisfying people's physical needs, which are, respectively of their importance, food, shelter, and clothing (*Republic*, 369d). The crafts that are involved with making the tools needed for farming, building, weaving, and cobblering are categorized under the main crafts as being instrumental to them (370d). Socrates groups under

these a tertiary set of crafts, those concerned with supplying the resources necessary for the other two groups, including that of building
and maintaining the physical strength necessary for building, loading
cargo, and so forth (370e–371e).

In this hypothetical original city, then, the crafts are all perfectly
ordered with respect to their goals, and their goals are perfectly ordered with respect to their uses: eating, warmth, and shelter. In this
city, the citizens' conceptions of goodness are unmuddied by the need
for beauty and their craft is unmuddied by art because their activities
are all purely and clearly functional. Their food, their clothes, and
their homes do not serve any cultural or artistic functions over and
above meeting their physical needs; they are not designed with imitation, fashion, or pleasure in mind, and so they can be said to serve as
purely natural signs of the satisfaction they aim to produce, much as
smoke naturally signifies fire. Spinach and peas, for instance, naturally signify farming because farming actually produces them. Thus,
all objects of craft are natural or unproblematic signs of the skill (or
lack thereof) of their producers.

In the Platonic ontology everything is a sign of the good to some
degree, and so is like the good to some degree because the form of the
Good is for Plato the highest existent and the creator of all things.
Every distinction of something from the good (i.e., everything that is
to some degree not so good) is distinguished from the good primarily
by *how* it represents or signifies goodness.[6] In artistic imitation as opposed to craft, for Plato an object's signification or representation of
goodness is confused; its good, in other words, is not so clearly apparent as for objects of craft and needs to be investigated. In other words,
all art for Plato requires interpretation and to that extent should be
understood as operating on the model of language. Art has the capacity
to misrepresent and so requires skeptical observers. Unlike the spinach
or peas of farming, a painting's signification is open to criticism.

In the primordial city, then, no one need make the fine critical
distinctions between signs and signifieds that will become necessary
once artistry is introduced into human existence; in other words, no
one need really exercise judgment in a city of pure, functional craftsmanship. No such city exists, however, in human experience. The rational ordering that results from the city's pure functionality fades
when the city becomes "civilized." For this is not as yet, of course, a
human city, but what Glaucon, the interlocutor at this point, calls a
"city of pigs" (*Republic*, 372d). It is a city that does not yet clearly
evince injustice or justice or any of the vices or virtues that specifically
characterize a human soul.

Callicles echoes Glaucon's quandary over this simple style of craft in the *Gorgias* (490d–1a). It seems unjust to Callicles that social status, marked by lush gardens and numerous and beautiful shoes and clothes, should be accorded on the basis of the craftsmanship of the person who made them. He, like Glaucon, seems to feel that natural signs of human skill are less valuable and less human than conventional signs of social status. Yet Socrates claims that this city of pure craft is "the true city... like a healthy individual," in which people live "at peace and in good health" (*Republic,* 372d). Socrates considers this the healthy city precisely because domestic aesthetic practice is perfectly skillful, or perfectly craftsmanlike there. The products of the farming, weaving, cobblering, and building in this first city are purely functional, not decorative; purely necessary, not luxurious; purely good (i.e., useful or beneficial), not just pleasant. They are therefore the products of pure (or "true") craft, or as pure as human craftsmanship can be unmixed with art. The "pig city" is healthy, just, and peaceful, but it is not available to human beings.

When its food, clothing, and shelter become *decorated,* the city takes on the character of art, described in the dialogues as either imitative (as in *Republic,* Books III and X) or routinized (as in the *Gorgias*). The citizens of the human city are carnivorous and luxurious; they now need "hunters and swineherds, chefs, cooks, and spices" (*Republic,* 373a). Their homes are painted and contain "couches . . . and tables and other kinds of furniture" (373a); their personal appearance is "beautified" (373b); they use "wet nurses, dry nurses, beauty parlors [, and] barbers." All the kinds of things that are luxuries and overabundances, things beyond what is necessary—all the "falseness" of fiction (which leads Socrates to advocate censoring it), or in other words, all those things I've described as "decorative"—are represented here as "imitation" and "routine," all of it "art" in the Platonic sense. Thus, in this passage of the *Republic,* art is not first and foremost fine art, as we understand that term today; art is first and foremost a transitional, decorative realm in which things signify both conventionally and naturally. This is not a city of beauty or fiction, plain and simple,[7] but primarily one of luxury, convenience, and attractiveness. For instance, hunting is represented among the arts here.[8]

When their activities become artistic endeavors rather than craft, the citizens of the city take on an ambiguous character. The citizens here are confused both about what they need and about how to satisfy their needs. Here, for the first time, the citizens must develop judgment in order to determine the value of their endeavors. They no longer share a conception of the good, no longer lead a meaningfully shared life. They suffer from the internal and external conflict that contrasts to the "harmony" that, in Book IV, Socrates calls "justice." "After hunting and art," Socrates declares (*Republic*, 373e), for example, "our next step is war."

Moral judgment seems to arise, then, with the ambiguity, the unclarity with which citizens are able to distinguish between needs and their satisfaction, forgetfulness and memory, bad and good, longing and fulfillment, and so forth. All of these dichotomies that citizens of the human or artistic city confront can be summed as a burgeoning gap in consciousness between knowledge of the good and apprehension of the appearances of good. The development of human nature is marked by the move from an undecorated, purely functional personal aesthetic to a decorated, both functional and pleasant one, that is, a metamorphosis from craft to art in the production of food, clothes, and shelter. Humans' newfound ability to make judgments comes with the unpleasant realization of the need to do so, the realization that they do not fully apprehend goodness. This conflicted human soul, unlike its counterparts in the life of pure necessity, needs to order itself toward the good. To do this task well requires a clear conception of that good. In this passage Plato describes this effort toward moral improvement as the attempt to make its activities more craftsmanlike and less artistic. Plato's vision of the origin of the moral consciousness here is the yawning of a gap between the idea of the Good and individuals' knowledge of it, something not unsimilar to what I have called *phenomenological distance*, and its cure is developing skill at making judgments as a part of one's personal routine.

In *Republic*, Book II, Plato demonstrates through Socrates's construction of the city of art from that of craft that the capacity for moral judgment arises along with the need for aesthetic judgment. Both moral and aesthetic judgment are described in surprisingly domestic terms as manifested in people's different ways of feeding, clothing, and sheltering themselves. In addition, Plato implies that the achievement of justice, the "health" of the city of craft, is attributable to something quite like what I have called *phenomenological intimacy*, achieved through the physical closeness and shared projects of its citizens; similarly, the capacity for injustice and the need for judgment are described in terms of the unclarity of notions and appearances of goodness in the city of art.

In *Gorgias*, Socrates and his interlocutors, (Gorgias, Polus, and Callicles) turn their attention specifically to personal health and beauty, both fleshing out in detail the analogy of these to the health and beauty of the soul and working out the status of that analogy by really attending to the role of cooking and cosmetology in the examined life of the philosopher and in the life of the virtuous person. The discussion is cradled within a dialogue about the definition of *rhetoric* and its role in moral education. The dialogue—itself a part of the literature of moral education—is therefore profoundly self-reflective. Indeed, its most striking feature is its almost existentialist comparison of two kinds of life, the rhetorical and the philosophical.

At the climactic point of the dialogue, Callicles breaks into a conversation between Polus and Socrates, not with a comment about the purpose of rhetoric, but with a personal criticism of Socrates's rhetorical style. "It seems to me that you run wild in your talk, like a mob orator, . . . Socrates, . . . you actually drag us into these tiresome popular fallacies. . . . Abandon philosophy and rise to greater things. . . . When a man who is growing older still studies philosophy, the situation becomes ridiculous" (*Gorgias*, 403a) Callicles's claim is that Socrates is a bad artist and a vulgar, tiresome rhetorician. Socrates, he claims, has a confused image of the good and is a bad judge of his own and others' character. Callicles's tone turns a civil conversation into a nasty competition. It boldly marks the fact that this dialogue deals with personal, intimate concerns. As a dialogue, it is directed most explicitly perhaps of all the dialogues (except probably the *Symposium*) at the characters and relations of the interlocutors themselves. The characters in this dialogue not only discuss personal aesthetics and its role in moral well-being, but they get personal while doing so. Thus, in *Gorgias*, we read not only a dialogue about different styles of the moral life, we also see several examples or scenarios play themselves out before our eyes.

In the beginning of the dialogue, Socrates engages the great rhetorician Gorgias in a debate about the value of rhetoric as an art (hence, the title of the dialogue). Gorgias claims that rhetoric is "the greatest and noblest of human affairs" (*Gorgias*, 451d). Socrates expresses his difference of opinion here by considering seriously the words to an old drinking song in which health, beauty, and honest wheat are represented as the greatest human blessings.[9] Through this rhetorical move to more humdrum topics (by Gorgias's standards), Socrates changes the tone of the conversation to one of jocular self-reflection. He gets away from the high rhetoric that draws the attention of the interlocutors away from themselves, their character, and their habits, and returns to the simplest, lowest form of communication. This is clearly a personal insult to Gorgias, the "high" rhetorician, and Socrates echoes this insult in the content of his claim, saying that personal well-being, not beautiful speaking, is the proper goal of a human life.

As Socrates and Gorgias try to consider the uses of rhetoric for good or bad, they are interrupted by Gorgias's student Polus, who at several points in the dialogue attempts to talk his teacher out of a tight spot (therefore both imitating and backhandedly complimenting Gorgias). With Polus the parallel raised between the health and beauty of a person and the health and beauty of words is drawn again, this time in considerable detail. Socrates and Polus lay out an entire taxonomy of human activity, of personal words and deeds. Rhetoric, says Socrates, is a kind of routine, like cooking, which aims at gratification and pleasure, (*Gorgias*, 462b–3a). As such, rhetoric and cooking are labeled as parts of "flattery," (in which, as we have just seen, Polus is engaged with regard to Gorgias and hence Socrates offers Polus an occasion here to self-reflect).[10]

In this dialogue, flattery is associated with routine. Flattery aims, according to Socrates, at the pleasure and the gratification of both the recipient and the speaker, and it is offered in ignorance of what is really good for either of them. Gorgias and Polus want to define rhetoric as a craft or skill but Socrates maintains that it is just a routine, which is to say it is an imitative art. "The activity as a whole [of rhetoric] it seems to me, is not a [techne or craft] but . . . I call it 'flattery.' Now it seems to me that there are many other parts of this activity, one of which is cookery. This is considered a [craft] but in my judgment it is no [craft] but only a routine and a knack" (*Gorgias*, 463a). Flattery, as a routine and a knack, is what a person does automatically, irrationally, and unconsciously. It is a mere talent, much like the idiot savant's that I described in chapter 1. And, like raw talent, the good of rhetoric or flattery in general is not clear; its value remains undetermined until it can be known what its effect will be on the souls it reaches. "And rhetoric I call another part of this general activity, and beautification and sophistic—four parts with four distinct objects. *But I shall not answer whether I consider rhetoric a good thing or a bad* until I have first answered what it is" (463b, italics mine).

Of what would the good or bad effect of this talent consist? Flattery is not a craft, but an imitative art, according to Socrates, using the very same principle here as in the *Republic*. Crafts are concerned with the good of their objects. They are fully ordered toward their objects, either because they are the results of pure appetite or because they are the result of pure rationality, and therefore, they are directly teachable. "To the pair, body and soul, there correspond two [crafts] . . . that [which] cares for the body comprises two parts, gymnastics and medicine, and in the political [craft] what corresponds to gymnastic is legislation, while the counterpart of medicine is justice. . . . There are then, these four [crafts] which always minister to what is best, one pair for the body, the other for the soul," Socrates states (*Gorgias*, 463b–c). Flattery belongs to the category of routine (the Greek term is *empeiron* or something "done by or through experience") and is a "semblance" of craft. It is an imitative

art and as such is not directly teachable. "But flattery perceiving this—
I do not say by knowledge, but by conjecture," he continues, ". . . in-
sinuating herself into the guise of each of these parts, pretends to be that
which she impersonates" (463b–e).

It seems, however, that flattery may be *learnable* through the
mimicry of a teacher or model and by experience with a medium.
Presumably, if routine is a part of imitative art, it is that part in which
activities are performed again and again, and through which, by this
repetition, one becomes increasingly facile (whether at a routine that
is good or bad for her). The routines described here are the four parts
of Flattery (the routines aimed at pleasure): rhetoric, sophistry, cooking, and beautification, and they are the semblances of political and
health crafts. Needn't the crafts of health and politics, however, also
be performed again and again? After all, legislators, judges, doctors,
and coaches devote their lives to their practices. *Legislation, justice
medicine,* and *gymnastics* are like "true" rulership in the *Republic*: they
are crafts—aimed at the good, rule governed, and teachable—but they
are human nonetheless. Therefore, they are never practiced perfectly
and without mistakes. A mistake, once made, will have to be corrected, and because the mistake itself belies the agent's true craftsmanship of the good life, she will probably have to correct her failings
through critical reflection on the examples of others. Thus, contrary to
many of Socrates's stated claims for Polus and Gorgias, there must be
good routines.

Evidence that Socrates believes there are good routines, despite
what he says to Polus and Gorgias, can be found throughout the Platonic dialogues. Socrates repeatedly praises the good friend or teacher,
the earnest student, the tactful host, the naturally moderate eater and
drinker, the honest critic, the graceful gymnast. These would seem to
be people with a knack for goodness, people with good habits, from
whom one can learn, *if* one is a self-reflective, critical judge and not a
mindless, rote imitator.[11] In *Gorgias*, despite its otherwise standard
Platonic criticism of art, the imitative arts are discussed very sympathetically. Talking to Polus, Socrates insists upon the value of explanation and principle over imitation. Speaking to Gorgias, however,
Socrates appealed to the wisdom and authority of an old drinking
song. This juxtaposition of rhetoric severely weakens Socrates's criticisms of the imitative arts. This is brought out when Socrates reflects
on his own rhetoric, remarking that the taxonomy he has developed
with Polus is geared to improve Polus's particular vision of the good.
"[I]f a cook and a doctor had to contend in the presence of children or
of men as senseless as children, which of the two, doctor or cook, was
an expert in wholesome and bad food, the doctor would starve to

death. This, then, I call a form of flattery, and I claim that this type of thing is bad—*I am now addressing you, Polus*—because it aims at what is pleasant, ignoring the good, and I insist that it is not a [craft] but a routine . . ." (*Gorgias*, 463a, italics mine).

Socrates's claim here that rhetoric is bad is quite contrary to his admission, not a page earlier, that the value of rhetoric is an open question until it can be defined. We can only surmise, then, that Socrates judges rhetoric to be bad for Polus because Polus is not yet an adequate judge. Socrates indicates this reading when he tells Polus, "when I spoke briefly [before], you did not understand" (*Gorgias*, 465e). Socrates admits, in other words, that he speaks differently, presents his views differently, depending on the level of understanding that he judges his interlocutor to have. Thus, his criticisms of imitative art or flattery or routine are all shown to be contingent upon Socrates's assessment, as himself a judge, of the judgment of his audience.

We see here in the rhetoric of the dialogue, despite its content, that the imitative arts as the dressing and decoration of words and deeds attract and therefore motivate students toward certain teachers and to the things they teach. Imitative art sets the style and creates the mood of a human life and therefore is the medium through which a life may be transformed. Here in the *Gorgias*, as in the *Republic*, then, routine, art, and flattery, despite comparing badly to craft, do have their uses as important tools for moral learning and can be judged better and worse according to their success in guiding agents toward the better practice of virtue. The best routine or imitative art comes across as being that which most nearly approaches the limit of routine (i.e., most closely approximates a craft), which is to say that its products represent their own value as obviously as possible.

Routine—here including cooking, cosmetology, interior decoration, rhetoric, sophistry, flattery, and so forth—because it comprises most of our ordinary human behavior, therefore ought to be one focal point of any inquiry into virtue and the teaching of virtue. Accordingly, cookery and beautification are Socrates's foci for the two succeeding paragraphs.

> Cookery, then, I say, is a form of flattery that corresponds to medicine, and in the same way, gymnastics is personated by beautification, a mischievous, deceitful, mean and ignoble activity, which cheats us by shapes and colors. . . . Sophistic is to legislation what beautification is to gymnastics, and rhetoric to justice what cookery is to medicine. But, as I say, [these] . . . tend to be confused with each other. . . . For if the body was under the control, not of the soul, but of itself, and *if cookery and medicine were*

not investigated and distinguished by the soul, but the body instead
gave the verdict . . . medicine and health and cookery would be
indistinguishable. (465d, italics mine)

Cookery and beautification (which include both fancy dress and
makeup) are described here (at much greater length than just the
passage I have excerpted) as the very most personal and most bodily
of the imitative arts, the semblances of medicine and gymnastics, the
most personal and bodily of the crafts. They are the rhetoric and sophistry of the body, where rhetoric and sophistry themselves are imitations of justice and legislation respectively. For those whose souls rule
their body (i.e., for fairly advanced critical judges who love virtue and
begin to achieve it), the distinction between imitation and original is
fairly clear. For those, however, who still love pleasure without regard
for the relation of pleasure to goodness (i.e., for those whose conceptions of ends are fuzzy, like Polus's), this distinction is quite confused.
In their hands, cookery and beautification threaten to corrupt the body
by covering up its failings or its illnesses.

Cookery and beautification, however, *in the hands of a doctor or a
trainer* respectively, are conspicuously not discussed here, that is, for
Polus. With Callicles, however, who is able "to test adequately a human soul" (*Gorgias,* 489a), "a godsend" (486e), and "fully competent to
decide" (489a), Socrates does not exclude routine activities from a discussion of virtue. When Socrates restates for Callicles the taxonomy
that he worked out earlier for Polus, he retains all of the distinctions
and their principles, but he leaves out the derogatory adjectives that
he used when talking to Polus. With Callicles, Socrates directly associates flattery with the other imitative arts, such as flute playing, poetry, and theatre. Finally Socrates capitulates to Callicles, granting him
that "one part of [rhetoric] I suppose would be flattery and shameful
mob appeal, while the other is *something fine*—the effort to perfect as
far as possible the souls of the citizens . . . " (503a, italics mine). It
becomes clear at this point that flattery is neither good nor bad in and
of itself, but a tool whose value is dependent upon the goals and skills
of the particular person who uses it. These flattering products of craft
bear some similarity to my previous description of the decorative arts;
they make both useful things and useless things alike seem attractive.
Therefore, the flatteries can be dangerous or helpful, depending on the
real good of the things they decorate and the judgment of both decorator and audience.

Callicles and Socrates decide that what is tasty and filling for a
body well-ordered with its soul, what gives pleasure to it, is what is
good for it and that doctors allow healthy patients to eat whatever

they choose (*Gorgias,* 505a, b). We might say, analogously, that teachers allow healthy minds to choose their own books and speeches. Note that this stands in contrast to Socrates's earlier claim to Polus, that a doctor with senseless patients would starve if she competed with a cook. The doctor whose patients know enough to trust her, on the contrary, can trust both them and their cooks. Flattery, however, is a good tool indeed for "doctors" (and judges and legislators) whose job it is to produce the good of senseless patients. All the doctor's, politician's, legislator's, or trainer's skill is wasted if she does not have at her disposal the artistry necessary to make medicine tasty, exercise interesting, punishment meaningful, or laws inspiring for the people she aims to serve (i.e., if she is not a good decorator as well as a skillful craftsman).

Cooking, beautification, rhetoric, and sophistry, then, would seem to be both legitimate and praiseworthy when they improve a soul, and illegitimate and blameworthy when they damage it. They are not only the most dangerous of tools in the hands of a foolish or vicious person; but also—so we must believe if we are to believe, as Socrates seems to, that it is possible to learn virtue—the most beneficial of all tools in the hands of a good teacher, ruler, doctor, or trainer. The passage asks readers, as it asks the interlocutors, to reflect upon whether we are "as senseless as children" by looking honestly at our habits and our ideas of goodness. Will we be swayed by a fancy cook when our lives and those of others are at stake? Without good teachers and the mastery of good routines, the dialogue seems to warn us, the answer is likely to be "yes." In fact, I claim in parts II, III, and IV that this is precisely our condition today and for very similar reasons.

In the *Gorgias* and in *Republic,* Book II, then, we see two Platonic ethical theories that illustrate, in a way, how domestic aesthetic judgment can be understood to develop moral and aesthetic reasoning. It is through one's domestic aesthetic practices—here, daily personal routines that express and refine one's character—that she forms the conceptions of goodness toward which her other choices will be guided. What kind of style attracts a particular agent toward the good will depend on the conceptions she presently holds on the present state of her character. These dialogues not only imply that this is the role of the routines, they also demonstrate the use of such a principle in clarifying the reader's and the interlocutors' notions of the good as one reads. For they are not merely philosophical texts that inform and exercise one's reason; they are dramatic rhetorical vehicles that attract one's attention.

In art, these dialogues imply, the value of one's work may be the result of inspiration or ignorance, of good habits or bad, of helpful influences or corrupting ones, of deliberate and reflective thought or of irrational and unconscious habit; but because we are human, our actions are likely to be the result of some combination of these influences. As artists, which humans necessarily are, we run the constant risk of mistaking imitation for original, luxury for necessity, pleasure for usefulness, and so on. A person's best work, the dialogues imply, is performed when her conceptions of good, of the object in question, and of herself are all clear and easily judged correctly when she is in a state something like what I have described earlier as phenomenological intimacy and what Plato represents as approximating a craft. It is good for us, then, to be guided in our artistic endeavors—including eating, abiding, wearing, and expressing our needs to each other—by knowledge of their limits in the realm of craft and therefore to produce the most rational and self-conscious art we can. It is also important that we try consciously to surround ourselves with good art, good artists, and good interpreters of art because these will teach us better about the good.

ARISTOTLE

Of the eleven moral virtues listed by Aristotle in the *Nicomachean Ethics*, seven are quite explicitly described in terms of aesthetic judgments: temperance, magnificence, pride, right love of honor, and all the "virtues of social intercourse"—friendliness, truthfulness, and wit.[12] We may take it in our reading of the *Nicomachean Ethics* as a whole that Aristotle's notion of moral and political judgment (essentially practical wisdom) has an aesthetic component. Aristotle even remarks, in closing, about the Sophists: "They say it is possible to select the best laws, as though even the selection did not demand intelligence and as though right judgment were not the greatest thing, as in matters of music" (*NE*, 1181a15–20), implying that the practical judgment of the good statesman is the same kind of aesthetic judgment as one sees in the good musician.

Temperance and magnificence probably most clearly represent the domestic aesthetic aspect of practical wisdom. Temperance, according to Aristotle, is the mean with regard to appetite. Aristotle understands temperance, however, not just as a matter of general prudence or restraint, but as requiring an aesthetic judgment of the quality of the objects we desire. *Temperance* is the predisposition to refine one's experience of the *sensual* pleasure of the sensation of *touch*. "Temperance and self-indulgence . . . are concerned with . . . touch and taste. But . . . the business of taste is the discriminating of flavors, which is done by winetasters and people who season dishes; . . . the actual enjoyment . . . in all cases comes through touch, both in the case of food and in that of drink, and in that of sexual intercourse. This is why a gourmand prayed that his throat might become longer than a crane's, implying that it was the contact he took pleasure in." (*NE*, 1118a25–27).

Temperance is a moderate aesthetic appreciation of pleasurable tactile sensations, such as enjoying the feeling of food in one's stomach, slight inebriation, or being touched. The temperate man is not, as the word connotes for moderns, the one who eats what is good for him despite its tastelessness or who avoids tasty things on principle. Rather, like Plato's "good patient," Aristotle's temperate man is the man who finds a healthy, well-cooked meal, the stimulation of exercise, and the comfort and excitement of good sex to be enjoyable. The temperate man is one whose taste is refined in a particular way, not one who curbs his actions in spite of his tastes. Furthermore, temperance is the most personal and domestic of aesthetic sensibilities, regarding as it does the pleasures of table and bed. The temperate man is specifically the layman, the homegrown or domestic aesthete. According to the previous passage, the professional aesthete is, like the gourmet, likely to be a temperate man; however, he has in addition to temperance a virtue specific to his profession, the ability to make fine discriminations in taste. Thus, what distinguishes temperance as a moral virtue rather than an intellectual study is specifically its amateurism or its domesticity as opposed to its professionalism.

Magnificence, according to Aristotle, is "fitting expenditure" where what is "fitting" is explicitly what is *tasteful*. "The magnificent man is like an artist, for he can see what is fitting and spend large sums tastefully; . . . And he will consider how the result can be made most beautiful and most becoming rather than for how much it can be produced and how it can be produced most cheaply" (*NE*, 1122b9–10). Although a poor man cannot be magnificent, the magnificent man is not concerned primarily with economic influence, but with style.

That the aesthetic nature of magnificence is domestic or personal is perhaps best shown by a look at its vice of excess, "vulgarity," by which Aristotle seems to mean what we would call *tackiness* or *ostentation*: "The vulgar man engages in showy expenditure; . . . he gives a club dinner on the scale of a wedding banquet, and when he provides the chorus for a comedy, he brings them onto the stage in purple, as they do at Megara" (*NE*, 1123a20–25). Because *vulgarity* is overdressing, overdecorating, and overfeeding, we can say that *magnificence* is dressing, decorating, and dining elegantly and appropriately. It is almost as if we have found in magnificence Aristotle's explicit claim that good domestic aesthetic judgment simpliciter is a moral virtue.

While magnificence, however, is akin to the domestic aesthetic as I have defined it, it is not confined exclusively to the home. In some passages, magnificence appears to be a very public and political virtue: "Magnificence is an attribute of expenditures of the kind which we call honorable, i.e., . . . all those that are proper objects of public-spirited ambition, as when people think they ought to equip a chorus or a trireme" (*NE*, 1122b18–20). The magnificent man, then, is something like the good host, both for his municipality and for his home; in fact, we see in Aristotle's magnificent man how the distinction between what is public and what private is differently cast by the ancient Greeks from how it is today, and therefore, how the household plays differently into the political good for the ancients than we envision it to today. In a host (or, more commonly today, a hostess) we find that person whose job it is to gracefully introduce the private and the public sphere. "Of private occasions of expenditure, . . . the most suitable are those that take place once for all, e.g., a wedding or anything of the kind, or anything that interests the whole city. . . . the receiving of foreign guests and the sending of them on their way, and gifts and counter gifts, for the magnificent man spends, not on himself, but on public objects. . . . A magnificent man will also furnish his house suitably to his wealth (for even a house is a sort of public ornament)" (1122b39–1123a7).

The passage is interesting on many counts. First, it indicates how much wider and balder the distinction between the private realm and that of the public has grown since Aristotle's time, in part because moderns no longer value the good host or hostess as a model of moral virtue. Today, the private realm of the household is the sphere of wild abandonment to our pleasures; in Aristotle's household, on the contrary, it is simply assumed of the good citizen that he "has his house in order." Similarly, we see in the passage that for Aristotle every citizen is a host, every home is a public ornament, every servant is a diplomat. In a sense his city has no "private citizens" at all; more important for my purposes, however, neither does it have any citizens whose public duties encroach upon their private lives. Rather, as we will see in the *Politics*, a good city-state is, for Aristotle, a necessary condition for intimacy, friendliness, and justice between citizens and members of households alike.

The passage also reminds us, as we may today be inclined to forget, that a great deal of the work of relating the private realm intricately and in an ordered way, to the public realm that was done in Aristotle's time by religion is achieved not just because religion dictated moral duties between persons, but because religion has ceremonies, activities for which people dress up and make special food. This observation can inform our notion of the devaluation of domestic aesthetic skill; for instance, one way contemporary Americans promote a general cultural and moral secularism is through contemporary designs in habits and priests' frocks, which are not only uniform and dull, but also deliberately made to look not very different from ordinary street clothes. By contrast, all other things being equal, the increased care and value invested in the preparation of food in a kosher than in a nonkosher home and so forth sustains the religious spirit in the members of kosher households. In other words, Aristotle shows how we, even today, can be understood to mark the moral value of the religious realm in part by our domestic decoration.

"The magnificent man is liberal, but the liberal man is not necessarily magnificent" (NE, 1122a–30). The elegant life in which the magnificent man can participate, but the merely liberal man cannot, is higher and partakes more of virtue than does the virtuous use of modest means. The distinction that Aristotle makes between magnificence and liberality shows that because striving to be virtuous is the moral obligation of men, we are morally obliged to surround ourselves with good, valuable, and beautiful objects to the extent possible within our means. Because, according to Aristotle, however, it may be crass to earn the money to live well (see the following discussion of ambition), those without large inheritances must take it as their lot in life that the highest virtue is closed to them. On such people falls an added moral responsibility: because they must strive to be as virtuous as they are capable of being with limited means, they must try to get the best things at the best price. This is exactly analogous for instance, to the situation of a person with a physical or mental handicap; indeed, Aristotle seems to think of insufficient wealth very much like a moral handicap: "for it is impossible, or not easy, to do noble acts without the proper equipment" (1099a30). In the Politics, however, Aristotle claims that a citizenry that is dominated by the middle class is the politically best situation because, among other things, it reduces the risk of revolt (Politics, 1295b35–40). Thus, we may surmise that how one deals with a "middle income" is important because virtue requires living within one's means, seeking the best in life, and being a good citizen.

Proper love of honor, about which Aristotle says quite little, is the virtue of dealing rightly with one's class situation. It is to pride as liberality was to magnificence. It "dispose[s] us as is right with regard to middling and unimportant objects" (NE, 1125b5). Although its vice of excess is "ambition," nonetheless "sometimes we praise the ambitious man as manly," and although the vice of deficiency is a lack of ambition, "sometimes we praise the . . . unambitious man as moderate" (1125b10–15). Here Aristotle faces the difficult interrelation between public and private goods that surfaces in a socially mobile society. Negotiating between social order and just distribution requires careful judgment of the distinction between talent and merit. It is not the modest heel, in other words, whom we praise for becoming ambitious, but the modest natural leader. Similarly, we would praise the ambition even of the immodest natural leader; his love of honor would be rightly actualized even if he were overly prideful. Because our society is very flexible and mobile, the proper love of honor occupies our moral discourse much more than it does Aristotle's. In contemporary moral conversation, we very often frame ethical questions in terms of the trade-off between distributive and retributive justice in terms of the merit required for one's receipt of social goods, and this is essentially a discussion of how to distinguish admirable ambition from petty social climbing. That Aristotle confines his discussion of ambition to a couple of sentences is a sign that he has implicit faith in the organization of Greek city-states, in people's good judgment, and particularly in the judgment of governors. That we can't hear enough about it is a sign that we have very little such faith.

For Aristotle the social position the ambitious man seeks is a moral prerequisite, and one is morally obligated to seek a position in which he may actualize virtue. The ambitious man, concerned as he is with unimportant objects, is petty. He does not aspire to greatness, truth, or beauty, but only, like Rodney Dangerfield, to a little respect. The man who has all the accouterments of honor, but none of the characteristics of the good man, however, is a terror; as revealed in the famous passage from the *Politics*: "For man, when perfected, is the best of animals, but when separated from law and justice he is the worst of all . . . the most unholy and the most savage of animals" (*Politics*, 1253a32–3). Thus, we see that the justice that is necessary to achieving the right love of honor requires something very similar to the self-reflection of the good domestic aesthete. Proper ambition is a function of how and what we desire and deserve as ordinary and small-minded people.

Pride is like magnificence in that it requires a grand scale and the possession of great things, where grandness and greatness are aesthetic categories. Pride is to right love of honor what magnificence is to liberality in that pride is the knowledge of one's own personal worth, where one's personal worth is very great, but it is also the "higher" analog to temperance. "For he who is worthy of little and thinks himself worthy of little is temperate, but not proud" (*NE*, 1123b5–6). The temperate man, as we saw earlier, knows his physical limits in eating, drinking, and sex. The proud man knows his limits too, but has few of them. He is large, healthy, and attractive, worthy of the honor he properly loves. The proud man, then, is not just a skilled judge, but also a skilled practitioner of personal decoration. "He will . . . possess beautiful and profitless things rather than profitable and useful ones; for this is more proper to a character that suffices to itself" (*NE*, 1125a12). He is well bred, genial, and attractive, aware of his beauty and enviable position, and frank but not showy about it. In this the proud man is reminiscent both of the Confucian gentleman and the well-bred lady of modernity. The good householder, of course, will be a proud man, and so it is not surprising that we should see in pride certain character tendencies that are more common today in women than in men.

The virtues of social intercourse are the virtues through which we judge and maintain proper intimacy and distance in our relationships. We could say that as the skills by which we attach and detach ourselves to others in our communities, these virtues are the "glue" that holds the city together. In truthfulness, for instance, it becomes apparent that *nobility*, as Aristotle uses the term, refers essentially to an aesthetic criterion for action. "He will avoid falsehood as something base . . . [and] . . . inclines to understate the truth; for this seems in better taste, because exaggerations are wearisome" (*NE*, 1127b5–8). We praise the mock-modest man over the conceited one because he "seem[s] more attractive in character" (1125b22). *Wit* is defined by Aristotle as "tasteful intercourse" (1128a1), whose excess is "vulgar buffoon[ery]" (1128a5) and whose defect is "boorish[ness] and unpolished[ness]" (1128a9). Yet Aristotle associates wit with freedom in an almost Kantian sense. The witty man is "as it were, a law to himself" (1128a32). The buffoon, on the other hand, "is a slave of his sense of humor, and spares neither himself nor others if it will raise a laugh" (1128a34–5). Thus wit is a moral virtue that depends on a reflective aesthetic judgment through which one evaluates whether a joke is worth its cost.

Friendliness is but one of the virtues of social intercourse, a part of what makes life lived with others pleasant. As such, it is aesthetically and domestically enough founded for our purposes at present; yet this is still not as clear as it becomes when Aristotle revisits friendship in Books VIII and IX of the *Nicomachean Ethics*. As described in *NE*, Book IV, the friendly man makes aesthetic judgments—judgments about pleasure and pain—and he is good at finely discriminating intimacy and distance (*NE*, 1126b25–1127a6). Friendship, however, the affectionate relation modeled on friendliness (1126b20–5), is a fundamentally political function, and so the virtue of friendliness is an important part of the practical wisdom demonstrated by the good statesman. "Friendship seems to hold states together, and lawgivers to care more for it than for justice. . . . When men are friends they have no need for justice, while when they are just they need friendship as well, and the truest form of justice is thought to be a friendly quality" (1155a23–5).

Both justice and friendship are ways of getting along together, ways of sharing time, place, and property. The political and moral importance for Aristotle of living together and sharing the things that fill a life cannot be overstated. It is the very essence of good human functioning. Both *Nicomachean Ethics* and *Politics* promote this theme: the good life for man is a freely and happily shared one. "For what is the use of prosperity," Aristotle states in the *Ethics*, Book VIII, for instance, "without the opportunity of beneficence?" (*NE*, 1155a9). The aesthetic nature of Aristotle's friendliness and friendship, combined with this integral notion of sharing, make these characteristics particularly useful models of what I have been calling *domestic aesthetic* skill. This is because in good (i.e., friendly) relations of any depth, Aristotle claims, people share first of all their conceptions of the ends of human life; they share an interest in the sense of being interested in similar things, not in the modern sense of having similar social position. Sharing the instruments toward those ends, then, is relatively easy for them and does not require the intervention of justice. "Unanimity" for instance, ". . . seems to be a friendly relation. For this reason, it is not identity of opinion, . . . but we do say that a city is unanimous when men have the same opinion about what is to their interest . . ." (1167a20–5).

Furthermore, in good human relations, the conception of goodness that is shared is of the continuingly happy relationship. For although "we must honor the truth above our friends" (*NE*, 1096a16), still, one should break off a friendship "only if one's friends are incurable in their wickedness; . . . one should rather come to the assistance of their character or their property inasmuch as this is better and more characteristic of friendship" (1165b18–9). In this sense, the commitment that Aristotle claims one should have to a friend is similar to the commitment I have claimed one should have to one's conception of goodness; and because, for Aristotle friendliness is akin to justice and defined, in part, by reference to shared ends, we can see that for Aristotle friendliness is a kind of general moral skill, not unlike the skill I call *domestic aesthetic*.

For Aristotle, in addition, the good life is a life lived long in good relationships of varying intimacy, distinguished from each other in part by the quality and degree of friendship between the parties, and in part, therefore, by the property that their relationship requires them to share. Justice fails when the parties do not share a common interest in being together; when the "political friendship" or "unanimity" (*NE*, 1167b3) in which they share an interest dissolves (1167b13). Thus, injustice turns out for Aristotle to be the allowance by one friend to let something get between himself and his friend, which is at the same time to let something intervene between his own activities and their proper ends. Injustice here is not, therefore, at least in the first instance, the result of some sort of inequality, but rather of betrayal and abandonment.[13]

Because a person has different interests in the various people with whom she is acquainted, injustice will occur, as will justice, in different ways relative to different relationships. Between husband and wife, injustice will appear as "oligarchy, . . . for in doing so, [the man] is not acting in accordance with their respective worth. . . . Sometimes, . . . women rule, because they are heiresses, so their rule is not in virtue of excellence but due to wealth and power, as in oligarchies" (NE, 1160b32–1a5). Because the rule over children is monarchical, injustice appears there as tyranny (1160b28). Friendships of utility are contractual relations, as are some constitutions, and injustice in these arrangements appears as unfair exchange (1162b5–3a25). These, of course, are not true of perfect friendships, and the parties willingly and without resentment end them when the purpose of the friendship—their shared interest in being together—fades. For instance, however useful may be one's relationship to the doorman of her building, under ordinary circumstances, Aristotle might say, no one ought to be indignant if one's doorman does not keep in touch after one moves out of the building.

True friendship and the true injustice that follows from its abandonment is distinguished from lesser friendships by its closeness and longevity, or in other words, by its intimacy. Those in whom we invest little can betray us little. In a friendship where the parties rightly expect and want to live together, however, which is the nature of true friendship (see, e.g., NE, 1156b5–7b25), their investment and therefore their betrayal, if it occurs, is immeasurable. Thus, the various Aristotelian political relationships are defined and distinguished by their phenomenological intimacy, which Aristotle calls, almost identically to my term, their "closeness in consciousness" (1171b33–5) and duration. In turn, he defines justice in terms of that intimacy as proper to it and injustice in terms of proper justice. "The justice of master and that of father are not the same as the justice of citizens, though they are like it. . . . Hence, justice can more truly be manifested towards a wife than towards children and chattels, for the former is household justice; but even this is different from political justice" (1134b9–10).

Because intimacy is phenomenological closeness over time, it is temporal and at least partly physical. Indeed, some Aristotelian passages claim that intimacy at its best occurs within shared physical space. When that space is very small, like the bed shared by husband and wife, then the intimacy of the relation is very obvious. But if children, slaves, friends, and fellow citizens are also all defined by qualities of intimacy, as different sorts of "partnerships," then intimacy must be spread over quite large physical spaces. Sharing, then, has to occur over these spaces, and this is made possible through property.

Under the influence of classical economics and Marxism, we tend to think of property as exchangeable for money, and money, therefore, as facilitating exchange over great physical spaces and among great numbers of people. Aristotle accepts this theory as far as its explanation of money is concerned, but he does not understand property in terms of either monetary exchange or simple use and exchange. Rather, Aristotle conceives of the sharing of things as an integral part of friendly and just relations, whose ends in the happiness of the people who live together give value to the things they share. Thus in Aristotle's theory of property the physical objects that people share are at once both integral and purely instrumental to the moral framework of their relationships. Economic choices for him are an integral part of virtue and vice.

Because "the state is made up of households" (*Politics*, 1253a40), the first responsibility of a good man and a good citizen, according to Aristotle, is "household management" or acquiring the necessities of life for the members of his household to share. This includes overseeing the work necessary to that end. The good household manager needs to be good at understanding and organizing the work through which his household maintains the necessities—farming or herding, barter and sharing with nearby friends, weaving, sewing, cooking, and so on—and further if he can afford it, at decorating these decorative crafts. Aristotle thinks of the acquisition that is natural to household management as decorative: it is not "pure provision," which indeed is achieved by nature, but a further work upon the products of nature. "The manager of the household—who has to order the things which nature supplies, . . . may be compared to the weaver, who has not to make but to use wool, and to know, too, what sort of wool is good and serviceable or bad and unserviceable" (1258a24–27).

Household management, in Aristotle's sense, is much like the job now assigned to the housewife (except that she goes to the store for much of what Aristotle's manager provides on his own estate): yet for Aristotle it is paradigmatically a man's job. Which duties and jobs fall to the woman of the house are a function of the constitution of her particular state, not of her gender per se (*Politics*, 1260b10–20). Thus, household management, the first responsibility of the man who would hope to be happy and good, is a skill at decorating (like weaving), and it is aimed at enabling the life we live closely with others to continue long and happily. Good household management, according to Aristotle, is the prerequisite for virtue and good statesmanship. Again, this generalized skill at good citizenship is very much like what I have described as *domestic aesthetic* skill.

Unlike both classical and Marxian economic theories, Aristotle distinguishes ownership of property as but one qualitatively distinct type of its use.[14] Aristotle's distinction between ownership and other types of use is the distinction of one type of phenomenological engagement we have with objects from other types. *Value* therefore, is just a name we give to the phenomenological quality of our relationships with the objects with which we live. To own a piece of land, for instance, which one rarely visits and never uses, is to stand toward that property in a different way than if one were to live on the property that one owns and to oversee its cultivation. To merely own the land—perhaps just to sell it for a higher price later—is to own it without committing to any sort of relationship to it. "For each is a use of the same property, but with a difference: accumulation is the end in one case, but there is a further end in the other" (*Politics*, 1257b37). To own land as an investment is for Aristotle to use the land in a particular sort of vicious way because it reverses or perverts ends for means by using property as a tool to obtain a still more instrumental tool—wealth (*Politics*, 1258a1–7).

With this theory of property, Aristotle is free to conceptualize private ownership as consistent with communal use. In fact, that one privately own property and share it is integral to the virtues of magnanimity, liberality, and pride. For the good man does not just avoid miserliness and greed because they pervert ends for means; rather his character is such that he does not enjoy property unless he spreads it around. For Aristotle, justice, as a "friendly quality," is a sort of "right sharing" of property with one's friends; a sharing that is proper to each friendship. As such, justice here is less a commitment to principle than it is a social graciousness about property. Thus, fair exchange—justice in the distributive sense—for Aristotle has nothing primarily, but only derivatively, to do with value, market or otherwise. Justice in the first sense has really to do with the propriety of our economic transactions to the intimacy of the friendships in which they occur. "This form of Justice is not . . . absolute . . . but in relation to our neighbor" (*NE*, 1129b25).

"It is by exchange that they hold together. . . . For this is characteristic of grace—we should serve in return one who has shown grace to us, and should another time take the initiative in showing it" (*NE*,

1133a3–5). Monetary property exchange is not for Aristotle what many consider it today—the model on which we base our friendships, political associations, and household relationships. For him it is precisely the opposite. The gracious sharing that is natural to our friendships, political associations, and household relationships is the model on which we base monetary property exchange. Suppose, to use one of Aristotle's examples of a very distant relationship (1133a5–20), a doctor and a cobbler who otherwise do not know each other meet to do business. The exchange of money facilitates their otherwise awkward relationship by allowing them to maintain the distance proper to it. Thus, the exchange is natural. By using money to maintain this natural, mutually recognized relation, distant parties are acting justly. Without the ability that money provides them to return to their comfortable distance, they would be an irritation to each other to return the favor. When the exchange itself becomes the reason for their meeting, the relation is unnatural and unhappy.

This is an Aristotelian criticism of a credit-based economy. Just monetary exchange is a natural relation, but one short of true friendship. By sharing judgments about how to share property and maintain their natural social relations, people get along together and stay friendly to the degree proper for their social intimacy. Justice in all these cases is the lubricant that prevents social irritation and unrest in the city. When the more friendly relations that we would prefer are not possible, justice keeps us from falling into incivility. Money, then, approximates the virtues (liberality and magnanimity, friendliness and pride) that good people ought to show each other. For Aristotle money is not a tool for ownership as much as it is a tool for getting along amicably with people with whom we are not particularly close. It is one of the social bridges that we make over the various gaps between publicity and privacy.

For money to enter into the household or private relations is for Aristotle essentially unjust because money is proper only to more distant relations. In a household, all property ought to be shared throughout everyone's lifetime and over a rather small physical space. "For the members of the family originally had all things in common; later when the family divided into parts, the parts shared in many things, and different parts in different things, which they had to give in exchange for what they wanted. . . . [This type of] natural riches and the natural art of wealth-getting are a different thing [from retail trade—i.e., from monetary exchange]; in their true form, they are part of the management of the household" (*Politics*, 1257a21–1257b19–20).

Aristotle might well have predicted that the main topic of dispute today among couples not getting along would be money. He would not attribute the unhappiness as we might, however, to unjust distribution or appropriation of funds within the household. He would instead claim that the fact that money is distributed in any way at all within a household signifies that it is already an unvirtuous and unhappy household in which the members are not close to one another and do not share either a vision of the ends of their activities together or of the use of property necessary to those activities. To share meals, for instance, will enhance the citizens' friendly feeling and consequently will encourage the just relations that approximate friendship. But because it is so important, food like all property must be carefully regulated and ordered in the good city. A city cannot expect to enjoy common meals, for instance, if its population is very large. Thus, Aristotle compares the common meals in Crete favorably to those of Sparta (*Politics*, 1271a27–38). Yet in Crete, where the meals were publicly funded and so less likely to cause resentment, the government had to struggle to maintain a generous meal and to keep the population and their appetites at manageable levels, which is unpleasant and rude. In Sparta citizens were required to contribute, and so were encouraged to be generous. This of course would be consistent with Aristotle's general claims about private property. To be the beneficiary of a good man's generosity inspires virtue; to be on the public dole is merely better than starving.

Here in the economic realm, Aristotle defines types of *property* by reference to an analysis of different types of relationships to things distinguished from each other by the ends at which they aim, just as he defined types of friendships by reference to an analysis of the types of relationships distinguished from each other by their ends. A comparison of Aristotle's discussion of friendship to his discussion of property brings out the phenomenological similarity between his notions of love and of work, and how they consequently share a kind of aesthetic judgment that is integral to maintaining a man's just relations both with his fellow citizens and with his property. This demonstrates once again the similarity of friendliness to what I call *domestic aesthetic* skill. Food, clothes, houses, land, and even money are for Aristotle essentially morally weighted entities, practice with which defines the various relationships in which one's character is developed.

❧

In Plato and Aristotle, we have seen two examples—themselves quite different from each other—of workable moral theories that may be understood as recognizing the importance of what I call *domestic aesthetic* activities and skills; thus they also provide further exposition of the sort of thing I mean when I talk about this domestic aesthetic.

Both Plato and Aristotle take both beauty and virtue to be integrally related to that more fundamental good from whence both one's aesthetic and moral judgments get their content. The claims I offer here about the domestic aesthetic, therefore, can be seen not only to have philosophical support, but also to be well-founded in philosophical tradition, if in an alternative reading of it. This points to the contingency of modern and contemporary moral theory upon historical events. It shows that we need not have come to think of morality in the unhelpful way that we do now and that we may yet be able to touch base with a tradition through which we can find ways to think clearly about the good. My goal in what follows is to identify the unhelpful content of contemporary moral discourse, try to trace some lines of its development, and point to places in which one can still tap into the kind of moral thinking that takes domestic aesthetic choices as its base.

Part II

Theory, The Domestic Aesthetic, and the Historical Relativity of Moral Reasoning

O, Kate, nice customs
curtsy to great kings. . . .
We are the makers of manners.
—Shakespeare, *Henry V*

CHAPTER 4

POSTMODERNITY AND CHARACTER

> The Law, he [the man from the country] thinks, should surely be accessible at all times and to everyone, but . . . he decides that it is better to wait until he gets permission to enter. . . . The doorkeeper [of the Law] frequently has little interviews with him, . . . but the questions are put indifferently, as the great lord puts them, and always finish with the statement that he cannot be let in yet.
> —Franz Kafka, "Before the Law"

A conflicted attitude about one's humanity is arguably a state chronic to human nature. It is apparent, however, that the character of today's insecurity about the nature and worth of being human is more serious—it has a more practical and material bent—than that of our ancestors. What is represented in the media, informed by postmodern theory, as a sophisticated kind of identity crisis (on talk shows, for example, or on commercials marketed to Gen X'ers) I would instead interpret as a developing *confusion* about how to conduct a human life. In other words, I do not believe that self-identity is an outmoded concept; only that maintaining a human life requires a moral skill that has gone out of style. In the following chapters I examine the insecure character of contemporary moral discourse and, on the basis of my previous claims that moral reasoning is honed and degenerated through domestic aesthetic practice, investigate how both academic theory and economic practice in the modern period may have contributed to the moral confusion we so often experience today.

Consider the following summary of the postmodern condition by Jean-François Lyotard, a household name in postmodernism: "What, then, is the postmodern? . . . It is undoubtedly a part of the modern. . . . The emphasis can be placed on . . . the obscure and futile will which inhabits [the human subject] in spite of everything. . . . The emphasis can also be placed on the increase of being and the jubilation which result from the invention of new rules of the game, . . . The postmodern would be that which, in the modern, . . . denies itself the solace of good forms, the consensus of a taste which would make it possible to share collectively the nostalgia for the unattainable. . . ."[1]

Examples of the sort of empty aesthetic of sophistication that Lyotard describes (which represent contemporary life as "futile" in its efforts to order its choices and actions, denying itself a "taste" that would allow "collective life," ignorant of the limits imposed upon it by nature; indeed, "jubilant" about their absence), which have already for many years been fashionable in academic discourse, have now more generally become the rage and invaded popular political and moral discourse. The *me* generation of the 1970s and 1980s to which Lyotard's remarks here were presumably originally directed, with its self-defeating attempt to define the human good in terms that the Western economy could satisfy, has by now given way, beyond the merely self-violatory jargon of late '70s punk, to the strangely moralistic carelessness of alternative rock. Nike responded to the invasion from planet Reebok—where there were "no limits," where there was "no pain"—with ad campaigns in which athletes bleed, vomit, and display their scars: although these commercials at least recognize that athletic virtue is made meaningful by the physical obstacles it overcomes and not by the fantasy into which it lets us escape, this is certainly a skewed vision of the appeal of shoes, much less of a particular brand of shoes compared to others.

The manipulative advertising strategy of the 1984 and 1988 presidential campaigns with their sharply opposing rhetorical imagery of two kinds of the American Way disintegrated by 1992 into two indistinguishable series of confused montage, and this repeated itself in 1996 with less verve. The impeachment proceedings against President Clinton, coupled with the public's pervasive lack of support for them, are particularly revealing: The distinction between the concepts of the "good president," the "good husband," the "good employer," and so forth, required to clarify and judge the issue seemed beyond the abilities of the media; the prosecutors and U.S. Congress belied the sexual mores they appeared to advocate by publicizing the sordid details of the affair; and the consuming public, who bought the commodities whose advertising budgets supposedly dictated the ubiquitous sensationalistic coverage, expressing its preference for other entertainments and government expenditures, nonetheless did little to affect the coverage and continued to buy the products at an especially satisfying rate.

One might read this all as evidence of the meaninglessness of life, of the aimless dispersion of simulacra into which we have devolved or as which we now see ourselves. Despite their increasing attraction for the facile rhetoric of postmodernism, however, consumers, voters, and readers of theory are demonstrably unsatisfied by this sort of representation of goodness. Whatever the fashionable way to think about the good, people continue to try to order their lives toward a good they rightly imagine is humanly possible and yet difficult. Living creatures, at least most of the time, in general simply do struggle for organization and coherence, for survival and success, for clarity of purpose and its effective achievement. As I have argued in part I, we simply do not observe living creatures, certainly not those we call human, striving lifelong for entropy and degradation, although the fact that we do sometimes strive for these tragic encounters with the infinite may be among the things that give human life its potential for moral misdirection and its need for redemption, precisely because the tragic or euphoric loss of oneself is a fragile anomaly within the larger direction of life.

Were this not the case, advertising, however vague, deceptive, and empty, would not be able to sell products. The great appeal of the battered athletes in the Nike commercials is not their scars per se, but their willingness to acquire them in pursuit of athletic greatness, that is, the nobility of character the scars imply. The success of advertising to promote its many misleading images of the good life depends on people's innate desires to live rightly and well. As Studs Terkel in his deeply insightful reading of modern American life circa 1972, *Working*, sums the opinions of the 130 "average" Americans he interviewed: "I was constantly astonished by the extraordinary dreams of ordinary people. No matter how bewildering the times, no matter how dissembling the official language, those we call ordinary are aware of a sense of personal worth—or more often a lack of it."[2] Indeed, I argue in succeeding chapters *against* the now-familiar screed that advertising is a kind of mass deception, dumbing down the viewing public through a kind of rhetorical violence. Rather, I believe the techniques and effectiveness of advertising in our age, though not praiseworthy, are not the causes but just more symptoms of the phenomenological distance that plagues our judgment; they are not the intentional manipulation of consumers by producers and advertisers, but instead our confused, well-intentioned, social coproduction.

We find further evidence of moral effortfulness in the recent eruption in various media of references to old television shows, old commercials, old movies, and so on. The sophisticated satisfaction that is gained from this knowledge of trivia, of minutiae of nostalgia for an only recently passed history of mass entertainment seems to be one of the few good hopes people have nowadays for meaningful, challenging entertainment and a tie to a shared tradition. We want to demonstrate our knowledge, our historical consciousness, our entitlement to citizenship, and we eagerly await these opportunities to sharpen our wits and share a memory. Although this love for nostalgic intertextual references may be consistent with the postmodern analysis of ours as a society of signs, such an analysis does not by itself explain the nostalgic character of the signs, their quality as shared moments of recognition among members of a culture. The tragic euphoria Lyotard describes, the nostalgia for nostalgia itself, therefore, can be understood as an expression of the concerted efforts people still make toward value.

The postmodern claims, therefore, though disturbing, are sympathetic; perhaps increasingly so. More and more, we do witness people actually conducting their lives according to the very confused, dysfunctional vision that the postmodernism of mass culture too often extols, and, I will argue, we sense that this is attributable somehow to the "increase of being" such as Lyotard describes. Something about our relationship to *stuff,* as both workers and consumers, has gone desperately awry and has led to awkward relationships among and within us. Still, the postmodern analysis does not address ordinary people's actual behavior in that it does not acknowledge the unhappiness of the necessity with which today's constant reinvention of ourselves is mothered.

An Unsatisfying Freedom

One difficulty faced by contemporary thinkers when they try, both in and outside of universities, to sort out what it means to choose well what to do is that the concept of *freedom* (especially of choice) today carries more connotations than it can live up to. For different reasons, most contemporary Americans value quite immeasurably what they think of as freedom, and yet for most to be free means everything and nothing at the same time. This is because for most a first answer to the question, "What is freedom?" is "The ability to do what I please."[3] Yet on reflection, "what I please" is simply not a useful concept in the absence of any reflection on what is good for me to want and in what my abilities consist. Nevertheless, any suggestion that one's desires be refined or redirected, even by one's own moral reflection, tends to be rejected as an imposition on one's freedom.

I believe that this attitude is partly attributable to the language of the market, or what I describe as the "tactics of fashion," which have conflated what are already problematic political and moral notions of freedom with empty pseudoeconomic notions of *free choice* on the market. I believe that the vagueness of our contemporary notions of freedom, combined with the depth of our attachment to them, are immediate and core symptoms of the mistaken epistemology of moral reasoning against which I argued in part I, symptoms of the phenomenological distance under which our judgment is suffering. I will argue that our contemporary notions of freedom, although largely influenced by economics, have wholly moral and political connotations and are wholly abstract: they cannot be concretely imagined, nor therefore, can they be socially manifested. Whereas much of the vagueness of our notions of liberty comes, as I argue in parts III and IV, from mass-produced objects and mass-media representations, they are also influenced by theory—both directly, when the producers of these representations read theoretical works, and indirectly, when their teachers, bosses, and consumers do so. Thus, it is worth spending some time fleshing out some influential theoretical models of freedom and investigating their shortcomings and possible effects on character, on the way people actually conduct and evaluate their lives.

In his famous 1958 article, "Two Concepts of Liberty," Isaiah Berlin distinguishes what he claims have been the two major conceptions of freedom presupposed in Western political and moral philosophy.[4] What he calls "negative freedom" is essentially the absence of external human constraints upon one's actions, and his "positive freedom" is essentially self-mastery—"deciding, not being decided for."[5] Berlin insightfully claims that different conceptions of freedom entail different conceptions of self-identity; negative freedom requires a relatively simple free agent—nothing but the actor whose movements either can or cannot be interfered with.[6] Positive freedom, on the other hand, is linked to a conception of a divided self, he claims, part of which is a "rational" decision maker, a "higher" self that can ideally resist the internalized influences of others or of the "lower" self. In other words, Berlin's negative freedom is neutral with regard to the goals of any particular agent's actions, which according to Berlin may well be vastly heterogeneous. Positive freedom, by contrast, is linked to the notion of a self for whom some goals are better than others are, and, according to Berlin, to a rationalist or perfectible notion of self-identity. Indeed, Berlin claims that for the advocate of positive freedom, all goals of action must, ideally, logically entail one another.[7]

According to Berlin, "every interpretation of the word *liberty*, however unusual, must include a minimum of what I've called 'negative' liberty. There must be an area within which I am not frustrated."[8] According to Berlin, however, a political theory that advocates only the protection of negative freedoms, such as John Stuart Mill's, is not based in an accurate notion of self-identity: "The bulk of humanity," he responds to the likes of Mill, "has certainly at most times been prepared to sacrifice this to other goals: security, status, prosperity, power, virtue, ..."[9] One might suppose that Berlin advocates a certain minimal notion of positive freedom in any political theory, as he has negative, such that these more specific, higher goals are always acknowledged. Indeed, he does seem to believe that positive conceptions of freedom are at least psychologically ineradicable. Yet Berlin's position on the necessity of positive conceptions of freedom to political theory is less than clear. Although he admits that "it is a profound lack of social and moral understanding not to recognize that the satisfaction that each of them [positive and negative freedoms] seeks is an ultimate value . . . among the deepest interests of mankind," he also claims that theories that advocate positive notions of liberty risk paternalism, totalitarianism, or at least cooptation by such governments.[10] Citing Rousseau, who infamously claimed that a citizen can be "forced to be free,"[11] Berlin argues that "the common assumption of these thinkers [advocates of positive liberty] . . . is that the rational ends of our 'true' natures must coincide, or be forced to coincide. . . . Freedom is not freedom to do what is irrational, or stupid, or wrong. To force empirical selves into the right pattern is no tyranny, but liberation."[12]

Thus, although Berlin is sympathetic to personal or individual desires for self-mastery, or for social groups' desires for self-determination, he fears these desires when they occur on the part of political theorists or governments. Seemingly on account of this fear, Berlin ends the essay by sublimating *both* notions of freedom to the political systems in which they occur, stating: "I do not wish to say that individual freedom is, even in the most liberal societies, the sole, or even the dominant, criterion of social action."[13] Thus, ultimately, Berlin advocates "pluralism, with the measure of 'negative' liberty that it entails, . . . [as a] . . . truer and more humane ideal than . . . the ideal of 'positive' self-mastery by classes, or peoples or the whole of mankind."[14]

That Berlin ultimately backs away from liberty in either of the forms he delineates at such length in favor of a pluralistic political system is profound evidence for my earlier claims that no concept of freedom can live up to contemporary expectations and that an inflated investment in the notion of freedom is evidence of phenomenological distance. For Berlin defends his eventual backpedaling from liberty to pluralism specifically by reference, not just to the impossibility of moral perfection, on which I certainly agree with him, but also to the impossibility of moral learning. Indeed, Berlin equates all attempts to reevaluate one's goals to a kind of "inner totalitarianism" or what postmoderns might call *totalization*. "Human goals are many," he claims, "[and] not all of them commensurable. . . . To assume that all values can be graded on one scale, so that it is a mere matter of inspection to determine the highest, seems to me to falsify our knowledge that men are free agents, to represent moral decision as an operation which a slide-rule could, in principle, perform."[15]

This is a vicious circle, however, not so far from the inchoate "doing what I please," because if inconsistent human goals cannot be comparatively evaluated, as Berlin claims here they cannot, then whenever one sacrifices her freedom to the achievement of other goals, as he claims occurs for the "bulk of humanity," one must do so basically just because it pleases one. Thus, neither of Berlin's concepts of liberty yields a notion of self that is able to make the free choices that its brand of freedom protects. The self, in either case—whether it is an undifferentiated source of action as is associated with negative freedom or a ranked group of distinct sources of action as is associated with positive freedom—is just acting out. Berlin's version of the self is unable to self-reflect or self-evaluate, and so unable to *change its mind*— surely a prerequisite for the use of either kind of liberty. Its conceptions of the good function as mere premises of action, never entering into negotiation, or as Dilnot expressed it, into dialogue with their results or foundations in the sensible world; it can only do either as it pleases or as someone else pleases.[16] Hence Berlin's bald dichotomy between pluralism and totalitarianism. Berlin's self, then, suffers from a near complete phenomenological distance, acting out whims unreflectively despite its noble willingness to sacrifice to high ideals. Of course such a figure is in severe danger of becoming a dupe or a tyrant: She has no discretion. Hence Berlin's fear is well warranted by his conception of the self, but if his conception of the self is correct, no political system could protect us from the eventualities he fears.

Among contemporary theorists, Michel Foucault best captures our ambivalence and confusion about human freedom, especially in his last work, *The History of Sexuality*. There he finally gives rein to his intuitions that "power/knowledge" is a freeing as well as a repressive force.[17] He depicts its liberating power not unlike Berlin's positive freedom and resistance to it similarly to Berlin's negative. However, even with this insight, Foucault cannot manage to shake the baggage of his earlier works in which he analyzes very thoroughly the development of power/knowledge over history into an all-encompassing, repressive manipulator of otherwise free individuals.[18]

The case Foucault makes is compelling. He convincingly depicts the mechanisms by which power is imposed (which certainly do include many modern social institutions) and how the various claims of "science"—in one sense, at least, the general collection of "knowledge"—have been repeatedly used in that effort. However, because Foucault remains faithful throughout his work to the principles that "power [and therefore knowledge] is exercised rather than possessed,"[19] and that "there is no difference between marks and words,"[20] he is unable to depict how an individual might actually *use* power/knowledge to freely achieve her ends.

Because no one ever *has* power/knowledge, but rather only *exercises* it, power/knowledge is devoid of concrete content. Power/knowledge, on this model, allows one to engage freely in rigorous activity, to expend its great energy, but not thereby to *do* anything. Similarly, that words have no more or less meaningful content than marks, and marks no less or more meaningful content than words, speaking and writing (presumably, two important ways that power/knowledge is exercised) become nothing more than putting marks in the world, imposing them like a mere machine on the listener, the reader, the watcher, the self. Thus for Foucault as for Berlin, agents operate at an almost complete phenomenological distance, as good as unconscious.

In addition, these intellectual commitments of Foucault's by default lead him to define freedom and individuality essentially as resistance to meaning. No wonder acting on our own recognizance seems confusing, especially to the ever-increasing number of tacit Foucaultians, such as those who have popularized the power/knowledge trope. This empty notion of freedom cannot by itself give meaning to a life. These two principles of Foucault's provide a well-argued foundation for the pervasive belief that conducting oneself in contemporary society is nearly impossibly oppressive. Just like Berlin, Foucault's notion of the self is nothing but either the tool or the wielder of power/knowledge; what marks Foucault's position as postmodern is only that this empty, impossibly disparate notion of the self is explicitly valorized.

To investigate how these notions of the self and its free action fail us, both as theories and as moral influences, it would be well to contrast them to Aristotle who, I have argued, is truer to people's experience of choice making than contemporary theorists. Aristotle did not associate voluntary or free action either with wild or undisciplined action or with self-mastery, as Berlin claims he did (Berlin includes Aristotle among adherents of positive liberty), but instead with ability or "praiseworthiness"—the ability to discern and accomplish the virtuous actions that tend toward happiness. Foucault and—with regard to the pluralism he advocates—Berlin, understand freedom as something that is restricted by knowledge, directing our will along some paths and away from others. By contrast Aristotle claimed (contrary to Berlin's characterization) not that knowledge leads to freedom, but only that, in addition to compulsion, ignorance definitely impedes it (*NE*, 1110a1–5).

In other words, Aristotle understands freedom as a tool in one's attempts to achieve the good life, a tool that works best under optimal conditions, which for Aristotle include the absence of external restrictions to action and accurate or reliable knowledge. One might still achieve a happy life, though—or at least a fairly happy one, or at least the happiest one possible in one's circumstances—when one's freedom is restricted to a degree.[21] Although Aristotle claims that virtuous action must be voluntary (and means by this something like what Berlin means by its expressing positive liberty), not having the opportunity to act voluntarily in a particular instance, nor therefore to act virtuously, may or may not affect the goodness of one's life. Whereas never having the opportunity to act voluntarily would of course, according to Aristotle, limit one's possibilities for happiness, having no external restrictions upon one's choices would be just as devastating.

Indeed, Aristotle's main ethical discussion of free action occurs in the context of establishing the warrant for praise or blame, not in the context of decision making at all (*NE*, 1199b30–35). For Aristotle vast knowledge and unrestricted movement in no way imply good moral decision making because we could easily imagine them the possessions of a morally vicious, miserably poor, or profoundly unfortunate person. Thus, to bring Aristotle into the contemporary argument, we could say that although restrictions of freedom may prove to be obstacles to the achievement of a good life, they are not necessarily so; the possession or protection of freedom per se is relevant only as one among many factors that contribute to good moral decision making and the possibilities for a good life. Aristotle's conception of freedom, like Berlin's and Foucault's, implies a conception of self, but here it is a self such as I described in preceding chapters, able to comparatively evaluate various goods and to weigh the possibilities and value of achieving them in light of various obstacles—a self that is a conscious agent, albeit constricted in various ways, not the pawn of unconscious forces.

Although Berlin usefully summarizes many modern conceptions of freedom, then, in taking Aristotle (and Plato as well) to be mere advocates of positive freedom, he overlooks their emphases on the interdependence of self and other—in love and craft (for Plato), and habit and skill (for Aristotle)—that I discussed briefly in the last chapter. The disparate, unconscious self that is presupposed by both Berlin's and Foucault's analyses of freedom is a self so conceptually distinct, so alienated from its surroundings that it cannot do otherwise than obey them or dictate to them. For Plato and Aristotle, as in a domestic aesthetic theory, on the other hand, agents who are skilled in the conduct of their lives are understood to be able and likely to distinguish themselves conceptually from others and seek individual freedoms for some purposes, and to associate themselves conceptually with others and yield concern for their freedom—and not just in the contractual, or "positively free" sense—for other purposes. Out of love, devotion, sensibility, inspiration, and so forth, people give their attention or even their lives to things they believe to be good, as in the many examples of domestic aesthetic decoration, the gestures of love I discussed earlier, and as opposed to exchanging their time contractually.

To depict Plato's and Aristotle's treatments as theories of positive freedom, as Berlin does, or to see their notions of virtue and vice as just the temporary harnessing of power/knowledge, like Foucault, is essentially to see their theories of human decision making as contractual, self-determined. It ignores the different dramatic, moral, and political qualities of agents' activities, as well as the seriousness of agents' relations to their surroundings such as I discussed in the preceding chapter and identifies a person with and by only her empty freedom. This is a similar identification, here in terms of free agency, to the one I argued earlier was made by Hegel and Marx in terms of a person's relation to the objects of her labor.[22] It is essentially to conflate the human decision maker with the good; and in this case, I ask again, what guide can there be for self-improvement?

A newborn infant, for example, left entirely free to do as she pleases, will probably lie around gurgling, flailing, and crying for her mother. The right to bear arms or to speak freely may be this child's from birth if she is a U.S. citizen, but they are empty freedoms until the child can hold a weapon or form sounds into words. The right to blither meaninglessly and to be interpreted by others as they see fit, which we often seem to claim is desirable, founds a freedom that cannot be exercised. It is in this sense, I take it, that Alasdair MacIntyre will ask us to "consider the following possibility.... What would it be like if social control were indeed a masquerade? ... That what we are oppressed by is not power, but impotence...."[23]

Authority cannot be resisted or imposed successfully over the course of a life without the sensible content of character developed through domestic aesthetic practice. For an individual to offer resistance to external forces or to exercise self-determination she must have strength of character; there must be a reserve of concrete characteristics—serious, reflectively held likes and dislikes, but also skills, talents, particular physical characteristics, and so forth—available to her to pose against an internal or external threat. An individual cannot acquire any and all possible characteristics; some possibilities must be eschewed and some adopted. Consider, to revisit the analogy from part I, an actor with no conception whatsoever of the costumes, props, or sets in the play in which she is cast: one who cannot even call them to mind. Her character development will be exceptionally poor, merely a grammatical reading of the script. She would soon be eaten alive by the other actors, even if they only had the slightest bit more sense of the play. The forces upon which such a person could call to hold her position on the stage would be used up in an instant. Berlin, speaking in the person of the totalitarian advocate of positive freedom evokes precisely the misconception of the theatrical metaphor I have criticized previously—"I must, if I can, impose my will on them, . . . 'mould' them to my pattern, cast parts for them in my play,"—envisioning the playwright or director of a play as its totalitarian dictator, as if the production were not a joint effort to achieve a shared vision of quality in which everyone's contributions and their evaluative reflections are relevant.[24]

I argue that the postmodern has less to do with the "the obscure and futile will," or the "invention of new rules of the game," or the "denial [of] . . . the solace of good forms," as Lyotard surmised, less to do with the construction of identity or with the protection of freedom, in other words, than it does with struggling against the deterioration of a basic *skill*, the skillful discernment of useful or pretty objects and abilities from dumb, dull ones; the ability to decide one's conduct, rather than just to opt for—or worse yet, merely to ally with or evoke— one fashion over another. No human being is simply free to do whatever she pleases; only an infinite character is able to that, and our characters are not infinite. I am not free to be a seven-foot-tall man; nor would I be any more free to be such a thing just because the technology were eventually developed that enabled me to change both my gender and height and if my right to do so were protected by law. Without the development of a character, over time and through good judgment, which knew how to be a seven-foot-tall man, these physical changes would be as useless to me as setting the infant out on her own or plopping a script in the lap of a lousy actor. I could do nothing with it. This is the frightening position in which we too often find ourselves today because our setting, props, and costumes are just expressions of the thoughtless, desperate tactics of fashion.

I will argue that these conceptualizations of freedom and self-identity, models such as those offered by Berlin and Foucault, and many of the modern philosophers whose influences they represent, are gauges of the phenomenological distance typical of our age, and that these conceptualizations derive in part from the economies in which agents find they have to operate. Where we represent ourselves in theory as selves who are in no position to *use* the freedoms that we nonetheless want to protect, we express to ourselves our own dissatisfaction with the choices by which we find ourselves confronted and with the quality of life in which our choices have resulted. I argue below that this dissatisfaction derives from the meager opportunities for practice of domestic aesthetic skill that our economic, social, and intellectual climate have offered.

Despite the seeming cynicism of the foregoing analysis, however, I take it as a given that every person "seeks what appears to him to be good," as Plato's Socrates claimed. The success of postmodernism, deconstruction, and all the other morose, manic, or confused trends in academic discourse are evidence that their followers believe these philosophies to be in the service of what they consider the moral or political good. That people will make conscious efforts to rid their lives of meaning is a kind of weird evidence of the lengths to which people will go and the courage they will muster to do what they believe to be right. Political and philosophical schools do indeed now promote themselves in this country through the tactics of fashion, but to quote Kennedy Fraser, whom I discuss later, "our society is neither so naive nor so cynical as to hand itself over to fashion without in some way believing that fashion is a worthy guide."[25] Thus, I agree with Lyotard that the impending failure of domestic aesthetic skill is at least in large part a result of the "increase of being"—a glut of objects with which judgment can no longer keep up—and to this extent, I sympathize with many of postmodernism's sentiments and intuitions. We are beginning to suspect, on account of this increase of indistinguishable objects, that it doesn't matter what we do; that any choice we make is as good as any other; that any place we hang our hats is home. However, I do not attribute the increase of being, nor the tactics of fashion in whose spirit they are offered to us, to any malevolent, manipulative power. Rather, I believe that good judgment has simply become very difficult for us.

MacIntyre's Criticisms of Modern Ethics

This last claim is akin to the "disquieting suggestion" with which Alasdair MacIntyre begins his *After Virtue*—that our culture just plays at decision making among the rubble of a far distant moral scheme.[26] MacIntyre claims that modern moral reasoning and argument have devolved into bald, empty assertions and counterassertions of incommensurable moral claims. He attributes this to the historical development of what he calls the "emotivist self," a notion of moral agency, very roughly derived from Hume, which models it on emotional acting out. The contemporary individual's vision of herself, MacIntyre claims, of her own actions and beliefs, is of a jumble of preferences and whims. She envisions her own moral claims as nothing but the expressions of these feelings or wishes. MacIntyre claims, in other words, that the average person today simply accepts as a truism the initially radical philosophical claims of the emotivists, who, following Hume, claimed that morality was just an expression of sentiment. MacIntyre's disquieting suggestion obviously bears some resemblance to the claims I have been developing in this chapter, and his analysis of the situation has become a kind of paradigm in philosophical ethics. Hence, it will behoove me to clarify my position here by comparison and contrast with MacIntyre's.

According to MacIntyre, the degeneration of moral discourse is the result of the Enlightenment project—both philosophical and so-cial—of liberating the individual from the bondage of Aristotelianism. That project was always doomed to fail, he claims, because its goal is internally inconsistent. When we divorce the concept of the moral good from all particularities of ethos and so from all concrete concep-tions of human purpose or telos, he claims, it follows necessarily that human actions (i.e., facts) are without value. This *fact-value distinction,* according to MacIntyre, is absolutely unbridgeable in the absence of a belief that human agency functions toward an end. According to MacIntyre, the abandonment of a notion of telos makes moral dis-course fundamentally irrational. If value does not inhere in facts, if actions cannot be understood in terms of their efficacy to achieve cer-tain goods, then there are no reasons that can be given for any of our moral choices. Nothing that occurs, nothing that people do, can be argued to be good or bad; hence moral discourse devolves essentially into force—assertions and counterassertions with no rational support.

MacIntyre's analysis of contemporary moral discourse is ex-tremely acute. Teachers of applied ethics courses and followers of media treatments of social issues will find his reproductions of contemporary moral debate eerily familiar. Because I take a cue from MacIntyre in my understanding of the character of contemporary moral reasoning, however, it is worthwhile spending some time tracing his divergence from what I am arguing here. First, in his focus on the philosophical terms of debate in our moral disintegration, MacIntyre has overlooked people's aesthetic judgments and discourse, and consequently, his moral epistemology is inadequate to his analyses of both the deterioration of moral debate and its possibilities for redemption. MacIntyre's rejec-tion of anything like a domestic aesthetic moral epistemology is ex-plicit in that he grants the emotivist that aesthetic judgments, on which the emotivist models moral judgments, are jumbles of preferences and whims. MacIntyre, in other words, accepts that there really is "no accounting for tastes."

Second, even if MacIntyre is correct in his claim that that our problematic philosophical presuppositions derive from Enlightenment moral and social theory (a claim that he shares with others, such as the Frankfurt School critics), this would still explain neither how the "poison" of Enlightenment thinking has taken effect, nor why it has progressed at the particular pace it has. To do that, as MacIntyre rightly notes, one must be able to tie moral reasoning to physical objects and actions (i.e., values to facts). And although MacIntyre may be right that this tying function is effected by an ethos, we would need an analysis, absent from *After Virtue*, of the mechanism of reflection between material objects and concepts of goodness in order to explain what an ethos really is and how it occurs.

Contrary to MacIntyre on the first point, if my reasoning in part I is correct, the notion of *function* that founds our ability to reason morally from facts to values cannot be divorced so easily from its role in the aesthetic judgment of the value of facts. When one says that a concert is a fine one, one judges it able to do what a concert is supposed to do in the same way that one judges the "man of practical wisdom" able to do what he is supposed to do, in the same way that one judges oneself able to do what one believes one ought to do. The analogy of practical wisdom to aesthetic judgment is Aristotle's own, as I have discussed, and MacIntyre uses it to explain how facts may be understood as having values. MacIntyre is content, however, to leave the aesthetic parallel at a didactic analogy. My understanding of domestic aesthetic judgment, by contrast, is of a skill that is not only functional in the same way as moral judgment, but also is an exercise in generic choice making, one of whose more sophisticated species is moral judgment. Only through a domestic aesthetic moral epistemology, I believe, can we begin to understand how something we *do* affects something we *think*, and vice versa; regarding the second point, only when we understand this process can we adequately understand both historical and cultural differences of ethe and mores, as well as the change or the refusal to change, among those who hold them.

Despite MacIntyre's rejection of the literal theatricality of moral choice, however, his concept of "representative characters," the socially recognizable manifestations of theory, has affinities with a domestic aesthetic theory.[27] "Characters," MacIntyre states, "are the masks worn by moral philosophies."[28] MacIntyre takes up three modern representative characters who he believes exemplify the modern disintegration of the concept of virtue—the Rich Aesthete, the Manager, and the Therapist—and he claims that all three of these characters present moral reasoning as wholly instrumental and fundamentally bureaucratic in its organization. The Manager takes increased production, the Rich Aesthete connoisseurship, and the Therapist smooth adaptation to society as given unquestioned ends. Thus claims MacIntyre, these characters take their jobs to be wholly technical, nothing but conniving means to achieve these given ends. The ends, of course, MacIntyre argues, are themselves only instruments: in each case—production of what? connoisseurship of what? adaptation to what society?—the ends sought by these characters are empty of content, like Berlin's and Foucault's versions of the self and its freedom.

Still, although MacIntyre's Rich Aesthete, Manager, and Therapist are extremely informative about the moral logic of contemporary culture, we cannot understand their relation to moral reasoning or cultural trends if, like MacIntyre, we ignore their aesthetic qualities. For a society to understand and ruminate upon these characters, to make them "representative," individuals must call sensible images of them to mind; one perhaps runs through a little dialogue with this person in one's head, perhaps even has a passing olfactory image of each character's cologne, and so on. To clarify one's thinking about the "moral mask" that is being referred to in each case, in other words, as I have argued, one generally imagines a concrete sensible "mask" and plays out a scenario of action in it to consider the moral choices that fit with a certain character. A young person who gets a new job in management, for instance, will almost certainly buy a new wardrobe, and in an important sense, she does so *in order to* take increased production as an end, to devise means to it, and to designate work to others in accordance with it. MacIntyre's representative characters are both compelling and useful—although, as he argues, very possibly not optimally useful—precisely because they are as much dramatic, aesthetic, exemplars as they are moral ones. MacIntyre may well be right that these characters are only instrumentally rational, and that they serve society badly on that account. That they serve us at all, however, he does not adequately explain.

Material Conditions and the Historical Relativity of Values

How can we explain differences among ethe, though, or historical or cultural trends in moral reasoning? A domestic aesthetic conception of moral reasoning yields an effective framework for understanding these things, more effective than MacIntyre's or the Frankfurt theorists'.

Although fully fleshing out the concept of ethos is beyond the scope of this work, it is relevant that its prerequisite features are material conditions. Whatever view one might hold about the good itself, whether, for instance, it is relative or absolute, no one can argue that material goods change. Even the strictest rationalist, a Plato or a Descartes, does not deny that the objects of sense (even if they are wholly illusory) undergo constant change; in fact, their arguments for rationalism depend upon it. And no one can deny that many of the changes that material objects undergo, while perhaps only apparent, are brought about by human intervention, by technology of some sort. Thus, the MacIntyrean who claims that moral reason has deteriorated, who wants to understand this phenomenon without reference to aesthetic value—and so, without reference to the perceptual accommodation of the objects of sense—must accompany her claim with some kind of bald moral relativism. This is difficult to do if one wants to claim at the same time that there has been an objective failure of moral reasoning, but this is the route that MacIntyre himself takes.[29]

If we are going to deal with cultural difference rationally and capably, however, we must believe that people *have their reasons* for differing from one another and that we are each obliged and able to understand and evaluate those reasons. As MacIntyre rightly claims, this is the only basis for meaningful moral discourse. It is also the only basis for meaningful appreciation and sympathy for cultural differences; to put one self in someone else's position must be, if it is to be a meaningful moral idiom, to imagine oneself in her place, that is, to put one's aesthetic imagination to work on a concrete scenario.

If one allows oneself to believe that the way we judge moral goodness has to do integrally with the way we judge the objects of sense, then one is able to account for historical, cultural, and individual differences in moral reasoning without having to take a stand on the nature of the good. If one attributes changes in moral reasoning to material changes in history and culture, one is still welcome to be a relativist, but one also may continue to hold an absolute notion of the good and a categorical notion of good reasoning. A domestic aesthetic theory of moral reasoning such as I have described above allows that conceptions of goodness will differ, in part, according to differences in material environment and especially so according to differences in domestic aesthetic objects; in other words, it can offer a partial explanation of cultural difference that is consistent with either a relativist or an absolutist notion of the good. A judgment that is both aesthetic and moral is subject to the influence of historical and cultural changes in moral reasoning and historical and cultural changes in the qualities of objects. It is perfectly consistent then, with this vision of aesthetically detectable cultural differences, both that there be an absolute good of which they are all more or less clear reflections and that the good itself differs from place to place or from time to time.

Differences in the qualities of cultural objects can be considered in two ways. The first way, climate and landscape, can account for many regional differences in culture; the second, technology and economy, can account for how more fundamental cultural differences are developed through history into vast, complex, stylistic ones.

(1) *Climate and landscape*: Cultural differences are associated, ultimately, with the land, the climate, and the sensible character of people's natural surroundings. Indeed, if not, then there is simply no further cause of cultural difference to be sought beyond the arbitrary fact of the differences themselves; and without such a cause, maintaining that human beings are fundamentally similar in their reason and in the rights and privileges to which they are entitled is very difficult. Both moral absolutism and moral relativism, both "conservative" notions of moral value and "liberal" notions of neutrality toward conceptions of good, fail if we are not willing to base cultural differences in an interaction between human beings and their basic physical environments, and this interaction must take place through the mediation of sense experience, that is, through an aesthetic medium.

Of all the sensible, and thus, changeable things comprising our basic environment, the most stable are the land and the climate. Technologies that allow us to manipulate geography are of relatively recent origin; technologies of weather are still largely unable to go beyond prediction. Thus, we may say that the most fundamental cultural difference, one that is only with great difficulty and in small increments overcome, is the difference in the types of food, shelter, cloth, and sensible environment that particular lands and climates can produce. The different qualities—both aesthetic and botanical—of the native plants of different regions, and especially the different qualities of the cereal plants on which the world's peasant majority subsists, can have a profound effect upon cultural tastes, technologies, social organization, and economic systems.

Designer Victor Papanek, arguing that people "relate to their environment esthetically and psychophysiologically" through technology or artifacts[30] states:

> The kind of sunlight (compare a July morning in Greece to the autumnal sun setting over Stockholm), the chemical composition of the air (contrast the birch-scented breeze on an island in the Finnish archipelago with the heady aroma of Frangipani and jungle vines on Bali or the plastic air in a shopping mall); and

colors, shapes, materials, views, sounds, and odors affect everyone's physical well being, mental ability and cognitive grasp, sense of self, humanity, and, by extension, understanding of humanity's pressing problems and unfinished business.[31]

Economic historian Fernand Braudel cites statistician Paul Ladame in calling wheat, rice, and corn the "plants of civilization," which "profoundly organized man's material and sometimes his spiritual life. . . . They have exercised . . . the 'determinism of civilization' . . . over the world's peasantry and human life in general."[32] Michel Rouche discusses how medieval Europeans, both nobles and peasants, venerated bread and associated it with ideals of graciousness and strength.[33] And in the *Odyssey*, Homer identifies humanity and civility (i.e., Greekness) with bread eating to distinguish it from the inhumanity of the Cyclopes (*Odyssey*, 9:121, 135, 212).

It is notable, despite the differences, however, that human beings from different cultures often sustain themselves primarily, for instance, with grains, and that these grains, despite their different tastes, take similar positions in the common meals of their respective societies. Every culture is distinguished by a particular few materials in each of its food, shelter, and clothing. Yet we find similarities of form and overlap of materials across cultures, which are some of the things that make rationally accessing a culture very different from one's own possible. Everywhere in the world where people can live we find at least some minimal sunshine, precipitation, and earth.

Certainly people are able to share and refine one another's conceptions of goodness through conversation and by reference to worldwide similarities in the qualities of land and climate and in the form of human needs and ingenuity. Certainly both do occur. That there are qualitative cultural distinctions among groups of people, therefore, does not foreclose either the possibility that an absolute good exists and that general agreement about it can in theory be reached, or the possibility that goodness is relative and that people's moral differences can be discussed and accepted by one another. In fact, this opens up the possibility that both these positions may, in a sense, be true at the same time: An absolute good may be reflected in many beautiful landscapes and climates each of which can provide for human happiness in its own way when cultivated with more or less difficulty by imperfect but thoughtful creatures, each of whose actions is in theory understandable and reasonable.

(2) *Technology and economy*: Obviously, distinguishing technological differences from geographical, cultural from natural, and so on, is difficult and perhaps even impossible in many cases, and for my pur-

poses doing so is quite irrelevant. On top of fundamental differences in land and climate, however they are defined, we can nonetheless posit the different technologies that people have devised to live by their means. Fundamental physical objects strike those who live around them in different ways as pretty, as useful, and sometimes as good in their own right and worthy of worship. Needy, rational, and appreciative creatures that we are, people reflect in conjunction with these objects, certain notions of the good—or of usefulness, beauty, divinity, and so on as parts of the good—and work with the land and the climate to better bring out the potential for the good as they conceptualize it. This is the beginning of craft, or technology, through which conceptions of goodness are applied and developed through history.

Philosophers have sometimes figured technology as a struggle against nature or a struggle to dominate nature.[34] Certainly to work with anything other than oneself (or sometimes even within oneself) is to confront resistance to one's will, and to that extent it is a struggle. Certainly, in addition, the primordiality of our work with the land gives this struggle mythic qualities.[35] But to envision technology as a pure conflict between man and nature or a pure effort of domination is unfair. Indeed, this position takes phenomenological distance to be our natural state and does so contrary to the evidence. No farmer can afford to envision her work as the domination of nature because a farmer well knows that nature cannot be dominated. This misunderstanding of our relation to nature is reminiscent, of course, of the popular misunderstanding of women's relationship to domestic labor that I discussed in part I; what is characterized today as unadulterated oppression is, I have argued, properly understood as a complex and ambiguous compromise. A skillful farmer, like a skillful homemaker, is involved in an effort to work with nature, to bring nature into her confidence, to bring out the bounty of which the land is capable to the credit of both. Even the computer hardware designer cannot do otherwise than to join her own efforts with the possibilities of electromagnetism to create something she believes to be good.

By looking at the history of technology, then, one can investigate the history of conceptions of use and beauty and of our ability to think about and achieve these ends because these conceptions are parallel to, standards of, and supported or invalidated by each society's technology or means of production. As Lewis Mumford states in his introduction to *Technics and Civilization* (quoting his own "Drama of the Machines"): "If we wish to have any clear notion about the machine, we must . . . appraise its esthetic and ethical results. . . . Perhaps in the long run [what is] important . . . is [the machine's] spiritual contributions to our culture."[36] Klaus Krippendorf expresses something similar when he states that artifacts exist in "ecological interaction" with their users, who live in particular places and times and have certain habits and traditions. "Cars do not look like horses," he states, for instance, ". . . but early cars very much resembled horse-drawn carriages, probably facilitating substitution, just as personal computers now look very much like typewriters and television sets. . . . Designers must understand the dynamics of meaning that ecological interaction entails. . . ."[37]

To trace the history of technology is to trace a "spiritual economy," where the value of machines is judged according to their ability to satisfy the human need for the most pleasant, the most meaningful, the most beautiful possible a survival. These practical needs are always the guides of technology, which always follows them. Once produced, however, a particular tool or set of tools may in turn change the quality of the human needs that it was produced to satisfy. An understanding of economic systems, in the Marxian sense of the constraints that we put on our production of things, therefore, is of no small importance in understanding why people have at certain points in history conceptualized the moral and aesthetic good in the different ways they have.

We have a tendency to believe contrary to this, however, that technological progress occurs in an almost Darwinian way.[38] Indeed, today, many people see technology as achieving a kind of universalism that one never sees in nature. We sometimes talk as if inventions simply appeared on the market at certain historical moments as natural mutations where those that survive are those that, by virtue of their survival, denote the good. We sometimes talk as if technology and pure science are so closely linked as to be indistinguishable, as if technology were somehow a "discovery," as if every invention is a potentially good idea that will be recognized as such in its adoption by the market. José Ortega Y Gassett describes this as the profound "ingratitude" of the modern "common man": "They believe [that motorcars will in five years' time be more comfortable and cheaper than today] as they believe that the sun will rise in the morning. . . . The common man, finding himself in a world so excellent, technically and socially, believes that it has been produced by nature and never thinks of the personal efforts of highly-endowed individuals which the creation of this new world presupposed. . . . [This is] his radical ingratitude towards all that made possible the ease of his existence."[39]

But technological development has never been just a spontaneous result of our natures or of nature in general; it never has been synchronous with pure science, or for that matter, with pure (i.e., fine) art. Although we may or may not want to say that pure scientists provide a better view of nature and goodness than past views and therefore lead us along a path of progress, we would never want to say such a thing about technology. Mumford notes: ". . . All the critical instruments of modern technology—the clock, the printing press, the water-mill, the magnetic compass, the loom, the lathe, gunpowder, paper, to say nothing of mathematics and chemistry and mechanics—existed in other cultures. . . . They had machines: but they did not develop "the machine." . . . The machine [took] possession of European society [because] . . . that society had, by an inner accommodation, surrendered to the machine."[40]

Millions of interesting tools have been invented whose time (i.e., whose mass production or wide use) never came or whose time came only long after their invention. This may or may not indicate that they were poor inventions; all it really indicates is that they were out of synchronicity with the conceptions of use and beauty of their time or place. That this is all we can surmise is evidenced, as Mumford cites, by the fact that many technologies lay dormant in some areas of the world for many hundreds of years and yet were later rediscovered and put to use. Daniel Boorstin, in his 1983 *The Discoverers*, echoes Mumford, claiming that "what was possible technically was not always possible socially."[41] For instance, Chinese scholars were "dazzled by the wonderful 'European' invention," when Matteo Ricci, a Jesuit missionary, brought them precision clockworks in the sixteenth century, apparently unaware of the precision instrument invented by the Chinese Su Sung five centuries earlier.[42] Paper, invented in eighth-century China, didn't have a wide application in Europe until the fourteenth century. We cannot know whether old, unproduced machines that we consider laughably passé or trivial may not seem absolutely necessary to our great-grandchildren, or whether they may not have yielded a far better result than the technology with which we are familiar if they had been widely produced and distributed. Similarly, we can never know how many potentially useful inventions have never been dreamed of, or how many died with their inventor, never to have entered our world as products.

What we can know is that if something got produced, somebody, however wrongly or rightly, thought it would be a good means to some end. How the instrumental good is, in general, conceptualized at any particular period is therefore an integral factor in what gets produced. These general conceptions of the instrumental good are manifested in the ways people find to satisfy what they perceive to be their needs (i.e., conceptions of the instrumental good are partly manifested in economics). Hence, economic history can give a fundamental insight into the history of conceptions of goodness. To quote Lewis Mumford again, "Behind all the great material inventions of the last century and a half was not merely a long internal development of technics: there was also a change of mind. [There was] . . . a reorientation of wishes, habits, ideas, goals. . . ."[43] Along the same lines, Braudel prefaces the first of his three volumes: "In drawing up the inventory of [the] possible, we shall often meet with what I [have] called . . . 'material civilization.' . . . And material civilization has to be portrayed, . . . alongside that economic civilization, if I may so call it, which co-exists with it, disturbs it and explains it *a contrario*."[44]

In our own time, almost all the inventions we call *technological* result from very narrowly applied sciences; in other words, their application, the apparent needs that they fulfill, exist prior to the research from which the invention results. Most often today, of course, these needs—the goods that the products are supposed to serve—are dreamed up by corporate executives, market researchers, and advertisers, in order to sell products. So, while technology—and so, much of our manifest vision of the good—is still economically influenced, it is no longer influenced through the same economic system or mechanism it once was. The vicissitudes of technology and its applications over history are evidence of the phenomenological relation between the sensible qualities of objects and people's conceptions of goodness that I have claimed is at the core of domestic aesthetic judgment. These "slings and arrows" are also, therefore, evidence of how changes in material conditions, or in the production of artifacts, can adversely or positively affect moral reasoning.

This is by way of saying that today's operative definitions of self and of freedom cannot account for human behavior and are not helpful in satisfying human needs. Mass production and some of its attendant aspects, I will argue, at least partially account for their pervasiveness, as well as for the rather Darwinian understanding of technology and its relation to the good that they support. Even by the more cynical among us, technology may seem under present circumstances to be something that betters human life by fulfilling needs we didn't even know we had yet. We certainly find ourselves able to do things that our ancestors "never dreamed of." But when technology is understood always to be constrained by material and economic factors, which are in turn accommodated by human judgments, we can see that the production of useless items that plagues us today is not just an alien, unconscious force. It can be and needs to be evaluated.

CHAPTER 5

ETHICS AND THE LABOR THEORY OF VALUE

"There are two moralities," [Rodolfe] replied. "One is the petty,
conventional morality of men, clamorous, ever changing, that floun-
ders about on the ground, of the earth earthy, like that mob of
nincompoops down there. The other, the eternal morality, is all
about and above us, like the countryside that surrounds us and
the blue heavens that give us light."
                                        —Flaubert, *Madame Bovary*

I argued in part I that moral reasoning, as a skill developed in
individuals through the practice of domestic aesthetic activities, must
sharpen or degenerate over history in the same way as those activities:
through practice. In the preceding chapter, I argued that the character
of moral reasoning today seems to be rather phenomenologically distant and despondent and that this cannot be cleanly attributed to
Enlightenment moral philosophy, as MacIntyre and others have tried
to do. I have argued that we must look instead at the history of concrete practices and objects, which do not lend themselves to clean or
easy analysis, in order to understand the vicissitudes of moral reasoning over history. Despite my earlier criticisms of his conception of
freedom, I agree with Foucault here that the history of ideas, like the
history of technology, develops in fits and starts with anomalies and
inconsistencies and that we should therefore reject the "priority [of]
the observing subject . . . which . . . leads to a transcendental consciousness."[1] Foucault claims that attempts at such causal analysis belie the
myriad conscious choices and behaviors that mediate the "unconscious"
flow of intellectual forces that the historian aims to understand.[2] This
is consistent with Aristotle's perennially frustrating claim that in the
"subject-matter [of ethics] . . . precision is not to be sought for . . . any
more than in all the products of the crafts" (*NE*, 1094b12–5).

Nevertheless, I have argued that as a society we have let the
practice of moral reasoning deteriorate over the centuries, and an investigation of how theorists of the modern period understood this

practice will not be entirely unhelpful in figuring out how it degenerated. Although it can hardly be the singular influence that we might like, surely intellectual history is not irrelevant to individual behavior. Because theory is delivered in concrete objects—books and articles and classes—it would be as inconsistent with my claims thus far that philosophy should have nothing to do with ordinary moral reasoning as that it should conclusively determine it. Thus, before I discuss contemporary domestic aesthetic practice and objects in part III, it is incumbent upon me to say a few things about intellectual history. In this chapter, I will briefly investigate what I think are some relevant trends in some relevant seventeenth- to nineteenth-century thinkers' epistemological presuppositions; in the next, I'll do the same with some twentieth-century theorists. In both cases, I argue: (1) that the presuppositions that have gone awry are, importantly, not specific to philosophy, but shared by economics (in this chapter) and cultural studies (in the next), such that they can be understood to be pervading domestic aesthetic choice as well as moral decision making; and (2) that these presuppositions have less to do with historical conceptions of self-identity, moral good, or economic value than with historical conceptions of phenomenological intimacy and distance, and domestic aesthetic skill.

BACK TO MACINTYRE: RETHINKING THE EFFECT OF THE ENLIGHTENMENT

I have claimed that the particular kind of weakened judgment with which I am concerned is a modern phenomenon, and that I am partly sympathetic to MacIntyre's attempts to uncover its roots. According to MacIntyre's criticisms in *After Virtue*, the Enlightenment moral project failed inevitably because it set itself to derive purely rational moral rules, on the model of mathematics, from certain truths about human nature; yet it abandoned the Aristotelian notion of a human-specific function in favor of a concept of human nature that is in its very essence neutral with regard to conceptions of its own good. Thus the Enlightenment thinkers, according to MacIntyre, tried to get blood from a stone: they wanted to get particular moral rules out of a creature with no particular moral purpose.

According to MacIntyre, post-Enlightenment thinkers have used two routes to resolve the "no ought from is" problem that faced them when they adopted this doomed Enlightenment project, and neither attempt succeeds because the project cannot be sustained in any case. One route is the Kantian, which attempts to found the authority from which moral rules follow, that is, the human good, in "the nature of practical reason." The other is the Millian, which attempts to "devis[e] a new teleology," essentially by picking what seems like a reasonable concept of the good and calling *moral* whatever choices achieve it.[3] For MacIntyre, these moral theories fail because their conceptions of the good are empty; they cannot be socially manifested. For him, only a cultural ethos, in which is inscribed a conception of the human good and of the proper path to its achievement, can found a practical moral theory. And so he understands Kant's and Mill's failure as originating in their unwillingness to accept the necessity of a particular cultural ethos and their consequent avowals of a universal individual human nature.

Although MacIntyre's criticisms of the Enlightenment project are provocative, they lack the acuteness of his analyses of contemporary moral discourse discussed in the preceding chapter. In part, this is because MacIntyre's notion of human nature, such as it is, derives its moral content, including its rationality, rather much and rather directly from cultural ethos. MacIntyre is stuck, then, with an odd sort of relativistic notion of the good that depends on the stability and cohesion of particular societies. Yet these culturally relative notions must exist in his human individual alongside certain shareable or universal strands of rationality (e.g., those that enable people to function instrumentally at all). If there is no universal rationality, then MacIntyre's more intuitively satisfying claims about contemporary moral debate would have to be abandoned because they are based in the unused possibility of offering one another reasons for our actions.

MacIntyre's analysis also depends too much on a notion of history in which, contrary to the Foucaultian conception to which I ascribed earlier, certain turns have unavoidable consequences, one in which the Enlightenment project, in a certain sense, "had" to be tried and "had" to fail. "In this way," as sociologist Colin Campbell states, "the modern pattern is presented as immanent in history."[4] We might wonder, for instance, in the face of claims such as MacIntyre's, why the Enlightenment became "the Enlightenment" at all. We can certainly imagine a history, for example, in which Kant had been noted in passing and dismissed; in favor, for example, of an Anselmian renaissance.

It seems to me, somewhat as it does to Campbell and Foucault, that there is no definitive reason why our particular versions of capitalism or of postmodern discourse had to be our particular versions. Of course moral philosophy, in the form of books and conversations, provokes reflection about the good life and how to achieve it, and thus certainly affects people's thinking and behavior, perhaps even (as I believe), it does so better than many other objects of contemplation. But it does so, surely, *in roughly the same way* as any other such objects—read by individuals who live among many material and intellectual influences. Even intentionally polemical works or scholarly works available to only a select few are accommodated by their readers alongside a plethora of other theoretical, personal, and material influences; similarly, even the most unreflective novice essay adds a unique perspective to its platitudes.

"There are reasons for being skeptical . . . about the extent to which politico-economic theorizing can be seriously regarded as contributing to the justification of consumer behavior," argues Campbell against scholars who attribute the eighteenth-century consumer revolution to the likes of Smith and Mandeville.[5] Campbell instead suggests that the increased consumption of romances and Gothic novels, especially by women, just prior to and during the same period might be a significant contributing factor in this consumer revolution.[6] Campbell's point is well taken not only because certain consumer demands have romantic qualities, as he claims, but also because fiction, produced specifically for aesthetic appreciation and reflection, can so easily be understood to affect individual's conceptions of the good and of how they imagine achieving it. Indeed, according to MacIntyre's own theory of "practices," agents imbue their productions with value by artistry and technique; consequently, consumers and decision makers must find the value in them by aesthetic appreciation.[7] But MacIntyre's analysis of the breakdown of practices hermetically attributes them to the history of moral philosophy.

Campbell makes similar criticisms of hermetic economic analysis. He claims, for instance, that the economic phenomenon of modern consumerism is not adequately explained by reference to the increased supply of products during the Industrial Revolution, manipulation of the market, increased spending power among the middle class, the increased pace of changes in fashion during this period, or the emulation of the aristocracy by the middle class (the leading contenders among economic historians).[8] For one thing, he argues, these analyses presuppose one another in a vicious circle (the "fashion" hypothesis rests, for instance, on a hypothesis of market manipulation, which in turn presupposes a "fashion pattern").[9] Second, the evidence does not support them. It appears, for instance, that the consumer revolution originated with the middle class, making emulation theories suspect or at least incomplete.[10] Similarly, imitation of one's social superiors originated long before the eighteenth century, the pervasive social mores of the middle class at the time tended toward the ascetic and so on.[11] To understand why a long-standing practice would suddenly become dominant at a particular point in history, or why the behavior of members of a particular class at a particular time implied inconsistent beliefs, one must consider the complicated territory of people's desires and try to discern how individuals in that period typically conceptualized the good to themselves.

Although definitively determining the causes of a cultural worldview may be impossible, "describ[ing] an epistemological space specific to a particular period," such as Foucault claimed he tried to do, is possible and beneficial; as is perceiving, entertaining, and reflecting upon the ways human nature and goodness were conceptualized in periods precedent to, and influential on, our own, and doing so across different disciplines and practices.[12] With the goal in mind, then, of ferreting out the precedent conditions of today's situation, and in light of my argument thus far, I am particularly interested in the overlapping conceptual features of modern theories of ethical decision making and those of labor and consumer choice. The moral theories of Kant and Mill, of such interest to MacIntyre, share with the economic theories of Smith and Marx certain striking structural assumptions about what might count as good and about how human beings think, assumptions whose effect is far less striking when their cross-disciplinary character is obscured. The presuppositions that form this framework foreshadow the severe phenomenological distance depicted by Berlin and Foucault, which I have argued is the pervasive character of moral reasoning today. Although I do not think the nature of the subject permits a precise analysis of the relation between these theories and the development of real people's typical styles of decision making, I do think they can give an insight into the "epistemological space" of modernity, the space upon which the postmodern edifice I discussed in the preceding chapter is built.

I find three presuppositions shared by Mill, Kant, Smith, and Marx to be particularly telling. First, notions of the good are conceptualized as givens on the model of natural law. Despite differences in the notions of moral and economic goodness to which each of these thinkers ascribes—duty for Kant, utility for Mill, opulence for Smith, and humanity or "species being" for Marx—all of them take their respective goods and the faculty by which they claim people accomplish it to be significantly like natural phenomena, conceived as lawlike, which on that account can be harnessed, legislated, known, and so forth, but, and importantly, they can never be evaluated or corrected.

The conception of natural law to which these thinkers appeal is an early modern scientific one—one that has absolute but arbitrary control over behavior, such as gravity or Avogadro's number. According to this model, natural laws can be borne out or discorroborated through experience, but they cannot themselves be praised or blamed. Not only in cases of physical movements, but also in cases of choice, natural laws conceived thusly become like external authorities to us. Agents may *defy* the law: Kant, for instance, claims we may refuse to do what we know to be dutiful, Smith, that we may knowingly pay workers below subsistence, and so on. This is not the same, however, as *criticizing* the law, refining it, arguing with it, analyzing it. These four modern thinkers tend to depict human beings as subject to the moral or economic law as they are to the laws of physics.

Second, in all of these thinkers, qualitative distinctions are conceptualized as categorical ones. Mill's, Kant's, Smith's, and Marx's tacit epistemologies depict a human choice as between one or another different *type* of given object, not as between better and worse examples of a single type. In Mill, for instance, one opts for either intellectual or physical pleasures; in Marx, for the commodity relations of a worker or an owner. These thinkers depict a world in which there are no meaningful matters of degree; only a selection of ever-generic representatives of types.

All instances of a type, characterized and ordered according to the essence that marks the type, are equally representative of their type. There is no difference of degree in the exemplary status of individuals. Thus, the possibility apparently declines that a sharp judge of character might designate a particular brilliant porpoise or orangutan to be more human than a particular vegetative human being, or that a sharp judge will designate a particular inclined, unconscious action of hers as morally better than a particular intended, reasoned action, just as the possibility declines that she would think a particular beer more beerlike than another. Similarly, the failings of a particular individual within a category tend to be understood in terms of its lacking essential markers for membership in the category.

A world that is organized by natural law into inescapable categories such as is depicted by these modern ethical and economic theorists is, of course, a world that would discourage an agent from making refined evaluative judgments about it. In the world envisioned by these thinkers it is morally meaningful to weigh drinking beer against going to a concert, or economically meaningful, to weigh buying flowers for the mantelpiece against buying one's books for the term; but the differences between a night drinking Guinness with friends at home and one spent with new acquaintances in the back row at a Metallica concert are not morally relevant; the differences between ending a profound winter depression by buying oneself a bouquet of spring irises and the fleeting good conscience derived from laying down the same money on a logic textbook is not economically relevant. Subtle qualitative differences among several permissible courses of action, or among several affordable commodities with the same purpose, or among several human lives with the same social status—differences that require a practiced judgment to discern and articulate—are largely irrelevant to decision making as these theorists depict it.

Third and finally, in these thinkers different kinds of choices and different faculties of thought are straightforwardly represented as phenomenologically distanced from each other in consciousness. Mill, Kant, Smith, and Marx unanimously conceive of the standards of economic choices, aesthetic choices, and moral choices, respectively, as being entirely separate and incommensurable within the consciousnesses of agents. Neither Smith nor Marx nor Mill envisioned moral and economic choice as having anything to say to each other in the mind of the agent, and while Kant is a considerable improvement over them in that he implies, as I have discussed, that reflective judgment must base morality, Kant does not flesh out this interdependence such that his analysis would be of use to agents.

This presupposition is part and parcel of the preceding one: if all things are thought to occur in nature according to unshakable categories founded on essences, faculties of the mind should be envisioned this way, too. And that is exactly the background epistemological structure of the moral and economic theories in Mill, Kant, Smith, and Marx. Their epistemological framework precludes the existence of generic, moral-economic judgment such as the domestic aesthetic. By contrast, the ancients did not think of the "parts of the soul" to be incommunicado with each other; rather, they were seen precisely as "talking" to each other in an internal "dialogue," where agreement between conflicting "faculties" could at least in theory be reached. If, for instance, a person were faced with a decision between quitting smoking and caring for her sick mother—to do which she needed to concentrate her energies on her mother and not on quitting smoking— the relative damage to her health could be compared to and evaluated against the relative service to her parent, according to the single standard of the character of her life. It is not at all clear in the four philosophers being discussed here, however, how one would make this sort of decision, even where, on the face of it, as in Mill, it seems like the process should be crystalline.

The divided consciousness depicted here is unflinchingly but separately subject to moral, economic, and scientific laws. The modern consciousness, as described by these theorists, is pulled in different directions internally, seemingly unable to create a coherent vision of the world, of the good, or of itself. This is precisely the condition I have earlier described as phenomenological distance, a condition where conceptions of the good and interpretations or perceptions of objects that are supposed to express it are not comparable to each other in consciousness, making acute judgment difficult. Because the health risk of smoking is an unquestionable fact known to her cognition and the duty of caring for her mother is an unquestionable value to which she baldly adheres, in these theories the agent would have to sacrifice her health to observe her duty to her parent or sacrifice her duty to her parent to preserve her health. Within this epistemology the agent really would not be able to consider, as ordinary agents regularly do consider, that caring for her parent might significantly improve her own overall health, that her parent's recovery or state of mind might be benefited by being asked to give moral support in her child's no-smoking effort, or that she could stop smoking a few years down the road and still significantly benefit from it.[13] Furthermore, where the agent, understood by an ancient philosopher, would face a variety of choices because every way of handling the situation, from petrifying anxiety to angelic grace, would constitute a different choice, this modern agent would have only two: health or duty.

Now I turn to the texts of these thinkers to see how the three trends I have just outlined are manifested in each.

MILL

As is well known, Mill advocated as a moral good whatever action produces the greatest happiness for the greatest number of people. To defend this principle against accusations of hedonism, Mill posits a famous "quality distinction" between pleasures, claiming that some actually always possess a greater utility than others do. Contemporary philosophers willingly devote class time to criticisms of Mill's quality distinction in *Utilitarianism*, but rarely do they consider its phenomenological or epistemological aesthetic presuppositions, the distinction between the aesthetic qualities of categorically distinct activities (basically, intimate ones vs. social ones).

Mill's idea of high-quality pleasures is not of experiences of objects of very high quality. He does not claim, for instance, that there is a relevant moral distinction between very good sex and not-so-good sex or between very good beer and rather poor beer. Rather, Mill's distinction is a categorical one between intellectual and physical pleasures: "Now it is an unquestionable fact," he claims, that there is "a marked preference to the manner of existence which employs the higher faculties. Few human creatures would consent to be changed into any of the lower animals for a promise of the fullest allowance of a beast's pleasures. . . .[14]

Mill's "quality" distinction does not address the facts of ordinary experience. Consequently, he brings in a "happiness expert" whose opinion must be consulted whenever a theoretical question arises about pleasure quality and who uses the following notoriously ill-thought standard: "Of two pleasures, if there be one to which all, or almost all, who have experience of both give a decided preference, irrespective of any feeling of moral obligation to prefer it, that is the most desirable pleasure."[15] The "expert" conducting the "test" to which Mill appeals has, then, by stipulated definition no sense of moral obligation to prefer certain pleasures. This makes her distinctly unlike the ordinary people for the sake of whose choices she provides the data. For ordinary people take both the moral and aesthetic qualities reflected in different experiences of the same kind to mark a great difference among their various experiences of pleasure.

For most people, for instance, illicit sex is both more exciting and less safe than is licit sex; these factors, as well as their own and their potential partners' prowess and skill, weigh sometimes quite heavily upon the pleasure of the experience. For most people, beer is more pleasant and edifying to drink at a party or even while watching football, than it is to drink alone and out of alcoholic desperation; still more so if it is good beer, a good party, or a good game. Most of the time, aesthetic choice, which for Mill as we can see is prerequisite to moral choice, is not a quantitative procedure (and to the extent that Mill improves upon Bentham in this regard, he is to be lauded) but instead a true qualitative evaluation. But what Mill calls a distinction in quality of pleasant objects gets translated by his "expert" into a categorical distinction between general kinds of objects.

I mean by the Millian "expert" anyone, or any part of the self, who insinuates herself between the making of a decision and the personal and intimately shared ends or reasons by which that decision is guided, that is, anyone who in the name of beneficence creates phenomenological distance between agents and their possible objects of choice, including other agents. This does not mean only that moral reasoning is instrumentalized by Mill, as MacIntyre claims, although Mill's version of moral reasoning is emotivist in MacIntyre's general sense. By looking at the quality distinction, rather, we can see that bald aesthetic assertions underlie bald moral ones for Mill.

As undergraduate readers often vehemently note, for Mill choices are unfree even in the most narrow positive sense because they are made by the utilitarian decision maker. But underlying the affected parties' lack of autonomy at the hands of the decision maker is a deeper one, that of the decision maker at the hands of the pleasure expert. The utilitarian decision maker herself is a kind of aesthetic bureaucrat: she makes decisions for others based on the results of a sort of "scientific research" that she does not consider herself eligible to contemplate. The decision maker assumes moral authority, but the expert assumes aesthetic authority. She decides for others what is more and less pleasant and by how much, but not because of her skill. The expert's expertise is nothing itself but the application of a vague categorical distinction between "intellectual" and "physical" pleasures: she is less "expert" than "authorized," in fact, because she meets the empirical conditions of having tried both pleasures while being morally neutral toward them both.

I argue later that the phenomenological distance at which we presently find ourselves in making our domestic aesthetic choices is conceptually similar to that at which the Millian "expert" puts her "client." The Millian expert, then, is not just an instrumentalizer of choice, not just a mediator between pleasures and the reasons they are pleasurable. Beyond that, and more worrisome, too strict an advocacy of Millian theory deprives agents' pleasures of their pleasant qualities. A real Millian decision maker must become inured to fine distinctions of quality among similar objects and perceive only gross moral distinctions of kind: between designated physical pleasures, such as orgasms, and designated intellectual pleasures, such as the beauty of an elegant mathematical proof. Mill's expert takes pleasures out of their context in a life full of personal considerations, both moral and aesthetic, through which an agent derives her conceptions of the good. Surely this affects the agent's judgment. To use the dramatic analogy once more, what Mill advocates is similar to evaluating a character from a work of fiction or drama without regard to its role in the overarching effect of the literary work, and indeed similar to asking the actor who will play it to do the same. The performance of even a fairly good actor would surely suffer under these conditions. In sum, Millian theory divorces aesthetic judgment from moral reason in consciousness and simplifies aesthetic judgments to the point where they could provide little practical exercise or insight.

KANT

I have already discussed Kant's ethics to clarify my notion of the domestic aesthetic by way of comparison and contrast with his aesthetics.[16] Here, I concentrate on Kant's ethics in so far as it is distinct from his aesthetics. Kant claims that moral duty is given to an agent by reason as a "categorical imperative." The categorical imperative is a rule modeled on natural law; in one formulation, for instance: "Act as if the maxim of your action were to become through your will a universal law of nature."[17] Inclination, on the other hand, is according to Kant at the mercy of real natural law (i.e., the laws of physics and biology) and is subordinate to it in the same way that the understanding is subordinate to the moral law. "The laws of [natural philosophy] are those according to which everything does happen, while the laws of [moral philosophy] are those according to which everything ought to happen."[18] Basically he means by this that any attempt to rationalize morally impermissible behavior will prove to be self-defeating; that what he calls the "maxim" of a morally impermissible action (i.e., the reasoning behind it, or its statement of reasoned intention) is, at least according to the standard of what he calls, "perfect" duties, self-contradictory.

This means, however, that from the point of view of Kant's moral agent, duty appears to call "out of nowhere," even though its directive originates in the subject and is responsive to circumstances. Kant's notion of duty has an authority similar to Mill's expert, in this sense at least. Opposite to Mill, yet with a similar effect, in Kant's ethics pleasure and moral good are incommensurable. Under these circumstances, Kant's agent freely chooses whether to act in accordance with duty or whether to act in accordance with her happiness; but she is not able to command, for instance, as a moral agent, that her reason and her inclination negotiate an acceptable compromise. Kant claims that as a moral agent, "man must represent and think of himself in this two-fold way. . . . "[19] This is because Kant's agent is the legislator, but not the judge, of the moral law; she administers, devises, and evaluates the maxims of her action, but she cannot evaluate the moral law that is their standard. In a way similar to Mill's agent, the Kantian agent makes a kind of alliance with either her happiness or the good will, rather than negotiate qualitatively complex situations. As Nancy Sherman writes, "the idea of a unified life . . . is something Kant, for the most part, gives up."[20]

This is not to say that Kant denies that agents deliberate and reflect upon the good or that they decide, in a sense quite reasonably, to do things that are contrary to the dictates of the purely good will.[21] In fact, I tend to understand Kant to be primarily offering an analysis of just such deliberations. When one contemplates whether to lie to protect a friend who one knows is innocent of the malice of which she is accused, Kant knows, one may well decide to lie.[22] But if we take moral deliberation seriously, Kant claims, we must acknowledge the command not to lie with which this individual struggles in her decision. Kant asserts, in a sense, that there is not a rational person who doesn't feel the twinge of conscience when she lies. This is a very sympathetic claim, aimed to express the gravity of moral deliberation, but it does depict an agent who operates at a phenomenological distance. Kant's moral agent is autonomous, but she is not in an authoritative enough position to be both thoroughly well-intentioned and yet have no qualms in a particular instance about lying.

In fact, for Kant, it is essential to the moral worth of our actions that the moral good be in some sense beyond question: "The moral law is valid for us not because it interests us . . . but rather, the moral law interests us because it is valid for us as men. . . . "[23] As I mentioned, with regard to imperfect duties (such as developing one's talents), Kant implies that our adherence to the moral law is more like dedication to an ideal, and thus that an agent's moral thinking and achievement are subject in a qualified sense to judgment and revision.[24] But with regard to perfect duty, Kant envisions the good will as always perfectly rational. The categorical imperative, therefore, is not subject to the agent's revision, despite her position as its legislator. Kant well recognizes this problem for the "innocent" consciousness and closes the first section of the *Groundwork* by advising that she, like the client of Mill's pleasure expert, "seek help in philosophy"[25] to articulate the good to herself.

This Kantian phenomenological distance accompanies the claim that fine qualitative distinctions between two actions of the same type (in this case, between two inclined actions or two perfectly dutiful actions) are morally irrelevant. This is revealed in the difficulty of resolving conflicts between Kantian duties. For instance, with regard to the categorical imperative, Kant does not morally distinguish a "noble" lie from a malicious one. It is well worth noting, however, that Kant, like Mill, can make no moral distinction between two inclinations either; for instance, he cannot distinguish morally between a merchant giving a good price out of sympathy for the customers and her doing so out of competitive strategy.

Although Kant recognizes the value of character as the spring from which actions flow, he does not believe either that moral character can be built through education or that judgment has any role in improving the will.[26] In other words, Kant claims that to know as moral agents why our consciousness is conflicted in this way or anything else about the necessities that guide either our inclination or our reason, except to know that they are necessary is, impossible. Otherwise, he claims, "we do not see . . . how the moral law can obligate us."[27] The result for Kant is that the moral worth of our actions in a sense decline as we become better people. The more inclined one is to act in accordance with duty, the better one comes to appreciate the necessity of the moral law, the more partial one becomes in a sense to oneself. The character that, as it were, "speaks" to the moral law as if it were its peer, can seemingly no longer be its subject for Kant. "Hereby arises a natural dialectic, i.e., a propensity to quibble with these strict laws of duty to cast doubt upon . . . their purity and strictness. . . . Thereby are such laws corrupted in their very foundations."[28]

Again, Kant's intolerance for sanctimony here is sympathetic, but surely there must be a more direct argument against it. Furthermore, and as Kant himself acknowledges in the Third Critique, not all judgment puts the judge above the object. He states there, for instance, that "the reflective judgment [i.e., aesthetic taste] has to subsume under a law that is not yet given. It has therefore, in fact only a principle of reflection upon objects for which we are objectively at a complete loss for a law. . . ."[29]

In passages in the Third Critique, Kant clearly agrees that reflective judgment is necessary for good moral thinking. In the aesthetics we see that the conflict that moral agents, according to Kant, inevitably face is bridged. In the reflective judgment, as I argued earlier, Kant gives us a faculty that brings reason and will together so that they can achieve what each fails to achieve by itself: moral learning, development of character, reflection upon law. "The mind cannot reflect upon the beauty of nature without at the same time finding its interest engaged. But this interest is akin to the moral. This immediate interest in the beauty of nature . . . is peculiar to those whose habits of thought are already trained to the good or else are eminently susceptible of such training."[30]

A moral agent, however, according to Kant, not only cannot morally review the law, she cannot even so much as appreciate the law and its perfect authority. Because the ability to recognize how good the good will is is a function of the judgment and not of the reason, Kant's moral agent must take the word of reason about the worth of the law, just as Mill's agent must take the word of his expert about the goodness of pleasures. "If in addition, reason had been imparted to this favored creature" whose sole alliance is to natural law and who therefore achieves happiness instinctually, Kant claims, "then it would have had to serve him only to contemplate the happy constitution of his nature." [31] To maintain his conception of moral and natural law as having perfect authority, and yet still speak to the facts of an imperfectly moral and an imperfectly happy human experience, Kant had necessarily to paint the moral agent as radically internally conflicted. If natural law is perfect and we are entirely subject to it, we should be perfectly happy—but we are not. If moral law is perfect and we are entirely subject to it, we should be perfectly good—but we are not: Kant frames his discussion of moral reason in the terms of this flatly conflicted consciousness.

THE DEVELOPMENT OF THE LABOR THEORY FROM LOCKE

Smith and Marx ascribe to a labor theory of value, as did their predecessor Locke. But what one observes in these thinkers is actually a profound difference in the notions of value that labor supposedly founds, from a labor theory of *property* in Locke, to a labor theory of *wealth* in Smith, and not to a full-fledged labor theory of *value* until Marx. This difference parallels differences among them regarding the conception of the role of human judgment in economic behavior, gradually entrenching in economic theory the previously defined three modern presuppositions that I discerned in Kant's and Mill's ethics.

Locke's version of the theory, which designates labor as the source of property, retains a relatively close phenomenological link between an agent's qualitative conception of her own work and her qualitative conceptions of the concrete, material objects that she produces or works on. Smith, on the other hand, by designating labor as the source of wealth, by quantifying both wealth and labor, and by categorizing value supposes an agent who operates at greater phenomenological distance. Still, because Smith does not identify wealth with all or with intrinsic value, but only with political-economic value, he leaves agents' judgment of ends out of his analysis, which leaves them free to make the higher order decisions that guide their economic choices at greater phenomenological intimacy. Marx, highlighting the overwhelming influence of economic conditions on the human spirit, insists on designating labor as the source of value itself, and this accounts in part for the power of what we might call his "phenomenology of labor." But because of his attachment to his brand of historical determinism, Marx cannot account for the revitalization of noneconomic value after the proletarian revolution. Thus, the labor theory of value dwindles with Marx to epistemological implausibility.

※

Let me turn again to the texts of these political-economic thinkers to see how the three trends I have just outlined are manifested in each.

As I discussed in the first chapter, Aristotle thought of property, including money, as existing solely within the context of social relationships, as a public representation of their closeness and duration.[32] Locke retains much of this Aristotelian framework in his notion of property, diverging from Aristotle primarily only in his Christian understanding of economic freedom and autonomy. For Locke, the question of property is the question of distinguishing "mine" from "yours" in a world where everything belongs to God.[33] His labor theory is really an attempt to make that distinction by reference to nature, rather than convention or contract.

Locke's famous statement of the labor theory in its simplest form is, "'tis *Labour* indeed that *puts the difference of value* on every thing."[34] For Locke, as for Aristotle, however, value is not identical to property. The source of value, for Locke, is God; each person's property is a distinct value. Work is the source of *ownership*, a natural and qualitative relation between a person and the material with which she labors. What he means by "putting the difference of value on every thing" then, is really that the results of ownership—useful and pleasant things—become valuable through the ownership relation established by work.[35] For Locke, a person's initial investment in a thing obligates her to bear fruit with it by cultivating, improving, and working it, drawing out its latent possibilities that could not be made manifest without further investment.

Property relations themselves are not wildly free, but bounded and ordered according to conceptions of goodness—"use and convenience"—given by God.[36] Higher than the value of work, as Locke sees it, is that of "use and convenience," a pleasant survival something such as I described in part I. "But how far has He given it us? *To enjoy*."[37] Thus, Locke, like Aristotle, envisions an owner as having a moral relationship to her property, one that carries with it obligations to use it rightly. In other words, Locke's concept of our right to property founds a corresponding responsibility for it, and not just for its protection either, but for its moral improvement. This obligation is understood by Locke to be qualitatively, but not categorically, different from the agent's various other moral obligations. In all our moral relationships, which differ according to the quality and intimacy of the attachments that found them, agents are obligated to appreciate, enjoy, and improve the lot God has given them. Therefore, although the ownership of property is given by natural law and cannot be judged, which as I have stated seems to be the modern trend, in Locke, the use of that property is still subject to human judgment and requires that agents judge well, which harks back to an Aristotelian schema.

Importantly for Locke and similarly to Aristotle, our obligation to use property rightly is an obligation to share its fruits with others. The benefit provided by labor is never represented by Locke as an individual benefit, but as a benefit to family, country, and mankind.[38] Labor, on his version of the labor theory, is an ongoing physical, phenomenological, and morally obligatory relationship. This claim colors Locke's conception of rights. Ultimately one's right to one's property is only, for Locke, the right to be obligated by it. Ownership is just the right to work hard to do what God commands one to do. Locke observes that absolute monarchies deny citizens this opportunity for virtue, and in this way debase and enslave them; hence, his interest in establishing a natural right to it. Essentially, the ownership of property gives an agent a particular opportunity to do something good, an opportunity that poverty-stricken individuals do not have, much like how wealth provides the opportunity for liberality and magnificence in Aristotle.

For Locke we breach our obligation only when we either abandon our commitment to our property or overstep it. The former occurs when we make slight, ill, or temporary use of our property, and the latter when we own more property than we can make good use of. The former failure Locke seems to think would hardly happen to a good and rational man. The latter, however, is made possible by money. Although money has its use as a lasting marker of value (gold and silver are enduring), which facilitates the consumption of perishable goods, its value is given to it only by "Fancy or Agreement," that is, it is a conventional or symbolic sign of value.[39] The durability of money allows people to possess more property than they can use because it allows us to exchange perishable goods right now for other perishable goods later on. But Locke, like Aristotle, claims that this characteristic of money allows people to pervert their labor, directing it toward other than its proper ends.[40] Money, or exchange value, interjects itself between the laborer and her conceptions of the good.

In sum for Locke, natural relations with property are "phenomenologically intimate," such that all men in natural relations, according to the law of reason, properly pursue rightly conceived good ends—use and pleasantness—with their property. Conventional relations mediated by money, however, divorce property from its proper ends. Locke's version of the social compact aims to restore natural property relations after the introduction of money and to protect people's right to do what they can be proud of in the eyes of God. This is to say that for Locke, labor forges a moral relationship between a worker and what by her labor becomes her property. These aspects of Locke's labor theory mark it off from later developments of the theory.

SMITH

Quite in contrast to either Locke or Aristotle, labor for Smith represents the exchangeable value called *wealth*, and not the moral value that obligates us to our property. Wealth is "the quantity either of other men's labour, *or, what is the same thing*, of the produce of other men's labour, which it enables him to purchase or command."[41] Property that cannot produce anything is by itself neither wealth nor, therefore, value. Clearly, Smith radically distinguishes moral value from economic value, whereas Locke did not. For Smith the significance of the phenomenological relation between a person and her property is not relevant to economics or politics. What one chooses to keep instead of to hold for exchange (e.g., one's spouse) has nothing to do with value, according to Smith, at least not political-economic value.

"Wealth, as Mr. Hobbes says, is power."[42] Specifically for Smith it is the power to purchase or command the labor of others. For Smith wealth becomes meaningful only under conditions of the division of labor, which increases the production of the usable objects that comprise wealth. Although it can always be increased, according to Smith (as can, therefore, the wealth it produces), division of labor has always been our human lot.[43] Wealth, therefore, for Smith is natural in the way that property was for Locke; it is not a perversion of social relations, but a vessel for them. Thus, while Smith, like Aristotle, conceives of agents as naturally interdependent, he diverges from Aristotle by advocating an economic response to human imperfections that alleviates our suffering without correcting our faults.

Where for Locke possessing the fruits of another's labor above what one can oneself labor to produce is vicious and akin to slavery, for Smith it is a positive good, especially if it produces capital or circulating wealth. For Smith wealth commands or saves labor, but the labor it commands or saves (i.e., the labor of its possessor) is identical to the labor by which it is acquired (i.e., the labor of the producer) so that commanding one's own labor is equated politically and economically to commanding someone else's. Wealth has no natural limits in the moral sense; it is limited only by the state of production technology and the breadth of the market.

Furthermore, for Smith the quantity of "necessaries and conveniences" into which labor translates is not associated with goodness in the moral sense as it was for Locke. Where for Locke labor creates property, and through property, valuable goods and obligations, in Smith the wealth produced through division of labor is not subject to the review of moral judgment. Moral value, for Smith, is the result of a sentiment, a sentiment that is natural to all people equally and whose directive is independent of the political and economic goods that wealth represents. In other words, morality is for him a sentiment that acts upon us naturally like a physical law, one that may well conflict with the laws of economics, something similar to the way Kant's "inclinations" obey a law independent of the moral law. Although Smith's moral good is the result of a sentiment and not of a duty, its role in the consciousness of an agent is functionally similar to the role that duty plays for the Kantian agent.[44]

Use value, the material quality of possessions in hand, has simply fallen out of the Smithian picture or rather into its obscure background. "Nothing is more useful than water, but . . . scarce anything is to be had in exchange for it," Smith claims early in *The Wealth of Nations*, raising the concept of use value only to drop it immediately.[45] "The quantity of the necessaries and conveniences of life which are given for [a thing]," Smith calls the "real" price of labor, however, and the "real" price of a commodity is, in turn, the labor needed to acquire it.[46] The "nominal" price of each is its money-price. For Smith the real and nominal prices of labor and commodities are given, once again, like natural laws. Although the value of labor for Smith is independent of the quality of its products, however, Smith nonetheless claims that the economist should attend to the "true" meaning of labor—its real price—as opposed to its nominal price. This is evidence of Smith's mediate position regarding the labor theory. Although Smith no longer integrates political or economic goods with moral ones through use value, as Locke does, he does maintain a preference for realism over nominalism in economics that echoes Locke. Specifically, Smith notes repeatedly throughout *The Wealth of Nations* that clothing, household maintenance, and especially food are more useful than other commodities. Thus, labor is morally and aesthetically (i.e., "really") different from "necessaries and conveniences," but in economic terms they are translatable to each other, like synonyms in the same language.

Money, which gives labor its nominal value, is in a sense the metalanguage that makes the translation possible, standing equally for labor and for necessaries and conveniences, and obscuring the "real" difference between them. As with Locke, Smith envisions the use value of money to be derived from its relative imperishability (and its divisibility), and like Locke, Smith sees the purpose of money as wholly secondary to barter. Thus, Smith claims, for instance, that because corn rents for land are more stable from century to century than money-rents (which are more stable from year to year), corn is the better rent, and the situation with wages is similar.[47] Thus, Smith does recognize a natural relation between labor and its ends that is more valuable on some scale than money; but the real scale of value apparently runs parallel to the nominal scale, the two kinds of valuation never meeting in the consciousness of the agent, setting her at a phenomenological distance.[48]

Consequently, although they have effects on wealth (and, Smith admits, on workers' happiness), the physical conditions of labor, never seem to affect skill.[49] For Smith the "extent of the market," one part of demand, covers a spectrum of qualitative distinctions, such as skill, that he can include nowhere else in his theory. This is another Smithian parallel to Mill's problems with the quality distinction. Smith assumes that pins, for instance, lend themselves better categorically to divisibility than the products of "more complex" manufactures, such as farming. But for Smith, the category of "complex" trades is simply operationally defined as those that cannot divide their labor beyond a certain point.[50]

Like Mill, Smith justifies his economic theory on the assumption that "more [wealth] is better." To his credit, as we have seen, he, like Mill, qualifies this claim in various ways. Nonetheless, Smith understands the division of labor, for instance, as a kind of a natural mutation, and he sees it as necessarily beneficial in the kind of Darwinian way I discussed in the preceding chapter. Thus, labor division has a natural and absolute authority. "The division of labor . . . is . . . the necessary . . . consequence . . . of . . . human nature."[51] Hence for Smith, as for Kant and Mill, good decision making amounts to the self-legislation of rules that are already given by nature, like natural laws. For an owner of a sweater factory to divide by three the labor required to produce her sweaters, for instance, is for her to simply tap into a natural and necessarily good process and use it to her advantage, like tapping into the natural process of sap production in a maple tree to have tasty pancakes. Similarly, failures to achieve the good are for Smith basically technical failures (e.g., due to lack of equipment, lack of funding, inadequate division of labor) and not failures of judgment.

Furthermore, according to Smith, agents cannot legislate, much less judge, the "law" of supply and demand; they obey it by buying or not buying existent commodities, but their reasons for these decisions are not economically analyzable. Quality is defined by the market. Those sweaters, for instance, that meet demand are good sweaters by definition, and those that do not are not. Like Mill and Kant, Smith accounts for the quality of objects essentially through a kind of categorical, or at least operational, distinction and does not really address differences of degree. That Smith assumes that consumers express good judgment, however, marks him as a mediator between Locke's highly moralistic labor theory and Marx's highly cynical one.

MARX

Because Marx recognized that economic conditions can degrade agents' humanity and change the way we think about the good—a position with which I am obviously very sympathetic and on which I base many of my arguments—it is important to pause and reflect on the differences between Marx's background epistemology and the one I have been advocating. Marx's scientistic criticism of capitalism requires that he not only make explicit, but also adopt, capitalism's own tacit notion of the labor theory of value in which value evades refined judgment.

Both labor and commodities are, for Marx, properly understood in terms of their money value or exchange value. For Marx, as for Smith, use value is not relevant to economic laws; it is simply a presupposition of the system. Whatever can be sold, Marx operationally stipulates, is useful. One hundred eighty degrees from Locke, then, Marx equates the creation of value with economic exchange, not with individual human beings. And for Marx exchange value is a completely abstract value; a quantity of money always represents a quantity of "the average labour-power of society" or "abstract labour."[52] Marx stipulates that the evaluation of labor by money depends upon the "homogeneity" of all labor. Because of this adept definition, Marx makes no qualifications on his claim that labor makes value. For him, as for the nineteenth-century capitalists and workers he is trying to understand, all labor is mediated by money, which serves as a wholly quantitative representation of a wholly abstract entity. By averaging labor for the purposes of analysis, Marx avoids the distinction between its nominal value and real value; yet, unfortunately for Marx, it is precisely in that distinction, as we saw, that Smith maintained his vision of the human ends of labor as distinct from money making.

Consequently, neither exchange nor labor is guided or limited, in Marx's view, by any notion of the human good. Issues of morality, quality of life, and so forth stand completely outside capitalist relations. "Law, morality, religion, are to [the proletarian] so many bourgeois prejudices."[53] Although it reads like a scathing polemic against capitalism when Marx dismisses moral and aesthetic notions of the good, his position is not very different from the idealistic sort of natural scientist who pooh-poohs moral objections to science as just so much sentimentality. Marx means to criticize the naiveté of the belief in real value exemplified by someone like Smith. Because a unit of money is a purely abstract particular like any other commodity, however, Marx also maintains that money only puts on pretensions of importance by representing other commodities, revealing a tacit belief or wish that money express real—or at least sincere—value. This paradoxical position of money underlies Marx's famous and provocative theory of commodity fetishism. Because only exchange value is value for Marx, the phenomenological quality of a person's relation to her work or its products (which was so important, for instance, to Locke) is no longer of any significant economic value whatsoever; still Marx often waxes nostalgic about precapitalist relations on account of that very quality.

Marx recognizes that use values differ materially and that the labor embodied in them therefore differs qualitatively; he does not consider them just different sets of habitual physical movements, as does Smith.[54] Probably the most moving appeals made in the *Manifesto*, in fact, are to the past glory of the craftsman under feudalism and the corresponding loss of the distinctiveness of different work under capitalism. Late in volume I of *Capital*, Marx describes the life of the peasants of the fourteenth and early fifteenth centuries in similarly glowing terms. But Marx's evaluation of this life is purely nostalgic: unlike Locke and Smith, he does not think a free life laboring meaningfully upon the land is possible under capitalism. The capitalist relations of production, and consequently their debasement of owners and workers, are the necessary result of economic laws, as will be their supersession by communism. That Marx recognizes and is critical of this situation is obviously very much to his credit, but despite his distaste, he takes commodity relations to have the authority of natural law. Money value, as a universal equivalent to all things, bulldozes over all physical, qualitative distinctions, including that between a laborer and the product of her labor. In other words, money value necessarily undermines phenomenological intimacy and with it all other access to value. "The value of commodities is the very opposite of the coarse materiality of their substance, not an atom of matter enters into its composition."[55]

Hence, in Marx's eyes, no amount of moral reflection could any longer result in the agriculturally based economy of the past, nor of its benefits. Indeed, the ninth revolutionary measure of the *Manifesto* is the "combination of agriculture with manufacturing industries, gradual abolition of the distinction between town and country, by a more equable distribution of the population over the country."[56] But what could more fully obliterate the distinct character of types of labor than to abolish the distinctions between town and country and between manufacture and agriculture? What could more alienate labor from the laborer than to redistribute the population? Rather than merely stipulating average labor power for the purposes of theoretical analysis, Marx thus claims that a real identity of different types of labor is a natural outcome of capitalism. In Marx this results in full-blown labor theory *of value*, such that human labor is not subject to any moral or even aesthetic standard.

Furthermore, the commoditization of labor, according to Marx, necessarily exploits the worker. Because the capitalist buys living labor power as just one among the numerous commodities needed to produce the one she will sell, the capitalist is able to get more value out of these instruments than she originally paid for them.[57] The laborer is paid her exchange value or in other words, subsistence, but the laborer nonetheless is asked to give more than mere subsistence-level work to the commodity produced; she must create something more valuable than the total cost of the materials used in production, including her own work, or the capitalist makes no profit.

For Marx, however, when the capitalist gets more value out of the laborer than she exchanges for it in pay, this is just a good deal for the capitalist. The capitalist, on Marx's view, pays the going rate for labor, that is, pays the representative of a quantity of abstract labor power, but serendipitously gets a higher quantity of abstract labor power out of the laborer and into the product for sale. Because Marx understands the formula for capitalist exchange on the model of natural law, he does not analyze the exploitation of workers as unfairness or deceit on the capitalist's part; it is not an immoral act, but an exploitative relation hidden in the unflinching form of capitalism itself. For Smith, by contrast, there was nothing exploitative in the fact that the capitalist gets from the workers more than she gave them, as long as she gives them pay enough to live a genuinely decent life. Admittedly naively, Smith implied that any capitalist so unfeeling as to pay workers less than is required for such a life would be morally blameworthy, as well as economically deficient, because ultimately the goal of economic progress for him was to raise the national standard of living. For Marx exploitation is inescapable; there is nothing we can do to improve the experience of work for the worker.

Long a favorite section of *Capital*, the "Fetishism of Commodities" provides the clearest indication of how Marx manages to be both such an incisive and such an obtuse analyst of human nature. The fetishism of commodities—their mystery, their strangeness—results according to Marx from their nonphysical relation to each other, their social intercourse with one another independent of human beings.[58] In other words, the mysterious nature of commodities is their similarity to language, their ability to stand in meaningful relations to each other like propositions.[59] In the fetishism section, Marx gets a genuine pay off for dissolving Smith's distinction between real and nominal value; he shows that capitalism tends to "really nominalize" value, and he is persuasive that this is the case and that there is something eerie about it. However, Marx is unable to properly criticize this nominalization of value because, as we have seen, he does not recognize a concept of real value. Unlike Smith, Marx is reduced to the claim that our ability to nominally express value is itself mysterious and weird. He cannot say that some expressions of value are wrong and some genuine because he recognizes no right way to express value.

Marx's criticisms are apt wherever work under capitalism is exploitative and oppressive, but they go astray when he claims that work cannot (or can no longer) be otherwise. This is Marx's worst disservice to his followers: the vision of the good life he offers is one free of oppression, but because liberation apparently requires escape from the sensible content of labor that, according to his predecessors, is the source of all value, liberation is nothing to be proud of. It is pure resistance to oppression such as Foucault describes; and it is so because of Marx's insistence that the movements of history and economics be modeled on those of nature. For Marx conceptions of the good are wholly obtuse.

※

Why note these shared background strains in Mill, Kant, Smith, and Marx? The exercise tells us something, I believe, about intellectual history in general and about our own conceptual inheritance in particular. First, the similarities have a certain irony because the epistemological framework that each thinker, according to my reading, assumes implies that no such overlap between economic logic and ethical logic should occur. Kant, for instance, implies that the descriptive laws that dictate economic (or inclined) behavior are incommensurable with the categorical imperative. According to these four thinkers, economics and ethics should have little to say to one another. Yet, if we find the two kinds of reasoning to be similar, then we must think of an individual's ethical reasoning and her economic reasoning as running in parallel to each other, going the same route over completely different territory. And this is what these thinkers imply: that we think in similar ways about absolutely incommensurable subject matters, such that the similarity in reasoning is always empty and unhelpful.

But the irony is informative. However much an economic theorist might speculate about the laws of economics, her claims are constrained by empirical observations of material conditions. Of course economics aims to be predictive and to design techniques to achieve economic norms, but it must be grounded in description of real-world behavior. Ethics, we tend to think, is intellectually freer. What we ought to do, according to Kant for instance, has nothing to do with what we can or cannot do physically; it is unaffected by the givens of a situation, just as the laws of geometry are unaffected by the givens in a particular proof. But in light of the shared intellectual strains I outlined earlier, we can see evidence that perception (of material conditions) and moral reasoning must be in "conversation" with each other in judgment, not only over the course of a life, but also over history.

Although the first point, obviously, lends credence to my arguments in part I, the second is the most salient of the two for my present purposes. I argued in this chapter that even though attributing clear causation of behavior in intellectual history is impossible, characterizing important intellectual trends of a precedent culture is possible and useful. It allows us to understand better some of the formative influences on the way people think and behave today. The shared presuppositions of phenomenological distance, the categorical classification of qualitative distinctions, and the paradigm of natural law in these extremely influential ethical and economic theorists, I believe, have affected our own material conditions and the way we think about how to live in these conditions. In the next chapter, I attend to the important aspects of the twentieth-century legacy of the shared presuppositions I have cited here.

CHAPTER 6

LANGUAGE AND OPPRESSION;
THINKING AND WORKING

Fashionable minds in more significant fields blur the distinctions
between real and spurious quality, between actual life and make-
believe. . . . A nose for trend now rivals the power to analyze the
present and has surpassed the ability to store past memory.
—Kennedy Fraser, "The Fashionable Mind"

I argued in part I that moral judgment is founded in the practice
of making domestic aesthetic choices, choosing the food, clothes,
housewares, and people with which to surround oneself. And I argued thus far in part II that although MacIntyre's characterization of
contemporary moral debates is extremely persuasive, his vision of
intellectual history and his insular philosophical analysis of the degeneration of moral reasoning cannot explain as much as it promises. Still,
the four brief analyses in the foregoing chapter have, I hope, demonstrated some shared assumptions in ethics and economics in the eighteenth and nineteenth centuries, which, as part of the implicit
worldview of influential thinkers, surely have affected intellectual
trends in our own day. I have claimed all along, in addition, that the
particular style of disordered thinking that we experience today is
attributable to the increasing number and the increasing meaninglessness of the food, clothes, household products, and so on produced in
our society, so that the degeneration of moral reasoning can be given
a materialist explanation. It remains for me to deliver on this long-
standing promise and ferret out the mechanism by which these disappointing objects have so badly served society. To clarify my position
on these issues, which will occupy part III, let me first contrast it here
from other recent theories of "popular culture."

Most recent criticisms of clothes and food and other commodities have relied upon an analogy to language. The model of language
that most of these analyses use relies heavily on Saussurean theory,
wherein language is understood to be a system of signs independent

of any particular speaker and of the various individual uses of the words within it. The individual speaker uses what is given in the structure, tests and presses the limits of the structure from within it, bringing into expression many particular statements with particular styles and connotations; but the speaker does not, by that action, affect language itself. Saussure's structuralist model of language poses the language system as a socially derived entity into the necessity of whose use any particular speaker is born. It is, in a sense, beyond her control—almost, despite its social construction, like a natural law. An individual's use of the language ("speech") is always already part of the language system and cannot be understood separately from it.

Saussure's notion of language is of a purely conventional, as he calls it, "arbitrary" entity, not a natural one. To his credit, he did not believe that language is a collection of words really corresponding to objects (this may be part of his appeal); rather, he claimed, language structures the relations between concepts by linking them to signs in a systematic way, through similarities and differences that suit or eliminate particular words for particular places in statements—in other words, language is a system of categories or types. Language therefore does not pick out things in the world or relations among them, but instead (and notably, as if this were opposed to the foregoing) structures itself over history as an ordered interpretive schema within which the particular marks are related entirely arbitrarily to the things they signify in the language.

In other words, language for Saussure is a purely historical, purely conventional phenomenon, but it is not thereby something that human beings control. In the Saussurean version of language, signs or words are "mediated" from concepts by the structure of the language in which they are used, and in addition, the concepts to which words are used to refer are themselves social artifacts, a part of a conventional structure on which the linguistic structure is modeled.[1] Thus, Saussure's notion of language is reminiscent of the shared presuppositions I outlined in the last chapter—it depicts the language user as severely phenomenologically distant, and language as a system of categorically distinct words, nonnatural but with rules that carry the authority of natural laws.

It is easy to see both the attraction of applying structuralist analysis to cultural criticism and the problems inherent in such an exercise. Once language has been posed as a paradigm, and as a system that is beyond the control of its speakers and writers, lots of social enterprises that have similarities to language start to look like linguistic systems with structures and rules over which people have no control. And once it has been posed that this structure assigns value through difference and similarity, it starts to look like a lot of things we think valuable are assigned their value by a system, according to their similarities and differences (e.g., their cost compared to other commodities, their mainstream popularity in a society, their social class).

Indeed, Saussure's notion of language looks at language very much the same way that Marx looks at the capitalist economic system, as a system in which exchange value is understood to be of foremost importance to commodities and in which exchange value is given by the system in a lawlike fashion beyond the control of any particular workers or consumers within it. It is easy to see how theorists living in a highly advanced and degenerate capitalist economy, one which seems huge and systematic and beyond their control, could start to think it can be analyzed by analogy to language on something like the Saussurean model. Such sociological analyses depend, à la Marx, on denying the possibility or importance of the use value of objects. To see all objects purely as significators in a system of significations (usually a class system), one must deny that objects have the function or desirability that we ordinarily think them to have, that is, one denies that they have a use value, denies one's immediate perceptions of their physical qualities and the relation of those qualities to the good at which the objects aim.

To the extent that recent commentators such as those I discuss in this chapter take themselves to be doing cultural criticism of our society's particularly arbitrary uses of language or of objects, their point is well taken, but only to that extent. As critical analyses of culture in general, of objects in general, of Western culture, or even of capitalism, structuralist and poststructuralist analyses disappoint. Use value, as I have demonstrated, simply cannot be so easily dismissed, nor can a successful social movement be founded in the claim that the system it seeks to reform is beyond human control. This last catch-22 is similar to the state in which Foucault seems to depict us, opposing a restrictive power/knowledge just by harnessing its absolute authority to our purposes.

In consonance with my description of domestic aesthetic choice and its role in moral reasoning in part I, and with my previous criticisms of the four theorists, I want to argue against structuralists and post structuralists that relations between objects cannot be understood in terms of linguistic relations, at least not where language is understood as a system beyond human control. On the contrary, I believe that linguistic relations are themselves one kind of practical relation in which we stand to the world, and consequently that language itself is founded in domestic aesthetic practices. As such, language is properly understood as a tool, although not the only tool through which we pick out and express things as we understand them. Language poses a more or less frustrating mediation between objects and concepts, but as with other tools, we use it according to our judgment.

POSTSTRUCTURALIST DISAPPOINTMENTS: BAUDRILLARD, BARTHES, AND LURIE

Jean Baudrillard, who has much of value to say regarding the deterioration of domestic aesthetic judgment in his *For a Critique of the Political Economy of the Sign*, owes a great deal to Saussure, despite his seeming defeat of Saussure's notion of "arbitrariness" (the arbitrariness of the sign to the signified) in favor of a "pure logic" of signs.[2] Baudrillard claims that the "system of signs" is purely conventional; it is a system of class differentiation and nothing more. For Baudrillard, not only language but all objects, including the users of words, are mere signs, signifying mere social or conventional relations. Baudrillard goes so far as to begin his inquiry with the unargued claim that the "empiricist hypothesis is false," meaning that no natural relation exists between objects and the needs, uses, or feelings that they signify to their users and purchasers: that is, there is no such thing as use value.[3] "Use value—indeed, utility itself—is a fetishized social relation, just like the abstract equivalence of commodities. Use value is an abstraction."[4]

Baudrillard denies quite explicitly that there is such thing as human need, claiming that it is given arbitrarily as a limit value of the capitalist system by capitalism itself. Thus, he depicts himself as a further historical advance upon Marx's already overripe abstraction to take values as givens on the model of law. Baudrillard also quite explicitly denies that qualitative differences can exist among commodities of the same type; consequently he denies that human judgment, expressed in consumption, can pick out these qualitative differences. Rather, all differences are understood by him as grammatical, structurally given differences; in other words, as differences of exchange value that mark commodities only in terms of their social or conventional place and never in terms of their naturally signified purpose or good.

For instance, according to Baudrillard, the "common name" *refrigerator* designates a type, a category, a function, and "all refrigerators are interchangeable in regard to [their] function."[5] The "proper name" *my refrigerator*, designates an attachment to a commodity, a possession of it which is also, insofar as it is a proper name only, given by the system as a physical property of the object that is beyond the purview of the consumer, like a family name. The distinction that designates ownership for Baudrillard is that between the statements, "this is a refrigerator," and "that is the refrigerator at 1402 Eva Street." Choice, according to Baudrillard, is relevant only to "brand name," a purely symbolic accompaniment to the refrigerator indicating the class status of the object. Choice is basically the fetishization of brand names according to Baudrillard. Baudrillard's analysis of the present state of capitalist production is a biting one, but the criticisms that I have leveled against these assumptions where they occur in Marx apply doubly here. Baudrillard is unnecessarily cynical in his judgment of earnest consumers who are trying their best to pick things of genuine value on which to spend their money. He takes them to be mere promoters of themselves like so many of the role models under whose influence earnest shoppers are supposed to be enthralled. But the more apt criticism of Baudrillard here is substantive: To the extent that any commodity is actually better than others of its type, use value is still relevant to choice, and Baudrillard's cynicism is premature.

Although Roland Barthes, unlike Baudrillard, restricts his criticism to fashion as it is discussed in fashion magazines, and so to a type of literature or language proper, he nonetheless claims in his *The Fashion System* that the literature of fashion is constitutive of the relations among objects of clothing, not vice versa.[6] The use of the appellation *system* is evidence of Barthes's sympathies for the Saussurean vision of language and of the linguistic relation between commodities.[7] He refers to this system as the "vestimentary code," a system of meanings in combinations of clothes as interpreted, in this case, by the writers of fashion magazines.[8]

Barthes's analysis is a fascinating study in rhetoric: He offers an insight into the use of language by fashion writers to project a wealth of moral and aesthetic meanings onto clothes. Like Baudrillard's, however, Barthes's notion of language rests on the assumption that all meaning, all notions of function and beauty (in this case, the function and beauty of clothes), that is, all notions of use value, rest in the descriptive power of language itself. In other words, Barthes assumes that the significatory relation between things and words in the language of fashion is purely conventional and arbitrary.

> It would seem that for Fashion magazines, clothing and the world can enter into any sort of relation. This means that, from a certain point of view, the content of this relation is a matter of indifference to the magazine; the relation being constant and its content varied, we see that the structure of written clothing is concerned with the constancy of the relation, not its content; such contents may very well be fallacious (for instance, accessories in no way

make the Spring [as one magazine writer described them]), . . . in this way, the correlation is empty; it is nothing but an *equivalence:* accessories are *good for* the Spring. . . .[9]

The vestimentary code is itself a set of linguistic or grammatical relations from which the structure of fashion language grows. In other words, Barthes believes like Baudrillard, that the form or structure of language itself, in thought, must constitute the objects.

But Barthes's claim that the relation of spring to accessories can be false assumes that things in the world *do* have a discernible naturally occurring relation to each other (if not a causal relation) and that this relation can be picked out by the mind and expressed in language, à la the "empirical hypothesis" that Baudrillard explicitly, and Barthes implicitly, denies. If we can pick out the *falsity* of the relation, then surely we can pick out the *truth of the falsity*. Implicit in Barthes's criticism of the arbitrariness of the fashion system is his vision of a nonarbitrary relation among clothes or between clothes and other things. Thus, unlike Baudrillard, Barthes assumes on one level that fashion writing "takes on a life of its own," implying at least that fashion language exacerbates the arbitrariness of relations between objects. On another level, however, the level on which Barthes implies that fashion language could or ought to be criticized and changed, he clearly assumes the possibility of a more natural, better significatory relation. "Fashion is an order made into a disorder," he claims, uncovering a reality of clothing even as he claims that the "rhetoric of fashion" proscribes it.[10]

Furthermore, whereas Barthes believes that the particular rhetoric of fashion is a modern invention, he does not seem to believe that the linguistic structure of relations between objects per se has modern roots. Hence, although this rhetoric is approachable in some sense, rhetoric in general is beyond our control. But this insight—that we can't be "silent" in our linguistic relations including in fashion—will not produce an analysis or criticism of linguistic systems in general or in particular. The inability not to signify does not imply, as so many structuralists and poststructuralists seem to think it does, the inability to signify according to our deliberate choice; we may still have control over how we use language even if we are not free not to use it.

Barthes implies that there is not, or is no longer, an extralinguistic relation among objects in the world that different languages pick out or against the background of which we can differentiate one language from another. Rather, the very differences among languages are just signs in a grammatical system of differences. Barthes makes this explicit in his *Elements of Semiology*: "It appears increasingly more difficult to conceive a system of images and objects whose *signifieds* can exist independently of language. . . ."[11] Like Baudrillard, Barthes offers a nice criticism of certain uses of rhetoric for sales purposes, as well as of the worldview of the producers and advertisers of fashion. He has no justification, however, for his belief that these uses of rhetoric are the most fundamental points to be made in an analysis of human clothing choice. We may understand Barthes, for instance, as offering a provocative and possibly helpful interpretation of the thinking of a person who emulates the fashion models in magazines, as, in a sense, mistaking her own body, which actually has to work and sit and walk and cook in the clothes it wears, for the picture of the model's body in the magazine. But surely, even if this were a correct analysis, this is merely one among many relevant criteria, including use value, that the consumer of fashion takes into account; she cannot believe this falsehood, for instance, for a very long period of time and still fit the rest of the hypothesis about her, that is, that she is an ordinary consumer of fashion. No one denies that writers are able to use their rhetorical skills to influence the way readers make judgments or consumers make purchases. But these unsurprising facts cannot form the basis of a criticism of consumption or of consumers. Barthes gives a thorough analysis of the rhetorical skills of fashion writers, but he says little about the actual production or consumption of clothing. His analysis is belied by its own presuppositions.

Alison Lurie, in her 1981 *The Language of Clothes*, follows the trend of Baudrillard and Barthes.[12] Going without argument from the obvious claim that "once they begin to think about it, everyone knows that clothes mean something," and its more interesting unpacking, "you announce your sex, age, and class to me through what you are wearing—and very possibly. . . your occupation, origin, personality, opinions, tastes, sexual desires and current mood," to the patently ridiculous claim that "clothing is a language . . . [with] a vocabulary and a grammar like other languages," Lurie takes the primary value of clothing to be linguistic in the Saussurean sense.[13] It can only identify a wearer through similarity and difference within a system of signs given for this purpose.

Certainly it is true that clothes have meaning and certainly it is true that one of the things we do with clothes, particularly in a consumer society, is to identify ourselves with some social values and distinguish ourselves from others. And Lurie's analyses of many of the mechanisms by which we do so today are enlightening and helpful. Her historical analysis, however, is dull, and her cultural criticism is unsubtle. Lurie accepts that changes in the value of clothes are arbitrary; she just denies that they are trivial on that account.

This is demonstrated in her chapter on "Color and Pattern" in which she offers the useful insight that although "the decoration of clothing with symbolic designs . . . is almost as old as clothing itself, . . . the printing of actual words and phrases upon them . . . is a relatively recent development."[14] She is blind, however, to the importance of this development in the formulation of her own theory, understanding it instead as just one kind of structurally given signification, no more or less important than decorating with colors or crosses or jewels. The decoration of clothing with words instead of with nonverbal designs is, however, surely a crucially significant cultural development, and clearly one that is historically, not structurally, founded, as I have previously implied, and will discuss further later in this chapter. But Lurie is not adapted to discuss historical influences because of her attachment to the analytic profundity of an analogy to grammar.

For example, when women started wearing pants, according to Lurie, this indicated their emerging manly self-image, rather than any real increased interest in the beauty, practicability, or other decorative and functional possibilities of pants. The meaning, "pants = male-ness," according to Lurie, is beyond our control as mere users of the system, although we may invoke the meaning in particular instances to connote the maleness of things formerly unassociated with it, as a poet uses a new metaphor. Lurie assumes exactly as does Baudrillard in the case of class significations that the association of pants with maleness is a mere equivalence.

> Male clothing has always been designed to suggest physical and/ or social dominance. Traditionally, the qualities that make a man attractive are size and muscular strength. . . . Men's garments therefore tended to enlarge the body through the use of strong colors and bulky materials, and to emphasize angularity with rectangular shapes and sharp points.
>
> . . . Female costume, during most of modern European his-tory, was designed to suggest successful maternity. It empha-sized rounded contours and rich, soft, materials. . . .[15]

Although there is precedent in European history for the kinds of significations that Lurie cites here, they are under no circumstances monolithic in the way that Lurie indicates. We can find plenty of modern European examples of men's pink satin fashions or women's stiff, angular suits, such as seventeenth-century French male costume, which set the tone for most of Europe, and the Elizabethan female costume, which was also widely popular. Tights did not come into fashion for men until the fourteenth century and were as much a display of genital size as of strong legs (i.e., a sexualization of the male body for perusal by others including women).[16] Through most of Western history, both sexes have worn one or another type of loose robe; for example, Peter Brown mentions the "billowing silk gowns of senators" in A.D. fourth century Roman cities, noting the important difference from the classical period where physical comportment, not clothing, distinguished social classes.[17] Lurie's historical sense is an indication of her contemporary academic allegiances: Her criticisms, and indeed the entirety of her interpretation, of women's historical role, and thus of fashion, is posed within a framework that really only dates at most from the seventeenth century. Like Barthes and Baudrillard, Lurie ignores the real efforts that people make to live well in favor of the notion that their judgments are made for them by the system. This carries the modern presuppositions I described in the preceding chapter to an absurd conclusion.

BOURDIEU'S DISTINCTION

Perhaps because his approach is that of a scientific observer instead of a philosopher, Pierre Bourdieu, in his mammoth study of French taste and class, *Distinction*, manages to get much more sensible conclusions from presuppositions similar to the structuralists.[18] Like Barthes, Baudrillard, and Lurie, Bourdieu believes—indeed demonstrates—that certain kinds of commodities symbolize class distinctions. For him, however, the symbols can only be understood as social guides manifested through the many more and less thoughtful domestic aesthetic choices of individuals in different classes and with different backgrounds. In particular, Bourdieu tries to qualify our understanding of the "specific logic" of the "economy of cultural goods" by reference to the types and levels of education, tradition, family upbringing, geographical area, and economic class of the individuals in that economy who are its interpreters.[19] In this way, Bourdieu improves on the others in his ability to take account of and sympathize with ordinary real individuals and sets the phenomena he analyzes against a concrete historical background. "Because they forget that the apparent constancy of the products conceals the diversity of the social uses they are put to, many surveys on consumption impose on them taxonomies which have sprung straight from the statistician's social unconscious. . . . Though of course, no 'natural' or manufactured product is equally adaptable to all possible social uses, there are very few that are perfectly 'univocal', and it is rarely possible to deduce the social use from the thing itself."[20]

With this sentiment Bourdieu undermines considerably both the more popular efforts of someone like Lurie and modern classics like Veblen. Thus, although Bourdieu does use all the rhetoric of the code of symbols of class, he is at least careful to place the encoding processes in the context of the practical choices of living people. Thus for Bourdieu, the commodities themselves are not the markers of class, but rather the tastes of the individuals choosing the commodities.

For Bourdieu, things are not given universal meanings by a systematic and structured culture; rather, the meanings that any particular individual attaches to things are indicative (to her and some subset of other consumers) of her being or not being cultured within that society. Bourdieu takes a great interest in questions of character; tastes tell the experimenter not just about the cultural code, but also about the lifestyle and circumstances of the subject interviewed.

This is demonstrated in Bourdieu's notion of "the habitus," which he defines as "both the generative principle of objectively classifiable judgments and the system of classification of these practices . . . the relationship between the . . . capacity to produce classifiable practices and works, and the capacity to differentiate and appreciate these practices and products (taste)."[21] This description, in itself, is similar to the reflective stance that I described as that of the practitioner of domestic aesthetic skill in part I.[22] And for Bourdieu, as for myself, these practices and reflections upon practices take place within a sensible environment and a set of social relationships that gives concrete character to the habitus.

Yet Bourdieu's habitus is necessarily systematic—a "structured and structuring structure."[23] Thus, according to him, agents are not quite able to interpret their world in better and worse ways; rather, the system of signification itself is the real agent here, the "unifying, generative principle of all practices."[24] Like MacIntyre, Bourdieu takes ethos as fundamental to moral standards or character, leaving few possibilities for the analysis of changes in the habitus over the course of a lifetime or an era—even though in its "structured" mode, the habitus is clearly affected by changes in the taste of individuals within it. For Bourdieu, taste is, at least in one sense, its own kind of "invisible hand," directing the efforts of individuals toward their significations of class differences without any reflection on their part, seemingly without the ability to change the signification of anything simply through their choice or use of particular objects. Thus, although Bourdieu sets the significations of taste in the moral and historical contexts of choice and practice, thereby at least allowing the individual to make complex judgments, he does not have a conception of agency such that one can ever deliberately make choices of the good, which I have argued must be the case: "All the practices and products of a given agent are objectively harmonized among themselves, without any deliberate pursuit of coherence."[25]

Furthermore, for Bourdieu, apparently one's class is the only thing one can really signify: class or the goodness or use of things as they appear through the rose-colored glasses of class. Thus, Bourdieu seems, somewhat despite himself, to share with Baudrillard, Barthes, and Lurie the belief that signification is always modeled on language, such that a sign is a mere equivalence—" 'believing being well-fed is good' = 'being working class,' 'catalogue buying' = 'being low class.' "[26] What he adds, however, to their analyses is that the equivalencies are produced by and in terms of practices and are not simply relations of objects among themselves. The filtering effect of her practice with objects, however, is itself beyond the agent's control here. "The schemes of the habitus . . . function below the level of consciousness and language, beyond the reach of introspective scrutiny or control by the will."[27]

Hence, Bourdieu shares many of the assumptions of the structuralists, which by depicting an agent incapable of reflection upon her actions and upon the good, will undermine any attempt on his part to give any real moral content to taste. Nor can he explicate any epistemological relation between consumer choice and moral choice. Nonetheless, by at least recognizing that the interpretation of signs is a practice, conducted within a social, historical, and moral context, Bourdieu gives us a starting point by which to understand the haywire significations of our day and improves upon the other poststructuralist theories of consumer choice.[28] For Bourdieu is fully aware that interpretive schemata (i.e., theories) are working hypotheses expressed by every individual in her consumer choices and beliefs even if he does not recognize the ability of a consumer to revise her tacit social theories.

LANGUAGE AND THE DOMESTIC AESTHETIC

Bourdieu's sharp cultural analysis points out a striking reason for structuralism's and poststructuralism's apparent applicability to domestic aesthetic choice and their real inapplicability. In contrast to Bourdieu's empirical sociology, we see that the world that Baudrillard, Barthes, and Lurie describe is not so much the physical and spiritual world we live in as it is the textual and pictorial world presented to us in media and especially in advertisements. Theirs *is* a world of images, not of things; a world of significant objects, not of useful, pretty, or even lousy ones.

Certainly, the world in advertisements and the world from which we look at advertisements are related, and certainly these worlds have grown more closely related in recent decades. They are surely, however, neither identical, nor realms that we should want to be more alike than they are now. In fact, if my claims so far are right, consumers often struggle hard against considerable resistance to keep their real household distinct from the advertising world. To the extent therefore that theory analyzes the world by analyzing the advertising world, the advertising world inevitably will eat theory alive, and being informed by such theories inevitably will impede consumers' efforts to make choices independently of the media.

It is understandable, then, that structuralism or poststructuralism seemed a good theoretical basis for the analysis of domestic aesthetic objects. It is not, however, the treasure trove it may have appeared to be. But this is not to say that some model of language might not be helpful in this endeavor. Indeed, one can make a useful analogy between language and domestic aesthetic choice, but to do so, one would need a model of language itself other than that offered by structuralists or poststructuralists. One would need a model of language that would draw out alternate tendencies in someone such as Bourdieu and give a theoretical basis for the possible remarriage of taste, moral character, and economic circumstance. One would need a vision of language in which neither an abstract grammatical system nor an abstract rule of reference, but a set of concrete human choices, is posited as the fundamental nonlinguistic basis of language; one in which needs and shared human goals, rather than abstract social systems, are envisioned as the mediators between signs and signifieds. Only on such a model can we understand both in what sense domestic aesthetic choices are like language and how we could come, through certain twists and turns of personal and social experience, to think of domestic aesthetic choice as more like language than we used to or than it really is.

One assumption that is shared by the structuralists and poststructuralists, including, most of the time, Bourdieu, is that because language is a system of purely symbolic (i.e., conventional) signs, any linguistic system must also be purely symbolic. In this assumption one takes for granted that there is little difference between different uses of the same words or on analogy between different brands of commodities of the same type. There is little difference, so goes the theory, between two different appearances of the word *and*, just as for Baudrillard there was no difference between two refrigerators. The "producer" of a word, on this model, has to go to desperate rhetorical lengths to distinguish her *and* from others, like the producer of the refrigerator. This model of language, however, overlooks an important way that all uses of a word are *not* alike. For instance, on a first draft of this work, I was found in an instance or two by one reader to use the expression *and etc.,* and I was corrected for it. In this appearance, *and* is used incorrectly—redundantly and unbeautifully. Of course, I may decide I want to be a language reformer and argue for my use of the term against this reader. But the fact that I could engage in an argument about the use of a term, even if I decided not to, indicates that language is not an arbitrary and dictatorial system, but is instead subject to human practice and judgment.

This is, of course, how Kant understood aesthetic judgment. As what he called the "common sensibility," beauty was subject to human reason without thereby being a definite concept. In other words, people can argue about beauty, and the argument is both productive and rational, but it will never be finished. This is in contrast, Kant claimed, both to how we think about individual gratification and to how we think about logical concepts. It neither makes sense to have an argument about whether a particular person likes mayonnaise on her sandwich instead of mustard, nor to argue about whether two plus two equals four. But it does make sense to argue about whether this painting is beautiful, according to Kant, and it is precisely because we argue about it that we can know that beauty is found through the human practice of judgment, even if, as he claims, it cannot be defined. The fact that we argue about the correct use of a term, particularly the fact that we could continue the argument indefinitely, shows that language, like beauty as Kant understood it, can be conceived as founded in the human practice of judgment. And if judgment in general is, as I have argued, founded in domestic aesthetic skill, then language is founded in domestic aesthetic skill.

This model of language can indeed provide a useful analogy to commodity circulation because it brings use value back into the picture. Use value is a real value inherent in the sensible qualities of commodities, about which consumers exercise judgment, and people may meaningfully argue about the proper use and usefulness of a particular product, including things like its class significance, reflecting as they do so on both the product and their own tacit theories about how to understand it. When we focus our analysis on the use value of products and on the particular possible use values that may be given to products by different consumers, we see many more differences between objects of the same type than we would be inclined to do on the structuralist or poststructuralist model. Implicit here, then, is the model of judgment that I offered in part I, on which goodness is understood as being at least to some degree naturally, and not merely conventionally or symbolically, signified by objects of conscious-ness.[29] The mediation between sign and signified is provided by the reflective consciousness of human beings engaged together in eco-nomic practices and not by an inaccessible system of signs.

Shared conventions, traditions of signification or use, may make judgment easier or more difficult. In the terms I used in part I, they may "shine" or "dirty" the reflective surfaces of thought and its vari-ous objects. In this sense, the theoretical frameworks, the academic fashions, the books in current circulation, the current rhetorical styles in various arenas—in addition to the goodness of the various material objects available at any particular time—may certainly affect our judg-ment, both of linguistic signification and of language itself. Thus, we can be led to believe that natural signification is unimportant, unanalyzable, or even fictional, as theorists such as Baudrillard have been led. We may be made both less willing and less able to have the arguments about use value that might reform our use of particular products and signs; we may come to believe such arguments are futile exercises. But if natural signification does occur and if, in at least other realms of choice besides language proper, it is related to conventional signification, then one can be said to have been misguided if one has been led to believe otherwise. I believe I have made a sufficient case for the first claim—that natural signification does occur—in part I. Here, I argue the second: that natural signification is of primary im-portance in domestic aesthetic choice and that we have been mis-guided in believing otherwise, in part, by theory.

PEIRCE AND THE LATER WITTGENSTEIN

Peirce and the later Wittgenstein are modern examples of thinkers who attempted to flesh out the relation between linguistic "systems" and objects in the world by reference to human action and choice. Al-though it is hardly appropriate here to discuss their metaphysical theo-ries, nor would I want to espouse them in either case, their analyses of signs and human judgment will be helpful in the present endeavor. Peirce gives us a useful analysis of other significatory functions besides the symbolic one most paradigmatically given in language proper, and the later Wittgenstein gives us a view of how human choice connects words to the world nonarbitrarily and nontrivially, yet nonsystematically.

Peirce insists on the mediation of an interpreter (his notion of "thirdness"), which is necessary for any knowledge to occur or for anything to be a "sign" properly so called.[30] Peirce recognizes that for any signification to occur, the interpreter must always conceptually presuppose the external or "natural" existence of sign and signified and must understand her identity in contrast and relation to them. Thus, signs for Peirce as for Bourdieu are morally or practically analyzable as an interaction of consciousness with the natural world as a particular agent understands it. "What distinguishes a man from a word? There is a distinction, doubtless. . . . Men and words reciprocally educate each other. . . ."[31] Thus, Peirce takes consciousness to be in a dialogic relation to the world, and this is something like the reflection upon goodness that I have described. A language user for him is not a mere pawn of a linguistic, rigidly rule-governed, interpretive schemata. She is a part of a community with shared practices, not an exchangeable piece of a mechanistic, mindless whole.

Peirce's notions of "qualisign" and "indexical," "iconic" and "symbolic" signification are helpful to an analysis of moral reasoning about commodities, and I have been using them implicitly throughout my analysis. A *qualisign* is a quality of an object that serves as a representative of that object; objects may also be represented by a qualitative possibility, which Peirce calls a *rheme*. The redness in or of a red block is a qualisign, rhemically signifying redness and cubedness. An *indexical* or natural sign signifies by way of its physical contiguity in space or time to the object signified—à la smoke and fire. An *iconic* sign signifies by way of its resemblance to the thing signified—like a portrait painting. A *symbolic* or conventional sign signifies by virtue of human agreement or dictate that it should do so. Names, and language in general, are symbolic signs.

These categories are not entirely pure according to Peirce. For instance, there are signs that signify in two or more ways at the same time, such as shadows and reflections in mirrors (which are both indexical and iconic), and maybe the word *ouch* or a grunt of a certain sort (which could be considered both indexical and symbolic). Statements are symbolic signs, but sentences may also be indexical qualisigns of a speaker's cultural background for example. Despite the inelegance of his terminology, we can see that Peirce offers an analysis of language and of signification in general that allows for great complexity of judgment. The interpreter may take a sign to represent in a plethora of ways, which are not given only by her class or by the sign system, but depend instead on some relation between more or less socially based systems of signification and her reflective judgment. And her interpretation may be more or less appropriate in different situations, as borne out in part by its consequences or efficiency at communication. Part of what makes interpretation complex for Peirce is precisely that not all signification is strictly linguistic and that not all uses of language are systematic.

Roughly systematic sets of symbolic signs, however, can develop historically from natural signs. We might refer to Wittgenstein's example of construction workers and their slabs and beams.[32] A certain need on the part of a builder, signified indexically perhaps by his coming to a momentary halt in his labor at the moment a particular item is needed, turns this indexical sign into a symbolic one, an impurely conventional one, when he says to his pal, "Slab." In this way the development of symbolic signs and conventionally agreed-upon grammars for their use can be understood as one type of purposeful human action. It is morally analyzable, a subject of moral philosophy as much as of metaphysics. Indeed, a tradition existed long before Peirce or Wittgenstein of envisioning language as an outgrowth of need and judgment, for instance in Plato, as we saw earlier; it also appears in Rousseau, Hobbes, and other political philosophers who ground political communities in a concept of human nature. Wittgenstein gives a taste of this when, famously, he describes language as "a game," which develops here and there through human interaction, like a little town. "Our language can be seen as an ancient city: a maze of little streets and squares, of old and new houses, and of houses with addition from various periods; and this is surrounded by a multitude of boroughs with straight regular streets and uniform houses."[33] In this example, Wittgenstein shows how and to what extent language becomes systematic. Initially, it is built up here and there by a small community of users with particular needs to express to each other. When the community is larger and it comes to have new members who are born into the use of the language, the building of streets, pathways, houses, and so forth, is refined, tidied, and regulated. Eventually the community is so old that it seems like it has always been there, and the language users born there come to think of it as a given. Despite the sympathy that we may have for these perceptions on their part, despite the genuinely increasing systematization of the town, however, it is not the prison it may sometimes appear to be to its citizens.

In a semiotic theory of domestic aesthetic objects of this Peircean and/or Wittgensteinian bent, some concept or analogy of use value may be restored to its rightful place. Use value may be there understood as an indexical signification of need, purpose, good, or beauty revealed to consciousness by certain objects in ways upon which we may or may not agree and that we may or may not be able to know for certain, but about which reflection and argument seem to improve our knowledge. By virtue of some other or higher human need or purpose or good, the use values of objects and the ways we signify them iconically and symbolically may be developed, à la Wittgenstein's little town, into a group of signs with a roughly systematic grammar. The grammar, the system itself, exists before the user only because the user's ancestors shared some purposes and conceptions of goodness, as well as this instrument to their fulfillment (the roughly systematic signs), in such a way that they made something that can be shared with still more people after their deaths.

A good domestic aesthetic choice (the foundation of a good moral or aesthetic judgment), then, must be based in the concrete judgment of the use value of an object as what Peirce would call an *indexical qualisign* or *rheme*. In other words, it must be based in the recognition of use value as a sensible quality or possible sensible quality of an object. This natural signification of goodness in things needn't, as I have argued, indicate anything about the nature of goodness. Whether one takes good to be absolute or relative, objective or subjective, a natural or nonnatural property, it can still be signified naturally in that its relation to its sign can appear to the interpreter without reference to or even education in a system or a tradition of signs. For example, whatever the social conventions and the nature of goodness itself, the interpreter of a Brooks Brothers suit need not have learned beforehand that "fits me" = "good suit" in order to interpret a 34-inch waistband as "not good" for his 38-inch belly, even if he would have to learn that "Brooks Brothers" = "acceptable suit for the businessman." This vision of language explains how it is the case that one can know, if one knows the current signification of weight in our community of interpreters, that "fat" tends to equal "poor" here and yet at the same time recognize that this signification is kind of weird. One can recognize both the meaning and its oddness at the same time—and consequently can reflect upon both—because fatness signifies in this case at once symbolically and indexically (and here, it signifies indexically in a number of ways at once; say for instance, of one's having eaten high-calorie foods as well as one's having eaten cheap foods).

An indexical sign is phenomenologically closer to the interpreter than a symbolic sign. In its case, the interpreter is able to bring more fully into her consciousness, not only *that* the indexical sign signifies, but also *how* it signifies because the contiguity of sign and signified in time or space more closely associates the two in consciousness as well. The interpreter needs to do more work to "hold up" a symbolic sign next to its signified in consciousness to judge the goodness of the significator because it is mediated by a whole history and tradition of signification (although not necessarily thereby by a *system* of signification). Other kinds of signification are of course helpful in our endeavors to interpret indexical signs of goodness correctly, just as the symbolic signification of Brooks Brothers was helpful for the gentleman in the previous example.

To put this notion of phenomenological intimacy in MacIntyre's terms, we might say that it is easier to offer reasons for judging an indexical sign to be so, where it is more difficult to do so for a symbolic sign. To consider the first case, suppose someone asked why a particular refrigerator was good; we could say it kept food cold and fresh, and we could without much difficulty say why this is good. It might be so obvious to our interlocutor, in fact, that she might simply find the goodness we describe to her in the cold drink we hand her. If someone asked us, however, why people call football player William Perry "the Refrigerator," we would have to spend some time talking about the circumstantial physical qualities of refrigerators (e.g., they are usually pretty big), to give reasons for our interpretation of this iconic signification. If someone asked, on the other hand, why we interpret the word *justice* as signifying some sort of right action, the trail of reasons would take us into an explanation of why we have languages at all and what kind of tools they are, which is, for instance, the same trail of reasoning that led Socrates, Glaucon, and Adeimantus through the *Republic*.

The more signification becomes symbolic or conventional, the more the phenomenological relation in consciousness on which judgment depends is mediated or distanced. Consequently, judgment is made more difficult. The more difficult judgment becomes, the more distant conceptions of ends are from objects in consciousness, the harder these conceptions of ends are to "see," and the fuzzier and foggier they become to us. Although the increased use of symbolic signs make our shared lives easier in some ways and opens up expressive possibilities, the difficulty of interpreting and justifying them increases the risk of using them badly. Thus, to judge symbols rightly one needs to know how to judge indices rightly, and this, as I argued, requires practice. If my argument in part I is correct, then if one is unpracticed at interpreting indexical representations of goodness, one will do a poor job at interpreting symbolic representations of it. In other words, if we are entirely unpracticed for some reason in *using* things to make our shared life better, we will probably be rather poor at *buying* things with which to do so.

Neither one's control over language nor one's control over the market is total, but that one is not the dictator of language or commodity consumption does not mean that one may not be a relatively free citizen of language or of the market, that one does not even have a vote in how these ought and ought not to be used. We see a lot of individuals who exert quite a bit of power over language use, for example, good writers, popular writers, even advertising copywriters. Seeing language itself as a domestic aesthetic object makes transparent how it may be both under one's control and beyond it for the user of language, both nonarbitrary and changeable. It is the good life, then, that stands above language and domestic aesthetic objects and to which we submit our choices, but our judgments are not impotent on that account. They influence both the actions and the language use of our interlocutors and household members.

In the foregoing chapters, I have given further support for a domestic aesthetic theory and some ways to understand how domestic aesthetic skill might tend to atrophy (or sharpen) over history, as well as some sense of how theory, among a variety of other influences, might partly affect such trends in individuals' moral reasoning. In the next chapters I look at how recent and contemporary economic practices (i.e., how the production and sale of domestic aesthetic objects themselves) have affected moral reasoning. I claim that what I call the tactics of fashion, far from being a malignant totalitarian system, are desperate and haphazard activities that have worn down agents' attention to indexical qualisigns of goodness in the objects with which we are surrounded and affected our habits of conversation about the good and our skill at comparative evaluation. In other words, I believe the effect of fashion tactics in production, marketing, and sales has been to set consumers at a further and further phenomenological distance by focusing our attention on the symbolic signification of the social conventions of exchange value and away from the indexical signification of use value. As this trend increasingly pervades habits in the production, marketing, and sale of domestic aesthetic objects (e.g., food, clothes, household objects, possible friends), the prognosis for skillful judgment becomes that much more grave.

PART III

Techniques of Vagueness

It's you, amplified.
                    —Vidal Sassoon commercial

CHAPTER 7

FASHION TACTICS AND PHENOMENOLOGICAL DISTANCE

But once the elements of this kind of fashion have established credentials for honesty, they are subject to no further scrutiny. . . . Self-regulated conformists, unencumbered by the need for choice, forget how to choose and are thus in a vulnerable position.
—Kennedy Fraser, "The Fashionable Mind"

In previous chapters I have argued that the tendency among structuralist- and postmodern-influenced theorists to understand consumer choices on the model of language and to understand language as a desperately important but entirely arbitrary system that mediates between agents and the objects of human choice is itself a historical development that signifies a deteriorating sense of domestic aesthetic judgment. Structuralist and poststructuralist accounts of fashion, food, and language are themselves victims of the increasing tendency to view the world as distant, far away, and arbitrary to our choices, but as determinate of them nonetheless—the increasing dependence of theoreticians themselves on mediation by "experts" who today we might call "tacticians of fashion."

What I call *fashion tactics*—in production, marketing, and sales; in homemaking, intellectual life, and ordinary conversation—exacerbates the phenomenological distance of consumers and producers alike. As I define them, fashion tactics are the haphazard processes by which agents are distracted from the indexical signification of use value, or what I've called "the reflection of goodness" in objects. Fashion tactics essentially flatter us for being bored with reflection upon goodness. Allured by the symbolic signification of social conventions of exchange value, fashion tactics "linguisticize" human life. They encourage aesthetic judgment to skim its objects at the gross level and to take away from them vague inklings of the objects' basic affinities instead of interpretations of their meaning or use. I call these *tactics* because of their vague shortsightedness; fashion tactics seek temporary alliances with the objects of consumer choice, not lasting victories in the achievement of happier lives. I use the term *fashion* to connote their continuous rhetorical appeal to vanity. The shortsighted, tactical, vulnerable aspects of fashion tactics characterize them as desperate and well meaning, rather than malicious and conspiratorial, although they may often seem like the latter. As Kennedy Fraser, from whom I have partly borrowed the phrase, claims in her deeply provocative essay "The Fashionable Mind," "the greatest disservice that fashion does is carelessly to turn life's most precious and fragile assets into marketable products of transient worth."[1]

The tendency of Barthes, Lurie, and others to identify the language of fashion with the sensible qualities of clothing dates them as children of an advertising age, wherein people have really tried to do with words and pictures what, I have argued, can only be done successfully and skillfully with food, clothes, apartments, tchotchke, and so on—sensible objects in the world and their discernible qualities. Language proper is the model for commodities, not insofar as consumers use them but insofar as they are represented by advertisers and other promoters. Hence the uneasy similarity that sometimes seems to hold between capitalist apologists and their structuralist and poststructuralist critics. In a political economy where the exchange value of objects has largely overtaken their use value and in which the maintenance of households, families, and love goes on at great physical distances, of course domestic aesthetic choices will seem linguistic, like written contracts, telephone conversations, newspaper ads, or e-mail. Theorists such as those I discussed earlier, who accept this appearance as the essence of the commodity form, tend as much as their rivals do to promote themselves as "experts," reference to whom must be made by any student, writer, or thoughtful consumer trying to make a legitimate choice about something.

Judith Williamson prefaces the 1985 edition of her *Decoding Advertisements* with a comment upon the effect of semiotic theory on advertising strategy and vice versa, which is not unsimilar despite its different subject matter to Fraser's analysis of the fashionable mind: "[W]hat is so shocking in the academic world is the way theoretical work can be used as a weapon of intimidation: as if understanding theories was an end in itself, . . . these ins and outs of theoretical fashion are not arbitrary, but are linked to wider changes. . . . And advertising also began to show far more skillful, self-conscious use of 'semiotics' . . . so that many of the formal practices of advertising . . . are now explicit."[2]

Williamson attests here that theories that understand all significations as mediated by convention—or to the extent that they understand signification as mediated by convention—actually conventionally mediate signification. Like Heisenbergian observations, the positing of these theories has an affect on the phenomena under observation. Furthermore, in this case, the theoretician herself, as a maker of judgments about the existence of systems of signs, is one of the phenomena under investigation, herself affected by the plethora of such theories and of the mass-produced objects that such theories lead people to produce. Williamson's and Fraser's depictions of the role of fashion in intellectual life are similar to a sympathetic observation made by Baudrillard: "Fashion is one of the more inexplicable phenomena, so far as these matters go: its compulsion to innovate signs, its apparently arbitrary and perpetual production of meaning. . . . The logical processes of fashion might be extrapolated to the dimension of 'culture' in general—to all social production of signs, values and relations."[3]

Although unlike Baudrillard, I do not find a "logic" of fashion, nor do I think it has real rules, I do agree with him, as he does with Fraser and Williamson, that fashion has become a fuel for culture—it is not just a rhetorical flourish, but a serious productive force—and that fashion is an odd sort of productive force that is only apparently arbitrary and meaningless. Like these three thinkers, I claim that fashion tactics have now negatively affected much of our moral and political reason, reason that MacIntyre argued we have forgotten how to practice. In this chapter, I investigate how these tactics of fashion work, how they develop in conversation with theoretical analyses of mass culture, and how they have affected the salient qualities of the commodities with which we fill our lives.

WEIRD SIGNS

Our domestic landscape has changed very drastically and very eerily over the last few decades. Just a few years ago, for a first example, couture designers came out with the grunge look, where expensive silk and wool versions of plaid poly/cotton and wool-flannel shirts, shorts cut off below the knee, and expensive versions of leather workboots were sold in apparent emulation of what was already a middle-class teenager's sloppy, slumming-it look. Although chalking this effort up to cooptation by capital—certainly it is that—is reasonable, it is an odd sort of cooptation of styles that have already filtered down the economic funnel, a reclamation by the wealthy of styles that were originally gestures of the trickling down of opulence to the lower class. The woven poly/cotton- and wool-flannel shirts originally worn by working-class adults were taken up by middle-class teens and then were copied in printed poly/cotton over again for the working class. And then the silk *couture* versions. . . .

Simplicity Patterns recently came out with a series for the working woman: outfits that can be zipped-up on the sewing machine in two hours. Purposely designed without seam binding, without finishing, without tailoring, and without openings (i.e., *designed to be badly made*) these over-the-head hunks of junk look like plastic bags and will last half as long. What time and money is really being saved over shopping at department stores by the women using these patterns, who must after all, still buy sewing machines and peruse fabric stores to slap these dresses together is both impossible and silly to try to figure out. What individuality and originality of appearance is gained by wearing one of these items over wearing a T-shirt is impossible to say. Like the couture grunge, this is an odd cooptation of an originally working-class effort to improve oneself and upgrade one's appearance, now without even the know-how, the time, and the willingness to work that enlivened the original working-class effort and made it successful.

The 1993 AT&T ad campaign ominously threatened that "you will" put your baby to bed by phone, attend business meetings in your pajamas, ask directions from your car, and keep your medical history on a credit card. That the world of the future would be such that you would not be able to be at home in peace was presented by AT&T as unquestionably your preference—all that held you back, apparently, was that you just didn't dream it possible. Here again, what was originally the sad fate of working people—that constant work away from home kept them away from their households, distanced their relationships, kept tabs upon their person, and intruded upon their spare time— was presented as the future salad days of the middle class whose higher status is marked over that of the poor, apparently, only in that they can wear sloppy, comfortable clothes while they overwork instead of the tidy and constrictive ones that because heavy labor couldn't be done in them, used to be the markers of the upper class. In the same vein, Cisco System's 1999 campaign follows a line of children, shot in a variety of national costumes and against a variety of topological backgrounds, directing at the viewer their smiles and the question, "Are you ready?" as a narrator reports on what appear to be unstoppable trends in the Internet's colonization of the world. This is certainly not catching flies with honey; it's simple extortion.

Far more confusing and pernicious, however, than either of those campaigns are the 1996–1997 Heineken ads, which had several variations. In all of them, the camera remains fixed in place, focused on some items that give the viewer only the vaguest hint of the scene: in one, we see the outside of a brick building with a lighted window and the edge of a neon sign; in another, the corner of a table with party foods on it, and so on. No people appear in the ad, but we hear them talking. In every version, the two interlocutors are having an extremely unpleasant and stupid conversation, which they themselves acknowledge as such. In the "outside of the bar" commercial, they are arguing about who authored Moby Dick; in "at the party," they are arguing about whether the pink paté is salmon or liver. Printed on the bottom of the screen in each commercial is the answer to their dumb query, presumably at the largesse of the Heineken company, followed by the anthem, "their words, their world, their beer." There is no way around the fact that these commercials insult the target audience. What is shocking, however, is that the insult is put across as a kind of tragic cool. Again, beer—the cheap drink par excellence—has been coopted by the upper class and filtered back down, only half successfully, to the middle class. (How else to interpret the inarticulate reference to literature and the inept familiarity with paté, much less the imported beer?) This generation of fumbling would-be sophisticates, one would guess according to the ad, are supposed to feel good about the fact that they're already bored by their lives and the beer that accompanies it.

Over the past several years, the fast-food restaurants have all been turning toward mock-home-cooked foods and away from their reputation as kiddie restaurants. McDonald's Arch Deluxe, with its "adult" appeal, was marketed as the sort of thicker hamburger with fresh vegetables that one makes at home. KFC added roast chicken to their selection, a little more like Sunday dinner and a little less like a picnic (one wonders why they weakened their connection to their old Kentucky home). In all these instances, such as the AT&T and the Heineken campaigns, the unfortunate situation of the busy working class who must replace or imitate the comforts of home with a quick bite from the drive-through is the product's selling point. It is supposed to be in our interest to have our dwindling domestic practices taken away by mass producers.

As if this weren't enough, along with these eerie trends on the fast-food front, a march is being conducted against the home cooks. Over the last two decades, the big supermarkets began diversifying. Not only did they conquer the former territory of drug, hardware, stationery, photography, and liquor stores, they also made intrusions on restaurants, bakeries and "gourmet stores," fitting fancy deli shops, coffee bars, and self-service counters, at considerable renovation costs, under their roofs. The result was that far beyond just buying the misunderstood convenience of frozen foods, shoppers now pack up plastic cartons of prechopped, slightly old vegetables to take home and plop bottled salad dressing on as some sort of preferable alternative to chopping up a carrot or two at home. Or, alternatively, squishy bagels, prepackaged soup mixes (a plastic bag containing a turnip, a potato, a carrot, and an onion), pre-molded and squashed chuck meat in rolls so that your burger at home can look and taste just like McDonald's, strange-looking ready-mixed pasta salads in boxes to which one just adds water, prefilled coffee filters so that coffee at home can indeed taste just like the Bun-O-Matic, all save virtually seconds in the kitchen. Now one can spend those five minutes after work in the supermarket instead. A very little amount of reflection would demonstrate to anyone that such products save their consumers only a negligible amount of time while making their lives significantly less pleasant, comfortable, and intimate. How are producers, retailers, and advertisers getting away with it?

Although these practices smack of things such as the emulation of peasant food in, say, fancy French cooking, something in the contemporary version has gone amiss. The French chef never pretended she was doing the peasant a favor, and the peasant didn't forget how to make soup just because somebody else was getting paid to do it. Everyone knows that roast chicken, for instance, is really a cinch to make, even on a tight schedule and budget, and so is vegetable soup. That customers put this knowledge aside—enough for these establishments to sell their wares—is much more disturbing than economists, sociologists, or philosophers seem to realize.

The Veblen-esque principle of invidious consumption (i.e., the emulation of the upper classes by members of the classes below them through consumption for its own sake) if it ever constituted a thorough explanation of consumer behavior, does not seem to apply here at all.[4] Nor is this just, as Baudrillard might claim, that our current social landscape is a "system of signs." Certainly we depend on signs, but no system of signs is evident today—no rules, no goals, no organized force of oppression or ambition running the show. The signs through which we have to live just don't make any sense at all because the production and consumption of signs is entirely divorced in the consciousness of workers and consumers from any conceptions of ends, whether political, functional, aesthetic, or anything else. The circulation of signs occurs, as shown in these examples, through aimless, inappropriate attempts to copy what seems to be the rage, or to do something for someone, for a price. But the signs have an effect

nonetheless: increased phenomenological distance and the degeneration of domestic aesthetic choice.

Contemporary life is marketed as if it were the necessary and
desirable result of the uncontrollable force that is technological and
moral "progress," the Darwinian model of technology I discussed
previously. The confused significations of class, taste, leisure, intelligence, history, and political and moral good, including both the
working-class emulation of the middle class and its distaste for it, both
its social mobility and its egalitarianism; and, sadly, including the
working-class fatigue, its lack of leisure, and its shortness of cash,
without including its skill, its industry, its traditionalism, and its common sense, is one of the weird turns along which fashion tactics have
taken us. Baudrillard may again be helpful: "The 'liberation' of needs,
of consumers, of women, of the young, the body, etc.," he writes, "is
always really the *mobilization* of needs, consumers, the body, . . . a mobilization whose end is competitive exploitation."[5] *Competitive exploitation* is by definition, however, an instrument (exploitation must be
for something); it is not in any sense to be called an end. There is no
point, no system, to this weird sign language, as Baudrillard thinks.
Still, Baudrillard is quite right that many of the hard-earned freedoms
of the last decades have had the effect of making us more, not less,
dependent on social institutions and big companies; and this dependence, no matter how much of an income it accompanies, puts everyone in a lower-class position than that in which an independent person
would find herself, no matter how nice a gloss we put on it.

This is in part because, in line with my thesis set forth in part I,
our phenomenological distance from the things with which we find
ourselves surrounded has accompanied a clouding over of the average person's ideals, of her conceptions of goodness. The irritation of
a working person's life (regardless of how much money she is making), where her phone calls are monitored, timed, and budgeted by a
paternalistic employer; where her meat is cut with cereal and served
by an unhappy stranger, is pictured across the media and in many of
our own psyches, as the American Dream. The private house and the
two-car garage, the steak and potatoes, and the passel of happy kids,
is the laughing stock of the intelligent and tasteful working person
today whatever her class, but it is not very different from the dreams
that replaced it, which aim in the same direction, only on a much more
winding and overgrown path. For all that these commercials acclaim
and these commodities enable is our bittersweet resignation to the
confusion in which they claim we conduct our lives.

Perhaps the single most striking perversion of signification in
contemporary U.S. culture, noted by Fraser and by Paul Fussell,[6] (about

whom I have more to say presently), remark on, is that fatness has come to signify quite clearly the lower class, and, to a lesser extent, thinness the upper. To be fat is no longer, for us, the sign of wealth, comfort, complacency, and leisure—qualities that were at one time seemingly worth the toil of carrying more weight on one's body. Rather, the obese must bear the brunt now not only of their weight, but of unattractive clothing, the scorn of the health-crazed majority, and the obviousness of their low class. The thin now seem to have the world by the tail. This quite confusing occurrence is the result of two weird factors: one, the fact that only fatty and sugary junk can be afforded by the poor (the brands allowed by the WIC programs, for instance, are paradigmatic of this phenomenon); and two, because most people's work and neighborhoods no longer afford them any natural exercise it has become necessary to pay health clubs, equipment manufacturers, video producers, and sportswear manufacturers for the opportunity to exercise, and only those who can afford to do so may burn off calories. It is difficult to fathom the extremity of the contortions that we have made today in our reading of signs, that such simple and obvious signifiers as thinness and fatness have come to represent precisely their opposites in class terms.

This mock choiceworthiness of what was originally making do, this adoption by the mostly middle-class society of what was originally an imitation of themselves by the lower class, this entanglement of what might at one time have been explained as Veblen-esque invidious consumption, marks what Fussell, in his deeply insightful but rather unhopeful book *Class*, calls "prole drift."[7] It is a strangely recent phenomenon afflicting a society that for so long was successfully upwardly mobile in both their economic standings and their tastes. "Of course, much social sinking is not at all intentional. . . . After decades of moving up "the mass of Americans now find themselves . . . *bumped down.*" . . . In a melancholy sense, the whole society could be said to be engaged in a process of class sinking, . . . the tendency in advanced industrialized societies for everything inexorably to become proletarianized. Prole drift is an inevitable attendant of mass production, mass selling, mass communication, and mass education."[8]

In other words according to Fussell, class sinking, both in wealth and style, is attached to the "increase of being" that Lyotard cited. Prole drift, like the nouveau-riche phenomenon of which it is evocative, is not adequately explained by a theory of emulation, although it does have deep strains of Veblen's other famous principle, conspicuous consumption. For one thing, the conceptualization of "the life of the rich and famous" available for lower-class imitation today is mediated by the producers and advertisers of the commodities for the lower-class market. As Fussell notes, the truly wealthy American lives a very private life—she is out-of-sight, of even the members of the upper class who might hope to imitate her.[9] Second, as I've shown in the preceding examples, it is common for members of the upper-middle class, professional people buying prepackaged soup mix in supermarkets, to imitate the fashions of the lower class or at least to buy the imitations produced for them. Campbell's "Romantic ethic" and its twentieth-century heirs seem much more consistent with the data Fussell and I have cited than does invidious emulation.[10] Fantastic visions of the irreverence, bohemianism, and raw expressiveness of the proletariat, such as those cited by Campbell as Romantic motivators, easily make as seductive sales pitches as staid butlers and smoking jackets, although the latter certainly have a reliable appeal.

Campbell's analysis is useful here in three other ways as well: first, in what he calls after Weber, the "irony of history," he observes in the Romantics a discrepancy between agents' intentions—certainly related to their conceptualizations of the good—and the consequences of their actions.[11] In other words, he observes in the Romantic movement and in what he claims are its effects in the consumer movement of the eighteenth century what, if it were to become the habitual mode of deliberative action, would create phenomenological distance. He "suggest[s] both that 'meaningless' action might regain its ideal and transcendent significance, and that conduct undertaken for petty or self-seeking ends could develop into a genuine romantic idealism."[12] In other words, Campbell would be surprised neither that an antiestablishment phenomenon such as alternative rock would be a cash cow for record companies, nor that its middle- and upper-middle-class consumers might become genuinely less reverent of authority through its influence. Second, and as a consequence of his notion of *irony*, Campbell suggests that history repeats itself in a sense at least: romantic-type movements accompanied by rises in consumerism are recurring themes of modernity. "I became convinced . . . that . . . cultural revolutions [similar to those of the 1960s and 1970s] had occurred before, and that the world-view espoused by the counter-culturalists could only adequately be described by the adjective 'romantic' ".[13] Thus, with caution, at least, we may take Campbell's analysis as a model for the interpretation of other consumer trends. Third, as I mentioned in previous chapters, Campbell's analysis of consumer behavior takes into account the influences of art and style on individual consumers' choices, adding to the economists' rational actor a faculty of aesthetic judgment.

Whereas Campbell's analysis, however, might yield explanations of, say, the imitation by upper-class young women of the waiflike pathos of Calista Flockhart and Courtney Cox or of couture grunge, it is not applicable to less romantic consumer phenomena. The Heineken ads for boorishness, the packages of old turnips, Cisco Systems's straightforward threat of their consumers' personal obsolescence—we find nothing either idealistic or euphorically crass in these. In a palpable sense, products and ads such as these offer absolutely nothing. To come to terms with phenomena such as these, one must put into the mix of one's explanatory categories a certain amount of simple, desperate, confusion. What *fashion tactics,* as I use the term, add to Campbell's Romantic ethic, Fussell's prole drift, Lyotard's increase of being, and Baudrillard's compulsion to innovate signs, is its element of sheer, desperate bullshit in fashion tactics: producers, advertisers, and consumers alike are to a certain extent *bluffing* their moral, aesthetic, and economic decisions.[14] In this sense, then, the tactics of fashion are "techniques of vagueness."

When, in the late 1960s and 1970s (coincident with the Age of Aquarius Campbell cites and with Terkel's interviews in *Working*), it started getting more difficult for Americans to make and retain an improved "economic capital" (as Bourdieu describes pure economic class status), extra duress was put on both consumer and producer choice. Consumers were increasingly inclined to "fake" the lifestyle they either had become accustomed to or wanted to be accustomed to, spending less money for lower quality that still, but merely, gestured at a handsome life; companies had to advertise more manipulatively and aggressively, creating a new kind of "fake" demand for cheaply made commodities. A marketing researcher describes it from her side: "Companies moved from selling what they produced to marketing what customers would buy.... Our economic growth has slowed, reducing the odds for an average, or even a superior, product to succeed by simply being there."[15]

Fussell had observed that Americans fill their lives with frighteningly vague symbolism as a substitute for genuine value, and he identified this as an unambiguous mark of prole drift. For instance: "Whatever the reason for the unicorn's popularity among proles, the motif is an example of what literary critics used to denigrate as *pseudoreference.* The thing seems to refer, portentously, to something more specific than it does. I have before me a pretentious prole drawing which comes on as loaded with meaning. It shows a unicorn bursting fully formed out of an egg(!) ... Meaning? Well, there isn't any, as a matter of fact, but there seems to be, and that's a prole sufficiency, gratifying the dual desire for the portentous and the vague."[16]

This dual desire for the portentous and vague, the deeply meaningful and the fuzzy, is clearly the function of a purely symbolic signification, ungrounded by any index of goodness. If this was a condition for lower class status in 1983 when Fussell wrote about it (about which one might argue), it is clearly now a common condition among every rank of American consumer, including the very wealthiest among us. Donald Trump, no less than the unicorn admirer here, seems to fill his life with portentous yet vague purchases and wives in a seeming effort to look as rich as he is. Similarly, the difference between the foggy profundity of the abovementioned unicorn and that of the futuristic, proto-Nazi, S&M symbolism of En Vogue's 1995 *Free Your Mind* video, the faux Freudian, Gothic-Romantic symbolism of Guns N' Roses *November Rain*, or even the loving concern of TLC's *Waterfall* is scant. In fact, MTV, one long commercial for middle-class American adolescence, marketed to wealthy and poor alike, is perhaps the pinnacle of vague and portentous symbolism. The fashion of the present age is to symbolize this and that, for no reason and to little effect. One can see quite obviously on MTV a case where a pretended system of similarities and differences pretends to make plays of reference, but neither its audience nor its producers have any idea anymore what these symbols are similar to or different from. They are just symbols we happen to be able to conjure up and set to music to make the music seem meaningful and, consequently, seem worth the expense. A society in which even the upper-middle class and extremely wealthy *put on airs* is not a society in which a system controls us; it is a society in which signification has gotten way out of hand of what is signified, one in which there is no system at all, but only the vague symbolic gestures of a system.

THE PHENOMENOLOGY OF FASHION TACTICS

Fussell cites José Ortega Y Gassett as an early pioneer in this sort of class analysis. Ortega rightly discovered, states Fussell, that "the mass crushes beneath it everything that is different, everything that is excellent, individual, qualified, and select."[17] But Fussell updates Ortega's insight: "Time, however, has shown that . . . he . . . is not invading anything. Rather, the world on top is sinking down to fit itself to his wants, since purchasing power has increasingly concentrated itself in his hands."[18] What Ortega calls "the mass man" and what Fussell calls prole drift are indeed very similar occurrences, and they come about through a mechanism of production wherein symbolic representation of goodness, the projection of the vague inklings of the self-concept of an ordinary consumer or promoter onto the objects she can buy, like a bulldozer, flattens and makes obsolete indexical or natural signification of the good. This is true both of agents and of the objects they buy. The mechanism gets its originating fuel from the production of poorly designed, useless domestic aesthetic objects, and it is catalyzed by the adaptation of theory, which filters into the mass media through textbooks, political activity, and marketing strategies, which accommodates this process rather than reflecting upon it and improving it.

For Ortega, the mass man is the man who opposes himself to the past, and hence is both essentially rationalist and essentially revolutionary. The empiricist, in contrast, according to Ortega, ties herself to objects in the world that have phenomenal qualities on which to practice judgment; through them, she also ties herself to a historically traceable physical existence.[19] Ortega's mass man blurs distinctions, having no historical consciousness, no appreciation for the efforts of others who made the things, indeed the language, the very world, that he now uses; he takes what is in reality a hard-won world as a given of nature.[20] That there are microwaves, cars, nuclear power plants, pollsters calling at dinner, trips to the moon—indeed, that there is a nation, a culture, a society at all—all these are givens as the air is given, as if they were the results of natural laws. Their meanings are divorced from the human practices and traditions that compose them, and so they are divorced from the use value that clarifies their existence. They function for the agent solely as placeholders in a system of exchanges. "We live with our technical requirements, but not *by* them. These give neither nourishment nor breath to themselves, they are not *causae sui* but a useful, practical precipitate of superfluous, unpractical activities."[21]

Despite Fussell's complaint that he is out of date, Ortega's mass man acts upon culture in a very similar way to Fussell's prole—through his buying power, he models all production on himself without meaning to or even realizing that he does. The mass man *signifies* the individual *to himself*, knows only how to be an abstract symbol of an individual who has rights and possessions, and not how to exercise those rights or use those possessions. He is precisely the person in the market for a role model that is, unbeknownst to him, only a more vague, less powerful, less interesting version of himself—he becomes just the person who the marketers and promoters need him to be. "Life . . . consists primarily in living over the possibilities of buying."[22]

The world of such a person cannot help but *seem* structured and systematic and full of meaning, and yet *be* haphazard, confused, and insignificant because the mass man is a king who feels like a pawn. It is this quite confused person who "invades" everything without effort and who draws everything to her will without even having a conscious will by which to draw it. Through her very efforts to make a life that she can be proud of, she keeps getting a life that dissatisfies her, her own life only less so.

Thus, Ortega gets at another aspect of fashion tactics, the circular dissembling of the qualitative content of character, which results from the conflation of self and goodness one finds in today's producers, advertisers, and consumers. I have previously cited this as a presupposition of Hegel's and Marx's, as well as a modern development traceable in Mill, Kant, and Smith. Campbell cites something like this as a Romantic trend.[23] Whatever its modern source, it is evident that the fashion tactics of contemporary consumerism are thoroughly practiced in a sort of circular flattery. The consumer herself—with her whims, her weaknesses, her talents, and her possibly vague ideals as she is depicted by market analysts—is characterized by the products and advertisements from which, in part, she derives her conceptions of goodness as one–dimensionally good. This characterization is put forward in the grossest way, as a categorical, symbolic representation of the ideal consumer of the product at issue. Only this indistinct appeal to a badly represented vanity could explain how something such as the abovementioned Heineken campaign could sell beer. And this appeal to vanity, perhaps especially when it is bolstered by philosophical theory, surely works directly against the development of good judgment and moral decision making; it is difficult to imagine how anyone would not be confused by it.

To return to the metaphor I used in part I, Ortega's mass man is similar to an actor—chosen to play the lead role in a play, who has no concept of his character, or of the setting, props, plot, or other characters. Such a person should be, and indeed believes herself to be, without the wherewithal to play her part. Yet the play today seems to go on without noticing her failure; the other actors say their parts equally without any sense for their characters; the props and scenery seem mixed up and offer no help to her in establishing her will or in resisting the whims of the other players, the playwright, or the director. Of course such a person will believe the production proceeds from beyond her control. But she will be wrong. The reason the production is so confused is precisely because *she* is the playwright and the director, and yet does not recognize herself as such. It is her own ill-considered, unskillful choices that keep appearing on the stage with her, and she doesn't recognize them.

This, what I've called *eerie feeling*, is much like Freud's notion of the "uncanny," indirectly and unsurprisingly related according to Freud to Romantic or Gothic literature.[24] According to Freud, the feeling one sometimes gets of "uncanniness," whether when one is reading horror stories or just getting the creeps, is something like déjà vu. One finds a strange familiarity in something to which one is, one thinks, unrelated, or, conversely, a strange alienation from something with which one thought oneself identified. Under conditions of fashion tactics, we often feel this uncanny, alienated familiarity with ourselves as abstract entities; we identify both with the inadequacy that is the prerequisite to desire for the commodity and the omnipotent power behind the market to which the advertisements appeal. Under such conditions, decision making is reduced to guesswork and rewarded for its confused character. Through fashion tactics, living is emptied of its skillfulness in favor of desperate, confused stabs at acceptability, treading water.

The new wave of car names is a blatant example of phenomenologically distant, vague symbolic signification. *Impreza, Integra, Achieva, Lumina, Windstar, Rav4*—the list goes on—have replaced *Mustang, New Yorker, Cougar, Dart,* and *Thunderbird.* Granted, names must be symbols, but here what were once at least the names of icons or indices of strength, speed, urbanity, or cuteness are replaced with nonsense names that simply gesture toward mere abstractions that we may or may not want to see instantiated in a car. *"Integra?"* Not even the most determinedly thoughtful consumer could know what to do with that. Perhaps these are grandchildren of the exceedingly unfortunate early automotive name change, from the cute, indexical *Esso,* (onomatopoetic for the abbreviation of Standard Oil) to the affected, then-futuristic, now-dated, *Exxon.* The ongoing, "It's What's for Dinner" promotion of the Beef Council, for another instance (which gives only the names and cooking times of various dishes) valorizes customers who do not know that names and time consumption are not particularly relevant to good butchery or dining. Rybczynski introduces his book *Home* with a discussion of Ralph Lauren's incredible marketing success: "To call Ralph Lauren a tailor is like calling the Bechtel Corporation a builder. . . . Lauren is an orchestrator of images."[25] Rybczynski demonstrates that Lauren did not produce accurate period replicas in his Old West and Bermuda lines; he produced only vague symbols gesturing at what people think these periods and places looked like—largely cribbed from movie sets.

In these cases objects are marketed to make the consumer's evident confusion about use value seem like an asset. More and more this wild abandon of production and marketing is geared, not only to palm off junk, but also to sell junk as a glorification of the consumers' ignorance, gleaned from her very own "buying trends"; producers of these objects promote themselves as experts at living, experts because they "bring good things to life" where the consumer can only buy things ready made. The producer of objects takes the market trends to be authoritative, and the consumer takes the products available to her as authoritative; in reality neither is guided by anything but vague symbolic gestures at vaguely understood goods.

Of course, fashionable restaurants, fashionable clothes, and fashionable interior decorators can be found throughout the modern era. But today's methods of style setting are different. Fashionable things today are neither modeled for us by the wealthy, leisure class as Veblen would have suggested, nor are they very interesting or beautiful or even really very expensive. Today's fashions are precisely the fashions that are *not* novel because they are not set by or for people with leisure. Rather, today's fashions are purely intertextual: empty rehashings of what was popular last decade, last year, or last month dressed up to look as though they were deeply, profoundly imaginative and affecting. They can't be just pretty or helpful; they must be violently rebellious or right-minded. They can't be just comfortable or easy to take care of; they have to "change the way work is done forever." A quick survey of prime-time television ads will reveal the large number of companies that have adopted as their mottoes something such as "No boundaries" or "The rules have changed." On the one hand these sound very sophisticated, as if these companies would be our sci-fi, high tech, avant-garde liberators, but they also depict life or business as wholly unknown territory through which it remains questionable whether these companies or products can guide us. The tactics of fashion are the methods by which supposed experts keep their jobs: by consoling consumers in their confusion and instructing them in how to get by without really knowing how to take care of themselves. The experts are only "supposed," though, of course, because they are consumers, too; as consumers, they are just as confused as their marks.

Fashion tactics substitute vague symbolic signs of goodness for clearer indexical ones: the designer label on the dress replaces the cut as a sign that it will flatter; the washing instructions on the tag replaces the texture of the material as a sign that it should be dry cleaned or that it earns its expensive price; the list of natural ingredients on the shampoo bottle replaces the shine of the hair to signify natural beauty; the nutrition information on the side of the food package replaces its taste as a source of satisfaction; the Surgeon General's warning on the side of the bottle replaces the hangover as a sign of the unhealthiness of drinking alcohol; the slogan plastered across the T-shirt replaces the actions of its wearer as a sign of her moral commitment. In all these cases, vague, purely symbolic gestures at something vaguely connected with what was or might be thought good in some circumstances are crowding out any sensible appearances of goodness in the objects they describe, accompany, or represent. "The paradigm of the fashionizing process is the New York commonplace of a fashionable young man taking over from an unfashionable old man the ownership of a real nineteenth-century saloon, tearing out its insides, and replacing them with a stylized imitation of the insides of a nineteenth-century saloon."[26] In the same way that computerized cash registers have robbed cashiers of the ability to count change, the techniques of vagueness in our domestic aesthetic products is weakening consumers' common sense by covering castaway fashions in cutting-edge wrappers.

A typical example of vagueness techniques can be found at any newsstand for the price of a fashion magazine. The fall 1997 issue of American *Vogue*, for instance—the "730-page Fall Fashion Blockbuster"—touts "four great designers' . . . Outlandish! Unreal! . . . radically different visions."[27] In the first, John Galliano "spoof[s] ancient Egypt as seen through the eyes of Hollywood." The first two-page spread shows some models dressed up in long, slinky 1930s-style dresses that look kind of Egyptian. What's the "spoof" here? In the next spread, Yohji Yamamoto "conjures up . . . a play on fifties couture. . . . " Except that the models' hairstyles include uncovered multiple bobby pins, it is impossible to see how this is a "play on" anything—Yamamoto has basically just copied some cuts, shapes, and colors from 1950's movies and scruffed them up. The next presentation is actually entitled "the cutting edge." On it, we see seven outfits by Rei Kawakubo for the fashionable Comme des Garçons. Despite that the models, in a kabuki gesture, are sporting birdlike sprouts of hair and the oversized blocks of dark, unnaturally colored eye shadow that seems to be *Vogue*'s favorite makeup for 1997, there is nothing here that one hasn't seen before. To Kawakubo's credit, her designs are at least a reference to something ordinary women actually find to be of aesthetic interest, evocative of little girls dressing up in their mothers' clothes. But we find nothing cutting edge here: the hairstyles and makeup are revamped punk; the dresses, revamped housedresses.

In the last spread, Jean Paul Gaultier "puts a tongue-in-cheek spin on androgynous street style and hip-hop haberdashery." This is a gesture identical in form to the faux grunge shirts I described earlier: the models—who, by the way, are all African-American—are simply dressed up as pimps and prostitutes with 1920s overtones. Here, we have only the oldest of ideas about the oldest profession: it is fun to dress up like a harlot. Two women are wearing men's suits (one must assume this is what is meant by the androgyny of the design); the difference between this and Claudette Colbert in her men's pajamas, or for that matter from George Sand, of course, is slim. More disturbing still are the euphemisms with which this "cutting-edge" fashion magazine feels it must put forward these standard tropes in order to sell the clothes, calling the clothes' unambiguous reference to pimping and prostitution, and the bald association of this low-class life with African-Americans, street style, and hip-hop.

What passes for approaching-the-millennium innovation here shares exactly the sensibility of Fussell's "middle-middle" class: bland, slightly embarrassed, watered-down gestures toward the urbane. In addition, its techniques of vagueness redigest low-class styles for the consumption of the upper-middle classes (e.g., the price of the simple sleeveless black velvet minidress worn by one of the models is $905). Here, the tactics of fashion play themselves out to a T, offering not-especially-nice outfits from earlier decades for the most part with simple tailoring that any one of the magazine's readers could probably do herself if she took the time to do so. All four of the captions admit the derivative nature of the clothes, even as they designate them "new" and "cutting edge" by describing them as "a spoof of . . . ," "a play on . . . ," "a send up of . . . ," and "a tongue-in-cheek spin on. . . ." The outrageous prices charged are the sole remaining evidence of the high-class and expert knowledge that the designer is supposed to have. The fact that they are, despite their expense, just copies of prostitutes' attire and housedresses, shows that they are not for a higher class of people than the reader.

This confused, circular vagueness in fashion proper was beautifully captured by Fraser more than twenty years earlier: "In her 1975 "Couture," Fraser writes: "The two sides [couture houses and fashion writers] are in cahoots to get outsiders to believe that something is going on that is not going on: novelty."[28] The tactics of fashion, Fraser indicates here, are the ability, effected through marketing, to present the same old thing to consumers year after year under the guise of the radically new and original. Fraser describes the collections of that year, demonstrating in case after case that they consist of the same designs that women were already wearing, presented as if they were heretofore unheard of, wildly ingenious, and completely obligatory novelties. Why?

Because the women customers on whom the clothing designers and manufacturers depend for a living have sense. They are working women and mothers with families to support. They have certain kinds of needs and habits in clothing that they want to satisfy. They will not buy what is outlandish, cannot afford to buy what will be outdated in a year, and do not want to buy what is not pretty, comfortable, and nicely fitted to them—that is, mustering their remaining domestic aesthetic skill, they will not buy what is actually completely new (and why should they?)—but they also will not buy what they already have, what they can make themselves, or what they can get of equal quality for less money off the rack at J. C. Penney's. Hence, in desperation, the couture houses (which by 1975 were already mostly a front for ready-to-wear lines) and the fashion writers (who by 1975 were already mostly the pawns of advertisers) had to promote the idea that what they have to sell are both the ordinary everyday work clothes that any middle- or lower-class woman even fifty years ago could have made herself *and* the novel and highly specialized professional fashion for the privilege of wearing which she will have to depend on a designer. (Of course, it isn't even really the designer she depends on, it's the designer's staff of underlings.) Thus, the desperate advertisers must try to replace indexical signification of the goodness of certain clothes with words, without really changing the clothes. The more domestic aesthetically skillful the consumer, the more their jobs are in jeopardy; but because domestic aesthetic skill is exceedingly hard to eradicate, they must appeal to it nonetheless.

In most cases today, language proper is the medium of symbolic substitution. Fashion as often as not replaces the sensual qualities of touch, taste, and odor with words and pictures. "The concept of the multitude is quantitative and visual," claimed Ortega.[29] Many actual products today have been replaced by their names. Nike is one of the most proficient at this, which, in its infamous 1996 campaign (the vomiting campaign) explicitly claimed it was selling a name and the mood that name evoked. Or, of course, there is Tommy Hilfiger. Indeed, a whole gamut of commodities that are now sold primarily as self-expression (as Lurie, for instance, understands the primary function of clothes)—haircuts, decorations, CDs, makeup, beer, cars—are all victims of the "linguisticization" of objects for sale. Anything good about these things must be reducible to words and pictures. Actually using clothing or household or office decorations as mere fodder for printed slogans (a ubiquitous practice at this point) is perhaps the clearest and most important way that producers and marketers deteriorate human judgment.

No wonder, again, that the tactics seem systematic and beyond our control; many of the fashions I have noted originated as rebellions against a merely fashionable capitalist production. The political slogans on T-shirts, the natural ingredients in the shampoo, the U.S. Surgeon General's warning, all these were once antifashions that have now been sadly coopted by producers. But today, antifashion is just its own sort of fashion; everything one does seems to have a place set for it, a notch on the scale of similarity and difference already waiting even as one first thinks of something to do or buy. But one can also see here how these tactics are indeed quite unsystematic—the symbols do not represent any consistent things, half the time, nor are they ready and waiting before some poor ad assistant under the gun decides she can get a sale out of them. One can see despite the hype how they are more or less direct consequences of individual human choices.

For instance, Van Halen's famous 1991 *Right Now* video, which was at the time critically acclaimed as a politically radical, profoundly meaningful, novel piece of work, consisted mainly of peculiar phrases with possible political or philosophical associations (all beginning with "Right now") written out on the screen. The song and video idea were, of course, perfectly suited to the advertising milieu and were almost immediately snapped up by Crystal Pepsi. This was not the result of some anonymous cooptation by the forces of production or capital; Pepsi simply copied the video. No oppressive machine forced the hand of the well-meaning rock group; someone made a confused judgment, that's all. What often seems to be the uncontrollable production of signs by some unseen and powerful force can be traced one individual consumer at a time answering a market researcher or buying a product.

Still, the techniques of vagueness have a discernible debilitating effect. Presumably on the model of Van Halen and Pepsi, for instance, it has become the fashion in a variety of advertisements (e.g., station identification, ads for local news, and prescription drugs ads) to flash across the screen during a commercial a few words from the sentences contemporaneously overdubbed by its narrator. Invariably, the written words neither make grammatical sense nor express the main thought of the narration. The noun and predicate of the spoken sentence, for instance, are often eschewed in favor of decontextualized prepositional phrases. What is going on here? This is not a linguistic system conquering the former territory of freedom, quite the contrary: it's incoherent babbling for its own sake. It seems "cool" precisely because of its adolescent meaninglessness.

Fashion Tactics and Entertainment

The confused, circular flattery of the tactics of fashion is sometimes the case today, not just with advertisements or the dramas that ordinary people play out within their own homes and neighborhoods, but also in the dramas that they go to see in theaters or watch on television. The popularity of talk shows and game shows in which guests appear as themselves and "real-life" dramas, comedies, and commercials in which nonfiction dilemmas cribbed from newspapers or polls appear on television as stories for our entertainment, not to mention the new wave of "reality shows," evince the same desperate uncanniness as the sales techniques I described earlier. They cull from previous viewing trends and real-life occurrences what they dish back up as novel entertainment. An article in *Harper's* magazine a few years ago describes the miserable state of Hollywood screenwriting in exactly these terms.[30] The article delineates how movies made in the last few years almost always get their impetus and inspiration from journalists and marketers (who are themselves increasingly interchangeable with each other).[31] "The first thing we need to decide," states a marketer before the movie even begins production, "is how we're going to position this movie to the journalists who are going to write about it early on."[32] Before shooting even begins, contracts for promotional tie-in sales, trailer commercials for the film, ad copy for the posters, and so on, are all set in motion. But based on what? Where do the marketers get their cue for these things? From market research, in other words, from "consumers" of the film themselves (what the marketers in the article call "the audience") before they've seen it and can make a judgment about it.

The moviemakers' sensibility here is identical to that of Dick Ebersol, the head of NBC's sports division, who designed the coverage for the 1996 Atlanta Olympics, which I will discuss later. Applying the "expertise" of a businessperson a little too steeped in vague theories about what people want, theories that are themselves derived from a generation of market analysis, Ebersol weighted the coverage of the Olympics toward the personal stories of female athletes to increase audience identification and heighten drama, and against coverage of the impressive feats of the athletes.[33] What is shown on the movie and television screens in these cases are just poorly thought, vague, and careless symbolic versions of the audiences' own real prior buying trends, funneled through a market analysis and dished back up as a leftover of a now very old meal.

That most consumers, when asked—as Ebersol's researcher did ask, thousands of times—explicitly state their preference for something more meaningful, something that would expand their experience and their character instead of regurgitate it, is irrelevant. Because this opinion does not fit with the scientifically derived "data" of their buying trends, marketers can assume that people simply don't know their own minds. "In interviews," states Ebersol's researcher Nicholas Schiavone, "people will say they want all sports and all live. But you have to listen to what people mean more than what they say."[34] Similarly, in *The Player*, the movie discussed in the 1993 *Harper's* article, the studio executives go to the newspapers for their inspiration (which, in this case, adds to the plot twist because one of their ranks is involved in a murder) again offering up hardly fictionalized "real-life" stories onto the silver screen so that the consumers can watch their own fates in brighter colors with a louder soundtrack. The commercial jingle for Vidal Sassoon's campaign of a few years ago, which I have used as my epigraph here, sums up the tactics of fashion: What is their product? "It's you, amplified. . . ."

Obviously, the increase in television talk shows, reality shows, comedies about death and divorce, and commercials in which severely untalented "real" people (many of them actors) give their anonymous but authentic endorsements (think of the Saturn campaign, for example, where supposed real-life employees of Saturn talk about how happy they are in their work) or tell their not-particularly-interesting real-life stories to the audience (think of the Discover Card campaign, for example, where celebrities share their itemized Discover Card bills with us) just add to the vague symbolic representations of abstract versions of ourselves offered up as commodities, which comprise the offerings of fashion tactics. Nothing we do not already know, nothing that will expand our capabilities, nothing in which we are interested, nothing that requires or occasions thought, that is, nothing that we can really use, appears to us for reflection in the programs.

Still, neither television nor advertising per se can be "blamed" for their abuse at the hands of fashion experts. Like the philosophers I discussed in preceding chapters, media programming and the advertisements that continuously interrupt it, live among a plethora of aesthetic influences found around the house, on which people reflect as they go about their lives. Viewers will make different judgments of them for different purposes and with differing effects in their lives. And many media offerings provide excellent opportunities for serious contemplation, even among the ads. The effect of fashion tactics on our judgment comes in part, as I have argued, from our own good intentions to make our lives better, the kind of concern expressed by the people Ebersol's researcher interviewed.

Stanley Cavell compassionately critiques the aesthetic form of television, in his 1984 essay, "The Fact of Television," noting its "amount of talk, [and] . . . the massive repetitiveness of its formats for talk."[35] Cavell remarks on the ubiquity of talk on television as a kind of practical guide to gracious conversation. "I am struck by the plain fact," he writes, "that on each of the game shows I have watched, new sets of contestants are introduced to us. What strikes me is not that we are interested in identifying with these ordinary people, but that we are introduced to them. The hardest part of conversation, or the scariest part, . . . is repeated endlessly, and without the scary anticipation. . . ."[36] Cavell claims that the unique aesthetic form of television is its ordinariness, the relative directness of its applicability to real life. He calls this its appropriateness for *monitoring* rather than for *viewing*, like movies, and he relates this monitoring format to television's propensity for serialization.

Like the tactics of fashion that I have attributed to sales-oriented aesthetic objects, Cavell's "fact" of television is composed of well-intentioned, useful formats that are simply unusually vulnerable to the circular flattery of the tactics of fashion. Although television allows one to monitor world events, Cavell is interested in how it enables us to monitor social customs, to hone our skills at conversation, to visit and revisit representations of ordinary people doing ordinary things such as talk about politics or sports, or to tell jokes or play games. This is in contrast to the form of movies that, complete in themselves like live theatrical dramas, lend themselves to viewing and so, Cavell implies, do more of their aesthetic work visually. The form of television, then, has the potential to assist domestic aesthetic practitioners greatly by letting them watch and observe the repeated practice of others.[37] Even the regular interruption by commercials, according to Cavell, is consonant with the best potential of monitoring. It is not its form, then, but television's qualitative content that is so susceptible to the tactics of fashion. Cavell agrees that the form of television has potential that its content has not tapped: "The medium *must* have more in it than has so far been shown."[38]

The sign that fashion tactics has encroached on television programming can be observed wherever the characters, whether fictional or real, flatteringly demoralize the audience. Wherever the characters and their aspirations are gleaned by the producers from the viewing public's prior viewing trends and lessened as individuals by that characterization, while at the same valorized because of their identification with the beloved audience, viewers' domestic aesthetic skill is at risk. Where the game-show questions, for example, are not difficult, so that the audience is encouraged to disdain the contestants even when they win, one can see fashion tactics at work.[39] Or one finds fashion tactics at work where the talk-show guests are actors pretending to be "real" and deeply unhappy people, such as on the infamous *Jerry Springer Show*, where the show's producers evidently put their guests in harm's way and leave them emotionally damaged. Wherever one sees the valorization of patently needy and flawed characters mixed with the tacit claims that these characters represent the audience's "true" desires and the audience is congratulated for desiring this life, one sees fashion tactics at work. Fashion tactics put us at a phenomenological distance by conflating characterizations of the good life with characterizations of us and by characterizing both us and the objects of our contemplation as emptier of qualitative content than they are in real life.

The techniques of vagueness that fuel fashion tactics lead people, in their buying trends, to copy their own unreflective hunches at judgment, their own desperation, their own insecurities, which have been given as data to producers through the market trends and polls of the prior year—or these days, that week or even that day. The tactics of fashion are the methods by which domestic aesthetic skill is chipped away, molded to the extent possible into downwardly spiraling helplessness in the most ordinary business of life. The tactics of fashion deliberately replace independent craftsmanship with dependent consumership. Because few sensible people would want to make that trade, it has taken time to succeed; but, I argue, it is finally gaining ground.

CHAPTER 8

MASS PRODUCTION, NATIONALIZATION, ADVERTISING, AND VAGUENESS

The free man always has time at his disposal to converse in peace at his leisure. . . . The orator is always talking against time, hurried on by the clock. . . . He is a slave disputing about a fellow-slave before a master sitting in judgment. . . . Hence he acquires a tense and bitter shrewdness; he knows how to flatter his master. . . .
—Socrates, in Plato's *Theaetetus* (172d)

As I have argued, I do not think that fashion tactics are inherent in capitalism, modernity, television, advertising, or any of the usual suspects, however much these may enable it. Rather, since the Industrial Revolution and with a marked increase since World War II, particular production and advertising choices regarding almost the gamut of domestic aesthetic products have taken up a new style in which these tactics have come into play. Three fields of fashion tactics—mass production, nationalized economies, and especially, the independence and "new ethics" of the advertising industry—have severely skewed the proportion of judgments that we make based on symbolic representation of goodness relative to those based on indexical representations. So habitualized are we, not to the "meaninglessness of life" (nothing as romantic as that), but merely to the vague, insidiously frustrating stuff we find to buy and to the success of these commodities regardless of their adequacy or inadequacy, that we hardly know anymore what to do with a simple, useful commodity when we find it.

Consider this very common experience described by Donald Norman in his amusing *The Psychology of Everyday Things*:

In England I visited a home with a fancy new Italian washer-drier [*sic*] combination, with super-duper multi-symbol controls, all to do everything you ever wanted to do with the washing and drying of clothes. The husband (an engineering psychologist)

said he refused to go near it. The wife (a physician) said she has
simply memorized one setting and tried to ignore the rest.

. . . If the design was so bad, why did the couple purchase
it?[1]

Or consider this historical note by the Hesses in their classic *Taste
of America*:

Before World War II, only a relatively few Californians and Flo-
ridians, and Latin communities in the Northeast, ate avocados.
The thin-skinned, ripe fruit arrived bruised but heady with perfume and flavor. After the war, gourmet writers helped make it
snob fare, hence popular, and agribusiness made it stable. A
leather-skinned variety was developed that is picked stone-hard
and can be shipped almost like coal. It never bruises. It hardly
has any taste, but the gourmets haven't noticed.[2]

As Baudrillard claimed, we tend to believe today that any equally
caloric nutrients, any equally priced coverings, any similarly situated
coop apartments are interchangeable, not because they *are* interchangeable, nor even because we cannot perceive the difference between them,
but because we live with them at a phenomenological distance. However impressive the washer-dryer Norman describes (and he makes
clear that it was actually very impressive), the consumer who uses it
makes the washer-dryer functionally equivalent to other washer-dryers,
for her, by using it in the only way she knows how. It is not capitalism
by itself that leads consumers to depend on symbolic signs of price,
fancy high-tech buttons, chrome, or designer names. It is the vagueness of their presentation, simple bad design.

August Morello claims something similar to this:

Today, competition between enterprises is implicitly considered
more important than service to users; . . . As marketing success is
based on incident contribution margins, the apparent differentiation of products is the only means to maintaining competitiveness.

There are many direct consequences of such a syndrome:

1. *an overcomplication of performances:* . . . without adequate
information about use, and through a poor semiotics of products;

2. *the dominant idea that design is mainly a way to communicate:* . . . to include design in the area of "signals" and not the
"indices" of enterprises; that is, in the area of promotion and
advertising. . . .

3. *the separation of product form from structure and the reduction of design to styling:* a sort of "job impoverishment" of the product. . . .[3]

People have needs that they would like commodities to fill easily and beautifully. If they settle for fancy-seeming stuff that does not satisfy their needs, as Morello notes, it must be because consumers believe that this is the best they can expect. The progress of mass production, nationalization of the economy, and especially of a certain high-mindedness in advertising has slowly lowered the expectations and the real abilities of consumers so that today, often, what we get really *is* the best we can expect. More and more often, one only has an option of more and different kinds of vaguely distinguishable and slightly irritating products. One searches vaguely at the grocery store today for the least of several vague evils: a hard, corky-tasting avocado or three kinds of similar, tasteless spaghetti sauces. But as the Hesses note, the Michiganer who can buy some semblance of guacamole is not a larger person for it.

Norman's washer-dryer is a fine example of a commodity that might have—and really has—made life easier in a genuine sense but has become, thanks to mass production and advertisers, a constant, necessary-seeming disappointment. The washing machine has proven marketability just as it is: laundering is an unpleasant, time-consuming, labor-intensive activity, which is both necessary and unmysterious. Yet today, one only has an option between indebtedness to Maytag or Sears for a machine with unnecessary functions that requires her to buy harsh detergents to too-quickly ruin her clothes or interminable quarter rolling and basket hauling to a hot room-full of such machines. That commodities sell under these conditions is due, in large part, to there not being anything else available for most people; this in turn is attributable partly to the mass production of these household products, partly to the vast decrease in the number of households where someone is at home during the day to spend time on household chores, and partly to the legitimated rhetoric of the ads for them. Thus, the deterioration of domestic things and skill is a vicious circle, a downward spiral of judgment and commodities enabled, although not exactly caused, by certain capitalist relations.

At the limit of the informed consumer is the independent craftsperson. The more one can do oneself, or the more one can accomplish working together with a small set of skilled craftspeople in one's household or neighborhood, the less one's dependence on producers and advertisers, and the more genuine, or free, the choices one has in how to conduct one's life. The ideal limit case of the independent craftsperson is the person with the most choice possible, the most freedom possible, the perfectly and fully skilled jack-of-all-trades.[4] Not everybody does everything or does everything well, and what we spend our time doing, and what we do well, is what makes us suitable or unsuitable for the various roles we consider playing in our lives. What we do and what we do well are what make us both genuinely distinct from one another and genuinely close to one another in that we are, through them, both in need of and able to continue together in the same "play."

But very basic domestic aesthetic skills are very difficult habits to break. It takes a most unusual, prolonged effort to get people to forget, for instance, how to make food or clothes. Capitalist production could not, by itself, degenerate domestic aesthetic judgment. Rather, the particular things produced and the methods of their sale must work with private ownership to infect these very stable and fundamental skills. These three factors of fashion tactics (mass production, nationalized economies, and especially the independence and reputability of advertising) are among the ways that we are made into weaker consumers. These factors, what I call *techniques of vagueness,* work together to displace consumers from the physical circumstances of their lives, to disorient them about the world, and to degenerate their skills at taking care of themselves. Without strongly developed domestic aesthetic skills, one is hard put to resist these influences.

MASS PRODUCTION AND NATIONALISM

". . . The most important fact about modern warfare," Lewis Mumford claims, "is the steady increase of mechanization from the fourteenth century onward: here militarism forced the pace and cleared a straight path to the development of modern large-scale standardized industry."[5] Although the ties between technics and militarism are very old according to Mumford, it took the modern state, and the enormous standing army required to maintain it, to motivate mass production. The military beginnings of mass production accompanied nationalization: "The first large-scale demand for absolutely standardized goods," claims Mumford, was for Louis XIV's army.[6] A sewing machine for housewives to use to make their families' clothes was not produced for another two centuries. Thus, because modern nations conducted warfare on a large scale, mass production was from the start associated with national spending for the standing armies. The states funded the factories that made armaments and uniforms; they funded the distribution trades to bring these commodities to the soldiers; they gave the initial kick-start to mechanized, uniform, systematized production. "An army is a body of pure consumers," Mumford adds, "[and a]s the army grew in size it threw a heavier and heavier burden upon productive enterprise: for . . . it does not, like other trades, supply any service in return except 'protection' in times of war. In war, moreover, [the army] produces 'illth', . . . misery, mutilation, physical destruction, terror, starvation and death. . . ."[7] Similarly, Jane Jacobs calls government investment in military production a "transaction of decline."[8] Thus, the "spirit of consumerism," as Campbell calls it, is attributed by Mumford and Jacobs, at least in part, to mass production and the nationalization of economies.

As Jacobs understands it, one basis for the foolhardiness of such investment is that it perverts the natural, inventive course of production and economic growth by directing it to national ends. For Jacobs the natural unit of economic growth is obviously the city. In cities, the particular needs, talents, and tendencies of an interdependent and cohesive group of people of a particular geographic region with its particular capabilities, develop and improve through what she calls "import replacement"—starting to produce what it formerly had to import—not through increased wealth, and by ingenuity in attending to its own local needs. Import replacement must proceed through practice; "a process of continually improvising in a context that makes injecting improvisations into everyday life feasible."[9] In other words, for Jacobs the health and well-being of a municipality is signified by its independent, skillful functioning, not its wealth relative to other political entities: The city that can take care of itself, not the city that makes wealth for its country, is a city that will long survive as an interesting, thriving hub.

Jacobs's claim is echoed by designer Victor Papanek, who addresses: "The success of old and the failure of modern community design: . . . ancient planners, recognizing the invariable Aristotelian purpose of why people live in communities, put all their talent into building the communal nucleus: inns, churches, and city halls. The rest of the settlement then followed naturally. In contrast, modern designers are forever building the rest of the city. But without a nucleus, nothing can be held together."[10]

Papanek goes on to discuss the "esthetic factor" in site selection for cities, which is "ignored" by modern urban designers. Modern urban planners, attempting rational designs for universal applications, undervalue the site specificity of cities, Papanek claims, thereby overlooking what makes the citizens of successful cities happy. He notes succinctly, "where it is good to live, it is also beautiful to live."[11] A nationalized economy saps the energies and resources of the nation's major cities and weakens their internal mechanisms for satisfying their needs for the sake of external, more distant, and less germane goals. Nationalized economic policy can't help but treat rural regions as their bread and butter, claims Jacobs, and will always tend to subsidize them nationally at the expense of the cities. Thus, rural regions, detached from the cities of which they are the natural complements, become pure agricultural regions. These new pure producers of our most fundamental staple consequently become a distant, secondary, marginal citizenry in a nation in which most people create wealth by trade and manufacture. Thus, the natural interdependence of city and country, and of agriculture and industry, the natural variety and order of human life built through a history of economic interaction, is dissolved by a national economy; both regions become dependent on far away federal forces to sustain them.

The effects of the shared goals and judgments of a city, its "economic energy," according to Jacobs, have a certain reflective relation with its production, a kind of phenomenological intimacy writ large. Left to itself, a city stays within its means and exercises its talents, or it dies. Its economic health (import replacement) is an indexical sign of the wisdom of the economic judgments of its citizens and civic leaders. When the effects of the city's choices are exported by the federal government to regions unseen and imperceptible to the municipality, or when the source of productive employment is imported by the federal government from regions unseen and imperceptible, the cues on which the judgments of the city's members depend are phenomenologically distanced from them; they become linguisticized, uncanny.

Jacobs, like Mumford, links the decline of cities to "prolonged and unremitting military production."[12] Such a "transaction of decline," however, was impossible for European nations before the seventeenth century. With regard to the United States, Jacobs claims, "if we discount the pause of five years after the ending of World War II (a pause during which Marshall plan aid partially took the place of military production), we can think of military expenditures as being unremitting drains upon the earnings of American cities since early 1941, when lend-lease supply to Britain started."[13] The economic effect cited by Jacobs is contemporaneous with the shift in emphasis, such as Morello notes, from design to styling in the field of industrial design. Along the same lines, Richard Buchanan summarizes a thesis of fellow designer Jeffrey Meikle: "He compares the situation of industrial design in the 1920s and 1930s, when entrepreneurial consultant designers operated with a degree of independence from corporate structure, with the situation after World War II, when design professionals were absorbed within corporate structures . . . [in which they] often lost their voice in significantly affecting decisions about products."[14]

In a nationalized economy, vague symbolic signs of economic health—money in citizens' pockets, federal contracts, lots of fancy imports from other regions of the country, lots of fancy communications and exports to other regions, an so on—replace the indexical signification of wealth provided by the feedback of the economic decisions made by a healthy independent city: healthy, secure, happy citizens. Instead of having a strong, independent urban or rural character full of specific regional qualities, a close interconnection of businesses, and a citizenry of resourceful individuals the purpose of whose work is perceivable and clear, the city supported by and for the sake of a national economy necessarily weakens. Such a city grows confused, it loses its distinction from other cities, and consequently its pride of place, its culture, its cohesiveness; the citizens feel themselves to have greater loyalties to their employers or to the federal government than to their households and neighborhoods or to the quality of their own labor; their successes and failures no longer belong to them.

Furthermore, by interpreting farms as producers for the nation rather than for their shared "city region" and by acting upon this interpretation by exporting agricultural produce all over the nation and the world, nationalized economic policies have led farmers to breed "the taste out of [their products—in this case, tomatoes]. . . . They gave up taste for yield."[15] To produce shippable goods in mass quantities to feed the nation, farmers have been led to develop crops for hardness and freezability instead of for taste. Not only the deliciousness of the produce, but also the distinctiveness of the flavor of region and season is bred out of crops when a nationalized economy requires farmers to mass produce. The Hesses' avocado example earlier and the tomato example here are but two of thousands of cases of produce whose distinctive flavor once gave regional cuisines their interest and beauty, and that gave the changes of the seasons their character and mood. The nationalized economy gives us a life in which many kinds of foods are readily available (i.e., the number of categories of food has increased), but the individual foods are bland and boring cases of their types, representing little of the season or the land or climate and obfuscating consumer's sense of taste. Because the varieties of foods available are distinguished categorically instead of qualitatively, the number of tastes available to an ordinary citizen has actually decreased. "We are now so conditioned to cottony strawberries and tomatoes in January that we have forgotten the pleasures of anticipation, and the excitement when they finally came in, ripe, tart, and delicious. . . . Even in the most difficult months, January and February, Washingtonians in Jefferson's time could buy at least fourteen kinds of fresh fruits and vegetables."[16]

The mentality of such production is linguisticization—more of certain kinds of things are produced without regard to goodness within types. Such produce will of course lead to "new" (i.e., unfamiliar) tastes, but not necessarily more or better.

Phenomenologically similar, today one memorizes one's size, one reads the washing instructions, and one has one's color chart done because rarely anymore does are feel confident about what shapes, cuts, colors, and materials are actually flattering or pleasant to wear or comfortable or appropriate for the seasons; and even if one did know these things, getting clothes to meet these requirements would be difficult because almost no one has the time or skill to make custom clothing, including tailors. Almost nobody has a tailor anymore; the few old fossils that remain now mostly work in the back room of Barney's or the dry cleaner's. But tailoring surely is a timelessly useful, highly skilled profession if there ever was one, particularly so in a day and age when nobody can buy clothes that are flattering as they come off the rack or that last more than a couple of seasons. The only explanation for the decline of tailoring is a general degeneration of judgment.

In a similar way, one finds vague "viva Mexico" gestures in nacho-cheese concoctions or prepackaged guacamole; a similar puff of smoke is cooked up in a vaguely Greek meal, Greek because Athenos packaged feta is crumbled over the cube steak or iceberg lettuce. In this nationalized economy everybody, no matter where she lives, no matter her traditions or the season, eats everything, and hence everyone eats the same thing only in a more bland, more vague, more confused version than the ancestral habits that they randomly evoke. Of course, a skilled cook will be able to mix the ingredients of different regional cuisines and come up with a discernibly delicious dish she can quite rightly claim credit for inventing; but we should not depend on the producers of Combos or La Choy, or for that matter the owners of Dominick's or Food Lion, to make decisions for us about the fundamentals of international cuisine.[17] As Waverly Root and Richard de Rochemont note in their thorough history *Eating in America*, mass production and national distribution of food (and one imagines, of other things, too) obscures the line between production and advertising. "The package had become part of the product. . . . Is treating a tomato with ethylene gas to give it the bright red of ripeness, though it has been picked green and is destined to be sold green, except in color, a subtle form of packaging?"[18]

Similarly, the mass production of clothes is a perennial source of humiliation for the wearer, partly because the distinctiveness of her office, traditions, and tastes is obliterated by it and partly because this indistinction is a sign (both indexical and symbolic) of her subordination to a higher official. Thus, even in the seventeenth century, army officers "considered it demeaning to wear any man's livery, even the king's."[19] Terkel remarks on his interlocutors' distaste for any type of uniform[20]; uniform wearers from fast-food places to utility companies complain that they are demeaned by their attire.[21] Any clothes mass produced and nationally or internationally distributed, however, are thereby more or less uniforms.

This uncanny, unpleasant uniformity is the hook of a recent McDonald's commercial: printed across each item in a montage of diverse teenage McDonald's employees, recognizable by their uniforms, is their future contribution to society (e.g., "future aeronautics engineer). In the last scene, we see a very young customer, identified as "future McDonald's employee." Sadly perhaps, one must assume this commercial has a resonance with national audiences. Even where traditional dress in a particular region or profession is not much different from that of its neighbors, hand sewing, home spinning and weaving, custom tailoring, the personal histories of scraps or materials, and friendship or kinship between the wearer and the maker, and so forth used to make each article a unique achievement. One may have had fewer clothes under such circumstances, just as one may have had fewer types of food; one gestured at fewer traditions through them. But the clothes one possessed served the life in which they participated more meaningfully.

Mass production has effects not only on the pleasure or use of modern eating and dressing, but also on the whole domestic landscape of contemporary life. The layout and architecture of towns, the qualities of the seasons, the daily habits of household members, merchants, craftspeople, and farmers, and indeed, the physical health of the city's inhabitants, are all intricately bound up with the production and sale of the food, clothes, and everything else in the region on which their daily life depends. City and regional economies in the past always centered on the square, market, or fairground; in many old European cities and towns the flavor of the city is still defined by the great square of the city market.[22] The very term *market* stems from these local meeting places, physical entities that represented indexically and clearly the economic health or weakness of the region and its distinctive cultural style and that marked home for their inhabitants.[23]

In a nationalized economy, on the contrary, linguisticization is the norm: names—the names of companies, the names of large political entities such as that of one's country or state, the names of social groups identified by a shared national interest, the names of nationally advertised products, the names of nationally broadcast T.V. shows and characters—come more and more to do the job of the market square. These symbolic entities, within which we move around detachedly from location to location, are increasingly the recipients of our allegiances, love, and interest. In this way, today's commodities express, more than anything, alliances, dividing the landscape between friends and enemies. More and more the recognition of someone as friend or foe depends on the vague symbolic connotations of her clothing or other possessions, and more and more often, any outfit indicates a foe.

This is quite explicit in the relatively new commonplace of wearing actual words instead of (or, really, on) clothes—what Lurie remarks on but does not analyze and what Fussell calls "legible clothing." There is, to my mind, no clearer evidence of a phenomenologically distant mentality than this trend to actually write one's "name, rank, and serial number" on one's outfit so that others can identify one's alliances. Fussell identifies this tendency as evidence of his prole drift. Just a few years ago, only the working class wore actual words on their attire (presumably at least partly because shirts and golf caps with advertisements on them are so often given away free by manufacturers). For the upper-middle class, "the understatement principle begins to operate, [and] the words gradually disappear, to be replaced . . . by mere emblems, like the Lacoste alligator."[24]

One can distinguish the classes now only by increasingly abstract cues, the subtle connotations of the various statements that appear on clothing and how this is affected when worn in particular contexts. A Harvard T-shirt, for instance, means one thing when worn by someone who went to Harvard, or at Harvard, and another for her little sister, who went to NYU. To wear a Nike or a Reebok T-shirt may indicate the presence of an athlete, but it may also indicate an upper-middle-class identification with the students on sports scholarships or a thrift-shop purchase, depending on what else goes into the outfit. Things get still more complicated in their identifications—just as explicit, but just as ambiguous, too—with clothes that have long statements written upon them. Legible clothes of whatever sort are the most akin to uniforms of any mass-produced clothing, and our increasing dependence on reading people's alliances off their chests before we meet them, or instead of meeting them, mimics battle conditions.

The same holds for the increasing linguisticization of household objects. The shampoo instructions to "rinse, repeat"; the boiling time on the back of the spaghetti package; the recipes on the back of the chocolate chips package indicating the necessity of other products by the same company; the profusion of warning labels; the long list of mysterious or natural ingredients; all these and so many other verbal coverings on the things we use every day do the same work as designer names across shirts. They purport to identify for users' benefit the trustworthiness of the product, and they purport to demonstrate that the producer is on the up and up, but in actuality they add to the mystification of the consumer and further her dependence upon what she is told by producers instead of on what she herself judges to be true.

Linguistization and Advertising

Fussell cites the origin of what he calls *"rhetorical fake elegance,"* another marker of his middle-class prole drift, in advertising:

> The middle-class loves to use words which have achieved cliché status in advertising. . . .
>   . . . Because of its need for the illusion of power and success that attend self-conscious consumerism, the middles instinctively adopt advertisers' *-wear* compounds, speaking with no embarrassment whatever of the family's/footwear/nightwear/leisurewear/. . . .
>   Because it's a staple of advertising, the middle class also likes the word *designer*, which it takes to mean *beautiful* or *valuable*.[25]

The roots of this terrible misguidance by advertisers of their middle-class audience lie in the nineteenth century, where they manipulated upward mobility quite deliberately by translating clear descriptive words for their products into awkward, vague, fancy-sounding jargon.

> No one can read the advertisements of this period without marvelling at the cumbrous Latin compounds, the grotesqueries of "Greek" with which the advertiser sought to impress his public. Teeth were stopped with "mineral marmoratum" or "mineral succedaneum"; raincoats were "siphonias"; hair cream was an "aromatic regenerator"; hair dye was an "atrapilatory." There were "pulmonic wafers" for the chest; there were Aethereal Oleine, Elmes's Arcanium, Winn's Anticardium, Olden's Eukeirogenion, and Rypophagon Soap. Some critics feared, as many have feared

since, that the English language would never recover from the abuses of the advertiser.[26]

Nineteenth-century advertisers realized that more money was to be made from the "mass" of middle- and working-class consumers than from the wealthy alone. One presumes that this was not only because these classes had so many more potential customers, but also because they were thought less discerning, had no servants to do the things that the new products could do, and were assumed to be more easily impressed by the false promise of social status. The habits and common sense of members of the private household—and the faith that most people had in their own judgment—were intruded upon by quacks and fly-by-nights of all sorts; women were shamed into buying products of which they were suspicious and that they likely neither needed nor understood; the comparatively moderate budgets of middle- and lower-middle-class households were sapped; wild promises of vague social or moral import were made in unintelligible and unbeautiful language. Thus, the linguisticization of commodities was achieved in the first instance through advertising.

As advertising developed, every page of the newspaper, every usable surface, including boat sails, farmers' fields, and even the White Cliffs of Dover, were covered with the names of products. Names (mostly just names until the twentieth century, when jingles and logos came into prominence) were pasted everywhere. The landscape became a writing surface. This penchant for flashing the names of products across any and every available surface changed entirely the landscape of modern life. Today, every trip in a train or car, every box that sits on our kitchen shelf, every store window, every magazine page, the back pages of books, and all the surfaces that people pass as they go about their business carry the name of something to buy. The names, ultimately, started to replace the things they named. How could it be a surprise that in the next century we would find theorists who would call everything a *text*? This coup on the advertisers' parts has taken from the users of products a degree of intimacy in their relationship to the things about their own house. The use of the brand name, establishing familiarity with it rather than with the thing it names, begins the job of replacing use value with exchange value in the consciousness of agents.

The increasing acceptance and reputability of independent advertising agencies has contributed significantly to the effect of advertising on phenomenological intimacy. In the persona of charlatans, even very successful advertisers are limited in their moral authority. Until the end of the nineteenth century, however, that was their basic disposition: most manufacturers handled their own advertising campaigns. In the early years, companies were reluctant to delegate this important function to a disinterested other, and before the agents came to control advertising, many of the most interesting and original advertisements were still self-made. Many companies, in addition, "feared that, to their business associates an advertisement would be interpreted as a sign of distress. . . . There is also evidence that the heads of some businesses secretly sighed for a ban to be imposed on advertising, especially out of doors, to save the drain on their purses."[27]

Particularly in the United States, however, the agencies eventually revolutionized advertising into a "scientific" field based on "research"; it became a kind of social service, an artistic enterprise of "salesmanship in print."[28] Leiss, Kline, and Jhally, the authors of *Social Communication in Advertising*, cite Patten's *The New Basis of Civilization* as a landmark in the moral legitimization of advertising: "He argued that society should preach not renunciation of desire but expansion of consumption and should accept as its goal the attainment of a general state of abundance."[29] With the agencies and their advocates came a whole new psychological, artistic, and philosophical aura to advertising. "Marketing emerged as a recognized professional activity, and corporations established marketing departments in their organizational structures."[30]

The governments used ad techniques for recruitment, as well as to ease domestic tensions and complaints during World War I, implicitly imbuing them with political legitimacy. Employers who might have been angry about losing their workers, women who might have been reluctant to send away their husbands and sons, were approached by advertising to sympathize with the effort. Thus, because both were associated with the advertisements, national pride and product consumption eventually became conflated. Today, buying as a way of doing one's bit for one's country is often painted as a patriotic sacrifice akin to enlistment (certainly it is so in economic hard times). This was of course a popular line of attack between the wars, especially during the Great Depression. Advertising grew much more aggressive in its appeals during the 1930s. Not only was the public made to feel guilty and that buying was a civic duty, but the downright poor were tapped as a market. Tobacco and wine advertisements and the use of free gifts flourished as tactics for capturing the unemployed markets. With radio and its accompanying technology, the reactions of consumers could be charted amazingly quickly, and products or commercials could be revised and perfected almost as fast. Neilsen and the earlier "Hooperatings" funneled viewers' opinions back to industry quickly, and marketing researchers "tested" advertisements for success before they went on the air. This decreased the need for the time-consuming production of actual objects, because production could be largely replaced by new advertising angles, a new stage in replacing objects with words.[31] The ad agencies . . . "employed cooks and dietitians, doctors, economists, tabulators, sociologists, psychologists, and psychiatrists. The more research-minded had their coast-to-coast consumer panels, their testing theatres, their computers to process the results of "nose-counting" forays. No information, it seemed, was unavailable."[32]

ADVERTISING, GENDER, AND DOMESTIC AESTHETICS

Most of the test participants, like most of the consumers, like most of the protagonists of the commercials, were women. "Indeed, unlike the old-style work, consumption was an expandable task. . . . The thrifty housewife could always go to yet another store for yet another sale, clip yet another coupon from yet another magazine, read yet another article about yet another kind of appliance. It was the perfect task to occupy the full-time housewife. . . ."[33]

The development of advertising, then, as I discuss later, has paralleled not only the development of mass production and the nationalization of economies, but also the designation of domestic aesthetic activity to women. Truly the new guru, the new evangelist, the figure of the ad man personified this sexual aspect of advertising. We have invested the ad man, as much any male character in our social drama, with the morality of male conquest.

Several movies of the Madison Avenue period study this character, but perhaps none so clearly as the 1961 Doris Day–Rock Hudson classic, Delbert Mann's *Lover Come Back*. Equally a romance and a satire on the advertising industry, the plot of *Lover Come Back* hinges on a direct link between the wiles of the wolf and those of the ad man. "This is Madison Avenue," the movie begins, "nerve center of the advertising world. Here in these steel and concrete beehives are born the ideas that decide what we the public will eat, drink, drive, and smoke; and how we will dress, sleep, shave, and smell." Hudson's sophisticated character, Jerry Webster, embarks upon a deliberate plot to undermine the efforts of a rival ad executive, smart but naïve Carol Templeton, played by Day. To get her goat, he sends her on a wild goose chase to get the account for a fake product that he has made up, "Vip." She begins the campaign as an effort to win the account, and Jerry is under pressure to come up with a product to release by the date Carol has indicated in her ads. A down-on-his-luck scientist is enlisted to come up with the product, which turns out to be a powerfully intoxicating alcoholic candy. Everybody at the agency, including Jerry and Carol, try the candy and get roaring drunk, and the lead couple find themselves together in an out-of-state motel the next morning, married.

All the questionable techniques of the advertising industry and all of its questionable overtones are beautifully represented in *Lover Come Back*. The ad man, a wolf in sheep's clothing, takes advantage of the woman and the public at the same time. He is suave and sophisticated while they are well-intentioned, professional, and smart, but too naïve for their own good. The products sold are relatively insignificant; they are invented as afterthoughts once the selling has been taken care of. Furthermore, and perhaps most significantly, the product, once invented, is an intoxicant, and its effects are responsible for the marriage of the ad man to the hapless woman against her will or even without her knowledge.[34]

The advertiser took it upon himself to wine and dine potential clients as a part of his job description. Taking clients out has provided comic material for many advertising movies and television shows, especially when woman's honor was at stake. *Bewitched* is perhaps the best example of a television show devoted to fleshing out the intricacies of the advertising industry, particularly its associations with alcohol and its antagonistic position toward domestic aesthetic skill. Advertising, of course, is represented as a kind of lame witchcraft in the show to be distinguished from Samantha's ingenuity. Darrin is the hardworking, honest, American father whose job is a strenuous and strict meritocracy; he envisions his work at an ad agency to be as sober, serious, and important as the independent farmer or the village elder. The witch Samantha, on the other hand, wiggles her nose and effortlessly achieves much more striking miracles. The witches' spells, however, are thought by Darrin to be intrusive, distracting, irritating interruptions of his "real" life. But as Darrin's boss, Larry's attitude toward the job clearly demonstrates, advertising is thought to be nothing but a politic remark placed here and there, and the stuff it produces is ridiculous fluff. Much of the show's humor, then, is derived from a comparison of the effects of this real and effortless witchcraft in the hands of the women, to those of the fake, slogging advertising and alcohol in the hands of the men; ultimately, the phony magic is always shown up for what it is, a dull, goofy imitation of the real world it purports to improve.[35]

THREE TRICKS OF THE TRADE

Three particular recent techniques helped advertising confuse judgment to the extent we experience today: (1) the modeling of television

news on T.V. commercials; (2) the commercial product tie-ins with movies and television, including the paid promotion of goods used as props
in the films; and (3) the "ad-ization" of the commodities themselves
through packaging, market research, and decoration with words and
pictures. Through these phenomena, which appear with increasing ra-
pidity, real domestic aesthetic objects with which we find ourselves
surrounded have been transformed into commercials for a deteriorated
version of the lives we already live.

The news: In the late 1960s the "happy newsman," who had be-
gun to appear on the evening broadcast, engendered much scorn. At
the time, it was even noted that this was influenced by advertising.
The situation today, of course, is much more severe. The newscasts do
not so much advertise the political stance of those in powerful positions, as a cynic might imagine, as they relate to viewers the current
trend of public opinion. The networks constantly sponsor polls modeled on market research to such a degree as to be indistinguishable
from it, and results are reported back as some kind of enlightenment
the very evening of the day they were taken. On ABC's *Prime Time* the
polls are taken by telephone or internet during the show. The polls
seem to "inform" the viewer (i.e., they seem to help the viewer make
some sort of decision) based on other people's hasty, inchoate opinions. As often as not, the lead stories involve a review of "America's
reaction" to news of the event, often before the event itself has even
been reported. Thus, the news encourages viewers to make news, under
the pretense of reporting it—precisely the mechanism of fashion tactics. Worse yet, as often as not the news is mere self-promotion; Dan
Rather defends the actions of the media on the news program; the
local news stations give news "teasers"—commercials—throughout the
day under the auspices of up-to-the-minute reports; weekly special
reports on the national broadcasts focus "up close" on things such as
the relation of the news media to the politicians. Recently some coun-
ties near my home suffered a terrible flood; the very evening of the
flood, one of the local network affiliate news programs was running
ads about how up-to-the-minute and informative its own news coverage of the disaster was.

In addition, what are essentially commercials are now often presented in a newscast format. The MTV news, the movie reviews on
various channels, *Entertainment Tonight* and so on, all take on the tone
and style of news reports and seem to be informing the viewers or
even providing critical analyses. Among the most flagrant were the
Buena Vista movie commercials, which were put forward in a form
identical to the movie reviews on newscasts. But all these amount to
are plugs—even the real shows. How is a viewer supposed to distin-

guish a report on a presidential speech, delivered in exactly the same style with exactly the same inflections against the backdrop of very similar images, and closed with the very same dryly witty remark, from Tabitha Soren plugging a band's new tour? It is sometimes difficult indeed; in fact, the viewer is quite right to think them largely indistinguishable, because the news differs little anymore from commercials.

Paid promotional tie-ins: This trick has been popular since the 1970s and was, at that time, thought controversial; nowadays we take for granted that a television show, movie, or sports event is just an opportunity for the sales of further advertising ploys about itself, represented as usable commodities. In itself, this is an irritating and somewhat seedy practice, but there have always been those, and yet people have retained their judgment. What the promotional tie-in effects is a false belief among the audience and consumers that the world represented in the movie or show is a coherent world that reaches into our real lives. The tie-ins appear, furthermore, to verify the commercials' false representation of themselves as art.

Burger King's *Hunchback of Notre Dame* cups were doubtless the same cup design as its *Pocahontas* cups the year before. The T-shirts sold outside the Clint Black concert surely differ little from those sold outside the Hole concert. The action figures that look like the aliens in *Independence Day* are not an ingenious improvement over the Teenage Mutant Ninja Turtles, the Transformers, or for that matter, Gumby. What gives the promotional tie-in its more magical effect is that it produces advertisements-as-commodities or that it makes the movie or television show into just an advertisement by another name. Where, in a regular commercial, a product that exists independently of the ad is magically transformed into a copy or a reference to something vaguely represented as good in the ad, the promotional tie-in goes the other way. In promotional tie-ins, something that exists only in the fictional world is magically transformed into nonfiction—it is actually produced in the three-dimensional, real world. This effect is very similar to the fashion tactics of television shows discussed earlier, only more pernicious: the promotional tie-in directly attacks the ordinary functioning of aesthetic judgment.

The promotional tie-in makes it appear to the consumer that the fictional world produces things in the real world, it produces three-dimensional objects with which people have real social relations. It is the culmination of the advertising industry's attempt to legitimate itself as a producer of goods for the nation, the most blatant cooptation of Marx's notion of commodity fetishism, the most straightforwardly "uncanny" of advertising's effects. Of course, it is not the ad agencies that are producing this stuff, exactly, which is why promotional tie-ins are so debilitating to the judgment. Promotional tie-ins are really Descartes's "evil genius" hypothesis come to life. They reach into our minds and convince us that this coffee cup, for instance, exists, and coddle us in this knowledge, but they are lying. What appears to be an existent useful commodity for which one has paid good money, is really a fiction, a rhetorical exercise owned by someone else. Promotional tie-ins destroy the reflective distance of artworks and so undermine their artistic purpose.

The ad-ization of commodities: The ad-ization of a commodity occurs whenever a "new" commodity is created through new positioning instead of through a new product design—including changing only the words or pictures printed upon the package—and in general, the ad-ization of commodities has contributed to the deterioration of judgment most significantly of any vagueness technique because by seeming to render good design unnecessary to sales, it directly diminishes the actual quality of the things produced.

This trick, of course, primarily involves linguisticization techniques. Like *Lover Come Back*'s Jerry Webster, the producer of the commodity comes up with a name, not a design. It is the name that is salable, the name that will be plastered across the screen. This was the case with Hägen Dazs, for instance; L'Eggs was also invented by the packager.[36] One may add to ad-ization all the "make your owns"— cards, books, salads, records—that are just names waiting until the consumer gives them content. The ad-ization of commodities, however, is most commonly effected by the substitution of package design or brand name for product design. The design of products is, of course, already greatly inhibited by mass production and a nationalized economy, but the capper is put on bad design by the increasing stress on packaging over that of the usefulness or beauty of the packaged objects. This is, of course, a radical development of Morello's second consequence of using design to promote goods—that design be thought of mainly as a way to communicate.

Packaging experts J. Roy Parcels and Herbert M. Meyers do indeed call brand names "communicator[s],"[37] and Parcels is quite severe in his admonitions against the manufacturers trying to handle the difficult business of naming:

> Actual development of candidate names is often a very sophisticated process. It may involve the use of focus groups, computer generation, and careful exploration of possible root word, prefix, and suffix opportunities. These and other aspects of the task take time and an orientation which is the special talent of the trained and experienced professional. For this reason, use of an outside professional is recommended for this task especially.

... The mere fact that people within a corporation have other responsibilities detracts from their ability to give such a project their total attention.[38]

Few claims could be more degrading to domestic aesthetic judgment than Parcels's here, that the manufacturer of a product is not expert and professional enough to name the thing she's made and that naming household products is the proper work of highly trained professionals in rhetoric rather than the ordinary people who use them. Nor could any claim be more classically sophistic. Of course, Parcels does to some degree describe a true situation—professionals, not ordinary, thoughtful people, do name products. One result of this is that the names are confusing and stupid, associating the products with vague symbols of goods that may have little to do with their use; this, I take it, is the point of exploiting "root word, prefix, and suffix opportunities." Another result is that consumers by now are so resigned to not being able to tell how to use a product from its name or package, that they feel helpless to alleviate their confusion. This is brought to an extreme realization in the Claritin and other prescription drug commercials, which provide nothing but the (usually horrible) name of the product and a vague indication that your doctor will know what it means. Consider, for instance, the name *Propecia,* or the granddaddy of these ads, *Rogain;* it took professionals to come up with those.

Meyers continues Parcels's line of thought in an analysis of package development for Burger King's chicken tenders:

- A design which ... positions the band in the form of a ribbon surrounding the package similar to a gift package, thus elevating quality perception.

- A design communicating a "fresh from the farm" image.

- The selected design based on the popular chicken-in-the-basket concept. This communicates a festive, fun image ... to communicate appetite appeal.[39]

Here, in its full glory, is the transformation of a food into a commercial for food. "Appetite appeal" is offered instead of taste, "quality perception" is produced instead of chicken, " 'fresh from the farm' image" is sold instead of freshness, a "popular concept" bases the design instead of a culinary tradition. Surely, in this case, consumers can only be buying the commercial because the food no longer exists. Into this general category as well, go T-shirts with only a picture or a trademark or a slogan on them; golf hats with the same; jeans with a name on the pocket; celebrities' names attached to products; key chains, coffee mugs, pens, throw pillows, ashtrays, and so on, which are distinguishable solely on the basis of the corny joke, travel spot, or kitschy event that is verbally declared upon them. These products really have no functional design differences from one token to the other of their types. Essentially such products are only advertising used as decoration. They cover a three-dimensional world of objects more or less useful or pleasant with a two-dimensional one of words and pictures more or less meaningful. Little could be more debilitating to judgment than these sorts of commodities. No skill whatsoever—not even the ability to read—only a familiarity with advertising symbols, the fashions of the day, is required to get out of these objects everything there is to get.

Packager Mona Doyle defends this "packaging revolution."[40] "This revolution is shopper/consumer driven. Their wishes helped determine its direction and their buying behavior is keeping it going."[41] But Doyle cannot even maintain this argument through the opening paragraph of her article. The consumers she describes as directing this revolution are "complex, contradictory, and frequently fickle." If they are contradictory and fickle, how can they express a general trend of wishes? The truth is, they cannot and they do not, and Doyle's article is as full of stories of failed packaging strategies that received complaints or had other than the expected results, as otherwise. "Cereal," she states later, "is perceived as a terrible buy in an inconvenient package. . . . [But] cereal sales and profits have been running at all-time highs, [so] it may be fair to conclude that packaging that consumers don't like is sometimes great business strategy."[42] She gives no reason why we should conclude this—certainly not the obvious and reasonable one, which is that people like cereal.

THE ART COMMERCIAL

The culmination of advertising's techniques of vagueness occurs in what I call the "art commercial." Essentially a music video made exclusively to sell a product, the art commercial uses the technique of promotional tie-ins an ad-ization to make the viewer think that she is being entertained instead of sold—or, what is far less awful but probably more dangerous, really only to entertain her. For years Coca-Cola has spent millions of dollars on lavish multimedia art commercial campaigns. Original music with distinct performances for each commercial, extravagant special effects, intricate combinations of positioning for different markets, and phenomenal photography have marked its campaigns for more than a generation. The Coke ads, however, make a very strange gesture because they cannot possibly have a significant effect on the sales of Coke at any time in the foreseeable future; indeed, Coke has thousands of more ordinary ads do to that, should it need to. But Coca-Cola's sales are in little danger of falling from its heaven-knows-how-many-percent worldwide market share even if all its advertising were suspended—certainly there is no need for the epics in which it indulges. One can only assume that Coke has something nonmonetary invested in its image as a producer of art commercials, that Coke fancies itself a sort of artiste.

Most disturbing, ever since the monumentally important "I'd like to teach the world to sing" ads, Coke has been involved in making socially conscious art commercials with seeming aspirations toward saving the world. World music and consciousness-raising have marked the Coke commercials for more than twenty years, and this really has become the trend in art commercials. The volume could not be higher on this United Nations appeal than in the recent "Always Coca-Cola" campaign. Consistently the finest jingle composer, Coke depicted itself as omnipotent and eternal with this unmistakable ditty. In many of the commercials, the theme is played without any lyrics, assuring us that the ad has little to do with selling and everything to do with testing our cultural literacy.

Although Coke may be the most flamboyant case of this sort, it is far from the only one. Levis, Reebok, Calvin Klein, Nissan, and of course, Nike have invested millions upon millions in art commercial campaigns that they can't possibly need. Is this a kind of metalevel conspicuous consumption, when the manufacturers buy lavish ads just to show they don't need to sell products? I would venture to think so were it not for the pomposity of this new breed of commercials. They are not showing off their power, but rather making vague counterculture gestures, or gestures of charitable largesse, by funding these groundbreaking artworks. Nike's 1996 Olympic ad campaign is a fascinating study in art commercialism, basically a set of sort of avant-garde anticommercials with insulting criticisms of potential customers who can't stomach their images of vomiting athletes. The short-lived Calvin Klein commercials, which imitated auditions for porn films, are another stunningly obtuse example of the anticommercial genre of the art commercial. The art commercial brings together the tactics of fashion at their most vague and morally debilitating because they seem to exist, as some think art does, for their own sake and to experiment in the affective power of representing repellent images. Worse yet, they appear to have been made with intention of edifying us. Art commercials, then, because their primary function does not seem to be to sell products, appear to be mere social experiments on the part of advertisers and industrialists. They seem to be simply expressing themselves.

The existence of art commercials is a sign that manufacturers themselves are swept up in the presuppositions of their own advertisers: they have come to believe, seemingly, that it is their place, their role, as corporations to entertain the masses. They seem to believe it is more valuable to make a statement in the vague symbolism of advertising—they believe it has more effect—than, for instance, to lower the prices or improve the quality of the things they produce or even simply to privately contribute to political campaigns or sponsor artists such as the patrons of old. Here, the companies are consumers, too: consumers of advertising itself. They too appear to want to buy the life toward which the commercial inadequately gestures. The corporation, it then becomes apparent, is composed of people trying to make prideworthy lives out of vague representations of ingredients, just like the consumers who have to buy their products. In the art commercial we see the advertisers, the manufacturers, the consumers, all trying to look smart or inconspicuous, authoritative or pliable, trying to figure out what to do with the indecipherable symbols of the play into which they have been cast.

Many commercials today explicitly attach vague moral goods to the products as if buying the product were some weird charitable contribution. One recent ad for a spray-on stain remover would have us believe that we are sending tax-deductible funds to a Down's syndrome foundation, showing a gauzily photographed youngster suffering from the disease, making difficult strides through his day—and spilling things on his clothes—while his "mother" remarks on what a rewarding experience is her life with him. Similar appeals to viewers' social consciences were made in the "baseball, hot dogs, apple pie, and Chevrolet" campaign of several years ago, in the almost unwatchable Gap "poetry-reading" session, in the inept "Levis for women" series, in GE's heartwarming gestures to the various developing nations of the world, in Nike's "Support Title Nine" commercials; the list goes on and on.

These techniques are advertising's magical qualities. The abilities to transform consumption, through an illusion, into apparent production and to transform production, through an illusion, into an apparent symbolic significance are advertising's special tricks. According to Williamson, "magic is not a single unified referent system, . . . but a process, a . . . means of *doing* things. . . . It does not involve a particular area in relation to which we may be misplaced by ideology—it represents the misplacement itself. . . ."[43] Thus, for Williamson, the commercial's magic is that it makes something unsystematic seem systematic, apprehensible. It makes the consumer produce the commodities it advertises, while it makes her feel like a passive receptacle, just as if it took a quarter out of her ear.

As commodities, through the commercials, are further cheapened into vague linguistic symbols and sold as charity to the poor, and as both the number of holders of actual wealth in our society and the number of people who can take care of themselves by exercising strong domestic aesthetic skill continues to diminish, the world depicted in the commercials can be distinguished only with increasing difficulty from the real world. Physical objects, the commercials would have us believe, might as well be mere words and pictures. In the same way the commercial might as well be the show, the show might as well be the commercial; the T.V. world might as well be one's life, one's life might as well be lived on a T.V. talk show. The T.V. commercial, especially the art commercial, directly attacks the judgment in its efforts to distinguish art from life, and it is in a position to bother one at home. Thus, many of the ills of the fashion tactics to which I have referred, which have chipped away domestic aesthetic skill, can be traced if indirectly to advertising, especially on television. First of all, T.V. advertising has contributed more than any other ad medium to the redirection of judgment from the indexical signification of goodness to vague symbolic signification of unrecognizable traces of ourselves. In this way advertising in general turns *things* into *connotations*, turns a world of objects and agents with various real, social, emotional, and direct physical relationships into a world of signs associating in purely linguistic ways. The commercial is in a uniquely auspicious position to hide our judgment from us and discourage us from using it in our buying choices by leading us to believe that goodness attaches to products symbolically, like a meaning attaches to a word. Television commercials are the most intrusive, the most repetitive, and the most domestic of advertisements, and as such, their negative effects on phenomenological intimacy are the most palpable and unremitting.

Television commercials tend to lead the viewer to believe that she will get everything good symbolized in the commercial when she buys the product precisely because the reverse is the case—she has already gotten everything symbolically good in the product in the commercial. This is the ultimate culmination of their fashion tactics. If one wants to satisfy one's guests with a scent-free cat litter box, if one wants to feel that sense of success and relief, such as it is, one does so as a catharsis while watching the commercial. If the viewer wants to get something of the cool zing of a fast car with none of the stress—or the skill—of driving it, she gets that thrill and then some by watching the artificially sped-up, roaring, sound-enhanced image of driving in the commercial. The product is turned by the T.V. commercial into something of nominal relevance—literally—so that buying the product becomes, in the mind of the consumer, a reference to the commercial rather than the commercial a reference to the product. The consumer's reaction to the artistic, audio-visual, linguistic world depicted in the commercial replaces her reaction to the product.

Campbell compares something like this effect, what he calls the phenomenon of "modern autonomous imaginative hedonism," to daydreaming.[44] Like the effects of her purchase, Campbell claims, a person's daydream is "the imaginative elaboration, in a pleasurable direction, of a forthcoming or anticipated, real event. . . ."[45] Although Campbell's point is well taken with regard to actual consumer behavior regarding products, the T.V. commercial's relation to daydreaming would make it basically an art form according to Freud.[46] For Freud, only the anticipation, not the event, can be real in a daydream: art's distinction as art is that it allows one's wishes to be satisfied by fictional fulfillment. Thus, to the extent that the commercial, with its depiction of a desirable life, is still a commercial, that is, to the extent that it still depicts the full realization of its daydream as dependent on the purchase of the product, it can never really be the artwork it aspires to be. Because it cannot be truly a commercial and be truly fictional at the same time, the television commercial's affectation of art is pernicious. The commercial undermines viewers' faculty of aesthetic judgment precisely to the extent that it genuinely entertains them.

✻

Although many, perhaps most, ads offer us vague signs of instruments to shrunken, unidimensional, faded regurgitations of people's attempts to be happy, we must remember that people still attempt to be happy, and both their purchases and their sales rhetoric are still motivated by that goal. Just as successful lying, as Kant pointed out, depends on our basic faith in the truth, fashion tactics and the vagueness techniques that serve them leech off our earnest effort to do what we believe is good. That effort, to do what seems to one to be good, as long as domestic aesthetic activity is still pursued with some seriousness by enough people to affect our general social consciousness, is likely to make its way into commercials. I have argued that domestic aesthetic judgment, despite the onslaught it has faced, is still alive and difficult to kill. Were it not for the good judgment still evident in new, perfectly good commercials, one might have to think that mass culture or advertising culture was a monolithic system of deception and that it had won the day. To imagine these human practices as such, however, would undermine my claims that decision making—the decision making of the individual advertisers in this case—is refined through domestic aesthetic skill. Happily, though, for my thesis as well as for our happiness, we still see, even among television ads, earnest attempts to help one another make good lives.

What, then, to be fair, does a good commercial do? It follows from my argument in this chapter that what is most debilitating to domestic aesthetic skill is actually not that the ads have somehow expanded their influence into the nonfictional world of news and education and into the physical objects that they depict (although this is extremely disturbing), as that they have themselves taken on the fictional status of art and offer themselves as aesthetically valuable. This is most damaging to judgment, I have claimed, because precisely to the extent they are commercials, they are never just art. Hence, beyond lying about the particular product they advertise (if they do lie, which is not always the case), such commercials lie about the aesthetic good itself. For the viewer with close phenomenological intimacy, this won't be much of a problem; she will judge such a commercial as art along a different scale than that on which she judges the value of buying the product. The judgment of a phenomenologically distant viewer, however, is vulnerable to them in a kind of wholesale way.

Hence, a good commercial, especially these days, is one that addresses the phenomenologically distant viewer. The best commercials are the ones that admit, despite their beauty or entertainment value, that they are trying to sell particular, real products. The acclaimed "Got Milk?" campaign, consequently, earns its praise: it never veers from its representation of the specific good qualities of milk. The Volkswagen "Antilock Brakes" ad, depicting a young couple who realize while driving home from the video store that they have returned their pornographic home video, and stop the car on a dime—cute and entertaining as it may be—patently exists to sell cars. The Corona "On the Beach" campaign, wordless and beautifully photographed, depicts the peaceful enjoyment of beer. The Iams commercial, which traces a dog and his girl going up a flight of stairs together over the course of the dog's long life, expresses the simple claim that its dog food is very healthy and people should buy it for their dogs.

Inventors, advertisers, and product designers who engage in careful reflection on people's homely skills and practices—or better yet, practice some themselves—still come up with some genuinely novel, useful, beautiful products that better our lives in discernible ways. It is important to remember, then, when we are accosted by worse efforts, that the life depicted in bad commercials is just a weak tea brewed up from the dried, chopped-up fragments of the lives we already lead. The T.V. commercials' particular techniques of vagueness are in the service of fashion tactics. There's nothing essential in advertising's use of the techniques of vagueness, just something overwhelming. It is important to remember in the path of this storm that what the vaguest commercials are selling are only roundabout, watered-down reproductions of real, old, ordinary things—things human beings have done and needed and seen myriad times before.

Marketing research just mocks good judgment and ignores the researchers' own experience, and in its dumb understanding takes our repetitive behavior—repetitive because we try purposely to continue and to try to improve timelessly necessary practices or to incorporate known goods into our lives as well as we can—to be an opportunity for the sale of false novelty. Despite all its ills, bad advertising is still just a hapless, clumsy, desperate attempt to do what's right. The worst advertising has simply made being confused seem attractive.

PART IV

Women, Character, and Domestic Aesthetic Choice

The presence of friends, then, seems desirable in all circumstances. Does it not follow then, that . . . for friends the most desirable thing is living together?

—Aristotle, *Nicomachean Ethics* (1171b27–33)

CHAPTER 9

FOUR REPRESENTATIVE
WOMEN CHARACTERS

> This is why men are so sad, why they feel so cut off, why they
> think of themselves as orphans cast adrift, footloose and stringless
> in the deep void. What void? she asks. What are you talking about?
> The void of the Universe, he says, and she says Oh and looks out
> the window and tries to get a handle on it, but it's no use, there's
> too much going on, . . . so she says, Would you like a cheese sand-
> wich, a piece of cake, a cup of tea.
> —Margaret Atwood, "The Female Body"

We must at some point face the fact that the tactics of fashion
and their legion of vagueness techniques that I have described in
preceding chapters have not been gender neutral in their affront. They
have by and large been aimed at women, and women have by and
large accepted the responsibility for judgment that mass production
and advertising have dumped in their laps. Fashion, whether in or
outside the context of its effect on moral reasoning, whether it forms
the subject of study for a Barthes or for a Fraser, is by and large a
woman's concern, and the authors who discuss it focus largely on
women's clothes. Campbell, in his general discussion of consumerism,
concludes his arguments on the Romantic ethic with a reflection on its
interplay with gender:

> We have already had cause to note the prominence of women
> among readers of romantic and sentimental fiction in the eigh-
> teenth century, something which has remained true for that genre
> down to the present day; whilst many of the activities identified
> as most compatible with romantic values—notably education,
> child-care, welfare work and, to a degree, the fine arts—have all
> traditionally been regarded as "women's work."[1]

Campbell remarks as well upon the relation between romanticism and fashion in virtue of the "close association, both in time and place, between romanticism, especially in its social form as Bohemianism, and a dynamic upsurge in cultural consumerism. Paris, for example, is both the spiritual home of Bohemianism and the historic fashion capital of the world. . . ."[2] In light of my arguments so far about generic choice making and the domestic aesthetic, this should be unsurprising. Because, at bottom, the goods we need are household goods, one should expect the encroachments of mass production and advertising on human judgment in such an advanced stage of fashion tactics to aim at the household laborer.

I have suggested that the designation of domestic labor to women, although perhaps understandable, is not logically necessary. Rather, I have suggested, along Aristotelian lines, that aspects of an individual's character, including her gender, are defined like everything else interdependently with the character of her society and especially with the members of her household. In other words, I believe our notions of womanhood per se, like our notions of freedom and self and goodness, as I have discussed these, are indirectly influenced by our economic behavior and social practices if only, as is sometimes the case, antagonistically. Furthermore, and consequently, I believe that the economic and intellectual trends I have traced over the course of modernity and postmodernity have actually tended—in their attempts to create new markets for goods in an economy of mass production and contrary to our contemporary mythology—to increase the distinctions we tend to make between the sexes by encouraging us to characterize them categorically rather than as matters of degree. In other words, living the life of a woman or man, I think, is a kind aesthetic practice, refined or atrophied through domestic aesthetic activity; thus it is subject like all such practices to the tactics of fashion. In this chapter, I trace the vicissitudes of the conception of gender under the onslaught of fashion tactics by way of characterizing the situation of the domestic aesthetic as it faces us today: in representations of women.

MacIntyre may well be right that his three representative characters (i.e., the Rich Aesthete, the Manager, and the Therapist) are only instrumentally rational and that they serve society badly on that account. Hence the rather unhopeful tone with which MacIntyre concludes his case: "We are not entirely without grounds for hope. . . . However, the barbarians . . . have already been governing us for quite some time."[3] If my arguments are right, however, that the domestic aesthetic skills whose practice sharpens moral reasoning are very deeply ingrained and therefore hard to eradicate, then we should find among our representative characters at least some who still struggle to contemplate and live a good life. If I am right, in addition, that the affront on domestic aesthetic skill is being aimed particularly at women, then we should find among women representative characters some who have lost the battle against fashion tactics and who demonstrate the consequent weaknesses of their moral reasoning in particularly instructive ways.

MacIntyre claims: Characters "are, so to speak, the moral representatives of their culture, and they are so because of the way in which moral and metaphysical ideas and theories assume, through them, an embodied existence in the social world."[4] I have argued that MacIntyre's understanding of these characters, although provocative, falls just a little short the even imaginary "embodied" existence MacIntyre rightly claims they must have in order to be socially influential. I have claimed that to be influenced by the theories a character instantiates, one calls a sensible image of a character to mind, runs through a little dialogue with this person in one's head, imagines her attire, and so forth. To clarify one's thinking about the "moral mask" to which one refers in each case, in other words, I have argued one generally imagines a concrete sensible "mask," and I have argued that in general, one dons that sensible mask and plays out a scenario of action in it to consider the moral choices that fit with a certain character. A representative character, I have claimed, must be a dramatic, aesthetic exemplar, even as she is a moral one: the appropriate "props" and "costumes" must be imagined with her and have a significant influence on the outcome of one's deliberation.

Thus, I intend to include in my characters more of their sensible qualities, more of their dramatic tone, and more examples of their closest approximations in the drama really depicted in our social imagination through media representations than MacIntyre did his, focusing as he did primarily on the theories that informed them. To do this, I combine with a MacIntyrean model of abstract characters, influences of Stanley Cavell's analyses of the concrete dramatic characters in American movies. In his *Pursuits of Happiness: The Hollywood Comedy of Remarriage* and its later companion piece, *Contesting Tears: The Hollywood Melodrama of the Unknown Woman*, Cavell discusses several, as he argues, influential American movies of the 1930s and 1940s, concentrating in both works on the lead female characters.[5]

In both books, Cavell compares movie genres to myths, as types of explanatory exercises, working out philosophical or social hypotheses by testing out scenarios of action.[6] Thus, he claims, characters in these movies will have mythic qualities through which we may examine in historical context the perennial values and problems of human life. In *Pursuits of Happiness* Cavell claims that the 1930s comedies address the relatively specific question of women's happiness after the success of women's suffrage and the possibility of women's living in states of both equality and marriage with men.[7] In the 1940s, he argues in *Contesting Tears*, the genre of tearjerkers comes into its own in American movies, studying tragic—indeed melodramatic—women's characters. In these movies, he claims, women are depicted as rejecting the possibilities for happiness in marriage, accepting instead the tougher but more powerful role of mothers, sacrificing their happiness for the sake of their children, and gaining a kind of divine joy in return, that is, the women are tragic heroes.[8] In the remarriage comedies, he claims, "the woman's mother is never present (with illuminating exceptions that prove the rule), and the woman of the principal pair is never herself shown to be a mother. . . ."[9] In the melodramas, by contrast, we see "the woman's search for the mother,"[10] "the negation of marriage itself— . . . marriage . . . is transcended and perhaps reconceived. . . . this alternative integrity is still creation, or . . . metamorphosis—some radical, astonishing, . . . change . . . of her identity."[11] Thus, for Cavell, these characters are studies, at least in part, of how women discover or develop their own identities by reflections on their relationships to their husbands, children, parents, and others in their lives.

Like Cavell, and in accordance with my arguments about phenomenological intimacy and distance, I think it is important not to look at representative characters as entities existing independently in an abstract realm, but instead to consider their characters interdependently with those of others, particularly with domestic products and members of their households. Similarly, I want to investigate representative women characters, first, because as I interpret them they themselves understand their characters and their decisions as developing within a social context, and second, because the quandaries that we see women characters facing today as they are represented in art and advertising are paradigmatic of the struggle of both men and women to retain phenomenological intimacy in an age when it is under attack.[12] In addition, and quite aside from MacIntyre's use of the concept, it seems to me that as domestic aesthetic practitioners we generally take gender to be relevant to our decision making, just as on my running metaphor the playwright or director of a real theatrical production takes the gender of the characters, most of the time, to be relevant to the production. Thus, gender neutral representative characters are not quite representative.

Four representative women characters in particular can give us a picture of the state of domestic aesthetic judgment and of the concrete possibilities for living that we, as a society, envision to ourselves: they are the *Feministe*, the Model, the Mom, and the Working Woman.

The Working Woman and the Mom are opposite sides of a coin, and they are often instantiated to different degrees in the same person. I argue that these representative characters, although contemporary, share some features with Cavell's comic and tragic heroines, and thus can be understood as developing some of the lines of thought drawn by those characters and the movies in which they appeared, developing lines of thought about the possibilities for women's happiness, and for men's and women's lives together. The Working Woman and the Mom occupy a good position to occasion our moral reflection, but, like the tearjerkers in which the second group of heroines Cavell investigates appear, they are sometimes "somewhat condescended to, specifically as [if they] do not know their effect, the desire that is in them, and do not possess the means for theorizing . . . for entering into the conversation over themselves."[13] Following this line of argument, however, I would say that these characters have maintained some semblance of domestic aesthetic skill partly because they have been resistant to the temptations of fashionable theory.

Before turning to them, however, I investigate the *Feministe* and the Model, who are also opposite sides of a coin, although they have fallen some distance into the contemporary whirlwind of vagueness. Like the Working Woman and the Mom, they are also often instantiated in the same person. The *Feministe* and the Model, however, are more recent developments, taking their inspiration from domestic mythology of the 1950s. Consequently, I believe, they offer a nice study in the ways domestic aesthetic skill has been affected in recent decades. In all four cases we should note that these women representative characters are *only* representative characters; like MacIntyre's Therapist, Manager, and Rich Aesthete, these four women *only hypothesize* moral directions for people traveling various paths in contemporary life. They are not real people; they are informative fictions.

The *Feministe*

Quite aside from any meaningful political gains achieved for women by visionary feminist leaders, for which I am very grateful, the *Feministe*, as I hereby coin the term, is simply a character well entrenched in our social consciousness, quite as predictable—even more so—in her behavior and beliefs to the average American as is the Manager or the Therapist. She, like them, is already sent up in television shows, textbooks, and comic monologues; she is taken up by the faux alternative media as a model for living for countless young and middle-aged women. She is the protagonist of many ad campaigns, a sure sign that she represents an imagined target audience. Take, for instance, the 1996 Olympic Nike commercials in which unnamed villains who give a little girl a doll and tell her she is precious and beautiful are vanquished by equally anonymous heroes who give her a ball and tell her she is tough and strong, and consequently give her a "chance." Vague and ill thought as this message is, to be sure (a chance to do what, why can't she play with a doll and a ball and countless other toys, and so on), it demonstrates that the *Feministe* is, in a word, a type.

Genuine political or social actions that achieve meaningful goods, including protection from abuses, for anyone, women or men, is laudatory. Many actual feminists are still able to achieve these meaningful goods. But the *Feministe* life that is projected into our social consciousness by the *Feministe* as a character, and that is emulated by many real individuals, is denuded of these meaningful ends by the tactics of fashion, so that now it is not much more than what Baudrillard called a liberalism "in the guise of a disturbing attack on the system."[14] The *Feministe* is the vague theme who informs in varying degrees the public personages of such disparate individuals as Madonna, Tabitha Soren, Roseanne, Elizabeth Dole, Hillary Clinton, and Alanis Morissette. What these lesser idols all share to varying degrees is an inarticulate attachment to the "struggle" behind their own achievements as women, qua women's achievements, a struggle that somehow socially legitimates their successes. This difficult self-image to which so many people today, women and men, are inarticulately attached, I call the *Feministe*; and like the Model, it exists primarily on the plane of fashion.

Who is the *Feministe* and how does she tell us what is happening to our economy and our moral judgment? The *Feministe* is a kind of feminist who is particularly well suited for mass consumption. In a sense that may be said to include all the most bland, and hence, salable, strains of feminism of which it takes advantage, we may describe the *Feministe* as a figure who espouses beliefs that "promote the interests of women." She is envisioned in our literature and contemporary mythology exactly this way—as a promoter. The operative principle of this definition—certainly one with which many people today would want to ally themselves—is that it presupposes an understanding of what women and their interests *are*. And this is precisely the Weberian bureaucratic position in which MacIntyre found the Therapist, the Manager, and the Rich Aesthete, making the *Feministe* a fit companion for them. The *Feministe*, like them, is a purely technical character; she works to achieve presupposed ends. She is an agent, a lobbyist, an organizer. Thus, the *Feministe* is, every bit as much as the Manager or the Therapist, the moral mask of a certain type of bureaucratic character, one that is a big player on the stage of contemporary society. Her morality is certainly "emotivist" in MacIntyre's sense—a bald assertion of women's entitlements or unique experience without any clear articulation of the ultimate ends or reasons for seeking these entitlements or having this experience.

To understand the advent of the *Feministe* as she stands in our contemporary drama of signs, then, we have to consider in what sense she represents or signifies women's interests. We might suppose, which would be most commonsensical, that the *Feministe* promotes the self-interest of individuals within the group "women." But to the extent that this is possible in any meaningful way, it is the job of individual (perhaps feminist) lawyers; the *Feministe* loses her character as the representative of a group once she takes up the cause of any real individuals. To the extent that she is invoked in the interests of individual women, a vicious cycle is set into motion because the *Feministe*, insofar as she is emulated by individuals, has contributed to their individual self-images and so, informed their interests.

Surely, in addition, and at the very least, any individual's self-interest includes that she eat well and have a satisfactory home and clothing. There is no way meaningfully to understand an individual's "interest" as not at least including basic subsistence. And going about satisfying this lowest level interest in a human way is what I have described as domestic aesthetics. Now, an individual or her advocate might go about seeking adequate food, clothing, and shelter (putting aside for the moment the question of who supplies the raw materials, and looking only at the question of labor) in three ways: (1) the individual woman could see to these subsistence needs for herself, (2) some familiar private individual other than herself could see to it (e.g., a family member, a friend, a neighbor, a member of her congregation), or (3) these things could be provided by some public institution (e.g., the government, a corporation). Surely, these three possible ways of meeting survival needs are given in a descending order of their effectiveness; if one is able to take care of oneself, one is better off, assuming one has the necessary means, than if one has to depend on someone else and better off still than if one has to apply to some bureau or employer to support her.

If we now add to these reflections consideration of the supply of means, the order of best to worst case scenario is similar. One is best off if one is independently wealthy (or has a secure supply of means coming in for work that one does on one's own initiative and for its own sake). Although in the current social climate dependence on those close to one is a particularly risky business, surely one is generally worse off when one depends on someone else than when one can take care of oneself. Let us say that a person is worst off if she depends on some public institution and its inevitable bureaucracy, particularly if she has put herself in the hands of strangers because those close to her have done her harm. Although we could debate about the ranking of the various middle scenarios, surely a woman is worst off if she has to apply to a government agency or for a job or a handout and has to depend on someone else to take care of her and her home.

The *Feministe* has nothing to say about or to a particular woman who is independently wealthy or who has a secure dream job because this woman's position is immune to her promotions, and promotion is her raison d'être. Among the practicable means to subsistence however, the *Feministe's* goal, as a representative character, is precisely to undermine the best-case scenario and promote the worst-case one for the majority of women who find themselves somewhere in the middle. She doesn't promote knowing how to take care of oneself because her character requires her to depict domestic labor as utterly slavish.[15] Instead, she promotes mass-produced signs of women's empowerment—Levi's for women, government funding for women's issues, megaconcert tours for women artists—and thus, like all promoters of mass-produced commodities, she ultimately furthers women's dependence on anonymous strangers. Granting the *Feministe* that the government is less likely to abuse a woman physically than is her husband, father, or boyfriend (although it is not entirely unlikely to do so), still the *Feministe's* position does not include the best-case scenario of women's subsistence survival.

What interest, then, is the *Feministe* promoting for women? What interest is actually achieved through her promotional schemes and mythic example? It is an interest in working outside of one's household and therefore at a job that is "important," which "contributes to society," which "is valued by society"; it is an interest in competing with men for the things for which men "traditionally" compete with each other (e.g., promotions at work, victory in a game or sport, sexual or military conquest) or, alternatively and at the same time, an interest in scorning these competitions. It is an interest in being as empowered as anybody else to do what anybody else does; an interest in abstract freedom and equality, in exactly the problematic modern senses that I described as Berlin's and Foucault's. It is an interest in power, ultimately a class interest. But there is no distinct content to the character of the life that exercises this power or to the members of the class seeking it. As such, the interest promoted by the *Feministe* is not a moral end; it is a pure instrument.

Furthermore, it is an instrument to tacit ends that are both unrealistic and, for most people I would argue, undesirable. No matter the degree to which the *Feministe* pervades the contemporary consciousness, most people, men and women, will have relatively close, interdependent relationships with other people, including their families. And most people would, on reflection—or so we must believe—prefer that these small lives and relationships be happy, interesting, and worthy of pride than that they have to seek legal protection of their individual "interests" against the abuses of their families, employers, and spouses. In other words, what the *Feministe* promotes is really a negative interest, an interest in avoiding or seeking recourse against the abuse of power by others. It is not a positive interest in exercising power to achieve an identifiable end. It is really the sort of aimless exercise of freedom I discussed in the beginning of part II. Thus, to the extent that real women follow her example in their lives, the *Feministe* leads them away from the meaningful achievements that would give them reasons to be proud. The *Feministe*, consequently, undermines the accomplishments and debases the social goals of actual feminists by painting them over in a rhetoric of fashion.

The *Feministe*, as a representative character, is therefore just another lobbyist in the failed tradition who seeks a contentless freedom and equality; a sameness and therefore an emptiness for all. The life that she advocates for women may yield them an equality with men, but at what? The life she advocates for women is just the instrumentalized, empty existence of the Manager, the Rich Aesthete, and the Therapist. The life that real individuals achieve by emulating her may well wield a power for women equal to that of men of a similar class, but it cannot be happy just by virtue of its emulation of the *Feministe*.

Worthy of note, then, is the predominance in *feministe* rhetoric of representations of unhappy women, as in the 1996 Olympic Nike ads I mentioned. In Jane Campion's 1993 *The Piano*, for instance, immediately taken up as a *feministe* anthem, we find the utterly incoherent story of a miserably unhappy woman. In a similar vein, a recent campaign for the cereal Special K, deliberately addressing complaints from *feministe* quarters that its depictions of ideal women's bodies advocated a male feminine ideal by making them too skinny, tried to sell this diet product by depicting husky male characters complaining pitifully about their bodies in "typical" feminine ways while an overdub points out the irony of it all, how supposedly socially unrestricted are men's body images. The ads, in other words, express pity for the product's target audience, specifically by contrast to men, who, so the ads imply, would rightly feel silly for talking about themselves as women do. (The manufacturer switched to a celebrity-endorsement campaign—problematic in its own way, but far preferable—in which the slender but hardly anorexic Cindy Crawford is depicted enjoying the taste of the cereal.)

Of course the *Feministe* must depict women as unhappy; happy women don't need the products she has to sell. Young women athletes, for instance, will buy the shoes that their good judgment as skillful athletes lead them to buy; young women happy doing something else have no reason to buy athletic shoes. The *Feministe* engages in a weird kind of fashion tactic in which female audience members are flattered for their unhappiness, a tactic of moral self-congratulation for suffering under the monolithically oppressive conditions for women in a male-oriented society, or alternately for not suffering under them any more. That this rhetoric has influenced individual aesthetic judgment has been demonstrated to me several times, in the reactions of some viewers, women and men, to two of the movies Cavell discusses in *Pursuits of Happiness*, George Cukor's 1940 *The Philadelphia Story* and Howard Hawks's *His Girl Friday*, made the same year, which I teach in a junior-level college class every other year.

Invariably someone interprets these movies as sadly indicative of women's dependence on men in our society. Granted, the main female characters in both *The Philadelphia Story* and *His Girl Friday* (Tracy, played by Katherine Hepburn, and Hildy, played by Rosalind Russell, respectively) are eventually convinced by their ex-husbands (played by Cary Grant in both cases) to remarry, and granted, neither is represented as perfect, nor as completely self-sufficient, nor as seeking or respecting other women's advice. But to overlook that these characters: (1) are divorced, (2) remarry for love and not out of dependence, and (3) command authority over several male characters in each case, including their ex-husbands, and to overlook as well that (4) none of the male characters in either movie is represented as perfect, completely self-sufficient, or seeking other men's advice, either (although Mike (played by James Stewart) in *The Philadelphia Story* does seek from Dexter (played by Cary Grant) a revelation of his true feelings, and Walter (played by Cary Grant) in *His Girl Friday* and Bruce (Hildy's fiancé, played by Ralph Bellamy) *do* seek out Hildy's advice), is to interpret the movies myopically as social documentary rather than comedy and to overlook the aesthetic depth of every character. Furthermore, this kind of reading overlooks these factors for the sake of in this case an extremely vaguely connoted image of the good; some sort of women's independence. Independent of what? Of love, of men, of marriage? It is hard to imagine what of, which is precisely the point.

The *Feministe*, as I have described her, then, has taken on all the interpretive schemata of fashion tactics. She presupposes a notion of the good—"the interests of women"—without reflection on that in which women and their interests consist; in fact, because it is empty of particular content, the *Feministe*'s notion of the good is nothing but the female gender already possessed by the members of the target audience (i.e., it's them, watered down). She advises against making any qualitative distinctions or judgments among women's choices; what masquerades instead for her as a "quality" distinction among women's decisions or beliefs is really a categorical distinction between women and men (or "masculinists"), respectively. The *Feministe* endures a divorce in consciousness among the various faculties of judgment of moral, aesthetic, and economic good, which puts itself across as a unity of these faculties in which the instrumental moral good, the "interests of women," is thought to be the only standard by which aesthetic judgments can be rightfully made. She judges movies, books, paintings, and music, as well as food, clothing, and home decoration myopically according to their social portrayals of women. These portrayals themselves, however, are usually interpreted instrumentally according to the economic access, social role, physical activity, emotional appeal, and so on of the women depicted in them. Thus the moral standard in which the *Feministe* invests her judgment is really not an end at all but a means.

Playing the role of the *Feministe* will not be, as Baudrillard insists, to become a part of a "system of signs." This is because, as I've argued, the tactics of fashion are not systematized. The *Feministe* need have no worry that she is turning women into just a part of the system of oppression; she is merely leading women into a certain *kind* of haphazard life, no more or less oppressive than most other such lives. The *Feministe* merely represents a certain style of disorder and thoughtlessness. This style of disorder,[16] a term we might apply to many of today's moral masks, is delineated primarily by fashion. To be the *Feministe* is to be the pinnacle of fashion of a particular sort.

Increasingly, for instance, women's products that used to be sold on the basis of their contribution to women's attractiveness or to the cleanliness of their home or to the tastiness of their food are now sold on the basis of the freedom, equality to men, power, status, justice, or identification that they bring to women. A recent example is the NBC coverage of the 1996 Olympics in Atlanta that David Remnick discusses in the *New Yorker* article, which I have mentioned.[17] Remnick interviews Dick Ebersol, head of NBC Sports, who describes the coverage of the Olympics as explicitly, deliberately feminine. What does *feminine* mean for him? The *Feministe*.

"Ebersol's feminine Olympics," writes Remnick, "is a highly artificial construct, designed for maximum sentiment and ratings."

This notion of the feminine, whose use did succeed in capturing an as-yet-unheard-of 50-percent female viewing audience, includes as its second and third rings (the NBC policy is put across in "Olympic rings") Reality and Possibility. " 'Reality' NBC states, is 'the idea that anything can happen, both of an athletic nature and a human nature. People look for . . . relatability, things that apply to them . . . real life and real emotion. . . . ' 'Possibility' they claim, is 'self realization. The audience experiences the rise of individuals from ordinary athletes and their humble beginnings . . . [which] gives the viewer a reason he or she can 'make it through'."[18]

The upshot of these tenets of sports broadcasting was a diminution of the achievements of the athletes, female and male, in favor of a political and social legitimization of their seeming good fortune by reference to some personal tragedy in their lives—the "struggle" I described—and NBC explicitly designated this as "feminine."

Remnick rightly describes this as a soap-operatic turn in sports broadcasting, and he cites Carol Gilligan and Helene Çixous, real academic feminist authors, as evidence that this sort of narrative martyrdom does indeed speak to "feminine interests."[19] And the success of this marketing strategy with female viewers demonstrates that this "feminine" character is an influence on real American women (although perhaps not to the extent that Ebersol believes; there could be any number of other reasons for the increase in female audience). This character of the *Feministe*, then, is essentially a fashion, a marketing technique, and one that is often associated by its purveyors with real academic feminism and one on which real women try to model their behavior and beliefs. The *Feministe*, like any participant in a drama, dons her role through the style of props, costumes, and lines, as well as, and perhaps paradigmatically as, the style of "crowd" that goes with them. Similarly, those real women who choose to emulate all or some part of this character in their lives will do so by casting themselves, through these same props, into a scene in the *Feministe's* play.

THE MODEL

The Model is the parallel to and foil for the *Feministe* (although a recent trend in fashion photography and spokesmodeling has allied the two, another sign of the acceptance of the *Feministe* into the drama of culture). The Model has achieved a similar level of success as the *Feministe* in the weird significations of modern life, but with a very different technique. The Model represents to us, truly or misguidedly, a kind of absolute freedom, a freedom from the physical necessities of human life in the same way that the Rich Aesthete does for MacIntyre. As a representative character, she either doesn't need to work for health, glamour, love, acceptance, money, power, and so on, or else her efforts, unlike the viewer's own efforts at these very same things, are rather magically successful.[20] Everything comes easy for her. Thus, like that of the *Feministe*, the Model's vague tacit image of the good is simply a kind of vague instrumentality: desirability.

The Model's association with magic or ease come from the fact that the Model is actually glamorous, at least according to the tacit standards at work among the audience and employers who keep her in business. The Model, unlike the *Feministe*, naturally signifies something. Her body, actually, and not just the props, costumes, and crowd she acquires thereby, contributes significantly to her role as Model. Although the Model, then, lives in the pure world of fashion, she appears to be less subject to its whims, to its pure emotivism, as are other representative characters. She does have some reasons she can give for her behavior; the things she does must actually contribute to her good looks according to the popular taste, or she is out of a job. Of course, many actual models may indeed be out of a job simply because they can't maintain their looks or because the look they have is of fleeting interest. But the Model, the representative character, although she ages, always looks much better than other women her age; she has, at least so we presume, actual beauty secrets that really work. Whatever she puts on her face actually keeps her skin supple; whatever exercises she does actually tone her thighs; whatever shampoo she uses actually makes her hair manageable. The Model, then, we imagine to have a certain immunity to marketing, a natural gift by which she manages to wend her way through brand names and slogans correctly and actually get some good use out of the increased being that stymies the rest of us. This is one reason she is such a convincing marketing tool.

In this way, the Model is a deeply influential vehicle of fashion tactics. She represents in her person the success of a vast number of products marketed to women, and—where she appears as an accompaniment to them—also those of men. For an instance of the latter, a recent commercial for Ameritech cellular phone service depicts a chubby, balding man being laughed at by a posse of unbelieving male compatriots, who doubt his, as it turns out, true claim that his cellular phone was free. Among their taunts, the audience hears, "yeah, and your wife is really a supermodel (har har har)." The chubby, bald protagonist responds, "she *is* a supermodel," and as the commercial closes, the scene changes from him talking on his cell phone to his supermodel wife at home on the phone to him, expressing her love. Worthy of note, the supermodel in the commercial is an attractive actress playing a supermodel type; she is not a real supermodel; this is not a celebrity endorsement. Here, we see the representative character at work; the Model is the personification of the—in this case, male—audience members' personal validation. Here again, she is not a genuine end, but an instrument; she is neither an achievement nor a reward for achievement, but a mark of the protagonist's legitimacy to himself. Indeed, as I argue, this is her general function for both male and female audience members.

But the Model represents oddly, as oddly as any of our representative characters, and the oddness of her representation can be traced through the pages of old magazines and the memories of old commercials, which makes her again a particularly useful and interesting character study. The Model, as a representative character, has changed drastically in her social role over the last fifty years, largely due to the changes in the economy over that same period. Since World War II the mechanism through which she sells has increasingly evolved from that of associating in the mind of the potential customer the thought of the product with the thought of her glamorous body (as something at which the customer can gape or on which she can reflect), to that of associating in the mind of the potential customer the thought of the product with the thought of the life she represents (as something that the potential customer can live if she buys the product).

In other words, the Model has evolved from selling *as a model* or mannequin or decoration by wearing, holding, or standing next to the product to be sold, to selling *as a role model*, a dream, a life by playing out a vaguely evocative scenario for the camera with only the barest mention of the product that this life is supposed to sell. The Model has evolved from selling things by reference to the things' perceivable functions, convenience, and style, to selling things by reference to the things' hidden, magical, life-transforming properties. She has gone from being a natural significator of her own desirability as an endorser or attractive decoration for a functional or attractive product, to being a purely symbolic significator of potential *customers'* fantasies of *their* lives with little reference whatever to the product she sells. This is a very odd turn of events, quite in line with the analyses I have given: it is a trend toward unclarity of use value, both of the Model and of the products with which she is associated.

In a typical 1940s or 1950s ad, a woman stands before the camera in a striking position in a beautiful gown, holding a coffeemaker in a graceful gesture and an attractive gingham housedress, or sitting in a fancy convertible in cool sunglasses and a flowing scarf. We know what is happening in these images: a dress is being sold and shown to its best advantage on an attractive woman; a coffeemaker is being sold for homemakers to use to make coffee; a car is being sold for wealthy sophisticates to zip around town. Contrarily, in a typical ad today, the neck and half an eye of what appears to be a naked woman is dashed across the page; a group of laughing women is shown at the park, the wind blowing across their faces, their clothes. Now what is going on here? What is being sold? Why are we supposed to want it? What are we supposed to do with it? In contemporary ads, presumably, we are to want that moment of life evoked by the image, and—this is most important—precisely because it does nothing other than evoke a vague and fleeting memory of the audience members' own pasts. Because of the "relatability" (in Ebersol's sense) of the incoherent scene in which she appears, such ads assume, *we will* buy the product that evokes the Model's life regardless of what it does. The ad, the name of the product, the woman's body—these have little to do anymore even with the function of the advertisement and nothing at all to do with the function the product it supposedly sells.

Often nowadays neither the product nor the Model's body even appear in the ad. A recent Bud Dry beer commercial shows only two articles of clothing partying on a clothes line; a women was photographed in a dress, all reference to whom was computer edited out of the ad. A similar technique is used in a recent Levi's campaign in which the computer-animated bodiless clothing of a "sexy" supermodel type is depicted invading the apartment of a similarly bodiless young man's clothing and initiating sex with it. Another example is the station identification ad of a few years ago for the Comedy Central cable channel in which Denis Leary performs an entire monologue on the topic of Cindy Crawford, whose "beauty" is thus evoked and associated with Comedy Central although she never appears. Even more striking is when this ploy is used in fashion ads: Moschino, Christian Dior, and Calvin Klein among others, have for several years sometimes advertised their wares without any actual depiction of clothes, much less a human body wearing them. Not only does the Model today not sell the product but the life, the Model seems actually to be selling nothing at all and to be nothing all; her boss's ad is a pure exercise in technical salesmanship for its own sake.

The Model has gone from being an exceptional case of humanity by virtue of her desirability, then, to *representing* the *fantasies of ordinary people* by virtue of her abstract Modeldom, or in other words, her success. In this the Model has come to *seem* more accessible to ordinary men and women while she has come actually to *be* less accessible to them. The beauty secrets that she uses and the clothes that she is able to wear gracefully, were, in the earlier mode, occasions for reflection for the viewer. In admiring the Model's qualities as the Model's exceptional qualities and not her own, the potential customer was able, if she so chose, to decide which of them if any she was capable of duplicating in herself, and which not, and so to go about herself actually achieving the qualities she admired in the Model. Alternatively, where the Model was really just a display stand for a product (e.g., holding the coffeemaker) the viewer could simply decide not to identify with her at all. Importantly, regardless of the viewer's ability to achieve an approximation of the Model's style of glamour, the person looking at the ad could appreciate the Model as a kind of work of art and contemplate female beauty as occasioned by her. Importantly, with fashion ads of this earlier type, the potential customer could assess the clothes as well made, suitable to her body and style, beautifully colored, and so on, and even as imitable by her as a seamstress. The same for hairstyles, cosmetics experiments, and the like. Today, the viewer has no access through the ad to the criteria for this assessment or for inspiration in her own craftsmanship. Thus, qua model, the Model has fairly explicitly undermined domestic aesthetic skill by mystifying the crafts of using the products she sells.

Advertisers seem to address this situation by developing the new "real-life" fashion in fashion modeling and photography; note, for example, the increased incidence in the last few years of models who are chosen to model because they look "ordinary" and are not "made over" in the photographs. This is really just a furthering of the phenomenon under discussion here, however, in which the path from "there" to "here" (from the Model's life to the viewer's life and vice versa) is shrouded in mystery. In these ads, the Model seems to have gained her position wholly through connections or luck, and the viewer seems not to be in the ad only because she hasn't had the acquaintances and fortune of the Model. The Model in these ads, then, doesn't provide any vehicle through which the viewer might expand her own capacities or habits of self-decoration, doesn't provide any occasion for the viewer's imagination to expand or play; she persuades the viewer to buy the product, where she does so persuade the viewer, wholly according to an argument from authority—and unearned authority at that. "I am in an advertisement; you are not. Buy this." Where the impetus for this movement toward "real life" in modeling results in presenting a broader range of attractive-looking women, of various races and ethnicities for instance, on the pages of fashion magazines than in former times, simply as attractive models and without the self-congratulation, this surely does expand viewer's imaginations. But these efforts tend to use fashion tactics, undermining their ability to make any genuine aesthetic improvement in the fashion industry.

Similarly, the "makeovers" performed on the daytime talk shows promote the mystification of glamour; the "real-life" guests who receive them rarely look much better or even very different after their makeover than before, the "magic transformation" is performed entirely offstage by the show's unnamed "experts," and because of the presuppositions of the talk-show format, the makeover is represented in the shows as solving some sort of deep social or moral problem for the guests. By contrast, although superficially similar, viewers write into the E! channel's series *Fashion Emergency* asking for a makeover for a particular occasion. The producers of the show generally visit the guests and accompany them to upscale stores and salons in their home cities; the cameras accompany the guests as they try on outfits and talk with their dressers and cosmetologists. Although the stores and salons obviously offer their services for promotional purposes, the producers gear the options to the particular guest's expressed tastes and her or his looks and age, and the ultimate choice of outfit is left to the guest. The transformations effected are sometimes amazing and sometimes minor, but they are never mysterious—we see all the choices being made and all the artists at work. Although viewers may well not share the tastes of the producers or the guest, the show allows viewers to reflect on and to imitate or eschew them.

Still, the Model, the representative character, is depicted as unquestionably more desirable and successful than the women to whom the products she advertises are marketed. Without this presupposition, the sale could not go through; why would women bother to buy the products and get a little of what she has if they had it already? Nonetheless, the audience is often characterized as less only by their omission from the ad. Where, as is more common, the Model seeks the viewer's identification, of course, she is observing the straightforwardly flattering rhetoric of the tactics of fashion: "Like me, you are already desirable, and like me, you've relied on products like the one I am currently selling, not to become attractive, because we already are that, but because relying on these products is what desirable women like us do." This is certainly the rhetoric, for instance, of L'Oreal's "I'm worth it" campaign. Of course, it is a confusing rhetoric because the ad presupposes the difference between the Model and the viewer, even as it asserts their similarity.

Because she is still associated with glamour and success, women still attempt to interpret the Model in the old way, marking pretty magazine ads for reference and bringing them into salons and department stores. But the attempt is ill thought and uncontrolled and, so, ill fated. The viewer is no longer able to copy the things in the ads themselves or to reflect on or copy the female forms that the ads represent because neither the things nor the female forms actually appear in full view. Rather, the photographer has become the one with the secrets; she makes a work of art of her invention, using the Model as she pleases in ways that often have little to do with the Model's particular or exceptional looks. What makes the life that the Model represents glamorous is something hidden and mysterious, a magical quality known to the photographer and out of the potential customer's purview. It is a deus ex machina, something the photographer had to go to a special school to learn, something that the potential customer cannot figure out. The Model, her product, and her looks, rather than being presented in their best light by the photographer, are now deliberately obscured by the photographer according to rules to which the viewer is not privy. The ordinary woman's only hope is to be lucky enough to live that life wherein attractiveness is given by certificate, just like the men in the ads or the audience who dream of living with the Model.

The Model's exceptional good looks and the existence of the products she sells are now, like Millian preferences, absolutely essential to her role yet entirely arbitrary to it. She no longer presents a vision of feminine desirability on which potential customers may reflect, but instead, like a utilitarian decision maker, is at the mercy of "expert" photographers and ad executives. The life that the Model now signifies and for which she is envied is the ordinary life from which the sole distinction of the Model is that her looks are chopped up, covered up, disliked, and envied in the very photographs for which they uniquely qualify her. In short, the Model has become that woman whose attractiveness has allowed her to obtain a fancy, highly paid job—*and that's all.* Her job is presented as no more suited to her, no more elegant and leisurely, than anybody else's. Despite having to be glamorous to keep her job, her glamour does her no real good. She merely represents a certain style of success. Just like the *Feministe,* only with a less moralistic, less intelligent-seeming spin, the Model is a vaguely envisioned instrument to another instrument: fame, fortune, and men's attention.

The Model, then, as a pure instrument of sales of nothing at all but making good money at it, today represents that style of disorder that is, like the Rich Aesthete, that of *the lucky life.* The Model is that woman, not substantially different in character from the ordinary women to whom she sells products, who happens to have been lucky enough to have a good body and a pretty face, to have made all the right connections in the "industry," and to have no other obligations to take her away from living the easy life and being showered with admiration. She needs to have skill and to work hard to maintain her status as certifiably attractive, but that skill and work no longer appear in her photographs as a part of her character from which those who admire her can learn or take heart. Although she might be interviewed on talk shows and she may share some beauty tips with the audience, the results of her skill have an unclear relationship to the beauty tips. No one can just look at her and reflect on, tinker with, and copy some of her attractive qualities. Admirers will have to buy her video, from which expenditure they will still be disappointed because it will not provide them her life; she maintains the merely lucky, magical, and so, restricted, access to that.

The Model represents disorder, then, precisely because her cosmetic efforts are unrelated in both her and her viewers' consciousnesses to their ends in the lucky life, which of course is no end at all but an instrument, access to an impressive paycheck with nothing to spend it on but the clothes, exercise, and cosmetics necessary to sustain it. The Model's glamour represents today neither an end in itself nor a clear path to other things that might be ends such as happiness, serenity, wisdom, and so on. She just happens to have glamour and her glamour makes getting along in the same dumb life as the rest of us a little easier for her. It is her luck and convenience that we admire, not the things that these gifts allow her to *do*.

The Model brings fashion tactics to almost full expression: our heroes are melding together into one vague, bland, and sloppy representation of a well-paid version of those who once emulated them, their target audience. The ideal life that the Model models is just a better-paid, easier-to-live version of what we are already. Thus, by investigating the Model as a representative character, we have brought into relief the style of our general social disorder, the tactics of fashion. The development of the Model over the past decades demonstrates that these tactics are well-refined, much-practiced habits of wheel spinning: they lead us to emulate emulation as an end in itself; they evoke different styles in a haphazard, disorderly way with the effect of obliterating the differences between styles, of evoking all styles at once and regardless of their appropriateness to one's time, place, or circumstances; they lead their followers to want to be exactly and merely what they already are, only faster, easier, more.

A False Dilemma

The Model and the *Feministe*, then, are flip sides of the same coin. To make a home, as we have seen in part I, is to order one's life on some level, even on a neighborhood or governmental level. And this ordering of a life, this making of a home, requires a phenomenological intimacy, which in turn requires a clear conception of ends by which to judge objects of consciousness. Thus, to be led away from this reflective endeavor of ordering and choosing is, at the very least metaphorically, to be led away from home, a home of one's shared making. It is to be deliberately left to wander lost, without direction, alone among widely publicized but vague signs of value. The *Feministe* comes to her success through fashions in legitimization and the Model through fashions in attractiveness, both characterized to viewers as mystifying qualities that allowed these otherwise ordinary people like themselves to get more out of the "system." Thus legitimization and attractiveness, respectively, become for the *Feministe* and the Model and their followers, vague, circular, instrumental notions of the good life. To that extent, these two representative characters are flip sides of the same coin, leading us away from reflection upon the good and, consequently, from our own judgments.

I have argued that the household in which domestic aesthetic judgment first develops is a shared place, full of sensible objects available for one's contemplation, including the other people with whom one most intimately shares one's life. We must admit that in so far as the *Feministe* and the Model lead us away from "home," they represent a kind of alienation from other people. In so far as these two are women characters by definition, they especially represent alienation from men. In particular, both the *Feministe* and the Model represent a fading respect for men, in the way I defined it in part I, as a recognition of the values of particular men with whom they live, as reasonable and understandable values, even when they are unshared. The rhetorics of the *Feministe* and the Model both depict men's conceptions of the good as crass and morally vacuous, in the *Feministe*'s case expressly, and in the Model's by omission (just as both rhetorics must place the women in their target audience in a position below them, expressly and by omission, respectively). Thus, we can interpret the adolescent antics of the men on *The Man Show*, in the beer commercial, and so on, at least in part as evidence that the influence of these two representative women characters is powerful on both women and men alike. Representations such as these just embrace the depictions of men made fashionable by the Model and the *Feministe*.

Both the *Feministe* and the Model linguisticize men and women as categorically distinct creatures with different and unsharable notions of the good life, doomed thereby to live together, if they live together at all, at a miserable emotional distance. This vision of relations between men and women, of course, is perfectly consistent with

Campbell's Romantic ethic, which according to him is a motive force behind consumerism. "A romantic [male is] a male who, almost by definition, has refused to 'grow up' by the yardstick of normal 'bourgeois' values. . . . All of which suggests that the presence of the romantic ethic is of greater significance for adolescents and 'youthful' males than for the women and children for whom it is meant to apply."[21] To the extent that the Model and the *Feministe* collaterally inform the decision making of men, they cannot but have a demoralizing influence. In both cases what is put across as independence from men or, in words more appropriate for the Model, self-reliance, is really just a desperate but alienated attachment to "men," in the abstract and as morally inept. The characters of the Model and the *Feministe* are at least partly fueled by the characterization of the unworthy "men" their rhetoric tacitly projects. Were it not in the *Feministe*'s case for the evils of "patriarchy," and in the Model's case for "men's" insatiable and crude sex drives, these characters would have a difficult time occupying the stage of our social drama in the way they do.

Were it not for the tacit but powerful characterization of male consciousness projected in part by these two representative women characters, the women in their respective target audiences would have other things to worry about than abstract male oppression or their own abstract desirability. Perhaps they would have decisions to make about their ill treatment at the hands of particular men in their lives or particular bureaucracies; perhaps they would have decisions to make about how to deal with the size of their particular hips. Likely, the situations that would have occasioned these decisions are unfortunate, and maybe their causes can be traced to institutionalized sexual inequality or inveterate differences between the sexual drives of men and women. Still, as I have argued several times, abstract disrespect—the result of the conflation of the concept of the good with the notion of the self, which is the result of the fashion tactics in which the Model and the *Feministe* participate—is simply not effective in bettering particular individuals' lives. Where we are discouraged from contemplating the tacit analysis of social life that these characters represent, discouraged from reflecting on a moral "mask," and asked instead to simply buy and wear it, our phenomenological intimacy is at risk.

What we can see from the foregoing is that the Model and the *Feministe* represent equally although differently the faster, easier emulations of blander versions of ourselves that we are all today increasingly becoming. Each comes to her position as socially admirable by a mysterious circumstance to which her admirers do not have access or control, yet which is nonetheless essential to their lives. Thus, members of their target audiences will keep trying, and keep failing, to be like them—the perfect condition for manipulable consumers. Nice examples of this coin falling on its edge, thus demonstrating that the tactics of the *Feministe* are the same as those of the Model, may be seen in the growing number of public women who have embraced both lives. The MTV news anchor, Tabitha Soren is one such example; representing at once the promotion of women's interests and the lucky glamour of the spokesmodel. Other examples include all the MTV veejays, whose functional differences of character from someone such as Carroll Merrill (on the 1960s *Let's Make a Deal* game show) are imperceptible, but whose symbolic overtones radically diverge from their cleaner cut predecessors. Another example is provided by the women who inhabited the *Feministe* predecessor to Planet Reebok, depicted in their gym shorts and leotards stating "beliefs" such as that "70 is a long way from old" and that "sweat is sexy." Or, in a more subtle gesture, we might point to the catalogue models for J. Crew, Banana Republic, and L. L. Bean who, marketed to a target college audience, appear without makeup, with short hair, and sporty, but no less attractive by today's standards and no less attended to by men than the less enlightened models for Victoria's Secret or Calvin Klein.

That these seemingly new and progressive *Feministe* Models are little more than fashion tactics is demonstrated by their eternal recurrence on the fashion scene. Consider this description by Fraser, for instance, from almost thirty years ago:

> A legion of real women, after long months of oppression, is to come into its own in the fall. Who are these real women? . . . One New York department store caught the mood of the day in an advertisement that would not have appeared six months ago. "Glory Be for the Real Woman," ran the headline. . . . Beneath the text ("Sick of hearing about diets, exercise, and skinny girls?") was sketched, on suitably willowy forms, . . . corsets, . . . girdles, . . . this flowery praise of real women isn't going to change the world.[22]

Corset wearing aside, how different is this, really, from the J. Crew catalogues? Both are simply, and sympathetically, attempts to incorporate into the market for women's fashions a market formerly, and repetitively, hostile to "glamour."

Thus despite their opposition, the *Feministe* and the Model operate similarly within our social consciousness, not only to bring people both metaphorically and actually away from home into the "public" sphere, the sphere of social legitimacy, but also the sphere of access to marketing. In the public sphere, intimate relations between individuals of qualitatively distinct characters will no longer be necessary or relevant to making their life together; the arrangements of their lives can be referred to professionals. Once away from home, the followers of the *Feministe* and the Model are under the influence of the incoherent tactics of fashion; they will want to buy the props and professional services that will give them a public life as a right-thinking woman or a pretty girl. They will want to know how to get along outside the households, neighborhoods, and landscapes that provoke their thoughts and give their lives meaning, and a slew of advertisers and other paid assistants will be at the ready to serve them before going home themselves to a vague and overly public world in which their judgment is repeatedly accosted. As promoters of vaguely understood but strongly invested notions of the good, the *Feministe* and the Model are paradigmatic of the vague portentousness of our time.

A Brief History of the Woman-of-the-House

The characters of today's Mom and Working Woman, like that of the Model, are very different from their characters just a few decades ago. In that sense, the present incarnation of the Mom is a parallel to, and in part formed by and alongside, that of the Working Woman; they too are flip sides of the same coin. Both are the descendants of the early modern bourgeois woman-of-the-house, bringing together the authoritative position of the mother in an aristocratic family with the slavish position of a concubine or serf. Although actual working women and actual moms have been with us as long as human societies have existed, they have not always been the representations for us that they are today. Among Moms, Marge Simpson or Roseanne, their predecessor Edith Bunker, even the put-together Clair Huxtable or Jill Taylor—or more tellingly, the Moms who advertise minivans, dishwashing liquid, laundry detergent, floor wax, children's clothes and medicines, toys and diapers, convenience foods, and all the other family-oriented products on the market today—to varying degrees paint pictures of fatigued, conflicted, frustrated, laborers struggling to maintain a decent life for themselves and a herd of inconsiderate underlings with their own time-consuming problems. Among Working Women, the three female *Friends*, Elaine Benes, the kicky professional Ally McBeal, their predecessors Laverne and Shirley, or the Vassar-educated Jane Hathaway—or the working women who advertise Lean Cuisine, cellular phones, Victoria's Secret, hair dye and alpha hydroxy, cosmetic surgery, Woolite, headache medicine, and all the other coping mechanisms for adult women with full-time, stressful jobs—paint a similar picture except that the inconsiderate individuals they serve usually outrank them.

Lorna Opatow, speaking for the instruction of marketers, makes quite clear who these representative characters, defined for the use of marketers, are:

> For example, here is a target description [of the market for] a food processor . . . :
>
> —men *and* women who believe they are pressed for time
> —people living alone or in small families
> —users of specific types of convenience foods
> —willing to pay more for taste *plus* convenience but not for convenience alone. . . .[23]

The analysis demonstrates that it is taken for granted that homemakers, formerly conceived as women, are now shown to be both men and women, that they work and so "believe themselves" pressed for time, and that they are often single parents or working people living alone. Still more telling, they are people who, although they have been successfully convinced that they need convenience foods, cannot be talked out of their discriminating judgment of taste. As we saw in part I, this woman-of-the-house, a woman who both had household authority over a bourgeois household and did her own work, is a product of the seventeenth century.[24] Prior to this and in most of the Western world until industrialization, the woman's relationship to children and to others in the household was characterized very differently from our modern understanding.[25]

✷

Distant relations: "The paterfamilias was, in principle, head of the [Roman] household. It was he who, every morning, gave the slaves their orders and assigned them their duties, he who went over the accounts with the steward."[26] Throughout the Middle Ages, the household chores and the market trade, the farming and the cooking, were roughly shared by the members of the household. Women were as often as not the marketers, often supported themselves, often worked in the fields; men were often the cooks, the tailors, and the traders. In the Middle Ages, "several dozen persons lived at times in great, hangarlike wooden houses, where uncles and aunts, male and female cousins, children, slaves, and servants all slept together, naked, around a common fire."[27] Most children who survived infancy (two or three out of every twelve to twenty born) stopped playing children's games at age three or four, started to work at age seven or eight, married at age twelve or fourteen.[28] "Infants were treated more tenderly than older boys *and girls*, who were often disciplined harshly" (italics mine).[29] Married girls were not expected to be a burden on their husbands, nor were they expected to fulfill a separate set of household chores or children's caretaking; children, husband, and motley attachés all shared the various tasks done around the house.

There was a similar functional and communal style in clothes. Before the fourteenth century, "everyone wore tunics, sometimes shorter (to the knee) and sometime longer (to the ankle), but length was only a very rough indication of the sex of the wearer."[30] Distinctions between classes or professions, between men and women, between liturgical costume or royal costume and common wear, were marked (when they were marked at all, which was generally only for special occasions) by the luxuriousness or embroidery of the fabric or by jewelry, but only occasionally by cut.[31]

Beginning in the seventeenth century (in Holland, at least; in England and France the evolution was later) the composition and function of the European household began to change. The changes came from two directions, increased privacy and decreased use of servants, but from one source: capitalism. As the middle class began to afford private houses, they set their families apart, as social units, from other workers in their immediate vicinity. Domestic privacy as we know it is a product of the bourgeois era, and with it comes the woman-of-the-house as a categorically different kind of laborer than her husband, children, or unmarried friends. With the invention of domesticity in the modern, bourgeois sense comes perhaps the most important division of labor ever, the division of the labor necessary to maintain a household into domestic labor and labor away from home.

In Holland, bourgeois privacy carried attendant interests in freedom, the prizeworthiness of children, and thrift, which worked together against the use of servants or children for labor in the middle-class home.[32] Because Dutch law was favorable to servants ("Even the wealthiest household rarely employed more than three"[33]) and Dutch children were thought to be objects for affection and not discipline,[34] Dutch wives, at least 100 years earlier than wives elsewhere in Europe, had strict authority over their own households and did most of the work necessary to maintain them. This first incarnation of the modern woman-of-the-house was a decision maker, an expert laborer, a caretaker of children, and a hostess to guests. The idealization of this woman as Rybczynski describes her, was most likely from a Vermeer painting,[35] a picture of calm, graciousness, privacy, simplicity, and skill.

During the seventeenth century, the sexual division of labor was correspondingly reflected in women's fashions, and a whole new aesthetic erupted. Not surprisingly, France and Holland were the trendsetters for most of Europe.[36] The distinctions between the sexes were marked now primarily by cut: women's outfits were longer, closer fitting at the waist and wider at the hips, and had lower necklines.

Quite different from its spare, familial counterpart in Holland, the French domestic style of the eighteenth century (the Rococo period) was lush, soft, colorful, and sensuous. But for all its differences from the Dutch bourgeois household, it was still marked foremost by feminine authority. Following the style of Madame de Pompadour at court, Parisian ladies began to redesign their apartments from the multifamily, ill-furnished, professional workspaces of earlier centuries[37] to private dwellings overstuffed with soft, upholstered furniture with boudoirs for themselves and studies for their husbands, who now worked most of their day away from the house, affording their wives time alone to work and to entertain. Thus in the eighteenth century, home fashions became the woman-of-the-house's occupation. Whereas poorer dwellings and rural houses remained scantily furnished and unprivate into the twentieth century, the Parisian apartments professed privacy not just for the family, but within the family, and division of labor not just between domestic and professional labor, but among different domestic duties for household members. This was facilitated by smaller, more numerous rooms fit for new distinct activities.[38]

The eighteenth-century French woman-of-the-house developed an ability to wear many hats: the gracious and worldly advisor; the warm and loving mother; the beautiful, witty, and gracious hostess; the overseer of domestic architecture and interior decoration,[39] the housekeeper when servants were available, or the cleaning woman, cook, and seamstress when they were not. Thus, the legacy of the eighteenth-century French woman is, at least in part, her discerning judgment and authority, but it is also a legacy of overwork and internal conflict.

In England and the United States, division of labor between women and men, and between domestic work and other work, was the slowest to take effect. Throughout the eighteenth century both the running of the household and wage-earning labor were considered the responsibility and pride of both women and men. Oakley quotes a maid's manual from 1743: "None but a foole will take a wife whose bread must be earned solely by his labour, and will contribute nothing towards it herself."[40] In France bourgeois wealth was concentrated in Paris and urban style was the mode, in England and the United States wealth and luxury were spread over the countryside in estates, farms, and plantations. "The pre-industrial rural home," however, "was a center of production, not of consumption. . . . Even in noble house-holds an annual turn-out was preferable to daily chores. . . ."[41] Thus, in eighteenth-century England and the United States, prior to the consumer revolution Campbell takes as his object of study, the private life of grandeur, the private life to admire and copy, was the rural life of agricultural production. Keeping house in eighteenth-century England was apparently the pride and joy of the entire household. Through most of the century (until the development of the drawing room) furniture and interior decor were considered the jurisdiction of the man of the house,[42] and bookkeeping and hiring was as often as not the job of the woman.[43] In fact, according to Norbert Elias, "Marriage . . . of the seventeenth and eighteenth centuries derives its special character from the fact that . . . the dominance of the husband over the wife is broken for the first time. The social power of the wife is almost equal to that of the husband. Social opinion is determined to a high degree by women."[44]

Correspondingly, wives in eighteenth-century England and the United States had considerably more rights in marriage and independence than their counterparts a century earlier or later: they were able to sue their husbands for even threatened assault, they often shared their husband's business and its proceeds, and they were often sole executors of their husband's wills.[45] In addition, the lady of the house had an overall knowledge of every servant's duties and of how each contributed to the running of the house, including household production such as candle making, spinning, and cow milking, as well as the tasks that we now tend to associate with the woman-of-the-house, cooking, cleaning, and mending.[46] Housekeeping was highly skilled labor.

Despite accusations to the contrary, this eighteenth-century British woman-of-the-house remains the ideal for many middle-class men and women in the Unites States struggling to live graciously and well. Fussell remarks on how these faux nostalgic Anglophile ambitions motivate twentieth-century middle-class American catalogue shoppers (although he doesn't mention it, mostly women): "For the middle class with upward longings, the great class totem is 'Mother England,' as one catalog puts it. . . . 'The Kensington Candle Snuffer' . . . will add a touch of gracious English charm to your home."[47] Unsurprisingly, then, during this century the first fashion journals appeared. A flourishing market of relatively autonomous women, together with increased production of clothing and increased dependence on accessories, accelerated the rate of changes in style and of fashion trendsetting by ladies of standing.

This was also the century of increasing similarity between men's civilian and military dress, a slow simplification of the cut of men's clothing as compared with women's, and a generally slower rate of change of style for men relative to women. Men's dress became increasingly simpler, more uniform, and more stable, relative to women's, whose dress became relatively more sensuous, more changeable from year to year, and more exciting and varied visually and texturally, particularly with regard to cut. Women's dress slowly increased in variety of color and fabric, relative to men's, as well. While the sixteenth and seventeenth centuries already had the ruff, the enormous hoopskirt, the tall hair comb, and the overblown collar, the eighteenth century went wild for hats, gloves, feathers, removable wigs, cosmetics—a wealth of accessories and doodads, and increasingly only for women. In addition, over the course of the century stiff, stern, disciplined cuts and fabrics gradually gave way for women to softer, gentler lines, while the texture of men's fabrics tended to remain comparatively coarse and harsh.[48]

Thus, women's dress in Europe in the eighteenth century solidified the developing symbolic distinction between the sexes, paving the way for women's representation of the private retreat, the sensuous rapture, the comforting stability, the escape from the monotonous work of the male world; all these were put forward, alongside and interdependently with other social changes, through dress. Notably, the century saw less marked distinctions than in earlier eras between the dress of the members of different classes or countries or professions. An egalitarian and cosmopolitan standard became the vogue, and techniques of clothing manufacture endeavored to achieve it. But political egalitarianism was accompanied by sexual inegalitarianism, at least in dress. As the ways in which distinctiveness and character could be added to life through clothes decreased, the intensity of the effort along its few remaining avenues apparently had to increase, and the one important reservoir was gender distinction.

Thus in the seventeenth and eighteenth centuries began the dialectic between domestic aesthetic skill and the fashion tactics that seek to undermine it by inculcating vague thinking. With it were born the direct ancestors of the *Feministe*, the Model, the Working Woman, and the Mom. As fashion gained steam over the century, it gave aesthetic realization to both the division of labor between the sexes and the egalitarianism among the classes, playing down the sensible distinctions marking class and emphasizing those that marked sex. Women's clothing marked them, increasingly, for labor in the kitchen and the bedroom, as well as on the town, where men were clothed more and more for the front parlor and the office. Women's work was privatized, men's publicized; women's trivialized, men's made very grave and important.

✳

Family resemblance: The independence, authority, and skill of the industrialized woman-of-the-house (i.e., the housewife) were all undermined during the nineteenth century by the very technology that was supposed to make her life more comfortable and convenient. The nineteenth century became the century of domestic experts, to whose credentials the woman-of-the-house eventually bowed. As sexual division of labor saturated European and U.S. society, the distinction between housework and wage-earning labor was rigidified; men became imprisoned in the factories, in offices (if they were lucky), or on the farm, and women were, at least in word, imprisoned in the house.

The housewife was not, however, despite her interior exile, left alone to care for her home as she saw fit; the plethora of inventions that marked the century invaded the housewife's ever-narrowing realm so that she was not even the ruler of her ignominious kingdom. Law and morality gradually adapted to these new economic roles, distributing legal and moral responsibility for children's upbringing increasingly to the mother, while technologies of public education decreased her influence upon them and the new social roles under industrialization decreased her opportunities to support them.[49] The nineteenth-century housewife retained many of the ideals and traditions of her seventeenth- and eighteenth-century predecessors, but increasingly only as ideals and not as achievable practices; she had far greater responsibilities, but far less opportunity to meet them, than they had.[50]

To review quickly the second of Oakley's stages in "women's work" under industrialization:[51] Between 1841 and 1914 the call for child-labor restrictions was extended to women, because of working men's fear of their competition and because of a growing moral association of women with the home and children. Both the working- and the middle-class housewife of the period often also worked outside of the home, but the mythic association of women with the home, now firmly established, obscured the facts of most women's work outside the home, even to themselves. Ellen Tyler May describes the U.S. version of this situation as "the cultural form of [U.S.] Victorianism. Men usually worked in a separate sphere, away from their homes. Their wives comprised America's first leisure class. . . ."[52] Still, May claims, "[m]ost families with limited resources never experienced the economic autonomy that lay at the center of the . . . domestic ideal. . . . Their wives rarely had the luxury to be full-time moral guardians of the home; they often worked with their children in menial occupations."[53]

Increasingly, in addition, children were thought to be a source of pride and an obligation for the working head of a household who could now, it was presumed, afford to keep children immature longer.[54] The child was increasingly envisioned to be in need of the special attention of a practitioner with special skills. In aristocratic and very wealthy households, servants fulfilled this function. In the tidy, small, frugal middle-class nineteenth- and early-twentieth-century household, however, the housewife took over the job. Servants, with factory jobs available to them, were increasingly difficult for the middle-class house-wife to employ. The middle- and lower-class woman-of-the-house, unfortunately, however, was increasingly depicted as lacking in the skills necessary for the upbringing of children and thus as morally deficient; moral justifications for her unfortunate state flourished. The numerous household manuals, cookbooks, domestic devices, and out-spoken moralists of the era capitalized on her new duties, in the pro-cess convincing her of the presupposition of their sale, that by herself she was inadequate to the numerous household tasks for which she was entirely responsible. In accordance with the ideal advocated at the time, this was depicted as an anomaly rather than the norm, attributed almost across the board to women's increased work away from home.

With the care of the house and children increasingly delegated to a single adult woman, with increasing numbers of these women also working, either unrecognized or derogated, outside the home for pay, and with increasing need for the various new skills required for the new household technologies, the housewife's duties and responsibili-ties grew both more numerous and more specialized. The eighteenth-century French woman's hat wearing became the mode, but without the public fanfare or the possibility of graciousness. The housewife became the child caretaker, the cook, the seamstress, the buyer, and the cleaning woman, among others. These housebound tasks, now divorced except in wealthy homes from the more glamorous and public skills of the hostess, gardener, and decorator, defined the virtue of the nineteenth-century housewife, regardless of her wage-labor, which was discouraged, ignored, and for a period (Oakley's second stage), legally discriminated against. The housewife of Oakley's second stage was turned from a woman of broad capabilities and good judgment into a contracted household technician. The nineteenth-century theorists of domesticity asserted that only as long as a woman stayed at home and "kept up" with the "professional literature" of her "field" (cookbooks, housekeeping manuals, child-development manuals, technical manu-als for new appliances) could she meet the quite new and quite impos-sible ideal of virtue now forced upon her: maintaining a middle-class house and morally leading a middle-class family all by herself.[55]

It is important to note, however, despite the misrepresentation and misguidance by experts that she received, that the nineteenth-century housewife still strove admirably and with some success for quality in home life. She was not the mere dupe of producers, as twentieth-century critics might sometimes depict her, rapt in envy of the aristocracy and the upper class. Although invidious consumption clearly played and continues to play a role in her choices, and although items that were thought to be "aristocratic" did have a growing market among the lower classes,[56] this was not the end of the story. The nineteenth-century middle-class housewife was at least as thrifty and ingenious as she was ambitious.

This was because first and foremost she simply had no way to imitate the rich and aristocratic life fully without a large house and a staff of servants, and "by 1900 . . . more than 90 percent of American families employed no domestics."[57] The distinction of the middle-class woman-of-the-house, then as today, therefore, was that she did all or most of her own housework. The difference between the judgments of such a woman and those of a woman who has servants as to what constitutes a pleasant home should not be underestimated. Second, the nineteenth-century middle-class housewife, despite her wide-eyed awe at what the Jones's had, had in addition a set of middle-class ideals quite inconsonant with, and disdainful of, the lifestyles of the wealthy: simplicity, asceticism, efficiency.[58] These ideals, which Weber recognized at work in the middle-class Protestant sects, mitigated status seeking and directed women's efforts toward skill and competence even as they also emulated leisure, luxury, and pleasurable abandon.[59] Contrary, then, to much of today's mythology about both the viciousness of producers and advertisers and the helplessness of women against their economic force, we can see that a complicated struggle worked its way through the nineteenth century in which women fought, not unsuccessfully, to maintain the integrity of their homes and their own autonomy as household decision makers.

> Although frivolous gadgets would follow—electric carving knives and toothbrushes, for example—the earliest electrical appliances were distinguished by the authentic improvement that they achieved in easing the labor of domestic work. . . . If saving time had been [the] only advantage [of mechanization] it is unlikely that the electric iron and the vacuum cleaner would have become so popular so quickly. Nor was their rapid proliferation [more than one-half of homes with electricity contained a vacuum cleaner after it had been available less than a decade] the result only of marketing. . . .[60]

The housewife of industrialization was still taught by her mother and grandmother how to cook, garden, and sew despite all the factors that colluded against her. Isabella Beeton, writing in 1861, compares her, at least as an ideal, to the commander of an army, a moral authority perfectly well able to enforce her position.[61] Beeton, however, was writing in an effort to maintain for posterity a manual of skills that she felt were already growing rare, skills many of which only fell to the "mistress of the house" decades prior to her writing. Although Beeton's ideal of domestic virtue would not have been applicable even a century before she wrote, she does give an image of the powerful and respectable position still enjoyed by the woman-of-the-house in nineteenth-century middle-class society, as well as of her unquestioned moral surety.

By the time of the Lake Placid Conferences in Home Economics (1899–1908), however there was already growing concern over the housewife's loss of domestic skill and her consequent loss of moral authority and judgment. Marjorie Brown, summarizing the conference in her monumental *Philosophical Studies of Home Economics in the United States*, claims:

> Many household tasks were now being performed through industry; formerly one or both parents had done these tasks with the children thereby providing time for informal education of the children in values, in interpersonal understanding, and in understanding what was done in the home. Now the relatively leisurely pace of life in the home had disappeared except among families of wealth who could afford servants. Middle class housewives were doing their own housework; in poorer families, women often worked in the factories or on the farms leaving little time and energy for home activities.[62]

The Lake Placid representatives differed quite radically about the purpose and efficacy of home economics, but all agreed that home economics was in some sense necessary because women-of-the-house were no longer demonstrably able to win their struggle against industrialization and make happy, pleasant homes. Unfortunately, the home economists and the household experts who wrote manuals tended to model their advice on industry itself.[63] Thus, the methods sought by women's experts to ameliorate the increasingly disturbing situation of the housewife could not help but exacerbate the problem. The women's domestic skill and authority, newly won assets as they were, began to decline under industrialization. Mass-produced household goods; mass-produced manuals, magazines, and advertisements; moralistic crusades; and legal and social changes in her own, her husband's, and her children's work colluded both to keep the woman at home and to usurp her skill and authority there. Increasingly during this time, she was reduced to a mere household worker on the model of industrialized work. Although her debility was recognized, the unrealistic response of the industrialized society merely multiplied her difficulties.

Dressing during the nineteenth century was a greater obligation for the average woman, paralleling her increasing responsibility for domestic aesthetic skills in general. Women became the primary arbiters of taste through their choices of clothes, home decor, and so forth. As women's power over social distinctions and social role apparently increased, it was also more dependent on the whims of the producers and journalists of fashion. Thus, women's social power over the running of homes became intertwined with their economic and aesthetic dependence on mass production. The effect of the increasing mass production of clothes on the development of women's markets is especially clear in the distinction between couture and ready-to-wear, which occurred in 1858 with the first haute couture lines designed by Charles Frederick Worth.

For a decade before, clothing manufacturers had mass-produced clothing. In fact, couture arose out of, and as a contrast to, ready-to-wear lines. Prior to Worth's arrival in Paris, in the Second Empire and before, the fashion designers were women. Under Worth, French tailors (men) became the heads of fashion houses through whose bureaucracies French designs were distributed all over the world. Although there is no doubt that Worth was a design genius, he was also apparently a marketing genius, because couture, of course, was a wholly bourgeois enterprise. Women's jealousies and pettier aspirations were encouraged, while men's clothing allowed for a more functional, more egalitarian, more powerful, and more politically free gloss. Notably, Worth "was the first to stress the liveliness of his creations by employing young girls to wear his models for customers. It has been said that these 'doubles' . . . were chosen for their resemblance to his principle customers; his models were conceived for particular women, and not, as today, for a certain idealized type."[64] Hence, the first couturier originated the tactics of fashion in their early form: role modeling fancy versions of his customers to themselves as something more desirable than what they could achieve by their lonesomes.

Still, as May reminds us, "the ideal for family life in the United States was not invented by government agencies, media moguls, or Madison Avenue tycoons; it was the product of middle-class American aspirations."[65] Middle-class women in this new nineteenth-century fashion climate were subject to fashion production and motivated to put clothes in a position of personal importance in no small part to maintain their power and authority in the home. Yet fashion, despite its increasing importance, increasingly was considered a trivial accomplishment in virtue of its association with women in view of the profound change in women's status over the preceding century. Where eighteenth- and, to a lesser extent, nineteenth-century women's association with the home, with food, and with fashion had been signs of their social power as a leisure class and leaders of taste, after the onslaught of mass production, these same enterprises marked women as consumers, and as consumers, socially unproductive.

During World War I, tremendous pressure was put upon married women to take jobs while their husbands fought. Ernest Turner quotes one advertisement in the British war effort: "When the war is over and your husband or son is asked, 'What did you do in the great War?' is he to hang his head because *you* would not let him go?"[66] After the war, however, women's wage-earning labor was presented as a desperate measure that divided her consciousness irreparably, leading her to ignore her duty as a wife and mother, and signifying a disintegrating society. Thus, when World War I ended and husbands returned to reclaim their jobs, efforts were redoubled to encourage women to stay home.[67] These efforts had some success, but in combination with women's newly won right to vote, women's productive labor eventually won out. "Between 1880 and 1920 women went to work in unprecedented numbers. While the proportion of men in the work force remained fairly stable, the proportion of women rose 50 percent. This increase was not so dramatic among working-class women, for domestic work and factory labor were not new to them. The most striking increase was among middle-class women."[68] By the outbreak of World War II, "27 percent . . . of the labor force was made up of female workers [and the percentage] rose to 39 percent in 1945."[69] The number of middle-class women who work for pay has not decreased since.

Despite the fact that the woman-of-the-house now also worked outside the home, she was still modeled on, and judged by the standard of, what in reality was a fleeting phenomenon of the preceding century: the unpaid woman of leisure who took sole responsibility for the upbringing of children. Oakley cites the sociologist Mirra Komarovsky in describing women's situation during this period and after as "structural ambivalence."[70] Women's work outside the house came over this period to be an unrecognized, yet fully utilized, fact of modern society. The labor force increased and production increased in no small part because of women's contributions; yet society maintaned a whole mythical world of domestic leisure and grace. The woman-of-the-house carried both the economic fact and the moral myth of this society on her back.

Increasingly during this period knock-off schlock, rather than genuinely helpful devices, were sold to the housewife, taking advantage of her genuine desire to meet the domestic ideal with diminishing resources of time and skill. Increasingly, techniques for domestic efficiency and convenience were offered in print, although now more often magazines than manuals, by "experts," leading the woman who wanted to make a nice home away from the lessons handed down by her mother and grandmother and toward new, more "scientific" prescriptions. Increasingly, she found herself faced with a husband asserting his rights to domestic comfort and children led to believe that she owed them special treatment.

The woman-of-the-house towed the line for production both at home and in the factory while others got the honors for their work; she craved companionship and yet was obligated to provide it for those who craved it still worse. The housewife between the wars was characterized, perhaps for the first time, by Komarovsky's "ambivalence," ambivalence between work inside and outside of the house. We might say that during this period she internalized the division of labor initiated in the seventeenth century. Weakened by dependence on the mass production of the goods necessary to sustain her home and without the time to do otherwise, she became the audience for progressively worse junk. The vagueness with which women were characterized between the wars set the tone up to the present day.

Fashion itself has come to epitomize for us the anxious trivia of domesticity. "Fashion is in ceaseless pursuit of things that are about to look familiar and in uneasy flight from things that have just become a bore. Pretending, frenziedly, . . . it sells disgust for previous modes."[71] Men's fashions are very nearly uniform the world over and have changed only minimally from year to year since the end of World War I. The variations on the Western business suit offered up by even the most imaginative designers are infinitesimally minor. Very fine symbolic distinctions are required to mark a man's class through his business suits; neither cut nor color differs much or more than occasionally from suit to suit—even, increasingly, in uniforms proper, which begin to approximate middle-class attire more and more. After World War I, by contrast, women's fashion offered a vast variety. A new boyish look appeared: short hair, low or no-waisted dresses, unaccentuated bustlines and necklines, truly a workaday attire for "modern" women who had worked during the war and did not intend to stop. On the other hand, by the late 1920s a new set of couturiers offered a new "feminine" look, which returned to shapeliness, cut, and length. Now, however, unlike fashion shifts of the past, the two options were retained side by side. Increasingly, as well, designers worked international influences into the new fashions and attached cultural alliances to the "meaning" of an everyday woman's choice of attire. Individual women, as consumers of fashion, now made statements in their attire about their "philosophy" and way of life.

Thus in clothes as well as in social role, women saw themselves more and more as facing a dichotomous choice between "modern," "working," womanhood and "old-fashioned" domestic life. Now we can see, however, that the mass production of clothes was at least partly responsible for backing women into this corner. The fashion trends after World War II built upon this new ability of mass production to offer a plethora of vaguely significant options and to leave women on their own to negotiate this muddle. Increasingly, clothes were a set of complicated-seeming signifying options. Today, the consumer of clothing wends her way through a complex but ultimately meaningless array of symbolic gestures—at various cultures, at various sexuality, at various political opinions, at various class status, and the like—precisely through and because of the negligible actual differences among articles of clothing. A pair of Calvin Klein underpants differs little from a pair of BVDs. A leather bustier like the ones Madonna used to wear differs little from the satin or cotton brassiere older women wear. Status and fashion—indeed, for most, beauty—hinges on the symbolic association with the designer's or the celebrity wearer's name, or the vague connotation of a style from a magazine or MTV. One must memorize the significations to pass the fashion "test," just as one memorizes vocabulary for the SAT. Actually knowing and meaningfully using techniques for the achievement of beauty is decreasingly an option for the postwar fashionplate.

The complicated but silly symbolic associations on which fashion is now based make women's choices about clothes and domestic products, and so their lives, more difficult than those of women of earlier eras or than men's. Women must put more time, more money, more invested concern, more consultation, more restrictions of diet and exercise, and more moral reflection into fashion choices than ever before, in starker distinction than ever before, from men. But this world of fretting about clothes—along with the rest of the landscape of the woman's world, of fretting about food, decoration, relationships, and work—is for all its greater anxiety and greater requisite skill, still marked as a less important, less functional, less social, more private, and therefore more trivial world. Increasingly, she lives alone in it, identifying from a distance with other women in a categorical way instead of living together and sharing choices with her household members or community.

That we have so vigorously maintained the climate of moral ambiguity regarding our attitudes toward women's work in and outside the household that developed almost 200 years ago, that we generally continue to believe that that ambiguity is only three or four decades old, that we are still by and large committed to the belief that domestic labor is trivial and unproductive, and that only work outside the home is socially meaningful, evinces to me Fussell's theory of proletarianization. It is simply the attitude taken by a household that needs to increase its income and needs to delude itself to do it. Writ large, it is an ingenious attitude on all our parts that sustains a fragile market economy by promoting consumerism. It is ingenious because the woman who is torn between responsibilities at work and responsibilities at home is essentially two consumers at once. Like Zeus's decision to split the hermaphrodites in two (as represented in Aristophanes's speech in Plato's *Symposium*), in order to get both more and more vulnerable worshippers, mass production gets more and weaker consumers out of woman's conflicted character. She may not actually have the time to live two lives, but she does so symbolically through her buying trends.

THE MOM

I must note before I begin that today's Mom, the representative character, works outside of the house in addition to her Momdom. That a family household needs two incomes and that if it survives on one it is the Mom's have become mere facts in our representations to ourselves of modern life. Correlatively, the Mom is not a serene woman. Marked foremost by incessant labor and perplexity, the Mom today is a compendium of various low-paying professions (e.g., school nurse, short-order cook, dishwasher, daycare attendant, secretary) primarily subsumed under the job of errand runner. Her jobs tend to be wrongly conceived in her depictions as unskilled labor. Today's Mom is well aware that her various duties require skill, but she is also aware that she is often without the skill and entirely without the time to do them well.

Today's Mom, therefore, more than anything else, is harried. The Mom, likely the head-of-household of these small families, is a working, rushed, confused person, but she still seeks quality. Her role as a representative character is still that of a discriminating judge, a responsible decision maker, and an authority, but at the same time, she is a spacey, harried, conflicted person without help in either her decision making or her labor from anyone in her household. These marks speak to the Mom's lineage as purely middle class. Aristocratic representative Moms are entirely different: they are relatively disassociated from their children and house; the *Feministe* and the Model, by contrast, are what Paul Fussell would call upper and upper-middle class (as opposed to "top-out-of-sight" and "middle");[72] they "earn . . . quite a bit [of their money] . . . from some attractive, if slight, work, without which [they] would feel bored or even ashamed."[73] But the Mom is a middle-class phenomenon, as Fussell describes it. She is "earnest . . . and psychic[ally] insecure . . . and . . . obsessed with doing everything right."[74]

Cavell brings out some of these new Mom's dilemmas in his discussion of the "melodrama of the unknown woman." Charlotte Vale (played by Bette Davis in Irving Rapper's 1942 *Now Voyager*) and Stella Dallas (the eponymous hero of King Vidor's 1937 film played by Barbara Stanwyck) are examples of women's efforts to find recognition and joy, as Cavell states, in the roles of mothers and "to understand why recognition by the man has not happened or has been denied or has become irrelevant,"[75] that is, why that recognition has not been forthcoming from marriage. Whereas the "remarriage comedies," according to Cavell, are studies at least in part of women figuring out how to live happily with particular men to "become and stay friends,"[76] in these melodramas, "the woman's answer to that possibility of friendship is an unreserved No. . . . No to marriage as such . . . (unless it is essential for the benefit, or under the aegis, of a child under her protection). . . ."[77]

Using Cavell's model, we might quite fruitfully turn to a comparison of the characters played by Myrna Loy (Millie), Theresa Wright (Peggy), and Virginia Mayo (Marie) in William Wyler's 1946 *The Best Years of Our Lives* to investigate the evolution of our representative character, the Mom, after World War II. The movie follows three returning veterans (Al, played by Frederic March; Fred, played by Dana Andrews; and Homer, played by Harold Russell) through their period of readjustment to home. The younger two of the main female characters work outside the house, or did work during the war; for all three, their wartime occupations and habits pose a conflict with their happiness when the men come home. For Millie, the mature and worldly mother of an earlier generation, happiness is unquestionably found in the direction of her home and family to which her prior commitments hold fast. She yields the authority she has had over her household during the war and takes a mediator's role for her husband's difficult return to peacetime society. Despite its seeming submission by today's standards, Millie is a rock; she is the picture of serenity throughout the film, despite facing considerable challenges.

Millie's daughter, Peggy, on the other hand, is fighting against a crumbling society. She sees her world as posing a set of moral dilemmas (i.e., whether to steal Fred from his wife, how to freshly invent love and happiness after the war; whether to be a modern woman or an old-fashioned one) and her very interpretation of the world as such is depicted as morally rebellious. She wants to establish in peacetime a new, better world than the one to which Millie holds such strong commitments. In one scene, Peggy defies her parents precisely on the grounds that they "never had any problems," a belief used throughout the movie to characterize how members of the postwar generation view their parents. Early in the movie, for instance, Peggy explains to her father, who is discombobulated when he sees her doing housework, that the war has caused them to lose their maid. In addition to doing the housework, she works in a hospital where, her mother remarks to Al, she "knows more than we ever will."

All the returning veterans are shown attempting to return to work; Fred, with whom Peggy has fallen in love, is depicted as almost unemployable. If the family life Peggy desires is to become a reality, the movie indicates, it will be largely her responsibility to make it so, financially as well as emotionally. The clear moral end for this female character, whatever her reformist ideology, is the household. This is in marked contrast to Marie, Fred's wife and Peggy's rival, who thinks her ne'er-do-well husband is entirely expendable. She prefers her job to life at home, she prefers continued dating to her commitment to her husband, and she flaunts her breadwinning in his face. Marie is the "bad girl" in this picture, and she is the only female character in the movie whose job is depicted in any detail (she works in a nightclub).

Marie's villainy has nothing to do with class distinctions, although she is clearly a low-class dame. Fred's stepmother is of even lower class status than Marie (she and Fred's unemployed, alcoholic father live in a pitiful shack by the railroad tracks), yet Fred's stepmother is characterized completely sympathetically; she is almost a more troubled and haggard version of Millie. Rather, Marie is "low class" because her moral vision, her resolution of the choice between work and family commitments, is skewed. The movie implies that the postwar society will not be well served if the Mom follows Marie; rather, Peggy, despite her intention to break up Fred's marriage, is the hero of the film. Her choice, which is to work invisibly and without appreciation for the sake of a happy home life with a husband she loves, is depicted as the only moral solution for women in the postwar era. There is no going home, the movie seems to say, to the choices of Millie's generation; they are fossils of a happier, morally stable time to which the world cannot return.

Whatever one wants to say about the movie's tacitly advocating women's return to the home, *The Best Years of Our Lives* depicts Millie and Peggy as articulate, educated women with evident domestic skills and a friendly, sympathetic understanding of others. Despite their evident difficulties, even mistakes, in adjusting to the men's homecoming, they are heroic characters. Furthermore, despite their trials and errors, they are represented as knowing what they're doing: Millie and Peggy are depicted together making breakfast, shelling peas, and dancing and drinking with Al and Fred; Millie is pictured conversing with her husband about both important and unimportant family business; Peggy is depicted comforting Fred after a recurring nightmare. Whatever one might say about the value of their attachment to the home, there is nothing mysterious about how they maintain it. Their quest for happiness, and their problems and successes in that quest, appear on the screen for us to see and reflect on.

We find a quite different picture of postwar femininity, one in which domestic knowledge and household happiness are completely obfuscated, only three years after *The Best Years of Our Lives* in Joseph L. Mankiewicz's 1949 *A Letter to Three Wives*. Jeanne Crain, Ann Sothern, and Linda Darnell play three middle-class housewives (Deborah Bishop, Rita Phipps, and Lora May Hollingsway, respectively), each of whom fears her husband has run off with another woman (Addie Ross, who does not appear in the movie but is voiced-over by Celeste Holm). All three struggle with a sense of inadequacy toward their roles, and they each fear that something about her failure to play her part correctly has driven her husband to Addie. Yet where in *The Best Years of Our Lives* Marie actually fails in a determinate way to make her marriage work, in this movie none of the women has done anything depicted by the movie as wrong, none actually loses her husband, nothing is given up by any of them; and Addie, the independent femme fatale, magically goes home empty-handed.

Notably, however, in this movie, two of the three women work outside the home (even Rita, who has children), and the particularities of their jobs are a crucial consideration both morally for them and within the plot of the movie. In addition, their three quite different class backgrounds before marriage contribute to the intended universal message of the film, making them representative of a spectrum of American women. Rita Phipps grew up in the upper-middle-class suburb in which the film is set, Deborah is a farm-girl, and Lora May is from the other side of the tracks. But neither their class backgrounds nor their jobs seem to affect their relationships with their husbands in any way. Neither does their domestic labor have any bearing on the plot: Lora May is never shown doing any household labor; she is usually arguing with someone or other. Deborah, despite her farm upbringing, is never shown working, either in or outside of the home (although the background setting of the movie is some sort of community picnic at which they volunteer, and Deborah tries to make sandwiches at one point). Rita, who is a professional, is shown both hand sewing some last-minute adjustments onto one of Deborah's dresses and getting ready to host a party, but she also has a full-time maid (played impeccably, as always, by Thelma Ritter).

Furthermore, the three characters represent very different marriages with very different motivations on the women's part. Lora May is a hard-bitten gold digger (she went to work in her future husband's department store and succeeded in marrying up), Rita is a delicately bred intellectual (she is a writer for radio and her husband is a teacher), and Deborah is an innocent, old-fashioned farm girl unaccustomed to the country-club set (she met her husband in the Army where she served as a nurse). Lora May and her husband, Porter (played by Paul Douglas), constantly insult each other, even in public; Rita and her husband, George (played by Kirk Douglas), argue over the moral unworthiness of radio and her participation in it; Deborah and her husband, Brad (played by Jeffrey Lynn), seem perfectly happy. Yet none of this provides any insight for any of them into the question of their adequacy as wives and mothers any more than did their class backgrounds.

On account of its efforts at cross-section, the movie depicts all American women as being in this same boat. In all cases, their marriages can be threatened and their characters come under scrutiny by the least intrusion from any attractive other woman. No matter their success in maintaining or acquiring a prosperous life; no matter their resolution to the conflict between work and home; no matter their authority, their grace, their skill, their moral commitments, their treatment of their husbands; in any case whatsoever, this movie implies, a wife's happiness and the American home life on which it depends are continually threatened by completely mysterious enemies (even Addie, remember, does not appear in the movie). The postwar era looks bleak indeed for the household in this film: a continual state of anxiety.[78]

Yet, viola! everything turns out fine. Through apparently some mysterious secret technique known to these wives without their even being conscious of it, all their husbands love them and stay with them. The household maintains its unity and happiness. Postwar Momdom is depicted here as founded on *pure*, empty faith. Although no financial prosperity, no return to peacetime, and no graceful balance between work and home life can return her to a morally meaningful landscape, neither can there be anything to help a woman reason her way to a happy marriage. Women can only fret, this movie indicates, wait to find out what that their fates are, and, because the American marriage is a magic and impenetrable fortress, sigh in relief at their secure happiness.

Here, just four years after the end of the war, the postwar Mom is depicted as entirely out of control of her situation as is the world outside her door. No deliberate choice on her part can have any predictable effect on her happiness or on that of her household; none of her specialized talents, necessary as they are to her life in society, have any bearing on the smooth running of her shared life. The bare institution of marriage, the pure romantic love that motivated her husband's proposal, the prescribed habits of postwar life in the United States— these emerge as the "heroes" of this piece, calling the husbands back to their home life regardless of any particularities of their characters or that of their wives. The very foundation of the modern household— marriage—has become by the time of this movie a mysterious and categorical obligation completely divorced in our social consciousness from any and all of our concrete choices in life.

In these years Americans developed the sense, often attributed to certain kinds of conservatives today and, as we can see, rightly thought nostalgic of the 1950s, that social institutions, devoid of any character other than their traditionalism, hold the family and thus society together. This period consolidates the mythical, artificial, and mysterious senses of *tradition, commitment, faith,* and *love* in which Americans have invested their futures. In the 1950s, we see a generation of Moms whose real ties to the world before the war, whose real skills at caring for their households and their families, whose real union in marriage in a shared conception of the good of their household are emptied of power—seemingly as a matter of pure will. These women did not embrace conveniences and timesaving devices, they merely bought them. Habit, fear, and blind abandonment to the whims of outside forces typifies the 1950s Mom. Although at the end of World War I deliberate political and social efforts were made politically and socially to return the country, and particularly the structure of its households, to "normal," after World War II, a "normal" household was simply baldly asserted. Society insisted on it as a moral principle for an "emotivist" self.[79]

Every life requires many skills and activities of us, and in every life, they sometimes conflict. But the situation of the Mom, by the beginning of the 1950s, posed conflicts that were likely irresolvable even by the most reflective and masterful woman, the consequences of whose continued irresolution were severe: a broken home, an uncontrollable child, a ruined body that depended on its continued beauty for sustenance. These were high prices to pay and ones that could be afforded only by the achievement of a high economic status. The middle-class Mom pitted all her hopes on the eventual success of her husband, because only then could she be relieved of some of her duties, either in the house by servants or by not working. And so, as long as there was a genuine hope of widespread economic prosperity, a hope that continued through the 1950s, women worked and waited. This faith in economic salvation from their suffering allowed the women of this generation to bear their conflicted inner life with relative serenity and grace.[80]

Sadly, their patience allowed them to be run over roughshod by mass production and advertisers such that their judgment, skill, and authority was seriously threatened; this is the generation of Moms who embraced myriad useless household appliances, canned and frozen foods, ready-to-wear clothes, and mass-produced decor; consequently, this is the generation of Moms whose daughters and sons were as often as not not taught how to cook, sew, garden, decorate, or clean. Their daughters' and sons' generation—roughly that of the baby boomers—capture our imagination because it is the first generation who in a fundamental sense does not know how to take care of themselves and who apparently seriously adopted the belief that a good-paying job would do.

Today's Mom defines herself by reference to the 1950s Mom. The conflict between working and homemaking, which as we have seen is a development only three centuries old, has become so entrenched in our social consciousness that it is taken to have the force of a Western tradition. Today's Mom, the representative character, sees this modern kind of housewifery as old-fashioned, even primordial, and she sees herself as either or both simply accepting or simply rebelling against this tradition. She wants to do things differently, to work outside the household and to be proud of her job, to be glamorous, to be high tech, and to be assertive, and yet she has chosen marriage and children, and she feels drawn to the practice of motherhood and believes that the role of the 1950s Mom is the only way to achieve it. Thus, she is depicted as a sort of an unwilling throwback.

But the imaginary tradition of marriage and family into which she is thrown back requires from her both an intensity and a quantity of labor, and a level of skill, that are not humanly possible. In addition, it requires a commitment to ideals upon whose value she has not reflected, which are seemingly unrelated to the work ascribed to the role in which they have put her and to which she finds giving her full allegiance difficult. The Mom is fully conscious of the impossibility of her task, rightly full of complaints about the expectations that she fulfill it and admittedly inadequate to it; yet she tries to succeed at it anyway. One might think that this would make her a contemporary hero, but as in the world of *A Letter to Three Wives*, there are no real heroes in the home anymore. Rather, the Mom is envisioned in the commercials and the sitcoms by both her husband and her children as a well-meaning goofball, a superhuman domestic servant, or a domineering drudge because of her naïve and futile houseworkaholism. The Mom, for them, is either an overtaxed, endearing, slightly annoying necessity, a magical being with secret powers they will never master, or both. Today's Mom has little of the authority, skill, serenity, or taste of her predecessors, even of those of her mother's generation, but she is paradigmatically effortful.

A marked change in her character, from that of *bringing up children* to that of *keeping up with children*; from that of *comforting* her husband to that of *supporting* him; from that of *doing and making* to that of *buying* household necessities, has occurred. The Mom who advertises Playskool or Pampers or Robitussin or Mrs. Paul's is often saying things such as, "I work hard enough, and so I buy . . . ," and "There's so little time to spend with them, I don't want to spend it cleaning. . . ." Cascade's recent dishwashing detergent campaign shows, in one ad, a Mom dressed in a business suit proudly (rather snootily) asserting that she has her children do the dishes, cut with scenes of the kids wreaking havoc, making a royal mess out everything in the kitchen. Cascade, of course, has the secret power to wash the dishes despite her children's irresponsibility and her lack of a clue. In a minivan ad, the Mom is depicted as the chauffeur for several enormous troops of ungrateful and uncontrollably active family members, uncomplainingly taking out and putting in rows of seats and cups of soft drinks. In a sleeping pill ad, the Mom is depicted wracked by nightmarish memories of the preceding day—the plumber harangues her, her children taunt her, her friends insult her—she is exhausted, pained, and demeaned by everything around her, run ragged by the demands upon her life.

But despite the tremendous responsibility, stress, and knowledge required for her executive position in the family, the Mom is apparently unable to teach, distribute, or even streamline her labor, over whose necessity in her family's life she has no control whatsoever, other than as a consumer. The Mom who distributes her labor among household members, as well as the Mom who tries to bring pleasure to their lives, leaves everything to chance or to a product. There's no winning anymore for the Mom who fights to make something of her life as homemaker of which she can be proud. In a recent Ameritech commercial for a second line, the Mom is shown reading a magazine when her kids arrive home from school: apparently relieved that since the second phone line was installed her son and daughter no longer throw tantrums or tear each other apart over competition for the phone, she doesn't seem to notice or mind that her children barely speak to her before running off to their separate rooms to call their friends and play games on the Internet. "Kids," her face says to the camera, "They're incorrigible."

Obviously, this change is interdependent with changes in the representative characters of the American Child, who experienced very startling changes over the same period, and the Husband. They are now depicted in our shared consciousness as entirely at the mercy of their higher and higher high-tech whims. The child cannot tear herself away from her desperate desire for the PlayStation; the husband, from his desperate desire for gadgets and tools. In *Home Improvement*, Tim Taylor is the uncontrollable impulse shopper for tools and car parts. That he buys do-it-yourself tools and is a handyman is immaterial, however, because it is their manly signification rather than their usefulness (which, if it is ever demonstrated, will likely be so by his wife, Jill) in which he invests. Only the Mom still discriminates, and being the sole remaining judge in a failing society is a job she quite understandably both relishes and abhors.

Today's Mom lives in the middle of a daily struggle to maintain a vision of the good and pass it on to her children in the face of innumerable obstacles posed by the tactics of fashion in all its forms. On one front, fashion tactics work to convince her that she does not know how to maintain a household, but she must; on another, that she does not know how to raise her children. Ads for food and other household goods tell her she does not have the time to make dinner or to clean, while ads for cleaning products tell her she lives in a dream world if she thinks her children or husband can be trusted with the dishes. The television news opens whenever possible with a story of neglected or murdered children, whenever possible implicating the Mom. The Mom's choice in this impossible situation, whether she takes the "good girl's" alternative of buying the time saving products advertised for the home or not, is only and always to give up on the hopeless project of actually maintaining a happy household through the free practice and sage application of her skill.

With her attention already distracted by her job outside of the house, all the messages to which she turns for help, whether on the left or on the right, tell her to spend less time in the kitchen, less time changing diapers, less time getting ready to go out, less time with her impossible husband, and on and on; in essence, she is being asked to spend less time at home, where home is depicted as the locus of endless and purely unpleasant chores. In response, say these various marketers, to the Mom's impossible situation trying to maintain a household, nothing could be more desirable than to get her out of it completely. Of course, in most of the ads, this is represented as a perennially unrealized ideal or the consumer potential of the Mom would be used up. "Your life is full of frenzied, headache-producing drudgery; you wish you could relax in a warm bath or go out dancing; we understand, which is about as good as you're going to get; buy this."

The Mom is being pushed away from home, in some instances kicking and screaming; her house and children are being taken away from her by "experts," sometimes in the person of the manufacturers or advertisers of household products, sometimes as social services representatives, sometimes as children's entertainment. The Mom, at her most heroic, is depicted in our social consciousness as she who by her wise choices does battle with these experts to save her household as something that she and its other members autonomously and intimately share. Consequently, as a representative character, she struggles to save the household as perhaps the only remaining place where intimacy and judgment are still practiced. But all the factors at play around her, all today's fashions, work against this effort. The yearning for home, privacy, comfort; for meaningful, fulfilling work; for graceful and skillfully made gestures of love; this longing, for whose satisfaction we have now put almost sole responsibility in the Mom, is increasingly denied her by the hawkers of commodities, who put in its place the seemingly more easily satisfiable longing for a fashionable life.

As long as the Mom maintains her position as a knowledgeable household authority, little can be sold to her. As long as she believes she knows what she's doing, she'll do it herself. Today, however, the Mom's dippy and inexplicable but nonetheless stalwart insistence on making her own domestic aesthetic choices is increasingly expressed only in an informed consumerism, and not in skill, self-reliance, or an authoritative character. Fundamentally, the Mom, as a representative character, is the one who does the family shopping. It is by her choices at the store that her character in our social consciousness is formed and by these choices that U.S. households, now understood merely as the shared space of a nuclear family, are sustained. It is the Mom, as the primary domestic aesthetic judge and so the primary domestic aesthetic consumer, who is our most important figuration of domestic aesthetic skill. Her consumer choices, sadly, might right now have to

suffice as the most important way she is able to teach. This demonstra-
tion of her good judgment is the keynote speech in any workable class
in domestic aesthetic judgment. But to make a good life, the Mom
must retain her good judgment, her domestic aesthetic skill; and the
spacey, confused, slightly ashamed mentality that manufacturers encourage her to adopt, work against her doing so. Such a mentality is
an enabler, however, of advertisers, policy makers, and self-proclaimed
social leaders, whose full satisfaction is ever foiled by privacy and
people's faith in their own judgment.

Consequently, no character is more distasteful to the rest of our
pantheon of representative women characters than the Mom. Her skill
is considered demeaning, her closeness to her family Neanderthal, her
remaining serenity servile, her maternal authority oppressive to her
children. The more her distinct character as a Mom is obliterated, the
better she will get along with the rest of us as a fellow confused
manipulator of mass-produced signs. Today's representative character, the Mom, is engaged in a battle to be a Mom at all; thus, in this
era where we all face challenges to our domestic aesthetic skill, the
Mom marks a paradigmatic case study. Her fate is determinate for us
all.

Therese Carter, interviewed by Studs Terkel in 1972, sums nicely
the struggle in which today's Mom finds herself:

> What? I'm a skilled craftsman myself? I never thought about
> that. . . . Oh, gosh, I've been a housewife for a long time. (Laughs.)
>
> I never thought about what we'd be worth. I've read these
> things in the paper: If you were a tailor or a cook, you'd get so
> much an hour. I think that's a lot of baloney. I think, if you're
> gonna be a mother or a housewife, you should do these things
> because you want to, not because you have to. . . .
>
> Somebody who goes out and works for a living is more
> important than somebody who doesn't. . . . What I do is only
> important to five people. I don't feel like putting a housewife
> down, but everybody has done it for so long. It's sort of the thing
> you do. Deep down, I feel what I'm doing is important. But you
> hate to say it, because what are you? Just a housewife? (Laughs.)
>
> I love being a housewife. Maybe that's why I feel so guilty.
> I shouldn't be happy doing what I'm doing.[81]

Just as her 1950s predecessor was cast into the winds of fate, the
awestruck emblem of a faux-tradition who hoped that whatever she
was doing would hold her life together, today's Mom flails around in
a tizzy, struggling against myriad obstacles to her chosen work and to

her authority to do it. Characterized foremost as the family buyer, the Mom today takes discriminating consumerism as her first obligation, trying to buy products, not a dream life, off the grocery shelves or the clothes rack or the magazine display, and trying to make a shared life in which she and her family can be happy. Despite this shockingly weak position, the Mom today is our most independent, most discriminating, most skillful representative character.

THE WORKING WOMAN

As we have seen, women have always worked, as have men; until recently, both have worked for the sake of supporting their households. There is nothing new about that. To talk about the Working Woman as a representative character, as something distinct from women in general, however, would not have made sense to our preindustrial ancestors. As a character in our social mythology, the Working Woman was born in the last century and has only come to maturity since World War II. She can only be sensibly discussed as the contrast to the false "tradition" of domestic roles, invented and consolidated over the course of industrialization, climaxing in the 1950s. The Working Woman, as a character in our social pantheon, is like the Mom a woman-of-the-house; unlike the Mom, however, she is a recent phenomenon, almost as new to the scene as the *Feministe* and the Model. Yet she is specifically posed as a contrast to the Mom, even when the two characters are instantiated in the same person. At the most basic level, the Mom is distinguished from the Working Woman by her sheer motherhood—the Working Woman, like the Mom, may be single or married, but she does not have any children.

Both the *Feministe* and the Working Woman share an opposition to the "traditional" Mom's role of the 1950s, but the respective natures of their opposition are very different. Where the *Feministe* associates the oppression of women in domestic roles with a whole tradition of domination in Western culture and with men, the Working Woman has no necessary ideological disagreement with the "system," nor necessarily with traditional women's roles posed within it, nor does she depend upon an antagonistic characterization of men. Like the Model, the Working Woman is definitively linked to her job, but unlike the Model, her job has a content independent of her; her job is not an instrument of self-promotion. For the most part, the Working Woman does not oppose the Mom in principle, like the *Feministe* or the Model, but merely in practice. Hence the ability of an individual woman to characterize both and her consequent divided consciousness.

Like the Mom, the end that the Working Woman pursues, whatever its theoretical basis, is that of an ordered, good, personal life. She may still seek a monogamous romantic relationship or even marriage. She may still want children. She definitely still wants a pleasant home and a stable, functioning household. She definitely still finds being attractive, capable, and authoritative important. She retains, like the Mom, a weakening but still perceptible judgment on which her companions at work, like the Mom's family, often begrudgingly depend.

Cavell attends to something like the Working Woman's dilemmas in his discussion of the remarriage comedies of the 1930s and 1940s.[82] Characters such as Tracy in *The Philadelphia Story* and Hildy in *His Girl Friday*, according to Cavell, "struggle . . . for the reciprocity or equality of consciousness between a woman and a man, a study of the conditions under which this . . . is a struggle for mutual freedom. . . . This gives the films of our genre a Utopian cast. They harbor a vision which they know cannot be fully domesticated, inhabited, in the world we know. They are romances."[83] In other words, these movies study women's attempts to live happily (yes, ever after) with a man. They are romances, but less in the eighteenth- and nineteenth-century Gothic style in which Campbell finds the roots of consumerism (although they are that) as in the epic sense—these films are picaresque adventures not unlike the *Odyssey*; they are not, like the "motherly" melodramas and the Mom, about noble sacrifice and authority, but about compromise. The Working Woman, then, is a compromiser, a negotiator, an interlocutor: she seeks worldly happiness, not the transcendent joy of sacrifice. But unlike the gainfully employed heroines of Cavell's remarriage comedies, the Working Woman today has to earn her living.

Today's Working Woman works not so much because she wants to get out from under the thumb of her husband or her father, but because she sees herself as responsible for herself; today, her husband and her father simply cannot promise adequate financial support. She no longer expects to be taken care of, whether she marries or remains single. The modern character of husbands has changed as much as that of children, where the child has become a protected species requiring specialized care, the husband is characterized as a wage-earning lout who can with hope contribute income to the household but cannot be expected to care for himself, to aid in decision making, or to contribute to the maintenance of the home—evidence Ralph Kramden, Homer Simpson, Tim Taylor, or in a more refined style, Frasier and Niles Crane.

Adam Gopnik, in his short story "The Musical Husbands," shows a sensitive understanding of today's husband and his role in relation to the Working Woman:

It's certainly true that the longer they are married the more musical they become. At the same time, they enjoy acting the part of the husband. "She keeps me on a short leash," one will say ruefully to another when he is considering some musical purchase. "Yeah. Me, too," the other musical husband will say. "We made an agreement—one CD a week. But I think this leaves me a loophole for LPs. I'll stick them behind the sofa cushions." They never feel so happily husbandlike, in fact, as when they are buying music in secret.[84]

Given such a situation, the Working Woman today is just a realist. The Working Woman, for whatever reasons, believes that the pure life of the Mom will not be successful in achieving her happiness. Perhaps she thinks the Mom's life is unglamorous; perhaps she is reluctant to depend on someone else's income or skeptical of men's ability to support a household; perhaps, like Therese Carter, she feels that no pride is to be taken in the domestic labor of the Mom. Whatever her reasons, the Working Woman is an unguilty liberal; she's just doing her best to make a happy life for herself, going on about her business. The Working Woman has simply tossed her eggs in another basket than the Mom. Like the Mom, she still seeks the good life, and still, apparently, maintains a not-too-foggy vision of the good by which to seek it. Thus, because the weight of others' maintenance does not rest upon her shoulders as it does on the Mom's, she is freer than the Mom to pursue aesthetic standards; where the Mom is represented overwhelmingly through her responsibilities, the Working Woman is largely represented through her taste.[85]

The Working Woman is, in a sense, the star in the American cast of representative characters. This is because she is the primary market; almost anything sold in this country can—or must, if it is to sell well— be sold to her. The Working Woman in a high-paying, high-profile position takes twice as much responsibility as she needs to; the Working Woman in a low-profile, low-paying position does twice as much work as she is paid for. As such, as hardworking as the Mom, as responsible as the Mom, but with a salary of her own or a corporate budget to distribute, the Working Woman is both the most needy and the most discriminating of our representative characters. She needs the typing paper, the pantyhose, the wool suit, the comfortable desk chair; she will be interested in the face-lift, the hair-care products, the good rental car, the newest copier; yet she will also want the impressive stereo, the designer clothes, the exotic vacation, the best vodka. The Working Woman is laden with needs and desires and with decisions to make about how to satisfy them; she is the ultimate consumer

to whom both the status and the usefulness of commodities are important. The Working Woman today is a consummate decision maker.

One way to interpret the Working Woman, the "other side" of
"competitive success," which Carol Gilligan, agreeing with Georgia
Sassen, takes as evidence of women's "ethics of care," might be that she
takes the happiness of her personal life as the standard of her success
or failure at work.[86] Most of the women Gilligan interviewed in her 1982
In a Different Voice might better be interpreted as bringing domestic
aesthetic judgments to bear at work than as exemplifying an ethic of
responsibility. Take, for instance, Diane: "A part of [my] self-critical
viewpoint [is] saying, 'How am I spending my time and in what sense
am I working?' . . . I am sort of saying to myself constantly, 'Are you
taking care of all the things you think are important, and in what ways
are you wasting those issues?' "[87] Or Leslie, whose self-description is
very clearly in terms of virtue: "I am fairly hard-working [*sic*] and fairly
thorough and fairly responsible, and . . . I am sometimes hesitant about
making decisions. . . . I think maybe that is one of the biggest conflicts
I have had. . . . The other very important aspect of my life is my husband and trying to make his life easier and trying to help him out.[88]

These women, like so many in Gilligan's study, bring to their
work a concern for their characters, as a higher end affected by their
decisions. And by doing so, they offer an example for those around
them (likely men) whose decision making at work is more disassociated from the life in which that work takes place. Margaret Richards,
a real estate broker interviewed by Studs Terkel in 1972 makes the
connection between the domestic aesthetic basis of women's business
judgments and something like Gilligan's "ethics of care": "Being a
Realtor is something I enjoy very much. It probably has to do with
being nosy. The niftiest part is to be in on the ground floor of this
decision-making. . . . By and large, it's the woman who buys the house.
Most men, in my experience, let the wife decide, as long as the price
is right and the schools are okay and he can get to the train."[89]

Yet even as Richards extols the business acumen of women Re-
altors and their better knowledge of household goods, both as salespeople and as house buyers, her judgment of the goods of house
selling and house buying has weakened over the years of her experience into a more bald, "emotivist" position regarding rights to fair
competition without concern for their skill or talents at their work:

> About twenty years ago there were many part time ladies in this
> field. Ladies who had lunch with friends and somebody said,
> "I'm looking for a house." So you found them a house and this
> was your contribution and your workday. This is frowned upon

and no longer condoned. If you're going to hold a Realtor's license, you declare this is your occupation and you're doing nothing else. I think this is good. Men who are supporting their families doing this should not be undermined by the ladies luncheon Realtor.[90]

The journey that Ms. Richards made in her years as a Realtor is the journey that many, many working women are making over the course of their lives and from generation to generation. No amount of presence of mind can successfully combat the unending influx into the Working Woman's life of objects for sale and of people who take their sales as an end in itself, likely including her boss. Like the Mom, the Working Woman's life is an uphill struggle to maintain domestic aesthetic authority against increasingly stiff odds. The coordinated effects of bureaucratic work away from home and the constant intrusions of the tactics of fashion on her every and even most minuscule decision, lead the Working Woman away from the personal concerns that have tended to guide her at work; they accost her judgment.

The Working Woman is truly on the front line of the battle to reason well morally by practicing good domestic aesthetic judgment. Unlike the Mom who hides away at home to gain a moment's peace, the Working Woman has cast herself into the artillery fire of marketing. Without losing her sense of the personal, domestic standard that by her choices she tries to achieve, the Working Woman nonetheless conducts a public life. This accounts for the ubiquity, in the commercials and television shows in which the Working-Woman-who-is-also-a-Mom is the protagonist, of the scene where she first comes home and collapses on the couch or the scene where she gets ready to go out. Most likely, she is not only bombarded with pleas to buy all the objects that can be produced for sale to the woman-earning-her-own-living—clothes, quick-lunch solutions, office equipment, home- and car-security equipment, salon care for hair and nails, office decor and kitschy posters, exercise equipment, convenience foods and appliances, and if she's in a ranking position, also executive gadgets, fancy cars, and corporate credit cards, and if she is in a very high-ranking position, also corporate supplies, such as those sold by Archer Daniels Midland during *This Week with David Brinkley*—she is also badgered to put aside the goal of a good life, in order to keep her job. As a paradigmatic discriminating consumer who nonetheless lives a public life, as an authoritative buyer whose domestic choices do not place her in a position of disrespect like Therese Carter, the tactics of fashion have set their sights first and foremost upon her. She, like the Mom, is both a vanguard and a test case of the domestic aesthetic. If the Working

Woman loses this battle and becomes a domestic aesthetic weakling, judgment will be on the retreat.

If my analysis is correct and if the Working Woman increasingly adopts the language of the tactics of fashion and increasingly follows the lead of the *Feministe* and the Model in emulating promotion for its own sake—or, what is the same thing, emulating the promotion of ill-thought, vague, less satisfying versions of herself, then living a human life will be more difficult for all of us. The Working Woman is in a position both to lead the march to recover good judgment and to speed its demise. The Working Woman, then, who seeks a happy life in the company of good things and people of her choice without retreating from public life or from paid, "productive" labor, stands on the very edge of a coherent culture.

Thus, the Working Woman and the Mom form a "pair" of characters who pull our judgment back to domestic aesthetic issues—to judgments founded in the achievement of a beautiful, good, personal life. Where the *Feministe* and the Model are figures that lead us away from domestic aesthetic judgment, the Mom and the Working Woman, as figures in our social consciousness, are fighting to hold us to it. This is because where the *Feministe* and the Model are essentially promoters or salespeople of a "better" life, the Mom and the Working Woman are essentially decision makers, they are the people the promoters seek to sell these lives to. They are judges, not advocates. The Mom and the Working Woman are not posers, not styles of disorder for others to copy; they are craftspeople of lives. The Mom and the Working Woman are authorities within their home or workplace. They seek a good life for its own sake; pursue the practice of domestic aesthetics as best they can with what they have. They are not promoters of vague and portentous ways that others should want to live. The Working Woman and the Mom are remaining craftspeople in a world of salespeople.

Don't get me wrong: the Working Woman and the Mom are not ideal representative characters. But without the aesthetic vision of happy, shared lives that they as characters pursue, I don't believe we—real people reflecting on the characters available to us for contemplation—can live them. I believe, however, that if this aesthetic vision can ever be realized, it will have to be developed out of the current representative characters of the Mom and the Working Woman, because these characters, unlike the *Feministe* or the Model (or for that matter, the Therapist, the Manager, or the Rich Aesthete), are still represented as seeking good lives instead of promoting vague images.

MOTHERLINESS, FRIENDSHIP, AND CRITICISM

How explicit the coiffures became.
—Wallace Stevens, "The Ordinary Women"

I have tried to give a developmental theory of moral reasoning, a historical analysis of why there are so few occasions for us to make good judgments, and a sympathetic but stern criticism of the products, ads, and representative characters that command our attention as judges today. I hope that the analysis I have wrought shows that the reasons why judgment suffers today in the particular ways that it does are historical and indirect, a contingent combination of well-intentioned missteps that have affected the speed at which judgment tumbles into disuse. I imagine that relatively few of the unfortunate choices that I have traced along the path of modernity have been deliberate actions for which their agents can be held legally responsible or morally blameworthy. As I have argued several times above, then, I believe with Plato's Socrates and Aristotle, that everyone has done what appeared to her to be good. As I've argued, the domestic aesthetic activities that aim agents at pleasant and good lives are very fundamental and hard to eradicate; whereas some of the factors I've cited impede our ability to choose well, it would take a lot worse than them, I think, to make anyone want to choose badly.

I think it is important to repeat this belief. Despite my criticisms it is more consistent with my theory of moral reasoning than its contrary; also, however, the point of criticism is to do better; and there's no way for us to do better if moral reasoning and domestic aesthetic judgment cannot be resuscitated. Despite my criticisms of the "modern age," then, I do not think things today differ categorically from the sort of sophistry or vices of excess and defect criticized by Plato and Aristotle. Nor, consequently, should the way to counter the problems of contemporary culture differ radically in kind from the sort of suggestions made by moral theorists since antiquity. Plato and Aristotle, each in his way, and Kant to a degree, and many other traditional philosophers are perfectly well applicable to the problems we face today. In fact, contemplating the sheer timelessness of the household as a unit of human social organization goes a long way toward beginning one's practice at examining one's life.

Despite this timelessness, however, I would imagine that my focus on the household as the forum for practice in moral reasoning is somewhat untraditional by current standards. I hope that on this account it can lend a fresh and fruitful perspective to traditional moral philosophy, as well as provoke some ideas about practical contemporary avenues for bettering domestic aesthetic practice and moral reasoning. One does not need to reflect very long before one realizes that household chores, relationships, and entertainments are the common stuff of human life. This realization by itself can help immunize consumers against the tactics of fashion and the techniques of vagueness that affront their sensibility from all sides.

Indeed, to give some closure to my running metaphor, and to my frequent references to T.V., reflecting on the timeless, intimately shared settings of good comedy and drama, is worthwhile, especially in the contexts of the television series with which people so often share their daily lives. As Aristotle remarked, tragedy cannot occur "when the parties are indifferent to one another" (*Poetics*, 1453b18). Hour-long dramas and sitcoms on T.V.—surely one of today's more important domestic objects—invariably turn to the household or the workplace, not because their writers are unimaginative, but because this is what moves people to laughter or tears. The interactions of people who live or work together daily is what people want to see—despite their "unimportance," despite its having "been done." Hence the sensationalism in television journalism is always at the same time localism—family tragedies from the stations' home cities are preferred above all else for news ratings. Of course, television news is terrible, but the fact that the shared activity of people who live together is what people perennially want to be entertained by supports my thesis that people use their aesthetic reflections to contemplate how to live their own lives.

Hence the situations of situation comedies, the weekly events—the solving of the crime, the preparation of the trial, the treatment of the illness, even the encounter with the extra terrestrials—in hour-long dramas. "Tragedy," states Aristotle, "is essentially an imitation not of persons but of action and life . . . [because] *the end for which we live is a certain kind of activity*, not a quality" (*Poetics*, 1450b16–20; italics mine). In this way, Aristotle thought, audience members were able to glean the moral content out of tragedy and reflect upon it for relevance to their own carriage through their lives. Similarly, I have based my running metaphor on a conception of a "life" as an activity shared among certain people and objects in a household, toward which each contributes uniquely by her decisions and actions—as author, director, prop and set and stage manager—and from which, as an actor, too, each actively creates her character through her decisions and actions. Cavell makes a similar sort of claim when he discusses the "serial-episode" construction of television shows, including soap operas, and to a lesser extent, talk shows and game shows; in serialization, he claims, especially with the room it leaves for improvisation, "humanity [is] expressed by the power and the readiness to improvise, as much as by the power and the readiness to endure. The issue is how the hero and heroine can survive *this*, this unprecedented precipice; how the authors can get themselves out. . . . This . . . may . . . link . . . serialization with the idea or the fact of the popular."[1] Freud makes a similar point regarding popular literature.

> The less pretentious authors of novels, romances and short stories, . . . nevertheless have the widest and most eager circle of readers of both sexes. . . . One feature above all cannot fail to strike us about the creations of these storywriters: each of them has a hero who is the centre of interest, for whom the writer tries to win our sympathy . . . [or] place under the protection of a special Providence. If, at the end of one chapter of my story, I leave the hero unconscious and bleeding from severe wounds, I am sure to find him at the beginning of the next, being carefully nursed and on the way to recovery. . . . Through this revealing characteristic of invulnerability we can immediately recognize His Majesty the Ego. . . .[2]

It should be clear by now that, far from suggesting a wholesale rejection of television, I am a great advocate of the medium, and at least partly precisely on account of its ordinariness, its continual evasion of the status of "high art." Like the ordinary, repetitious, domestic lives we conduct in our houses and apartments, I believe that we derive candidate notions of the good life from television and learn how to reflect on those notions in part by reflecting on television programs. Thus, in addition to advocating television as the producer of domestic aesthetic exercises, countering the elitist claims against it is important so that viewers can learn and be encouraged to evaluate it critically as they would any other art form—indeed, I would argue, as they should evaluate everything. Critical reflection, in its domestic aesthetic, hence generic, form is the basis of the "examined life," any life other than which, Socrates claims, is not worth living.

Despite the criticisms, then, I take it as certainly true, and probably a very hopeful sign, that television has to all appearances enjoyed an aesthetic recovery in the 1990s. *The Simpsons,* I think it worth saying, is by my judgment one of the finest shows that has ever been on television, using as it does every inch of the medium's possibilities. Two or three other shows from the decade would easily make my top ten list. That cable companies can now regularly offer viewers a vast number of programs from earlier decades allows the medium to become really "literary," inviting viewers to comparatively study and analyze old television shows. There are even commercial campaigns that repay careful attention. It is possible of course, as I argued in part I, for a good domestic aesthetic practitioner with close phenomenological intimacy to benefit from reflection on even the vaguest fashion tactics.

✻

Even if one believes that there has been progress or deterioration over history that significantly affects the human condition, one can still find occasion for moral reflection in both the past and present. If one believes, for instance, that the quality of people's lives in earlier ages was come by through difficulties (e.g., against the plague, in spite of very cold houses, without running water, with fewer legal rights) all the more reason to appreciate the effort their lives required. If one believes that life is easier today, all the more opportunity to live it in an examined way.

As should be obvious from the foregoing, I do not believe that any national or international policy can speak to all the problems I have raised. No matter what sort of policies might be implemented on such a scale, the scale itself works against good judgment. In fact, if we are to do anything about the upsetting situation in which we find ourselves, we must suppose that it is unsystematic, and that particular individual choices on each of our parts, and the particular lives we share with those close to us, are meaningful and important. However objectionable one may find cooptation by capital, any organized or widespread political or consumer "movement" against it will have to use fashion tactics to market itself for backing, and this will dilute its significance.

No matter how much we seem to need mass movements, vast audiences, and widespread support for our endeavors, advocating for certain public policies and against others won't by itself affect the quality of our personal lives. We still cannot avoid the requirement that we live this life, with this body, with this household, with this neighborhood, with this landscape, let it affect however few or many it may. We simply cannot avoid the necessity of making choices and of trying to make a good life through them. Any positive project resulting from my criticisms, then, would have to focus on establishing good practices of moral reasoning on a small interpersonal scale, and so would primarily involve a theory of education. Although I am not prepared to put forward such a theory right now, I can say a couple of things about what it would look like.

The first response to contemporary stresses on judgment, like an actor's first response to a particular play in which she is planning to perform, is to get an idea of her own capabilities as a domestic aesthetic agent. This is what the lintel at Delphi advised Socrates.[3] First, therefore, a domestic aesthetic theory of education would focus on both the analogy and the real relation between crafts, particularly homespun ones, and the development of character in both fiction and real life, asking students to reflect on their own interactions with the objects around the house that they use or enjoy or by which they are irritated. When one buys something that seems fancy, for instance, knowingly unable to use it properly or to repair it, knowing no one personally whom one trusts who does possess these skills, and with no intention of learning them, the product can likely add little to one's life but headache and embarrassment. Such a person will wind up paying a lot of money for less-than-satisfying experiences, and should start reflecting on her interactions with her purchases as she tries to deal with her repetitive disappointments and save her money. As Cavell remarks in defense of the aesthetic evaluation of old movies, "to take an interest in an object is to take an interest in one's experience of the object, so that to examine and defend [it] is to examine and defend interest in my own experience, in the moments and passages of my life I have spent with them."[4] As a straightforward effort toward the examined life, this step in a domestic aesthetic theory of education is Platonic.

Second, such a theory would advocate actually teaching crafts, including skill in art performance and appreciation, thereby demonstrating both goodness in artworks and craftsmanship, and that such work results in real and evaluable objects and experiences. This is quite explicitly Aristotelian. After considering the good and bad aspects of various constitutions and states, Aristotle closes with a discussion of education; in particular, a discussion of education in music. He claims that "there is clearly nothing which we are so much concerned to acquire and to cultivate as the power of forming right judgments, and of taking delight in good dispositions and noble actions" (1340a15–20). Therefore, he argues, we should always teach music, both appreciation and performance, to children. I agree that the most important goal of education, including education in domestic aesthetic practice, is to teach people to "delight in good dispositions and noble actions," that is, to enjoy doing good things well. This should of course include, but not be limited to, participating in a household, a neighborhood, a city, and a state.

Third, by demonstrating that the products of human labor, including human characters and their moral choices, can be evaluated, a domestic aesthetic education would help individuals to put themselves in one another's place, to appreciate (aesthetically, morally, and intellectually) one another's reasons for behaving as they do. This sort of appreciation of character is pathos, the place where the moral and the literary-dramatic notions of *character* and *motivation* come together. That which is pathetic is both shameful and endearing. I believe we can appreciate and better our own and others' less-than-ideal behavior by being both ashamed of it and endeared by it, as we are provoked toward shame and endearment by the characters in comedies and tragedies.

Putting oneself in another person's place by sympathy, rather than, say, by trying to universalize one's maxim of action, I have argued, is an aesthetic exercise rather than a moral obligation. It is to exercise oneself in friendliness by extending one's friendship in the Aristotelian senses of those terms as I discussed them in part I. Aristotle explicitly describes "true" friendship as similar to "the good man's relation to himself" (*NE*, 1166a10), implying that friends, in a sense, do not so much put themselves in one another's place as simply feel themselves to be in one another's place, to "grieve . . . and rejoice . . . [and find] the same thing . . . painful, and . . . the same thing . . . pleasant" by virtue of their true friendship; "for his friend is another self" (*NE*, 1166a25–31). In a similar vein, Aristotle advises that the characters of a tragedy be like the "reality" (*Poetics*, 1454a25), so that audience members can find the characters' choices to be "necessary or probable" (1454a38), or in other words, to be reasonable and sympathetic, something that the audience members might do in the characters' places. It is precisely on this account (i.e., the expectation of familiarity, and hence of the "reality" of the characters to the audience members) that the playwrights, according to Aristotle, "still adhere to the historic names" in tragedy (1451b16). Thus character, according to Aristotle, "reveals the moral purpose of the agents" (1450b8).

My appreciation of the pathos of moral reasoning is Aristotelian, as well as Platonic and Nietzschean, but I also believe it is rather motherly, which is why I argue that the character of the Mom is such a useful representative character for contemporary emulation. By her day-to-day involvement with the business of making domestic aesthetic judgments, the Mom stands to appreciate the foibles of human nature in the most intimate and practical way, with humor and grief, scolding correction and playful teasing. We might well respond to the affront of the art commercial, for instance, as the Mom might respond to one of her children's moral mistakes—say, for instance, to the petty thievery of a candy bar—by appreciating its charm even as she refuses in no uncertain terms to allow it to go on. I believe this is one interpretation that can be offered for Aristotle's claim that the definition of friendship is exemplified by mothers:

> For (1) we define a friend as one who wishes and does what is good, or seems so, for the sake of his friend, or (2) as one who wishes his friend to exist and live, for his sake; which mothers do to their children, and friends do who have come into conflict. And (3) others define him as one who lives with and (4) has the same tastes as another, or (5) one who grieves and rejoices with his friend; and this too is found in mothers most of all. (*NE*, 1166a3–9)

Mothers, according to Aristotle, are the examples of the ability to wish another person well for her sake rather than for one's own, which is the kernel of true friendship, distinguishing it from friendships of mere use or pleasure. Friendship "seems to lie in loving rather than being loved, as is indicated by the delight mothers take in loving; for some mothers hand over their children to be brought up, . . . [and] seem to be satisfied if they see them prospering; and they themselves love their children even if these owing to their ignorance give them nothing of a mother's due" (*NE*, 1159a25–33). In the same breath, Aristotle gives this "motherly" friendship domestic aesthetic overtones, claiming that friends, by definition, live together and share tastes.

It is noteworthy, in addition, that Aristotle makes these remarks even though his ethics, including the books on friendship, are specifically intended for men because, among other things, ethics is a part of politics (*Politics*, 1252a1–7), and the "male is by nature superior, and the female inferior; . . . the one rules, and the other is ruled" (1254b12–15). Yet Aristotle seems to have little difficulty imagining a man identifying with his mother, recognizing in himself, in the quality of his true friendships, something of her. Hence, despite the clearly masculine slant of Aristotle's notion of virtue, he claims, "between man and wife friendship [of virtue, if the parties are good] seems to exist by nature . . . [because human couples] live together not only for the sake of reproduction but also for the various purposes of life" (*NE*, 1162a15–27) without, presumably, abandoning his claim that a friend is an "other self." Thus, the friendly quality of mothers is available to us all, men and women, according to Aristotle, and indeed, whatever his derogatory remarks about the female of the species, must be accessible to some degree by any man wanting to be a true friend in Aristotle's sense.

If Aristotelian true friendship has something of the Mom in it, then there is something of the Mom in his remarks on the question that faces us all: "If one accepts another man as good, and he turns out badly and is seen to do so, must one still love him?" (1165b12–5). A "man who breaks off such a friendship," Aristotle admits, "would seem to be doing nothing strange; for . . . [if one] is unable to save him, [one] gives him up" (NE, 1165a21–4). Yet "if they are capable of being reformed one should rather come to the assistance of their character or their property, inasmuch as this is better and more characteristic of friendship" (1165a18–20). Here, Aristotle reflects in a sense on what to do with our disappointments with our notions of self and of freedom, with mass-produced objects, and with the rhetoric of the shows and the ads that support and sustain them. If we are unable to save them, no one could blame us for talking revolution or for unremitting curmudgeonism. But it is better and more characteristic of friendship to come to their assistance through sympathetic criticism, the upshot, I think, of friendly, if not yet good, domestic aesthetic judgment.

NOTES

INTRODUCTION

1. Kennedy Fraser, *The Fashionable Mind* (Boston: Godine, 1982 ([first published Knopf, 1981]).

2. Richard Buchanan, "Wicked Problems in Design Thinking," in *The Idea of Design*, ed. Victor Margolin and Richard Buchanan (Cambridge, Mass., MIT Press, 1995), pp. 3–20; see also Richard Buchanan, "Rhetoric, Humanism, and Design," in *Discovering Design: Explorations in Design Studies*, ed. Richard Buchanan and Victor Margolin (Chicago, University of Chicago Press, 1995), pp. 23–66.

3. Stanley Cavell, *Pursuits of Happiness: The Hollywood Comedy of Remarriage* (Cambridge, Mass.: Harvard University Press, 1981); *Contesting Tears: The Hollywood Melodrama of the Unknown Woman* (Chicago: University of Chicago Press, 1996).

PART I. THE DOMESTIC AESTHETIC FOUNDATION OF MORAL REASONING

CHAPTER ONE. WHAT IS THE "DOMESTIC AESTHETIC"?

1. See Nancy Sherman, *Making a Necessity of Virtue* (Cambridge, England: Cambridge University Press, 1997), for a well-developed discussion of the issue of moral learning—particularly learning to exercise control over one's actions and emotions—as a point of comparison and contrast between Aristotle and Kant.

2. Readers of early manuscript versions of this book have read me as trying to gloss over a relativist position, in particular a "soft" relativism similar to MacIntyre's. (See Alasdair MacIntyre, *After Virtue*, 2d. ed. [Notre Dame, Ind.: University of Notre Dame Press, 1984].) For the record, I live in deep

uncertainty as to the absolute or relative nature of goodness, but tend when pressed toward a sort of aesthetic/moral realism.

3. This is only one possible reason, chosen to show the effect of geography on phenomenological intimacy.

4. Karl Marx, "Estranged Labor," in *Economic and Philosophic Manuscripts of 1844*, from *The Marx-Engels Reader*, ed. Robert C. Tucker (New York: Norton, 1972), p. 60.

5. Studs Terkel, *Working* (New York: Avon Books, 1974 [1972]).

6. Erik Erikson and Harry Stack Sullivan agree that some measure of success at intimate relationships is necessary to resolve the emotional tension between needs for intimacy and distance, even when the resolution suggests taking a distant stance in some particular situation. (See particularly Erik H. Erikson, *Identity and the Life Cycle* [New York: Norton, 1980 (1959)] pp. 94–103; Harry Stack Sullivan, *The Interpersonal Theory of Psychiatry*, ed. Helen Swick Perry and Mary Ladd Gawel (New York: Norton, 1953) pp. 263–89.) Similarly, then, we may imagine the person with a very weak phenomenological intimacy—deteriorated through its own atrophy—who reasons very poorly not only about the goodness of the objects of experience, but also about which objects warrant consideration of their goodness. This is the kind of person who has a very poor idea what is or is not her moral business or what is or is not morally important.

7. Hypothetical imperatives are, according to Kant, of two possible types. A *technical imperative* is an imperative whose necessity is conditioned by a particular end, such as, "If I want to see the seven o'clock showing of this movie today, I'd better leave the house around six." Kant calls these "rules of skill," which would appear similar to domestic aesthetic reasoning. An *assertorical imperative* is an imperative whose necessity is conditioned by the achievement of happiness, which according to Kant is a natural, although not moral, condition of human life, such as, "If I want to be happy—which I do— I should do the things that make me happy." That these imperatives aim one's action toward happiness also makes them appear similar to domestic aesthetic reasoning. See, for example, Immanuel Kant, *The Metaphysics of Morals*, trans. Mary Gregor (Cambridge, England: Cambridge University Press, 1991), p. 49.

8. Ted Cohen, "Why Beauty Is a Symbol of Morality," in *Essays in Kant's Aesthetics*, ed. Ted Cohen and Paul Guyer (Chicago: University of Chicago Press, 1982), pp. 221–36, esp., 228–34. "Purposefulness without a purpose" is Kant's infamous and puzzling "Third Moment" of the "Analytic of the Beautiful" in his *Critique of Judgment*, trans. James Creed Meredith (Oxford, England: Oxford University Press, 1952 [1928]).

9. Cohen, "Why Beauty Is a Symbol of Morality," p. 223. Cohen is quoting from the translation by J. H. Bernard, 2d ed. (London: Macmillan, 1892; 2d ed. 1914), sect. 8, p. 216.

10. Cohen, "Why Beauty Is a Symbol of Morality," p. 227.

11. This may sound like an implicit advocation on my part of a pragmatic theory of (moral) truth, but it is not to be taken as one. I am not opposed to such a theory, but I am not advancing it. Both Plato and Aristotle, for instance, because of their emphasis on learning and practice, might look like pragmatists if they did not claim that there is a notion of human life and human virtue that is absolutely, universally, excellent—and that on this account is always both more defensible and more successful than any other.

12. Kant's reluctance to include the reflective judgment in his moral theory is evidence of a more general failure in modern ethics, which I delineate in part II.

13. Immanuel Kant, *Grounding for the Metaphysics of Morals*, trans. James Ellington (Indianapolis, Ind.: Hackett, 1981), p. 36.

14. Kant, *Grounding for the Metaphysics of Morals*, pp. 36, 31.

15. "Freud was once asked what he thought a normal person should be able to do well. The questioner probably expected a complicated, a "deep" answer. But Freud simply said, 'Lieben und arbeiten.' " Erikson, *Identity and the Life Cycle*, p. 102.

16. Albert Borgmann, "The Depth of Design," in *Discovering Design: Explorations in Design Studies* (Chicago: University of Chicago Press, 1995), p. 20.

17. Kant, *Critique of Judgment*, no. 17.

18. Freud, for instance, claims that authors often or generally figure themselves as the heroes of their novels, even though they also appear to themselves in every character. Similarly, dreamers and daydreamers, he claims, figure at once both as themselves and as others in their own imaginations. "Creative Writers and Daydreaming," in *Philosophy of Art and Aesthetics from Plato to Wittgenstein*, ed. Frank A. Tillman and Steven M. Cahn (New York: Harper and Row, 1969), pp. 441–49, esp. p. 446. See also *Introductory Lectures in Psychoanalysis*, vol. XX, trans. James Strachey (New York: Norton, 1966 [1920]), and *Three Case Histories*, trans. Philip Rieff (New York: Norton, 1963).

19. For instance, in some of our arguments against the permissibility of suicide, in which we might claim that a person is not free to dispose of herself as she pleases as she is of her property. Similarly, although legally a person does own the "rights" to her life story, the moral repercussions of this are questionable and have been questioned, partly by friends and family members of the protagonists of biographical movies and books, who believe that the life in question is, in a sense, their life, too, and that they should have some say about its use as entertainment.

20. Arguments about abortion, from any position, lose none of their weight on account of this change of terminology, although the debate might presuppose different ground rules. We could still defend terminating a "soul" or a "consciousness," or we could still argue against doing so, with the same vigor as people do currently about terminating a life. I simply reserve the term

life here to describe the playing out of a character—of necessity defined inter-dependently—over time. My guess is that this characterization of a life could change for the better the terms of debate about dilemmas such as abortion, but it is not my intention to pursue such debates here.

21. Thus, I will claim in what follows, when I look at the history of households, that the development of the bourgeois household in the seventeenth century, which allows for more pleasant, less hectic, more private relations, has something to be said for it. This is not to say, however, that there are not other imaginable alternatives. Although the symbolic biological relation of parents and their children may seem more natural and more clearly definable for social purposes than the seemingly more amorphous relations of the household, it is actually much more difficult to define and to work with. Hence, the flabbiness of the Republican concept of family values, so easily, yet equally unclearly, countered by Democrats; hence, as well, the use of the unit of the *household* for real social policy applications such as taxes and the census, which have work to do and cannot be bothered with romanticized visions of familial attachments.

22. This is not to say that there is no such thing as overcrowding or getting in each other's way. We might refer again to our wife who has to cut her hair, or our husband who has to have his stereo, which points to the need to have "one's own space" in order to share a small space longer and better with someone else. Nonetheless, this might not be recognized as uncomfortable, and corrected, were it not for the clarity and nearness of the discomfort of the relationship brought to consciousness through physical intimacy. We can well imagine the members of, say, a farm household sharing lots of space over which to wander and with which to physically separate themselves from one another still coming together for shared meals, work, entertainment, and sleep, both more often and more closely than the average (i.e., their shared large space coexists with a voluntarily shared small space).

23. Clive Dilnot, "The Gift," in *The Idea of Design*, ed. Victor Margolin and Richard Buchanan (Cambridge, Mass.: MIT Press, 1995), pp. 144–55; p. 148. Of course, Dilnot's implication here that the work of some designers today is not at its best, and so may not be experienced as gifts given out of love, or as the media of human relations, will be of interest later on.

24. Dilnot, "The Gift," pp. 146–47.

25. I don't just mean to sound facetious having my man love a woman, and my woman love a house; rather, I think these two images conjure up clearly two ways to love that are familiar to everyone and are more similar than one might think without this juxtaposition. Perhaps, indeed, we are often loved as houses are loved, and perhaps we should want to be.

26. This is also MacIntyre's claim about meaningful rather than usury moral discussion (see MacIntyre, *After Virtue*, e.g., pp. 8–9).

27. In fact, I show later that human beings suffer a new kind of severe humiliation because of the modern turn toward conceptualizing all and only

human beings as ends in themselves. When, for example, one regularly throws in the garbage or destroys the inanimate household objects that one owns, one begins to feel surrounded by cheapness, to feel that one lives in a cheap, disposable environment, and that therefore one is oneself vulgarized, cheapened, by the daily experiences of one's life. Under such circumstances convincing oneself that alone among these objects one is intrinsically valuable is very difficult.

28. Aristotle touches on this as well when he argues that pleasure cannot be the end of human action because we cannot experience pleasure continuously: "... at no time can one find a pleasure whose form will be completed if the pleasure lasts longer... [because] of pleasure the form is complete at any and every time.... [And] all human things are incapable of continuous activity. Therefore pleasure is not continuous" (1174a15–1175a5).

29. See Jean-Paul Sartre, *Being and Nothingness*, trans. Hazel Barnes (New York: Washington Square Press, 1966 [1956]). See also MacIntyre, *After Virtue*, p. 73; MacIntyre discusses Sartre's conception of freedom and social role, p. 32.

30. *Facticity* is Sartre's word for those few things about which the human subject is not free—when she was born, for instance. For Sartre, we are not free not to be free. He puts this in the dramatic metaphor: "This inapprehensible fact of my condition, this inpalpable difference which distinguishes this drama of realization from drama pure and simple is what causes the for-itself, while choosing the meaning of its situation, not to choose its position" Sarte, *Being and Nothingness*, p. 131.

31. I say "at least prima facie" because we can imagine cases in which these would not be irresponsible choices, but admirable ones. As gestures of rebellion, for example, a tenants' rights meeting or a hunger strike, respectively, we might take these to be noble, tragic efforts.

32. Kant, *Critique of Judgment*, no. 17. Cohen also argues that this is analogous to the good will, which is, according to Kant, the only thing good in itself, and so, that which warrants respect as an end in itself. See Cohen, "Why Beauty Is a Symbol of Morality," pp. 231–33.

33. Kant, *Grounding for the Metaphysics of Morals*, p. 38.

34. See e.g., Friedrich Nietzsche, "The Heaviest Burden," *The Gay Science* trans. Walter Kaufmann (New York: Vintage/Random, 1974), no. 341.

35. Witold Rybczynski, *Home: A Short History of an Idea* (New York: Penguin, 1987 [1986]) pp. 51–75.

36. Yvon Thébert, "Private Life and Domestic Architecture in Roman Africa," in vol. 1 of *From Pagan Rome to Byzantium: A History of Private Life*, edited by Paul Veyne, trans. by Arthur Goldhammer; series editors Philippe Ariès and Georges Duby (Cambridge, Mass.: Harvard University Press, Belknap Press, 1987), p. 320.

37. Paul Veyne, "The Roman Empire," in *From Pagan Rome to Byzantium*, vol. 1 of *A History of Private Life*, edited by Paul Veyne, trans. by Arthur Goldhammer, series editors Philippe Ariès and Georges Duby (Cambridge, Mass.: Harvard University Press, Belknap Press, 1987), pp. 5–233; p. 71.

38. Veyne, "The Roman Empire," p. 97.

39. Rybczynski, *Home*, pp. 51–75.

40. Ann Oakley, *Woman's Work* (New York: Random House, Vintage, 1974), pp. 34–59. See also Lewis Mumford, who calls this same period the "paleotechnic phase" of technological history, one rife with social disruption and ills of this sort (*Technics and Civilization* [San Diego, Calif.: Harcourt Brace, 1962 [1934]); Fernand Braudel, *The Structures of Everyday Life*, vol. I of *Civilization and Capitalism 15th–18th Century*, Rev. trans. by Sian Reynolds (New York: Harper and Row, 1979); and Norbert Elias, *The Civilizing Process* (New York: Urizen, 1978) also echo this sentiment.

41. See also Betty Friedan's groundbreaking *The Feminine Mystique* (New York: Norton, 1963) for an analysis of this stage of women's work and its effects on social gender distinctions.

42. "Women are more involved than men in the 'grubby' and dangerous stuff of social existence, giving birth and mourning death, feeding, cooking, disposing of feces, and the like" Michelle Zimbalist Rosaldo and Louise Lamphere, *Woman, Culture and Society* (Stanford, Calif.: Stanford University Press, 1974), p. 31. See also Carol MacCormack and Strathern, *Nature, Culture, and Gender* (New York: Cambridge University Press, 1986 [1980]).

CHAPTER TWO. THAT MORAL REASONING IS DEVELOPED THROUGH THE EXERCISE OF DOMESTIC AESTHETIC SKILL

1. Dilnot, "The Gift," pp. 144–5.

2. See e.g., G. W. Hegel, *Aesthetics: Lectures on Fine Art*, (trans. T. M. Knox (New York: Oxford University Press, 1998 [1975]), Introduction, and Karl Marx, "The Fetishism of Commodities," in *Capital: A Critique of Political Economy*, vol. 1, trans. Samuel Moore and Edward Aveling, ed. Friedrich Engels (New York: International Publishers, 1967).

3. Immanuel Kant, "Analytic of the Subline," in *Critique of Judgment*, trans. James Creed Meredith (Oxford, England: Oxford University Press, 1952 [1928]), no. 45.

4. Kant, "Analytic of the Beautiful," in *Critique of Judgment*, nos. 10–17.

5. As I mentioned in note 6, chapter 1, part of the job of a well-developed judgment is to make decisions about the appropriate moral or physical or phenomenological distance to take in a particular situation; in other words, to make judgments about moral importance. Here, we can see that this is analo-

gous to the decisions a well-trained aesthetic judgment makes about the physical distance appropriate for viewing (or listening to, smelling, etc.) particular objects. Some paintings cannot be rightly appreciated very close up; some domestic aesthetic objects are good to admire in the store, but bad to take home; some of our fellows warrant our admiration, but would be bad to have as close friends, and so forth.

6. As I mentioned in the preceding note 5, some objects are not, in the sense used here, every particular agent's "moral business," and for her to spend undue time reflecting on such objects shows as poor judgment as for her not to reflect on some object that is morally important for her (i.e., her recognition of the moral unimportance of something that is morally unimportant is one of the things that should appear in reflection on it). For example, the yield sign on the access ramp to the freeway must not be placed too near to the freeway itself, nor should the driver on the big road be so dull as to pay prolonged attention to the sign, trying to determine whether it is intended for drivers on the freeway or the ramp.

7. Klaus Krippendorf, "On the Essential Contexts of Arifacts or on the Proposition that 'Design Is Making Sense (of Things),' " in *The Idea of Design*, edited by Victor Margolin and Richard Buchanan (Cambridge, Mass.: MIT Press, 1995), pp. 156–84; p. 166.

8. Victor Papanek, Donald Norman, Klaus Krippendorf, and other design critics whose reflections on bad design will give evidence for some of the arguments in part III all speak to this issue. See Donald A. Norman, *The Psychology of Everyday Things* (New York: Basic Books, 1988); Victor Papanek, *Design for the Real World* (New York: Pantheon Books, 1971); Klaus Krippendorf, "On the Essential Contexts of Artifacts or on the Proposition that 'Design Is Making Sense (of Things)'."

9. See MacIntyre, *After Virtue*, p. 44.

10. Sigmund Freud, "Creative Writers and Daydreaming," in *Philosophy of Art and Aesthetics from Plato to Wittgenstein*, ed. Frank A. Tillman and Steven Cahn (New York: Harper and Row, 1969), p. 443.

11. Freud, "Creative Writers and Daydreaming," p. 446.

12. See e.g., his "Differance," in *Margins of Philosophy*, translated by Alan Bass (Chicago: University of Chicago Press, 1982).

Chapter Three. Platonic and Aristotelian Ethics and the Domestic Aesthetic

1. This is not to say, as has now become a cliché, that "the personal is the political." In fact, I do not believe that the details, or even the broadstrokes, of anyone's personal life particularly belong in the classroom or the campaign literature. Aspects of private life, however, as a universal phenomenon in

which we all have a stake and about which we all have knowledge, ought to be discussed in the classroom, and I bemoan that it rarely is.

2. Consider, for example, Callicles's claim to Socrates in the *Gorgias*, 490d–491a: "By heaven, you literally never stop talking about cobblers and fullers and cooks and doctors, as if we were discussing them." Other important passages occur in the *Meno*, 70a–74b, where the topic is whether virtue can be taught; in the *Symposium*, throughout the discussion of love, effort, and flattery; in the *Protagoras*, 313a–314c, 319b–320b; the *Theaetetus*, 146d–147c; the *Philebus* 55d–58d; the *Lysias*; and the *Apology*. The list could go on and on. All quotes and line citations from Platonic dialogues are taken from *Plato: Complete Works*, ed. John M. Cooper, assoc. ed. D. S. Hutchinson (Indianapolis, Ind.: Hackett, 1997).

3. ". . . If virtue is some sort of knowledge, then clearly, it can be taught." (*Meno*, 86d–87c).

4. See e.g., *Republic*, 596e–598b.

5. For example, "There is in fact no defect or error of any kind in craft, nor is it proper to any craft to seek what is to the advantage of anything but the object of its concern . . ." (*Republic*, 342b).

6. This relation is made particularly explicit in the *Sophist, Republic,* and *Phaedo*.

7. Of course because both cities are "cities of words" in the sense that they appear in a piece of literature, they are in that sense (i.e., at the metalevel) simply fictional cities.

8. "All kinds of hunters and artists" will "swell" this city, says Socrates (373b). Hunting, then, is also represented here as an art in the Platonic senses of "imitation," "routine," and "luxury" (373b). Regardless of the ostensible anthropological facts that hunting and gathering were practiced before agriculture in the historical sense, Plato seems to be asserting the philosophical priority of agriculture over hunting; for example, because agriculture is a better way to achieve satisfaction of our needs for food than is hunting. In addition, hunting exerts a power over life and death that imitates the gods— and this is part of the description of art as mimesis that is given in this and the next book of the *Republic*. Often, indeed, and especially in the ancient world, eating meat served as much a symbolic function as a nutritive one (e.g., in animal sacrifices to the gods).

9. This (i.e., the theme of in vino veritas that Socrates here promotes), links the *Gorgias* to the *Symposium* and to Book II of the *Republic*. The *Symposium*'s relation is obvious: there, the characters do get "besotted," in both senses of that word, except for Socrates, whose tolerance for alcohol is noted. Here in the *Gorgias*, Socrates chooses to match Gorgias's tremendous rhetoric with a drinking song, not unlike the way Alcibiades's raw (and tragic) honesty in the *Symposium* is the match or response to Agathon's (comedic) imitation of Gorgias (the same as in *Gorgias*) in the *Symposium*.

10. Again the theme of flattery and its contrast to judgment or appraisal runs throughout the dialogues. It is especially nicely drawn in the *Symposium*, in which the interlocutors flatter their respective beloveds at the same time they try to impress them by inflating their own merits or flattering themselves. See, for example, Agathon's speech in which he spoofs this aspect of the earlier speeches (195a–199c).

11. Perhaps the clearest statement to this effect occurs at the end of the *Meno*, where Socrates and Meno, having established that there are moral heroes, cannot seem to find any moral teachers. They thus conclude that virtue has been learned, but not necessarily taught, and that these moral heroes can serve as moral guides for those able to learn from their example. Yet another similar claim appears in Book X of the *Republic*, in which Socrates argues that poetry should be readmitted into the good city if it "has any argument to bring forward to prove that it must have a place in a well-governed city" (607c).

12. Taste is requisite in all the virtues of social intercourse as we will see. This is noteworthy because Aristotle claims that "man is a social animal" and that friendliness is the model for Justice and an analogy for constitutions (*Politics*, Book VIII).

13. Injustice, even under this definition, of course may soon come to look like inequality, especially to the abandoned party. Its doing so will depend on what the "traitor" to the friendship has let intervene between them. If it is money, political power, the opinion of the neighbors, or some other "social good" for whose sake the friendship is let go, then the resulting enmity will look a lot like resentment of an inequality.

14. This is not a distinction between different kinds of value, such as the distinction between exchange and use value. Aristotle makes a distinction between exchange and use—that between a tool of a tool and a tool of a craft (see e.g., *Politics*, 1257b25–35)—but it is not a distinction between ownership and use. Ownership for Aristotle is one type of use value.

Part II. Theory, The Domestic Aesthetic, and the Historical Relativity of Moral Reasoning

Chapter Four. Postmodernity and Character

1. Jean-François Lyotard, Appendix: "Answering the Question: "What Is Postmodernism?" trans. by Regis Durand, *The Postmodern Condition: A Report on Knowledge*, trans. Geoff Bennington and Brian Massumi, vol. 10 of *Theory and History of Literature* (Minneapolis: Univeristy of Minnesota Press, 1984), pp. 79–81.

2. Studs Terkel, *Working* (New York: Avon Books, 1974 [1972]), pp. xiii–xxx.

3. The view is surprisingly strongly entrenched among college students, so that even when confronted with hypothetical examples of, say, pathological behavior, many remain firm in their convictions that the sociopath is acting freely and that her freedom is desirable in any circumstance. I have often found students maintaining this strong a valorization of freedom for its own sake.

4. Isaiah Berlin, "Two Concepts of Liberty" (reprinted in Isaiah Berlin, *Four Essays on Liberty* [London: Oxford University Press, 1969]), pp. 118–72.

5. Berlin, "Two Concepts of Liberty," pp. 122, 131.

6. Berlin, "Two Concepts of Liberty," esp. pp. 123–4.

7. Berlin, "Two Concepts of Liberty," esp. pp. 147, 168.

8. Berlin, "Two Concepts of Liberty," p. 161.

9. Berlin, "Two Concepts of Liberty," p. 161.

10. Berlin, "Two Concepts of Liberty," p. 166.

11. Jean-Jacques Rousseau, "On the Social Contract," in *The Basic Political Writings,* trans. by Donald A. Cress (Indianapolis, Ind.: Hackett, 1987), p. 150.

12. Berlin, "Two Concepts of Liberty," p. 148.

13. Berlin, "Two Concepts of Liberty," p. 169.

14. Berlin, "Two Concepts of Liberty," p. 171.

15. Berlin, "Two Concepts of Liberty," p. 171.

16. See the earlier brief discussion of Clive Dilnot, pp. 30–31 and 41.

17. Michel Foucault, *An Introduction,* vol. 1 of *The History of Sexuality* (New York: Vintage, 1980).

18. See especially Michel Foucault, *Madness and Civilization,* trans. Richard Howard (New York: Random House, 1973 [1965]); *The Order of Things* (New York: Random House, 1973 [1966]); and *Discipline and Punish,* trans. Alan Sheridan (New York: Random House, 1979 [1977]).

19. Foucault, *Discipline and Punish,* p. 26.

20. Foucault, *The Order of Things,* p. 34.

21. In fact, infamously, Aristotle claimed that some people's natural circumstances, (e.g., children's and natural slaves') were such that their achievement of something approximating happiness required their mastery by another (see e.g., *Politics,* 1253b15–1255b40).

22. See earlier, pp. 16–18.

23. MacIntyre, *After Virtue* (Notre Dame, Ind.: University of Notre Dame Press, 1984), p. 75.

24. Berlin, "Two Concepts of Liberty," p.146.

25. Kennedy Fraser, "The Fashionable Mind," in *The Fashionable Mind* (The article was originally published in *The New Yorker*, 1976) (Boston: Godine, 1982 [1981]), pp. 145–59; p. 147.

26. MacIntyre, *After Virtue*, pp. 1–5.

27. In part IV I look at several representative characters of interest to me.

28. MacIntyre, *After Virtue*, p. 28.

29. See e.g., MacIntyre, *After Virtue*, chaps. 17–19.

30. Victor Papanek, "The Future Isn't What It Used to Be," reprinted in *The Idea of Design*, edited by Victor Margolin and Richard Buchanan (Cambridge, Mass.: MIT Press, 1995), pp. 56–69; p. 57.

31. Papanek, "The Future Isn't What It Used to Be," p. 57.

32. Fernand Braudel, *The Structures of Everyday Life*, vol. I of *Civilization and Capitalism 15th–18th Century*, trans. by Sian Reynolds (New York: Harper and Row, 1979), p.107.

33. Michel Rouche, "The Early Middle Ages in the West," in *From Pagan Rome to Byzantium*, vol. 1 of *A History of Private Life*, ed. by Paul Veyne, trans. by Arthur Goldhammer, series editors Philippe Ariès and Georges Duby (Cambridge, Mass.: Harvard University Press, Belknap Press, 1987), pp. 411–549; pp. 446–47.

34. Although this sentiment has filtered down into grade school textbooks and PBS television specials, its most thorough advocation in academic literature can probably be said to have been advanced by Theodor Adorno and Max Horkheimer in their *Dialectic of Enlightenment*, trans. John Cumming (New York: Continuum Press, 1972).

35. For instance, Adorno and Horkheimer's interpretation of the *Odyssey* argues along these lines, pp. 43–80.

36. Lewis Mumford, *Technics and Civilization* (San Diego, Calif.: Harcourt Brace Javonovich; Harvest, 1962 [1934]), Introduction.

37. Klaus Krippendorf, "On the Essential Contexts of Artifacts or on the Proposition that 'Design Is Making Sense (of Things),' " in *The Idea of Design*, ed. by Victor Margolin and Richard Buchanan (Cambridge, Mass.: MIT Press, 1995), pp. 179–82.

38. This belief, that because of our society's technological sophistication, our society is objectively better than previous ones, like the belief that freedom is "doing what one pleases," is thoroughly entrenched among young American adults such as one meets in college classes. That person x claimed y before the invention of z technology is often and firmly posited as an unquestionable reason to dismiss claim y for instance.

39. José Ortega Y Gasset, *The Revolt of the Masses* (New York: Norton, 1957 [1932]), p. 58.

40. Mumford, *Technics and Civilization*, p. 28.

41. Daniel Boorstin, *The Discoverers* (New York: Random House, 1983), p. 56.

42. Boorstin, *The Discoverers*, pp. 56–64.

43. Mumford, *Technics and Civilization*, pp. 3–5.

44. Braudel, *The Structures of Everyday Life*, p. 28.

CHAPTER FIVE. ETHICS AND THE LABOR THEORY OF VALUE

1. Michel Foucault, *The Order of Things* (New York: Random House, 1973) [1966]; "Foreword to the English Edition," p. xiv.

2. Foucault, *The Order of Things*, see e.g., pp. xi–xii, 125–65.

3. Alasdair MacIntyre, *After Virtue*, 2nd ed. (Notre Dame, Ind.: University of Notre Dame Press, 1984), p. 63.

4. Colin Campbell, *The Romantic Ethic and the Spirit of Modern Consumerism* (Oxford, England: Blackwell, 1994 [1987]), p. 29.

5. Campbell, *The Romantic Ethic and the Spirit of Modern Consumerism*, p. 40.

6. Campbell, *The Romantic Ethic and the Spirit of Modern Consumerism*, see esp. chap. 9, "The Romantic Ethic," pp. 173–201, esp. pp. 175–9.

7. For MacIntyre's explication of "practices," see chap. 14, esp. pp. 187–192; for his advocacy of goods that are "internal to practices" see the last chapter, esp. pp. 256–7, and the postscript to the 2d ed., esp. pp. 272–7.

8. Campbell calls the last of these "Veblen–esque theories"; see e.g., *The Romantic Ethic and the Spirit of Modern Consumerism*, p. 19.

9. Campbell, *The Romantic Ethic and the Spirit of Modern Consumerism*, p. 23–24.

10. Campbell, *The Romantic Ethic and the Spirit of Modern Consumerism*, p. 25.

11. Campbell, *The Romantic Ethic and the Spirit of Modern Consumerism*, p. 20, 31–34.

12. Foucault, *The Order of Things*, p. xi.

13. This comparison of interpretations of a moral dilemma owes much to Carol Gilligan, particularly her discussion of the different ways boys and girls interpret Kohlberg's "Heinz" Dilemma in chapter 2 of her *In a Different*

Voice (Cambridge, Mass.: Harvard University Press, 1982). Although Gilligan's work remains controversial and is debated on many levels, the intuitive plausibility of her claims about different conceptual schemes in moral reasoning is particularly strong where she represents on the page partial transcripts of boys' and girls' responses to her queries. That the conceptual contrast she attributes to gender differences is similar to the one I am attributing to historical differences in intellectual climate raises questions about the relation between gender and the history of ideas and about possible differences between men's and women's economic and moral choices and economic history, questions which are of interest, for instance, to Campbell (see esp. pp. 171–72, 225–26). Of course, it also raises the question of whether the differences that Gillligan attributes to gender might not be gender differences at all, but instead historical, cultural, or just individual ones.

14. John Stuart Mill, *Utilitarianism*, ed. George Sher (Indianapolis, Ind.: Hackett, 1979), pp. 8–9.

15. Mill, *Utilitarianism*, pp. 8–9:

16. See previous, pp. 19–22.

17. Immanuel Kant, *Grounding for the Metaphysics of Morals*, trans. by James Ellington (Indianapolis, Ind.: Hackett, 1981), p. 30.

18. Kant, *Grounding for the Metaphysics of Morals*, p. 1.

19. Kant, *Grounding for the Metaphysics of Morals*, p. 57.

20. Nancy Sherman, *Making a Necessity of Virtue* (Cambridge, England: Cambridge University Press, 1997), p. 19.

21. For enlightening discussion of these complex issues in Kant, see e.g., Christine Korsgaard, "Kant's Formula of Universal Law," *Pacific Philosophical Quarterly* 66 (1985): 24–47, and "The Right to Lie: Kant on Dealing with Evil," *Philosophy and Public Affairs*, 15 (fall 1986); as well as Cohen and Sherman.

22. According to Kant, not lying is a clear example of a perfect duty. Kant, *Grounding for the Metaphysics of Morals*, p. 32ff.

23. Kant, *Grounding for the Metaphysics of Morals*, p. 60.

24. Kant, *Grounding for the Metaphysics of Morals*, pp. 36, 31.

25. Kant, *Grounding for the Metaphysics of Morals*, p. 17.

26. Kant, *Grounding for the Metaphysics of Morals*, p. 7.

27. Kant, *Grounding for the Metaphysics of Morals*, p. 52.

28. Immanuel Kant, *Grounding for the Metaphysics of Morals*, pp. 16–17.

29. Immanuel Kant, *Critique of Judgment*, trans. James Creed Meredith (New York: Oxford, 1988 [1928]), p. 35.

30. Kant, *Critique of Judgment*, p. 160.

31. Kant, *Grounding for the Metaphysics of Morals*, pp. 8–9.

32. See my pp. 27–28.

33. John Locke, *Two Treatises of Government*, ed. Peter Laslett (Cambridge, England: Cambridge University Press, 1988 [1989]), nos. 25–26.

34. Locke, *Two Treatises of Government*, no. 40.

35. Locke, *Two Treatises of Government*, nos. 40–46.

36. Locke, *Two Treatises of Government*, nos. 26, 31, 51.

37. Locke, *Two Treatises of Government*, no. 31.

38. Locke, *Two Treatises of Government*, nos. 32, 40–45.

39. Locke, *Two Treatises of Government*, 46, 47, 50. I argue in the next chapter that symbolic signification of value tends to promote phemonological distance and degenerate judgment.

40. Locke, *Two Treatises of Government*, nos. 37, 48.

41. Adam Smith, *The Wealth of Nations* (New York: Random House, 1937, Modern Library, 1965), p. 31 (italics mine).

42. Smith, *Wealth of Nations*, p. 31.

43. Smith, *Wealth of Nations*, p. 14.

44. See e.g., Adam Smith, *Theory of the Moral Sentiments*, in *The Essential Adam Smith*, ed. by Robert L. Heilbroner, with the assistance of Laurence J. Malone (New York: Norton, 1986) #I: V.

45. Smith, *Wealth of Nations*, p. 28.

46. Smith, *Wealth of Nations*, p. 33.

47. Smith, *Wealth of Nations*, pp. 35–36.

48. Smith believes that "nominal" price will approximate "real" price over the long haul, but he offers no defense of this position.

49. Smith is certainly concerned about the demoralizing side effects of the pursuit of wealth. He claims, for instance, that the urban situation resulting from increased industrialization can be debilitating for the poor: "The man whose whole life is spent in performing a few simple operations . . . generally becomes as stupid and ignorant as it is possible for a human creature to become" (*Wealth of Nations*, p. 734) and should be addressed politically by improved education. The point here is that exchange relations simply presuppose the equal good judgment of all concerned.

50. Smith, *Wealth of Nations*, p. 6.

51. Smith, *Wealth of Nations*, p. 13.

52. Karl Marx, *Capital: A Critique of Political Economy*, vol. 1, trans. Samuel Moore and Edward Aveling, ed. Friedrich Engels (New York: International Publishers, 1967), p. 39.

53. Marx, *Capital 1*, p. 344.

54. Marx, *Capital 1*, p. 42.

55. Marx, *Capital 1*, p. 47.

56. Karl Marx and Friedrich Engels, *The Manifesto of the Communist Party*, reprinted in entirety, *The Marx-Engels Reader*, ed. by Robert C. Tucker. (New York: Norton, 1972), p. 352.

57. See esp. Marx, *Capital 1*, part II, chap. 4, "The General Formula for Capital," esp. p. 193.

58. Marx, *Capital 1*, pp. 71–6.

59. This is also the starting point for Baudrillard in *For a Critique of the Political Economy of the Sign*, trans. Charles Levin (St. Louis: Telos Press, 1981). I look more closely at linguistic models in the next chapter.

CHAPTER SIX. LANGUAGE AND OPPRESSION; THINKING AND WORKING

1. For my summary of Saussure, I have relied heavily on Benjamin Lee, "Peirce, Frege, Saussure, and Whorf: The Semiotic Mediation of Ontology," in *Semiotic Mediation: Sociological and Cultural Perspectives*, edited by Elizabeth Mertz and Richard J. Parmentier, of the *Language, Thought, and Culture: Advances in the Study of Cognition* series (Orlando, Fla.: Academic Press, 1985), pp. 99–128. See also Roland Barthes, *Elements of Semiology*, trans. Annette Lavers and Colin Smith (New York: Hill and Wang, 1986 [1967]), pp. 13–16.

2. Jean Baudrillard, *For a Critique of the Political Economy of the Sign*, trans. Charles Levin (St. Louis: Telos Press, 1981), pp. 143–63.

3. Baudrillard, *For a Critique of the Political Economy of the Sign*, p. 29.

4. Baudrillard, *For a Critique of the Political Economy of the Sign*, p. 131.

5. Baudrillard, *For a Critique of the Political Economy of the Sign*, p. 68.

6. Roland Barthes, *The Fashion System*, trans. Matthew Ward and Richard Howard (New York: Hill and Wang, 1983).

7. Barthes, *The Fashion System*, pp. 17–8.

8. Barthes, *The Fashion System*, see chap. 3, esp. sects. 7–8.

9. Barthes, *The Fashion System*, pp. 23–24.

10. Barthes, *The Fashion System*, p. 301.

11. Roland Barthes, *Elements of Semiology* (New York: Hill and Wang, 1986 [1967]), p. 10.

12. Alison Lurie, *The Language of Clothes* (New York: Random House, 1981).

13. Lurie, *The Language of Clothes*, pp. x, 3–4.

14. Lurie, *The Language of Clothes*, p. 211.

15. Lurie, *The Language of Clothes*, pp. 215–16.

16. See Braudel, *The Structures of Everyday Life*, vol. I of *Civilization and Capitalism 15th–18th Century*, trans. by Sian Reynolds (New York, Harper and Row, 1979) op. cit., pp. 315–21.

17. Peter Brown, "Late Antiquity," in *From Pagan Rome to Byzantium*, vol. I of *A History of Private Life*, ed. by Paul Veyne, trans. Arthur Goldhammer, series eds. Phillipe Aries and Georges Duby (Cambridge, Mass.: Harvard University Press, 1987), pp. 235–312; p. 273.

18. Pierre Bourdieu, *Distinction: A Social Critique of the Judgment of Taste*, trans. Richard Nice (Cambridge, Mass.: Harvard University Press, 1984).

19. Bourdieu, *Distinction*, p. 1.

20. Bourdieu, *Distinction*, p. 21.

21. Bourdieu, *Distinction*, p. 170.

22. There I compared this reflection to Kant's notion of the reflective judgment. Bourdieu also relates his notion of the habitus to Kant's notion of reflective judgment, indeed the whole book, as the subtitle implies ("A Social Critique of the Judgment of Taste"), is a kind of critical reflection on Kant.

23. Bourdieu, *Distinction*, p. 171ff.

24. Bourdieu, *Distinction*, p. 173.

25. Bourdieu, *Distinction*, p. 173.

26. Bourdieu, *Distinction*, pp. 179, 378.

27. Bourdieu, *Distinction*, p. 466.

28. Bourdieu found two particularly important factors that determined consumer choice: *educational capital* (level of education) and *social origin* (father's occupation); in addition, among people with equal education, social origin was found to be a more important marker of class in matters of "personal taste" (i.e., domestic aesthetic choices), than with regard to the "fine" arts. This indicates, as is intuitively plausible, that domestic aesthetic choices are more steeped in tradition and more bound to one's family origins, to one's childhood economic circumstances, and to one's geographical surroundings than are one's tastes in the fine arts. This means that domestic aesthetic choices "give one away" (i.e., represent one's character) more strongly than choices in the fine arts, which may lend empirical support for the basic claims about the domestic aesthetic that I have put forward.

29. By the claim that the good is "naturally signified" here, I mean only, as I claimed in part I, that it *appears in* good objects. As in that earlier section of the book, I remain neutral regarding the reality of goodness, whether it is a natural, nonnatural, or artificial entity.

30. For my summary of Peirce, I have relied heavily on Lee and on Charles S. Peirce, *Selected Writings*, ed. Philip P. Wiener (New York: Dover, 1958).

31. Peirce, *Selected Writings*, pp. 70–72.

32. Ludwig Wittgenstein, *Philosophical Investigations*, trans. G. E. M. Anscombe (New York: Macmillan, 1953), p. 3e. This Wittgensteinian vision is not so different from the Platonic one we saw in part I, in which certain needs within the city of craft develop into arts, one of which is language.

33. Wittgenstein, *Philosophical Investigations*, p. 8.

PART III. TECHNIQUES OF VAGUENESS

CHAPTER SEVEN. FASHION TACTICS AND
PHENOMENOLOGICAL DISTANCE

1. Kennedy Fraser, in "The Fashionable Mind," *The Fashionable Mind* (New York: Godine, 1985 [1981]), p. 159.

2. Judith Williamson, *Decoding Advertisements* (London: Marion Boyars, 1985 [1978]), pp. 6–7.

3. Op. Cit., Baudrillard, *For a Critique of the Political Economy of the Sign*, trans. Charles Levin (St. Louis: Telos Press, 1981), p. 79.

4. See Thorstein Veblen, *The Theory of the Leisure Class* (New York: Penguin, 1979(1899]). See also my discussion above of Colin Campbell's criticisms of Veblen-esque theories, pp. 123–25.

5. Baudrillard, *For a Critique of the Political Economy of the Sign*, p. 85.

6. Paul Fussell, *Class* (New York: Ballantine, 1984 [1983]).

7. Fussell, *Class*, pp. 200–11.

8. Fussell, *Class*, p. 203 (Fussell quotes Paul Blumberg).

9. Fussell, *Class*, pp. 15–19.

10. See Colin Campbell, *The Romantic Ethic and the Spirit of Modern Consumerism* (Oxford: Blackwell, 1994 [1987]), esp. chaps. 9–10, pp. 173–227.

11. Campbell, *The Romantic Ethic and the Spirit of Modern Consumerism*, pp. 209–10.

12. Campbell, *The Romantic Ethic and the Spirit of Modern Consumerism*, p. 210.

13. Campbell, *The Romantic Ethic and the Spirit of Modern Consumerism*, p. 3.

14. For a very thorough, enlightening, and entertaining investigation of bullshit, see Harry Frankfurt's "On Bullshit," reprinted in *The Importance of What We Care About* (Cambridge, England: Cambridge University Press, 1988).

15. Lorna Opatow, "Marketing Research as a Strategy Tool" in *Packaging Strategy*, edited by Arthur W. Harckham, (Lancaster, Pa.: Technomic Publishing Co., 1989), p. 57.

16. Fussell, *Class*, p. 141.

17. Fussell, *Class*, p. 207. Fussell quotes Ortega from *The Revolt of the Masses*, in my translation (New York: Norton, 1932 [1957]), p. 18.

18. Fussell, *Class*, p. 18.

19. José Ortega Y Gassett, *The Modern Theme*, trans. James Cleugh (New York: Harper Torchbooks, 1961), chap. 2.

20. Ortega, *The Revolt of the Masses* (New York: Norton, 1957 [1932]), chap. 6.

21. Ortega, *The Revolt of the Masses*, p. 83.

22. Ortega, *The Revolt of the Masses*, p. 40, 44.

23. Campbell, *The Romantic Ethic and the Spirit of Modern Consumerism*, pp. 183–87.

24. See Sigmund Freud, "The Uncanny," reprinted in *General Psychological Theory*, edited by Philip Rieff (New York: Macmillan, 1963). Freud's most extended example of the phenomenon is taken from a story by Hoffman.

25. Rybczynski, *Home: A Short History of an Idea* (New York: Penguin, 1987 [1986]), p. 2.

26. Fraser, *The Fashionable Mind*, p. 151.

27. *Vogue*, fall 1997, p. 631. This is not a unique case. The 1997 Fall Fashion Issue of *Elle*, for instance, sporting "500+ pages of style," purports that a "seismic shift" has occurred in fashion. I could not figure out what the editors refer to here because the clothes are so absolutely ordinary. The same issue of American *Vogue* from which I have taken the "four designers" article has several other similar pieces. For instance in the article "The Thrill is Back," the models wear oversized dayglow eye shadow with off-the-rack suits and evening gowns. In earlier drafts of this work, I used earlier issues of fashion magazines; it's all essentially the same.

28. Fraser, "Couture," in *The Fashionable Mind*, p. 132.

29. Ortega, *The Revolt of the Masses*, p. 13.

30. *Harper's* Forum, Paul Tough, moderator, *Harper's*, June 1993, 34–45.

31. Note, for instance, the increase in movie reviews such as MTV's *The Big Picture* (the *E!* network has similar shows, and the end of network news offers short segments) which are indistinguishable from a commercial or a plug on a talk show. Interviews with the actors, plot summaries, and anecdotes about the production are all that the reviewer offers. Compare these, for instance, to the Buena Vista ad campaign, in which the production company

presented a pretend reviewer plugging its movies. The ads were so much like the reviews they imitated that the company had to run a small print warning that they were paid promotions.

32. *Harper's* Forum, p. 34.

33. David Remnick, "Inside-Out Olympics," *The New Yorker*, 5 August 1996, 26–28.

34. Remnick, "Inside–Out Olympics," p. 27

35. Stanley Cavell, "The Fact of Television," reprinted in *Themes Out of School* (San Francisco: North Point Press, 1984), pp. 235–68; p. 254.

36. Cavell, "The Fact of Television," p. 255.

37. I do not mean to imply by this that movies are ill suited to improving domestic aesthetic skill. Like any art object, a movie if it is good can teach its audience something about goodness. The presence of television at home, however, and the repetitive, talky quality of its programming, is especially practical. As I discussed in part I, and will address again, this practical aspect is a requirement of art's contribution to the achievement of virtue, according to Aristotle.

38. Cavell, "The Fact of Television," p. 237.

39. "They've made the questions very relatable," on the new game show *Who Wants to Be a Millionaire*? See the review by Paul Farhi, "Ask a Stupid Question and Millions of People Will Tune Right In," *Washington Post*, 6 January 2000, visited at http://www.msnbc.com/news/354398.asp?cp1=1 24 January, 2000. The apparent renaissance of the game show format is, on my argument, a clear triumph of the use of the television medium to hone skills, and because its success is responsible for this apparent renaissance, *Who Wants to Be a Millionaire* in particular is, to my mind, to be commended.

CHAPTER EIGHT. MASS PRODUCTION, NATIONALIZATION, ADVERTISING, AND VAGUENESS

1. Donald A. Norman, *The Psychology of Everyday Things* (New York: Basic Books, 1988), p. 8.

2. John L. Hess and Karen Hess, *The Taste of America* (New York: Penguin Books, 1977 (1972]), pp. 42–43.

3. August Morello, " 'Discovering Design' Means [Re]-Discovering Users and Projects," in *Discovering Design: Explorations in Design Studies* (Chicago: University of Chicago Press, 1995), pp. 69–76; pp. 71–72.

4. As I made clear in part I, such a perfect craftsperson with every possible characteristic honed to the highest degree is not a human being, but

an ideal for human beings. Plato seems to want to aim us toward an ideal something like this, for instance, particularly in Books I and II of the *Republic*, or in the *Gorgias*, the dialogues I discussed in part I.

5. Lewis Mumford, *Technics and Civilization* (San Diego, Calif.: Harcourt Brace, 1962 [1934]), p. 87.

6. Mumford, *Technics and Civilization*, p. 92.

7. Mumford, *Technics and Civilization*, p. 93.

8. Jane Jacobs, *Cities and the Wealth of Nations: Principles of Economic Life* (New York: Random House, 1984), chap. 12.

9. Jacobs, *Cities and the Wealth of Nations*, p. 221.

10. Papanek, "The Future Isn't What it Used to Be," in *The Idea of Design*, ed. by Victor Margolin and Richard Buchanan (Cambridge, Mass.: MIT Press, 1995), p. 64.

11. Papanek, "The Future Isn't What it Used to Be," pp. 65–66.

12. Jacobs, *Cities and the Wealth of Nations*, p. 183.

13. Jacobs, *Cities and the Wealth of Nations*, p. 185.

14. Richard Buchanan, "Myth and Maturity: Toward a New Order in the Decade of Design," in *The Idea of Design*, edited by Victor Margolin and Richard Buchanan (Cambridge, Mass.: MIT Press, 1995), pp. 75–85; p. 76.

15. Comment by a Florida tomato grower. Hess and Hess, *The Taste of America*, p. 41.

16. Hess and Hess, *The Taste of America*, p. 31.

17. The present commentary applies only to the mass production of food, clothing, and so on, and *not* to importation. In particular I specifically exclude the relatively small-scale production of ingredients and supplies for the benefit of immigrant communities maintaining some semblance of their home culture and for good restaurateurs of the cuisine of countries other than the ones in which they reside or other small businesspeople of this sort.

18. Waverly Root and Richard de Rochemont, *Eating in America: A History* (New York: Morrow, 1976), p. 244.

19. Peter C. Copeland, "Our Ancestors as Fashion Plates," in Lois M. Gurel and Marianne S. Beeson, *Dimensions of Dress and Adornment: A Book of Readings* (Dubuque, Iowa: Hunt Publishing. Co., 1979 [1975]), p. 71.

20. Terkel, *Working*, Introduction.

21. See e.g., *Dallas Morning News*, December 1993.

22. See e.g., Fernand Braudel, *Civilization and Capitalism 15–18th Century*, trans. by Sian Reynolds (New York: Haprer and Row, 1979), vol. I; and Mumford, *Technics and Civilization* (San Diego, Calif.: Harcourt Brace Javonovich,

1962 [1934]). See also Harvey Benham, *Man's Struggle for Food* (Lanham, Md.: University of America Press), chaps. 10–11.

23. Unsurprisingly, it was the women who were usually sent to market, while the men worked the land at home. See Hess and Hess, Jacobs, and Braudel. Hence, prior to the bourgeois era when independent craftsmen owned their own shops in town, and for farmers even afterward, women were often the ones who left home twice a week or even every day.

24. Fussell, *Class* (New York: Ballentine, 1984 [1983]), p. 54.

25. Fussell, *Class*, pp. 181–3.

26. E. S. Turner, *The Shocking History of Advertising* (Middlesex, England: Penguin, 1968 [1952]), pp. 57–58. See also Ivan L. Preston, *The Great American Blowup: Puffery in Advertising and Selling* (Madison: University of Wisconsin Press, 1996 [1975]), esp. chap. 3, "Puffery: Used Because It Works, Legalized Because It Doesn't," pp. 12–26, for a discussion of overblown diction in advertising.

27. Turner, *The Shocking History of Advertising*, pp. 132–3.

28. Turner, *The Shocking History of Advertising*, p. 150.

29. William Leiss, Stephen Kline, and Sut Jhally, *Social Communication in Advertising*, reprinted selection, "Advertising, Consumers, and Culture," in David Crowley and Paul Heyer, *Communication in History* (New York: Longman, 1999), pp. 206–11; p. 207. (Internal cites omitted.)

30. Leiss, Kline, and Jhally, *Social Communication in Advertising*, p. 210.

31. This claim shares some affinity with one of McLuhan's theses, especially about radio, in his landmark, *Understanding Media* , 2d ed. (New York: Signet, 1964), pp. 259–68. McLuhan claims on p. 267, for example, that "radio provides a speed-up of information that also causes acceleration in other media."

32. Turner, *The Shocking History of Advertising*, p. 233.

33. Susan Strasser, *Never Done: A History of American Housework* (New York: Pantheon, 1982), p. 251.

34. See Preston, *The Great American Blowup: Puffery in Advertising and Selling*, p. 97–99, and Judith Williamson, *Decoding Advertisements* (London: Marion Boyars, 1985 [1978], for discussions of advertising and drugs.

35. See Williamson, *Decoding Advertisements*, chap. 6, pp. 138–51, for a discussion of advertising's relation to magic.

36. Arthur W. Harckham, ed. *Packaging Strategy* (Lancaster, Pa.: Technomic Publishing Co., 1989), p. 9.

37. Harckham, *Packaging Strategy*, pp. 93–106, 117–49.

38. Harckham, *Packaging Strategy*, p.102–3.

39. Harckham, *Packaging Strategy,* p. 135.

40. Mona Doyle, "Consumers and the Packaging Renaissance," in Harckham, *Packaging Strategy,* pp. 67–81.

41. Doyle, "Consumers and the Packaging Renaissance," p. 67.

42. Doyle, "Consumers and the Packaging Renaissance," p. 71.

43. Williamson, *Decoding Advertisements,* p. 140.

44. Colin Campbell, *The Roman Ethic and the Spirit of Modern Consumerism* (Oxford: Blackwell, 1994 [1987]), chap. 5, pp. 77–95.

45. Campbell, *The Roman Ethic and the Spirit of Modern Consumerism,* p. 83.

46. Sigmund Freud, "Creative Writers and Daydreaming," *Philosophy of Art and Aesthetics from Plato to Wittgenstein,* ed. by Frank A. Tilman and Steven M. Cahn (New York: Harper and Row, 1969), pp. 441–49.

Part IV. Women, Character, and Domestic Aesthetic Choice

Chapter Nine. Four Representative Women Characters

1. Colin Campbell, *The Roman Ethic and the Spirit of Modern Consumerism* (Oxford: Blackwell, 1994 [1987]), p. 224.

2. Campbell, *The Roman Ethic and the Spirit of Modern Consumerism,* p. 206.

3. Alasdair MacIntyre, *After Virtue,* 2d ed. (Notre Dame, Ind.: University of Notre Dame Press, 1984), p. 263.

4. MacIntyre, *After Virtue,* p. 28.

5. Stanley Cavell, *Contesting Tears: The Hollywood Melodrama of the Unknown Woman* (Chicago: University of Chicago Press, 1996); *Pursuits of Happiness: The Remarriage Comedies of the Thirties* (Cambridge, Mass.: Harvard University Press, 1997 [1981]).

6. See e.g., Cavell, *Pursuits of Happiness,* pp. 30–34.

7. Cavell, *Pursuits of Happiness,* see e.g., pp. 16–19.

8. See e.g., Cavell, *Contesting Tears,* Introduction, pp. 1–20. The "definition" of tragic hero I am using contains aspects of both Nietzsche's analysis in *The Birth of Tragedy* and Aristotle's in *The Poetics.*

9. Cavell, *Contesting Tears,* p. 4.

10. Cavell, *Contesting Tears,* p. 14.

11. Cavell, *Contesting Tears,* p. 6.

12. Again, this vision of women's moral logic owes a debt to Carol Gilligan, not so much in her oft-cited claim that women observe an ethic of "care and responsibility," so much as in her subordinate claims that women envision the moral landscape as a web of relationships that, through their choices, they must negotiate. (See especially *In A Different Voice*, (Cambridge, Mass.: Harvard University Press, 1982), chaps. 2, 3).

13. Cavell, *Contesting Tears*, p. 7.

14. Jean Baudrillard, *For a Critique of the Political Economy of the Sign*, trans. by Charles Levin (St. Louis: Telos Press, 1981), p. 88. The 1997 Lilith rock tour is the piéce de resistance of this, what I call *faux-radical, Feministe* fashion.

15. Some comments on earlier drafts of this work have indicated surprise that I do not seem to deny that some domestic aesthetic labor, under any social conditions, is gross and tedious, and in a sense, slavish. Sure enough, I cannot imagine any recognizably human, good world in which some gross, tedious, slavish, and unpleasant labor doesn't have to be done by somebody, and better—better for the person performing it—that it be done out of recognition of its necessity and its role in a good life, than for financial compensation. It is our lot, as the kinds of creatures with the particular kinds of bodies and minds we have, that a certain slavishness is required in our conduct just to make do. This is one of Hegel's and Nietzsche's most useful contributions to the philosophy of human nature. As I argued in part I, what gives these activities their "free" character is when they are done for the sake of a recognized good end, and so can be chosen by their agent. In the world I might envision, full of people able to make good lives for themselves, I would imagine that this inevitable disgusting labor is so chosen in all the cases it is performed, and that in the best human world, such an arrangement would result in that labor's being fairly evenly distributed between women and men, young and old, and so on. But the wisdom of the choice, not the distribution of the labor, is the primary standard of the goodness of the result.

16. This may be thought evocative of Nietzsche's claim that the great philosophers were "types of decline." Nietzsche, "The Problem of Socrates," *The Twilight of the Idols*, in *The Portable Nietzsche*, translated and edited by Walter Kaufmann (New York: Viking/Penguin, 1954).

17. David Remnick, "Inside Out Olympics," *The New Yorker*, 5 August, 1996, pp. 26–28. As the reader may discern from this and other examples to follow, the 1996 Olympics were a real wellspring of fashion tactics.

18. Remnick, "Inside Out Olympics," p. 27.

19. Despite his sharp criticism of the NBC coverage and of the "femininity" that it espouses, I would claim that Remnick's reading of Gilligan, and to a lesser degree of Çixous, as "Ebersolian" is a misinterpretation.

20. Again, I must note that the Model is only a social type, and it is only as such that she does not need to work. I well recognize that real models work extremely hard, both to do and to maintain their jobs.

21. Campbell, *The Roman Ethic and the Spirit of Modern Consumerism*, p. 225.

22. Kennedy Fraser, "Back to Reality," *The Fashionable Mind* (Boston: Godine, 1982 [1981]), pp. 44–50; p. 45.

23. Opatow, in Harckham, *Packaging Strategy*, pp. 60–1.

24. As earlier, this review is largely dependent on Ann Oakley, *Women's Work* (New York: Random House, 1974), and Witolol Rybczynski, *Home: A Short History of an Idea* (New York, Penguin, 1987 [1986]). See also MacCormack and Strathern, Braudel, Elias, Mumford.

25. Since I have been discussing primarily contemporary Western, particularly American, society, this history focuses on European moms, especially Dutch, French, and English moms.

26. Paul Veyne, "The Roman Empire," in *From Pagan Rome to Byzantium*, vol. 1 of *A History of Private Life*, trans. by Arthur Goldhammer, series eds. Philippe Ariès and Georges Duby (Cambridge, Mass.: Harvard University Press, 1987), p. 72.

27. Veyne, "The Roman Empire," p. 465.

28. Oakley, *Woman's Work*, p. 25.

29. Veyne, "The Roman Empire," p. 462.

30. See Veyne, "The Roman Empire," pp. 453–57.

31. In addition to Braudel, I have relied for this discussion heavily upon François Boucher (with Yvonne Deslanders), *20,000 Years of Fashion* (New York: Abrams, 1987 [1966]); Veyne, "The Roman Empire"; Ellen Tyler May, "Myths and Realities of the American Family," in *Riddles of Identity in Modern Times*, vol. 5 of *The History of Private Life*, edited by Antoine Prost and Gérard Vincent, translated by Arthur Goldhammer (Cambridge, Mass.: Harvard University Press, 1991), pp. 539–92.

32. Rybczynski, *Home*, chap. 3.

33. Rybczynski, *Home*, p. 72.

34. Rybczynski, *Home*, p. 72.

35. Rybczynski, *Home*, chap. 3 gets its impetus from paintings of this style and mentions Vermeer often.

36. Rybczynski, *Home*, chap. 9.

37. Fernand Braudel, *The Structures of Everday Life: Civilization and Capitalism 15th–18th Century*, trans. by Sian Reynolds (New York: Harper and Row, 1979), pp. 277–82.

38. Braudel, *The Structures of Everday Life*, pp. 308–10.

39. Braudel, *The Structures of Everday Life*, pp. 308–10.

40. Oakley, *Woman's Work*, p. 22, quoting "A Present for a Servant Maid."

41. Christina Hardyment, "Introduction," in *The Housekeeping Book 1776–1800*, Susanna Whatney (London: Century Hutchinson, 1987 [1956]), p. 6.

42. Rybczynski, *Home*, chap. 5.

43. Susanna Whatney's notes reflect this; see also Oakley, *Woman's Work*, pp. 27–28.

44. Norbert Elias, *The Civilizing Process* (New York: Urizen, 1978), p. 184.

45. Oakley, *Woman's Work*, pp. 29–30.

46. Susanna Whatney, *The Housekeeping Book*, is particularly enlightening on this.

47. Paul Fussell, *Class* (New York: Ballantine, 1984 [1983]), p. 133.

48. See Boucher, *20,000 Years of Fashion*.

49. Oakley, *Woman's Work*, chap. 3.

50. See Parsons, *The Social Structure of the Family*, quoted in Oakley, p. 32; see also Alan Corbin, "Backstage," in *From the Fires of Revolution to the Great War*, vol. 4 of *The History of Private Life*, edited by Michelle Perrot, translated by Arthur Golhammer (Cambridge, Mass.: Harvard University Press, 1991), pp. 451–672.

51. See my previous discussion, pp. 48–49.

52. May, "Myths and Realities of the American Family," pp. 541–42.

53. May, "Myths and Realities of the American Family," p. 543.

54. Oakley, *Woman's Work*, pp. 25–29; see also Rybczynski, *Home*, chap. 3; Elias, *The Civilizing Process*, pp. 186–89; Braudel, *The Structures of Everyday Life*, pp. 277–88.

55. Oakley, *Home*, chap. 3; see also Rybczynski, *The Civilizing Process*, chap. 7; Elias, *Woman's Work*, chap. 9; May, "Myths and Realities of the American Family."

56. This is essentially Elias's thesis, although he dates the process as far back as the Middle Ages; see also, of course, Fussell's discussion mentioned earlier.

57. Rybczynski, *Home*, p. 155. He cites the 1949 *Encyclopedia Britannica* for the statistic.

58. See May, "Myths and Realities of the American Family," pp. 541–45; see also, Campbell, *The Romantic Ethic and the Spirit of Modern Consumerism*, e.g., pp. 217–27, in which he compares and contrasts the Weberian "Protestant" ethic of work with the "Romantic ethic" of consumption, both of which, he believes, obtain in parallel.

59. See Max Weber, "The Protestant Sects and the Spirit of Capitalism," reprinted in *From Max Weber: Essays in Sociology*, translated and edited by Gerth and Mills (New York: Oxford University Press, 1946).

60. Rybczynski, *Home,* p. 154.

61. Mrs. Isabella Beeton, *The Book of Household Management* (London: S. O. Beeton, 1861; facsimile edition, New York: Farrar, Strauss and Giroux, 1969), pp. 1, 18.

62. Marjorie M. Brown, *Philosophical Studies of Home Economics in the United States: Our Practical-Intellectual Heritage,* vol. 1 (East Lansing: Michigan State University College of Human Ecology, 1985), p. 247.

63. See Rybczynski, *Home,* pp. 167 and chap. 7; see also Oakley, chap. 3; Brown, *Philosophical Studies of Home Economics,* pp. 247–70.

64. Boucher, *20,000 Years of Fashion,* p. 385.

65. May, "Myths and Realities of the American Family," p. 540.

66. E. S. Turner, *The Shocking History of Advertising* (Middlesex, England: Penguin, 1968 [1952]), p. 168.

67. The men had a legal right to the jobs by the Pre-War Practices Act. See Oakley, *Woman's Work,* p. 58. It is noteworthy that here, as in textile manufacture during Oakley's second stage mentioned earlier, men saw themselves competiting with women for jobs.

68. May, "Myths and Realities of the American Family," p. 547; although May focuses on the domestic ideal and the character of family life, her analysis of the economic influences on women's self-characterization parallel's Oakley's analysis of "women's work" during the same time period.

69. Oakley, *Woman's Work,* p. 59; see also May, "Myths and Realities of the American Family."

70. Oakley, *Woman's Work,* pp. 80–81.

71. Kennedy Fraser, "The Secret Power of Dress," *The Fashionable Mind* (Boston: Godine, 1982 [1981]), pp. 7–10; p. 9.

72. Fussell, *Class,* p. 16.

73. Fussell, *Class,* p. 21.

74. Fussell, *Class,* p. 31.

75. Cavell, *Contesting Tears,* p. 30.

76. Cavell, *Contesting Tears,* p. 10.

77. Cavell, *Contesting Tears,* p. 10.

78. In the interpretation that I have given of this movie in class, I have suggested that Celeste Holm's character, Addie, as a figure for communism. With or without the explicit red metaphor, though, the movie poses the relation between husbands and wives in this period as an inescapable, intrahousehold, cold war—one in which one finds spies everywhere.

79. David Halberstam offers a very nice general study of this social mood in his *The Fifties* (New York: Fawcett Columbine, 1993).

80. See Betty Friedan, *The Feminine Mystique,* New York: Norton, 1963 for a sympathetic analysis still pertinent today.

81. Studs Terkel, *Working* (New York: Avon Books, 1974 [1972]), p. 398.

82. Cavell, *Pursuits of Happiness.*

83. Cavell, *Pursuits of Happiness,* pp. 17–18.

84. Adam Gopnik, "The Musical Husbands," *The New Yorker,* 31 August 1992, 38.

85. This is an important theme in some of the movies Cavell discusses in both books; when Stella Dallas, for instance, has a child, she completely abandons her own education in taste that she had undertaken when she married her wealthy husband. In *The Philadelphia Story,* by contrast, Mike's first attraction to Tracy occurs when she demonstrates her good literary taste. In a similar vein, in *A Letter to Three Wives,* Rita, the professional woman—though she is a mother—is constantly the arbiter of taste, the gracious host, and so forth, while Deborah, apparently now supported entirely by her husband, is represented as tasteless and out of fashion.

86. Carol Gilligan, *In A Different Voice* (Cambridge, Mass.: Harvard University Press, 1982), p. 15.

87. Gilligan, *In A Different Voice,* p. 99.

88. Gilligan, *In A Different Voice,* p. 159.

89. Terkel, *Working,* pp. 427, 429.

90. Terkel, *Working,* p. 429.

CONCLUSION. MOTHERLINESS, FRIENDSHIP, AND CRITICISM

1. Cavell, "The Fact of Television," p. 250.

2. Freud, "Creative Writers and Daydreaming," p. 446.

3. ("Know Thyself")

4. Cavell, *Pursuits of Happiness,* p. 7.

BIBLIOGRAPHY

Adorno, Theodor. *Minima Moralia: Reflections from a Damaged Life.* Translated by E. F. N. Jephcott. London: Verso, 1974 (1951).

Aristotle. *Categories.* Translated by E. M. Edghill. In *Works*, edited by Richard McKeon. New York: Random House, 1947, pp. 3–37.

———. *History of Animals.* Translated by D'Arcy Wentworth Thompson. Selections in *Works*, edited by Richard McKeon. New York: Random House, 1947, pp. 631–80.

———. *Metaphysics.* Translated by W. D. Ross. In *Works*, edited by Richard McKeon. New York: Random House, 1947, pp. 681–926.

———. *Nicomachean Ethics.* Translated by W. D. Ross. In *Works*, edited by Richard McKeon. New York: Random House, 1947, pp. 935–1112.

———. *Poetics.* Translated by Ingram Bywater. In *Works*, edited by Richard McKeon. New York: Random House, 1947, pp. 1455–87.

———. *Politics.* Translated by Benjamin Jowett. In *Works*, edited by Richard McKeon. New York: Random House, 1947, pp. 1127–316.

———. *Rhetoric.* Translated by W. Rhys Roberts. In *Works*, edited by Richard McKeon. New York: Random House, 1947, pp. 1325–451.

Atwood, Margaret. "The Female Body." In *The Female Body: Figures, Styles, Speculations*, edited by Laurence Goldstein. Ann Arbor: University of Michigan Press, 1991.

Baudrillard, Jean. *For a Critique of the Political Economy of the Sign.* Translated by Charles Levin. St. Louis: Telos Press, 1981.

Barthes, Roland. *Elements of Semiology.* Translated by Annette Lavers and Colin Smith. New York: Hill and Wang, 1986 (1967).

———. *The Fashion System.* Translated by Matthew Ward and Richard Howard. New York: Hill and Wang, 1983.

Beeton, Mrs. Isabella. *The Book of Household Management.* New York: Farrar, Strauss and Giroux, 1969.

Bellah, Robert N., et al. *Habits of the Heart: Individualism and Commitment in American Life.* Berkeley: University of California Press, 1985.

Benjamin, Walter. *Illuminations.* Translated by Harry Zohn, and edited by Hannah Arendt. New York: Schocken, 1976 (1969).

Berlin, Isaiah. "Two Concepts of Liberty." Reprinted in Isaiah Berlin, *Four Essays on Liberty.* London: Oxford University Press, 1969, pp. 118–72.

Best Years of Our Lives, The. Dir. William Wyler. Samuel Goldwyn, 1946.

Boorstin, Daniel. *The Discoverers.* New York: Random House, 1983.

Borgmann, Albert. "The Depth of Design." In *Discovering Design: Explorations in Design Studies.* Edited by Richard Buchanan and Victor Margolin. Chicago: University of Chicago Press, 1995. pp. 13–22.

Boucher, François. *20,000 Years of Fashion.* New York: Abrams, 1987 (1966).

Bourdieu, Pierre. *Distinction: A Social Critique of the Judgment of Taste.* Translated by Richard Nice. Cambridge, Mass.: Harvard University Press, 1984.

Braudel, Fernand. *The Structures of Everyday Life: Civilization and Capitalism 15th–18th Century.* Translated by Sian Reynolds. New York: Harper and Row, 1979.

Brown, Marjorie M. *Philosophical Studies of Home Economics in the United States: Our Practical-Intellectual Heritage.* Vol. 1. East Lansing: Michigan State University College of Human Ecology, 1985.

Brown, Peter. "Late Antiquity." In *From Pagan Rome to Byzantium,* vol. 1 of *A History of Private Life.* Translated by Arthur Goldhammer. Series eds. Philippe Ariès and Georges Duby. Cambridge: Mass.: Harvard University Press, Belknap Press, 1987, pp. 235–312.

Buchanan, Richard. "Myth and Maturity: Toward a New Order in the Decade of Design." In *The Idea of Design,* edited by Victor Margolin and Richard Buchanan. Cambridge, Mass.: MIT Press, 1995, pp. 75–85.

———. "Wicked Problems in Design Thinking." In *The Idea of Design,* edited by Victor Margolin and Richard Buchanan,. Cambridge, Mass.: MIT Press, 1995, pp. 3–20.

———. "Rhetoric, Humanism, and Design." In *Discovering Design: Explorations in Design Studies,* edited by Richard Buchanan and Victor Margolin. Chicago: University of Chicago Press, 1995, pp. 23–66.

Burke, James. *The Day the Universe Changed.* Boston: Little, Brown, 1995 (1985).

Campbell, Colin. *The Romantic Ethic and the Spirit of Modern Consumerism.* Oxford, England: Blackwell, 1994 (1987).

Cavell, Stanley. *Contesting Tears: The Hollywood Melodrama of the Unknown Woman*. Chicago: University of Chicago Press, 1996.

———. "The Fact of Television." Reprinted in *Themes Out of School*. San Francisco, Calif.: North Point Press, 1984, pp. 235–68.

———. *Pursuits of Happiness: The Hollywood Comedy of Remarriage*. Cambridge, Mass.: Harvard University Press, 1981 (1997).

Cohen, Ted. "Why Beauty Is a Symbol of Morality." In *Essays in Kant's Aesthetics*, edited by Ted Cohen and Paul Guyer. Chicago: University of Chicago Press, 1982, pp. 221–36.

Copeland, Peter C. "Our Ancestors as Fashion Plates." In *Dimensions of Dress and Adornment: A Book of Readings*, edited by Lois M. Gurel and Marianne S. Beeson. Dubuque, Iowa: Hunt Publishing Co., 1979 (1975).

Corbin, Alain. "Backstage." In *The History of Private Life*. Vol. 4, *From the Fires of Revolution to the Great War*, edited by Michelle Perrot, translated by Arthur Goldhammer, series eds. Philippe Ariès and Georges Duby. Cambridge, Mass.: Harvard University Press, 1991, pp. 451–672.

Cowan, Ruth Schwartz. *More Work for Mother*. New York: Basic Books, 1983.

Dallas Morning News, December 1993.

Deleuze, Gilles, and Felix Guattari. "Rhizome." In *On the Line*. New York: Semiotext(e), 1983.

Derrida, Jacques. *Margins of Philosophy*. Translated by Alan Bass. Chicago: Univeristy of Chicago Press, 1982.

Dilnot, Clive. "The Gift." In *The Idea of Design*, edited by Victor Margolin and Richard Buchanan. Cambridge, Mass.: MIT Press, 1995, pp. 144–55.

Doyle, Mona. "Consumers and the Packaging Renaissance." In Arthur W. Harckham, *Packaging Strategy*. Lancaster, Penn.: Technomic Publishing Co., 1989, pp. 67–81.

Elias, Norbert. *The Civilizing Process*. New York: Urizen, 1978.

Erikson, Erik H. *Identity and the Life Cycle*. New York: Norton, 1980 (1959).

Engels, Friedrich. *The Origin of the Family: Private Property and the State*. Chicago: Charles A. Kerr & Co., 1902.

Farhi, Paul. "Ask a Stupid Question and Millions of People Will Tune Right In." *Washington Post*. (6 January, 2000). Visited at http://www.msnbc.com/news/354398.asp?cp1=1. 24 January, 2000.

Flaubert, Gustave. *Madame Bovary*. Translated by Alan Russell. New York: Penguin, 1950.

Foucault, Michel. *Discipline and Punish*. Translated by Alan Sheridan. New York: Random House, 1979 (1977).

————. *The History of Sexuality.* Vol. 1, *An Introduction.* New York: Vintage, 1980.

————. *Madness and Civilization.* Translated by Richard Howard. New York: Random House, 1973 (1965).

————. *The Order of Things.* New York: Random House, 1973 (1966).

Frankfurt, Harry. "On Bullshit." In *The Importance of What We Care About.* Cambridge, England: Cambridge University Press, 1988.

Fraser, Kennedy. *The Fashionable Mind.* Boston: Godine, 1982; Knopf, 1981.

Freud, Sigmund. *Beyond the Pleasure Principle.* Translated by James Strachey. New York: Norton, 1961.

————. *Civilization and Its Discontents.* Translated by Joan Riviere. New York: Doubleday, 1958.

————. "Creative Writers and Daydreaming." In *Philosophy of Art and Aesthetics from Plato to Wittgenstein,* edited by Frank A. Tillman and Steven M. Cahn. New York: Harper and Row, 1969, pp. 441–49.

————. *General Psychological Theory.* Edited by Philip Rieff. New York: Macmillan, 1963.

————. *Introductory Lectures in Psychoanalysis.* Translated by James Strachey. New York: Norton, 1966 (1920).

————. *Three Case Histories.* Translated by Philip Rieff. New York: Norton, 1963.

————. "The Uncanny." *General Psychological Theory.* Edited by Philip Rieff. New York: Macmillan, 1963.

Friedan, Betty. *The Feminine Mystique.* New York: Norton, 1963.

Fussell, Paul. *Class.* New York: Ballantine, 1984 (1983).

Gilligan, Carol. *In a Different Voice.* Cambridge, Mass.: Harvard University Press, 1982.

Goldstein, Laurence, ed. *The Female Body: Figures, Styles, Speculations.* Ann Arbor: University Michigan Press, 1991.

Gopnik, Adam. "The Musical Husbands." *The New Yorker,* 31 August 1992.

Grazia, Sebastian de. *Of Time, Work and Leisure.* New York: Vintage, 1990 (1962).

Gurel, Lois M., and Marianne S. Beeson. *Dimensions of Dress and Adornment: A Book of Readings.* Dubuque, Iowa: Hunt Publishing Co., 1979 (1975).

Halberstam, David. *The Fifties.* New York: Fawcett Columbine, 1993.

Harckham, Arthur W. PDC, ed. *Packaging Strategy.* Lancaster, Pa.: Technomic Publishing Co., 1989.

Harper's, June 1993.

Harper's Bazaar, March 1990.

Hegel, G. W. F. *Hegel's Aesthetics: Lectures on Fine Art*. Translated by T. M. Knox. New York: Oxford University Press, 1998 (1975).

———. *Phenomenology of Spirit*. Translated by A. V. Miller. Oxford, England: Oxford University Press, 1977.

Hess, John L., and Karen Hess. *The Taste of America*. New York: Penguin Books, 1977 (1972).

Hollander, Anne. *Seeing through Clothes*. New York: Viking, 1978.

His Girl Friday. Dir. by Howard Hawks. Columbia. 1940.

Homer, *The Odyssey*. Translated by Robert Fagles. New York: Viking/Penguin, 1996.

Horkheimer, Max, and Theodor W. Adorno. *Dialectic of Enlightenment*. Translated by Herder and Herder, Inc. New York: Continuum, 1972.

Innis, Harold. Selection from *Empire and Communications*, excerpted as "Media in Ancient Empires" in *Communication in History*. Edited by David Crowley and Paul Heyer. New York: Addison Wesley Longman, 1999, pp. 23–30.

Irigaray, Luce. *This Sex which Is Not One*. Translated by Catherine Porter. Ithaca: Cornell University Press, 1985.

Jacobs, Jane. *Cities and the Wealth of Nations: Principles of Economic Life*. New York: Random House, 1984.

Kane, Robert. *Free Will and Values*. Albany, N.Y.: SUNY Press, 1985.

Kant, Immanuel. *The Critique of Judgment*. Translated by James Creed Meredith. Oxford: Oxford University Press, 1952 (1928).

———. *Grounding for the Metaphysics of Morals*. Translated by James W. Ellington. Indianapolis, Ind.: Hackett, 1981.

———. *The Metaphysics of Morals*. Translated by Mary Gregor. Cambridge, England: Cambridge University Press, 1991.

Korsgaard, Christine. "Kant's Formula of Universal Law." *Pacific Philosophical Quarterly* 66(1985): 24–47.

———. "The Right to Lie: Kant on Dealing With Evil," *Philosophy and Public Affairs*, 15(fall 1986): 325–49.

Krippendorf, Klaus. "On the Essential Contexts of Artifacts or on the Proposition That 'Design Is Making Sense (of Things).' " In *The Idea of Design*, edited by Victor Margolin and Richard Buchanan. Cambridge, Mass.: MIT Press, 1995, pp. 156–84.

Leiss, William, Stephen Kline, and Sut Jhally. *Social Communication In Advertising*. Methuen: 1986. Reprinted selection, "Advertising, Consumers, and Culture," in *Communication in History*, edited by David Crowley and Paul Heyer. New York: Longman, 1999, pp. 206–11.

Letter to Three Wives, A. Dir. Joseph L. Mankiewicz. TCF, 1949.

Liebling. A. J. *Between Meals: An Appetite for Paris.* New York: North Point Press, 1986.

Locke, John. *Two Treatises of Government.* Edited by Peter Laslett. Cambridge, England: Cambridge University Press, 1989 (1960).

Lover Come Back. Dir. Delbert Mann. U–I/Seven Pictures/Nob Hill/Arwin. 1961.

Lurie, Alison. *The Language of Clothes.* New York: Random House, 1981.

Lyotard, Jean-François. *The Postmodern Condition: A Report on Knowledge,* translated by Geoff Bennington and Brian Massumi. Vol. 10 of *Theory and History of Literature.* Minneapolis: University of Minnesota Press, 1984.

MacCormack, Carol, and Marilyn Strathern. *Nature, Culture, and Gender.* New York: Cambridge University Press, 1986 (1980).

MacIntyre, Alasdair. *After Virtue.* 2d ed. Notre Dame, Ind.: University of Notre Dame Press, 1984.

Marx, Karl. *Capital: A Critique of Political Economy,* vol. 1. Translated by Samuel Moore and Edward Aveling, edited by Friedrich Engels. New York: International Publishers, 1967.

———, and Friedrich Engels. *The Marx-Engels Reader.* Edited by Robert C. Tucker. New York: Norton, 1972.

May, Ellen Tyler. "Myths and Realities of the American Family." In *The History of Private Life.* Vol. 5 of *Riddles of Identity in Modern Times,* edited by Antoine Prost and Gérard Vincent, translated by Arthur Goldhammer, series eds., Philippe Ariès and Georges Duby. Cambridge, Mass.: Harvard University Press, 1991, pp. 539–92.

McLuhan, Marshall. *Understanding Media,* 2d ed. New York: Signet, 1964.

Mead, Margaret. *Sex and Temperament.* New York: New American Library, 1958 (1950).

Meilaender, Gilbert. *The Theory and Practice of Virtue.* Notre Dame, Ind.: University of Notre Dame Press, 1984.

Mertz, Elizabeth, and Richard J. Parmentier. *Semiotic Mediation: Sociological and Cultural Perspectives.* In *Language, Thought, and Culture: Advances in the Study of Cognition.* Orlando, Fla.: Academic Press, 1985.

Mill, John Stuart. *Utilitarianism.* Edited by George Sher. Indianapolis, Ind.: Hackett, 1979.

————. *On Liberty*. Indianapolis, Ind.: Hackett, 1979.

Molloy, John T. *The Woman's Dress for Success Book*. New York: Warner Books, 1977.

Morello, August. " 'Discovering Design' Means [Re]- Discovering Users and Projects." In *Discovering Design: Explorations in Design Studies*. Chicago: Chicago University Press, 1995, pp. 69–76.

Mumford, Lewis. *Technics and Civilization*. San Diego, Calif.: Harcourt Brace Jovanovich, 1962 (1934).

Nietzsche, Friedrich. *Beyond Good and Evil*. Translated by Walter Kaufmann. New York: Vintage/Random House, 1966.

————. *The Gay Science*. Translated by Walter Kaufmann. New York: Vintage/ Random House, 1974.

————. *The Genealogy of Morals and Ecce Homo*. Translated by Walter Kaufmann. New York: Vintage/Random House, 1969 (1967).

————. *A Nietzsche Reader*. Translated and edited by R. J. Hollingdale. London: Penguin Classics, 1977.

————. *The Twilight of the Idols*. In *The Portable Nietzsche*. Translated by Walter Kaufmann. New York: Viking/Penguin, 1954.

————. *Thus Spake Zarathustra*. Translated by R. J. Hollingdale. London: Penguin Classics, 1969 (1961).

Nishitani, Keiji. *Religion and Nothingness*. Translated by Jan Van Bragt. Berkeley: University of California Press, 1982.

Norman, Donald A. *The Psychology of Everyday Things*. New York: Basic Books, 1988.

Now Voyager. Dir. Irving Rapper. Warner, 1942.

Oakley, Ann. *Woman's Work*. New York: Vintage/Random House, 1974.

Ortega Y Gasset, José. *The Dehumanization of Art and Notes on the Novel*. Translated by Helene Weyl. Princeton, N.J.: Princeton University Press, 1948.

————. The *Revolt of the Masses*. New York: Norton, 1957 (1932).

————. *The Modern Theme*. Translated by James Cleugh. New York: Harper Torchbooks, 1961.

Ortner, Sherry. "Is Female to Male as Nature Is to Culture?" *Woman, Culture, and Society*, edited by Michelle Zimbalist Rosaldo and Louise Lamphere. Stanford, Calif.: Stanford University Press, 1974 (1983).

Papanek, Victor. *Design for the Real World*. New York: Pantheon Books, 1971.

————. "The Future Isn't What It Used To Be." Reprinted in *The Idea of Design*, edited by Victor Margolin and Richard Buchanan. Cambridge, Mass.: MIT Press, 1995, pp. 56–69.

Peirce, Charles S. *Selected Writings.* Edited by Philip P. Wiener. New York: Dover, 1958.

Philadelphia Story, The. Dir. by George Cukor. MGM, 1940.

Piano, The. Dir. by Jane Campion. Entertainment/CIBY 2000/Jan Chapman, 1993.

Plato. *Gorgias.* Translated by G. Zeyl. Indianapolis, Ind.: Hackett, 1987.

———. *The Collected Dialogues of Plato.* Edited by Edith Hamilton and Huntington Cairns. Princeton, N.J.: Princeton University Press, 1980 (1961).

———. *Complete Works.* Edited by John M. Cooper and assoc. ed. D. S. Hutchinson (Indianapolis, Ind.: Hackett, 1997.

———. *Meno.* Translated by G.M.A. Grube Indianapolis, Ind.: Hackett, 1976.

———. *Plato's Republic.* Translated by G. M. A. Grube. Indianapolis, Ind.: Hackett, 1974.

———. *Symposium.* Translated by Alexander Nehemas and Paul Woodruff. Indianapolis, Ind.: Hackett, 1989.

Polanyi, Michael. *Personal Knowledge: Towards a Post-Critical Philosophy.* Chicago: University of Chicago Press, 1958 (1952).

Popenoe, David. "A World without Fathers." *The Wilson Quarterly* (Spring 1996): 12–29.

Preston, Ivan L. *The Great American Blowup: Puffery in Advertising and Selling.* Madison: University of Wisconsin Press, 1996 (1975).

Remnick, David. "Inside-Out Olympics." *The New Yorker,* 5 August 1996, 26–28.

Root, Waverly, and Richard de Rochemont. *Eating in America: A History.* New York: Morrow, 1976.

Rosaldo, Michelle Zimbalist, and Louise Lamphere eds. *Woman, Culture, and Society.* Stanford, Calif.: Stanford University Press, 1974 (1983).

Rouche, Michel. "The Early Middle Ages in the West." In *From Pagan Rome to Byzantium,* Vol. 1 of *A History of Private life.* Edited by Paul Veyne, translated by Arthur Goldhammer. Series eds. Philippe Ariès and Georges Duby. Cambridge, Mass.: Harvard University Press, 1987, pp. 411–549.

Rousseau, Jean-Jacques. *The Basic Political Writings.* Translated by Donald A. Cress. Indianapolis, Ind.: Hackett, 1987.

Rybczynski, Witold. *Home: A Short History of an Idea.* New York: Penguin, 1987 (1986).

Sartre, Jean-Paul. *Being and Nothingness.* Translated by Hazel Barnes. New York: Washington Square Press, 1956.

———. No Exit *and Other Plays*. New York: Vintage, 1949.

Sherman, Nancy. *Making a Necessity of Virtue: Aristotle and Kant on Virtue*. Cambridge, England: Cambridge University Press, 1997.

Smith, Adam. *The Wealth of Nations*. New York: Random House, 1965 (1937).

———. *Theory of the Moral Sentiments*. In *The Essential Adam Smith*. Edited by Robert L. Heilbroner. U.S.: Norton, 1986.

Strasser, Susan. *Never Done: A History of American Housework*. New York: Pantheon, 1982.

Stella Dallas. Dir. King Vidor. Samuel Goldwyn, 1937.

Sullivan, Harry Stack. *The Interpersonal Theory of Psychiatry*. Edited by Helen Swick Perry and Mary Ladd Gawel. New York: Norton, 1953.

Terkel, Studs. *Working*. New York: Avon Books, 1974 (1972).

Thébert, Yvon. "Private Life and Domestic Architecture in Roman Africa." In *From Pagan Rome to Byzantium*, vol. 1 of *A History of Private Life*. Edited by Paul Veyne, translated by Arthur Goldhammer. Series eds. Philippe Ariès and Georges Duby. Cambridge, Mass.: Harvard University Press, 1987, pp. 313–409.

Turner, E. S. *The Shocking History of Advertising*. Middlesex, England: Penguin, 1968 (1952).

Veblen, Thorstein. *The Theory of the Leisure Class*. New York: Penguin, 1979 (1899).

Veyne, Paul. "The Roman Empire." In *From Pagan Rome to Byzantium*, vol. 1 of *A History of Private Life*. Edited by Paul Veyne, translated by Arthur Goldhammer series eds. Philippe Ariès and Georges Duby. Cambridge, Mass.: Harvard University Press, Belknap Press, 1987, pp. 5–233.

Vogue, September 1997.

Walsh, Elsa. *Divided Lives: The Public and Private Struggles of Three Accomplished Women*. New York: Simon and Schuster, 1995.

Weber, Max. *From Max Weber: Essays in Sociology*. Translated by H. H. Gerth and C. Wright Mills. New York: Oxford University Press, 1946.

———. *The Protestant Ethic and the Spirit of Capitalism*. Translated by Talcott Parsons. New York: Charles Scribner's Sons, 1958.

Whatney, Susanna. *The Housekeeping Book 1776–1800*. Edited by Christina Hardyment. London: Century Hutchinson, 1987 (1956).

Whitehead, Barbara Dafoe. "Women and the Future of Fatherhood." *The Wilson Quarterly* (Spring 1996): 30–34.

Williams, Bernard. "Utilitarianism and Moral Self-Indulgence." In *Contemporary British Philosophy*. Edited by H. D. Lewis. London: George Allen & Unwin, 1976.

Williams, Juanita. *Psychology of Women*. New York: Norton, 1977 (1974).

Williamson, Judith. *Decoding Advertisements*. London: Marion Boyars, 1985 (1978).

Wittgenstein, Ludwig. *Philosophical Investigations*. Translated by G. E. M. Anscombe. New York: Macmillan, 1953.

INDEX